MATHEMATICS OF BUSINESS

second edition
MATHEMATICS

Prentice-Hall, Inc., Englewood Cliffs, New Jersey

OF BUSINESS

Jay Diamond

Professor-Chairman
Marketing-Retailing Department
Nassau Community College

Gerald Pintel Ph.D.

Professor
Business Administration Department
Nassau Community College

Library of Congress Cataloging in Publication Data

Diamond, Jay.
   Mathematics of business.

   1. Business mathematics.   I. Pintel, Gerald, joint author.   II. Title.
HF5691.D5 1975   513'.93   74–17121
ISBN   0–13–564013–X

MATHEMATICS OF BUSINESS, second edition
Jay Diamond / Gerald Pintel

10   9   8   7   6   5   4   3   2   1

Printed in the United States of America

Prentice-Hall International, Inc., London
Prentice-Hall of Australia, Pty. Ltd., Sydney
Prentice-Hall of Canada, Ltd., Toronto
Prentice-Hall of India Private Limited, New Delhi
Prentice-Hall of Japan, Inc., Tokyo

CONTENTS

PREFACE   ix

ONE
BASIC MATHEMATICAL
COMPUTATION   1

1   FUNDAMENTAL OPERATIONS AND THE
METRIC SYSTEM   3

2   FRACTIONS AND DECIMALS   36

TWO
PERCENTAGES, ALIQUOT PARTS,
AND INTEREST   61

3   PERCENTAGES AND ALIQUOT PARTS   63

4   INTEREST   80

THREE
CONSUMER MATHEMATICS   103

5   CONSUMER LOANS   105

6   OTHER CONSUMER COMPUTATIONS   123

v

FOUR
RETAILING AND MARKETING MATHEMATICS 137

7 MARKUP AND MARKDOWN 139

8 MERCHANDISE AND PROFIT 154

FIVE
MATHEMATICS IN OFFICE PROCEDURES 169

9 SALARIES AND WAGES 171

10 COMMISSIONS AND DISCOUNTS 197

SIX
MATHEMATICS FOR ACCOUNTING 219

11 BASIC ACCOUNTING MATHEMATICS 221

12 INDIVIDUAL INCOME TAXES AND OTHER ACCOUNTING COMPUTATIONS 238

SEVEN
MATHEMATICS IN INVESTMENTS 261

13 INVESTMENT IN STOCKS 263

14 INVESTMENT IN BONDS 276

EIGHT
MATHEMATICS IN DATA PROCESSING 289

15 BINARY ARITHMETIC 291

16 ARITHMETIC IN BASE 8 AND BASE 16 305

NINE
MATHEMATICS IN MANAGEMENT 317

17 ANALYSIS OF FINANCIAL STATEMENTS 319

18 BUSINESS STATISTICS, GRAPHS, ANNUITIES, AND PRESENT VALUE 338

GLOSSARY 364

ANSWERS TO ODD-NUMBERED PROBLEMS 371

INDEX 383

vii

PREFACE

As was the case in the first edition of *Mathematics of Business*, this second edition has been written expressly for the purpose of reviewing arithmetic procedures and applying them to specific business functions.

An attempt has been made to simplify the book by treating individual topics in the most fundamental of terms. This is followed by extensive drill and problem solving to reinforce learning.

An unusual feature of the book is its extensive use of practical business applications wherever possible. This will make drill work more palatable and meaningful. Because business mathematics is an introductory course, business terminology and definitions are used extensively.

The growing importance of data processing in business is recognized by the inclusion of a unit on data processing arithmetic.

In an attempt to provide for the educational needs of the individual student, the sections of the text are organized to fit the curriculum needs of the particular student.

The first two sections are devoted to generalized arithmetic fundamentals required of all business students. The remaining seven sections deal with specific areas to meet the requirements of specialized curricula.

Although the book might be too comprehensive for completion in one semester, it is suggested that all students be responsible for the first three sections and whichever of the remaining units are pertinent to their field of interest.

Significant among the many new features of the second edition are the following:

1. A unit devoted to the metric system of measurement, added to familiarize students with what is an almost universal system, and what from every indication will eventually be the system officially employed in the United States.

2. In order to familiarize students with the arithmetic and fundamentals involved in income tax computations, a new unit on the subject has been included.

3. Each chapter now features summary problems in addition to those problems which follow the conclusion of each unit. These problems feature a mixture of the various types of problems found within the chapters and afford students the challenge of choosing the proper formulas by which to solve the problems.

4. The chapter on retailing and marketing mathematics features additional problems in order to provide sufficient drill work for those entering the field of distribution.

5. This text was written to introduce students to business terminology as well as to enable them to apply arithmetic to business functions. Thus the inclusion of the *Glossary* at the end of this second edition will enable students to familiarize themselves with terms that are significant in the business world.

An instructor's manual, complete with solutions, is available, as is a prognostic examination and tests, with solutions, for each unit.

MATHEMATICS OF BUSINESS

ONE

BASIC MATHEMATICAL COMPUTATION

Essentially, this is an arithmetic book. It consists of the application of basic arithmetic operations to common business situations. Because a strong arithmetic background is necessary for this course, the first section of the text will consist of drill on basic arithmetic operations. Most of the material will provide practice to improve your skill and speed in handling addition, subtraction, multiplication, and division. Students with computational weaknesses will find this section of the book to be remedial in nature. In any event, this is the most important part of the book, because an understanding of the business applications of mathematics depends upon the thorough understanding of the fundamental operations of arithmetic.

1

fundamental operations and the metric system

1. ADDITION
   a. Definitions
   b. Position
   c. Combinations of 10
   d. Proving addition
   e. Breaking columns
   f. Horizontal addition
2. SUBTRACTION
   a. Definitions
   b. Position
   c. Proving subtraction
   d. Horizontal subtraction
   e. Mental subtraction
3. MULTIPLICATION
   a. Definitions
   b. Operation—mental multiplication
   c. Operation—long multiplication
   d. Multiplication by 10 or powers of 10
   e. Multiplication when a factor ends in zero
   f. Multiplication when zeros appear within a numeral
   g. Multiplication with decimals
   h. Proving multiplication
4. DIVISION
   a. Definitions
   b. Operation—mental division
   c. Operation—long division
   d. Division by 10 or powers of 10
   e. Division when the divisor ends in zero
   f. Division when there are decimals in the divisor
   g. Division to prove multiplication
   h. Proving division
5. ROUNDING OFF
6. ESTIMATING
7. METRIC SYSTEM
   a. Linear
   b. Weight
   c. Volume

1. ADDITION   Addition is the most common of the fundamental operations. Adding with speed and accuracy is required of business people. This can be achieved only through practice. The following brief review and drill will improve your addition skills.

a. DEFINITIONS

The numbers to be added are called the addends. The result of the addition is called the sum or total. Thus:

$$\begin{array}{r} 6 \\ 7 \\ 8 \\ \hline 21 \end{array} \text{Addends}$$

21   Sum or Total

b. POSITION

Our numbering system is positional; that is, the value of a digit depends upon the position it is in, as well as the value of the digit itself. For example, the numeral 4 in the rightmost column equals the number 4, while the numeral 4 in second rightmost column equals 40. Therefore, when adding, it is necessary to arrange the numbers so that similar positional values fall in the same column.

ILLUSTRATIVE PROBLEM. Find the sum of $127 + 3746 + 12 + 923$.

4

SOLUTION:

$$
\begin{array}{r}
127 \\
3{,}746 \\
12 \\
923 \\
\hline
4{,}808 \quad \text{Sum}
\end{array}
$$

1.1 SOLVE THESE PROBLEMS: Add.

1. 3666	**2.** 17	**3.** 86
81	37	127
9	72	9
7842	36289	637
3	898	276
27	466	86
688	1	164
38476	378	97
927	9	472
	76	

In the case of numerals containing decimals, the addends must be positioned so that the decimals all appear in the same column.

ILLUSTRATIVE PROBLEM. Find the sum of $1.27 + 36 + 33.684 + 778.2632$.

SOLUTION:

$$
\begin{array}{r}
1.27 \\
36. \\
33.684 \\
778.2632 \\
\hline
849.2172 \quad \text{Sum}
\end{array}
$$

1.2 SOLVE THESE PROBLEMS: Add.

1. .3784	**2.** 1.2	**3.** 1.678
27.1	.374	71.4
3.63	12	.29
278	46	36
.14	9.268	4.72
3.6	8.3	.129
78	492	.8
9	36.9	3729
.8	.1274	.410

1.3 *SOLVE THESE PROBLEMS:*

1. The inventory of Bennincasa and Sons revealed the following: Style 608—46 pieces of green, 139 pieces of red, 2,746 pieces of blue, and 3,684 pieces of beige. Calculate the total pieces.

2. The Krinsk Building has the following space available for rent: 627 sq. ft., 3,780 sq. ft., 912 sq. ft., 96 sq. ft., 2,570 sq. ft., and 736 sq. ft. Calculate the total vacant space.

3. Tom held five jobs during the year. His earnings statements revealed that he had earned the following salaries: $628.40, $3,780.12, $68., $746.18, $2,764.15. Determine his total annual earnings.

4. The assets of the Right-Way Corp. consist of the following: cash in bank, $12,678.40; cash on hand, $125; receivables, $6,788.19; merchandise inventory, $7,663.47; delivery equipment, $4,627.14; supplies, $683.64; and prepaid insurance, $1,263. What are the total assets of the corporation?

5. Calculate the total weekly sales of Parker, Inc., if the daily sales are as follows: Monday, $463.14; Tuesday, $788.41; Wednesday, $636.; Thursday, $568.94; Friday, $13,688.19; and Saturday, $19,273.47.

6. The monthly payrolls of the Ryan Corp. were as follows: $3,748.12, $6,347.18, $2,147.22, $7,866.14, $9,268.72, $8,846.14, $2,789.41, $8,896.12, $3,368.31, $746.77, $126.70, $3,688.14. Calculate the annual payroll.

c. COMBINATIONS OF 10

Most competent arithmeticians do not add a column in a number by number fashion. Instead, they pick out combinations of 10 which they recognize instantly. The following are the two number combinations of 10 which you should memorize. These should not require you to think $6 + 4 = 10$ but the numbers 6 and 4 should be thought of as 10 with no intermediate calculations.

1	2	3	4	5	or	9	8	7	6	5
9	8	7	6	5		1	2	3	4	5

ILLUSTRATIVE PROBLEM. Add.

7
6
4
2
7
8

Without using combinations totaling 10, you would normally think 7, 13, 17, 19, 26, 34.

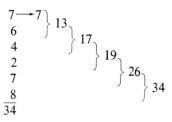

But by grouping into combinations totaling 10, you would think 7, 17, 27, 34. In other words, the steps in the addition would be as numbered below:

$$
\begin{array}{l}
7 \longrightarrow \text{Step} \quad 1\text{--}7 \\
6 \longleftarrow \\
4 \longleftarrow \quad \text{Step} \quad 2\text{--}17 \\
2 \longleftarrow \\
7 \diagdown \quad \text{Step} \quad 3\text{--}27 \\
8 \longleftarrow \text{Step} \quad 4\text{--}34 \\
\overline{34}
\end{array}
$$

Although this method may be cumbersome at first, it is worthwhile to develop. The authors estimate that 90 percent of all accountants add by using combinations of 10.

There are also many 3-digit combinations totaling 10 that should be instantly recognized. Some of these are:

1	1	1	1	2	2	2	2	3	3	3	3	4	4	4	4
1	2	3	4	1	2	3	4	1	2	3	4	1	2	3	4
8	7	6	5	7	6	5	4	6	5	4	3	5	4	3	2

1.4 SOLVE THESE PROBLEMS: Add, using combinations of 10.

	1.	2.	3.	4.	5.	6.	7.
	6	2	5	7	9	4	3
	7	8	6	8	8	2	9
	3	4	5	3	1	8	7

	8.	9.	10.	11.	12.	13.	14.
	16	81	16	77	94	14	39
	37	77	37	83	26	26	28
	24	99	74	34	83	37	11
	73	35	28	56	12	83	72

	15.	16.	17.	18.	19.	20.	21.
	312	416	126	984	827	297	632
	463	379	368	126	363	603	387
	738	694	984	378	289	816	723
	267	386	742	188	466	204	466
	849	724	866	732	634	497	643

22. 4783	23. 3762	24. 4636	25. 5277	26. 3788
3629	2328	2472	1833	1422
6317	7649	8968	4164	7366
5618	3618	2743	2946	2734
4492	8492	6357	7365	9648

27. 1642	28. 3822	29. 28364	30. 27362	31. 96427
2438	1487	12447	36187	34182
9960	7203	80793	83943	13673
8134	8678	26319	72473	42781
7676	2690	94601	26377	68309
		72688	38637	12784

32. 12796	33. 27988	34. 97233	35. 79006
37314	14129	33844	37118
27728	83001	10166	31894
12939	97273	28733	61902
14382	12469	71378	87377
98071	12837	82002	14736

1.5   SOLVE THESE PROBLEMS: Use combinations of 10.

1. Payroll checks for one week were: $127.63, $78.15, $229.17, $164.29, and $46.18. How much cash will be required to meet the payroll?

2. Calculate the total cash value of goods received if the individual bills were: $126.80, $782.19, $384.20, $1,308.91, $2,746.50, and $7,354.50.

3. The monthly rents of a small office building are $325.12, $168.98, $685.60, $429.40, $1,237.80, and $423.28. Calculate the monthly rent roll.

4. Determine the amount of cash needed to cover checks written in the amounts: $97.26, $4.68, $13.74, $3., $626.41, $2,484.62, and $47.88.

5. Tom Johnson is paid according to the number of pieces he produces. His production for one week was: Monday, 3,762 pieces; Tuesday, 2,648 pieces; Wednesday, 8,421 pieces; Thursday, 6,812 pieces; Friday, 7,288 pieces. What was Tom's total production for the week?

6. Calculate the total kilowatt usage from the following weekly totals: 27,626; 33,980; 80,404; 62,163; 38,942; 76,308.

d. PROVING ADDITION

Of the several ways of proving addition, reading in the opposite direction is by far the most common. If the original total was arrived at by adding the column from the top down, the proof would be accomplished by getting the same total by beginning at the bottom of the column and adding up.

Another method of proving addition is by adding the columns, writing the total of each column separately, and indenting one place left, then adding the column totals (partial sums).

ILLUSTRATIVE PROBLEM. Add and prove.

SOLUTION:

$$
\begin{array}{r}
1,527 \\
6,376 \\
1,429 \\
2,638 \\
1,726 \\
1,837 \\
2,618 \\
2,638 \\
\hline
20,789
\end{array}
$$

PROOF: Add each column separately.

$$
\begin{array}{r}
1,527 \\
6,376 \\
1,429 \\
2,638 \\
1,726 \\
1,837 \\
2,618 \\
2,638 \\
\hline
59 \\
23 \\
45 \\
16 \\
\hline
20,789
\end{array}
$$

   59   $(7 + 6 + 9 + 8 + 6 + 7 + 8 + 8)$
   23   $(2 + 7 + 2 + 3 + 2 + 3 + 1 + 3)$
   45   $(5 + 3 + 4 + 6 + 7 + 8 + 6 + 6)$
   16   $(1 + 6 + 1 + 2 + 1 + 1 + 2 + 2)$

Note that each partial sum is indented one column.

1.6   SOLVE THESE PROBLEMS: Add and prove.

1. 3728	**2.** 16,327	**3.** 63,808
1463	57,286	18,275
5936	38,194	28,998
2844	21,412	37,228
1526	67,808	16,189
3799	84,273	94,379

4. 289,736	**5.** 327,188	**6.** 975,263
374,263	187,989	236,632
185,317	963,274	178,188
263,362	147,741	169,961
203,848	208,343	907,163
278,417	369,774	187,521

e. BREAKING COLUMNS

It is frequently helpful in adding long columns of numbers to separate them into several parts, arrive at subtotals, and then add the subtotals. This method may also be used as a proof.

ILLUSTRATIVE PROBLEM. Add by dividing into subtotals.

3,726	3,726		
4,816	4,816		
2,978	2,978		
1,523	1,523	13,043	Subtotal
3,729	3,729		
1,866	1,866		
4,637	4,637		
2,619	2,619	12,851	Subtotal
		25,894	Total

1.7   SOLVE THESE PROBLEMS: Add by finding the subtotals where indicated and adding the subtotals. Prove.

1. 1,273		**2.** 3,896	
4,868		2,769	
3,729		3,728	
1,633		9,429	
2,788		3,768	
1,577		1,427	
	Total		Total

3. 1,627
7,836
1,568
_____
9,561
3,768
9,248
_____   Total

4. 1,877
1,926
3,747
_____
1,268
3,926
1,877
_____
4,236
7,233
5,726
_____   Total

5. 3,726
5,698
7,378
_____
7,561
1,627
2,478
_____
5,733
3,899
9,421
_____   Total

6. 37,263
54,379
73,187
_____
14,269
93,776
29,367
_____
34,429
14,477
26,376
_____   Total

f. HORIZONTAL ADDITION

Frequently business forms present numbers to be added in horizontal rather than in vertical form. To save the time required to relist these numbers vertically, business people often add horizontally.

ILLUSTRATIVE PROBLEM.

$$127 + 638 + 476 + 788 + 372 = 2401$$

SOLUTION: This problem is solved in the same manner as vertical addition, that is:

1. Starting with the rightmost digits, add $7 + 8 + 6 + 8 + 2 = 31$. Write the 1 and carry 3 to the second column _ _ _ 1
2. Then add the second rightmost digits, $3 + 2 + 3 + 7 + 8 + 7 = 30$. Write the 0 and carry 3 to the third column, _ _ 0 1
3. Then add the third rightmost digits, $3 + 1 + 6 + 4 + 7 + 3 = 24$. Sum $= 2\ 4\ 0\ 1$

1.8 SOLVE THESE PROBLEMS:

1. $786 + 375 + 682 + 747 =$
2. $376 + 147 + 966 + 525 =$
3. $472 + 638 + 395 + 716 =$
4. $635 + 727 + 994 + 126 =$
5. $737 + 617 + 884 + 237 =$
6. $127 + 774 + 918 + 758 =$
7. $875 + 376 + 889 + 443 + 712 + 658 =$
8. $926 + 137 + 644 + 127 + 633 + 526 =$
9. $127 + 371 + 363 + 188 + 347 + 156 =$
10. $362 + 464 + 163 + 927 + 138 + 929 =$
11. $445 + 721 + 633 + 277 + 641 + 292 =$
12. $296 + 263 + 576 + 146 + 279 + 898 =$

2. SUBTRACTION

Of all the arithmetic processes, subtraction is usually the easiest to perform and prove. Consequently, it will require the least amount of drill and review. Where the number in the subtrahend is greater than the minuend, 1 is borrowed from the preceding place in the minuend.

a. DEFINITIONS

$$
\begin{array}{r}
7 \\
\cancel{8}6 \\
-\ 27 \\
\hline
59 \\
\end{array}
\quad
\begin{array}{l}
\\
\text{Minuend} \\
\text{Subtrahend} \\
\text{Difference or Remainder}
\end{array}
$$

In the above illustration, the number 7 is greater than 6. 1 is then borrowed from the 8, making it a 7.

b. POSITION

As is the case in addition, our positional numbering system requires that numbers to be subtracted be arranged so that the positional value of each digit in the minuend and subtrahend fall in the same column. In the event that a problem is improperly set up positionally, it must be rewritten before it can be solved

ILLUSTRATIVE PROBLEM. Find the difference.

$$378 - 27$$

SOLUTION:

    1. The problem must be rewritten to place the minuend and subtrahend correctly.

    2. Then, subtract to find the difference.

$$\begin{array}{r} 378 \\ - 27 \\ \hline 351 \end{array}$$

1.9 SOLVE THESE PROBLEMS:

1. $317 - 6$	**2.** $194 - 23$	**3.** $781 - 5$
4. $216 - 19$	**5.** $3,622 - 129$	**6.** $2,755 - 1,675$
7. $3,977 - 295$	**8.** $2,788 - 84$	**9.** $4,633 - 2,611$
10. $7,879 - 341$	**11.** $8,265 - 8,252$	**12.** $9,733 - 8,526$

Where the numbers to be subtracted contain decimals, they must be positioned so that the decimal points fall in the same column.

ILLUSTRATIVE PROBLEM. Find the difference.

$$37.63 - 4.267$$

SOLUTION:

    1. Rewrite the problem to correct the positioning. Note that adding zeros to the rightmost column after the decimal point does not change the value of the number. If you find it easier to subtract or add figures with the same number of digits to the right of the decimal, you may add zeros.

    2. Then, subtract to find the difference.

$$\begin{array}{r} 37.63 \\ - 4.267 \\ \hline 33.363 \end{array} \quad \text{or} \quad \begin{array}{r} 37.630 \\ - 4.267 \\ \hline 33.363 \end{array}$$

1.10 SOLVE THESE PROBLEMS:

1. $3.76 - .127$	**2.** $.427 - .36$	**3.** $27.6 - 13$
4. $216 - 46.8$	**5.** $16.3 - 3.1$	**6.** $3.75 - 1.2578$
7. $.768 - .375$	**8.** $487 - .3256$	**9.** $.3756 - .2635$
10. $195.007 - .0063$	**11.** $727.185 - 3.76334$	**12.** $163.8544 - 1.726845$

1.11 *SOLVE THESE PROBLEMS:*

1. The Fit-Rite Dress Shop had 3,712 dresses in inventory (on hand) at the beginning of the week. During the week, 787 new dresses were received and 1,274 dresses were sold. What was the inventory at the end of the week?

2. Before paying the weekly bills, the Peters Company had $7,427.18 in the bank. The following bills were paid: $3,672, $4.65, $787.91, and $379.18. Calculate the bank balance after the bills were paid.

3. The Whitney Machine Shop had a production budget of 10,000 pieces for one week. The daily production was 2,637 pieces, 1,246 pieces, 1,597 pieces, 3,218 pieces, and 2,716 pieces. Determine the difference between the actual production and the planned production.

4. On the morning of March 19, the Mayflower Bank had a cash balance of $12,463,187.59. During the day they received deposits of $1,379,274.18 and paid out $1,972,364.78. What was the day's closing balance?

5. The gross monthly rents of a small apartment house are $1,746.18. The following rent checks were collected during the month: $127.12, $379.80, $268.75, $294.73, $312.65, $147.90. Calculate the outstanding rent at the end of the month.

6. The accounts payable (money owed suppliers) of Weinstein's Department Store is $263,412.15. The following checks were sent to suppliers: $3,578.86, $1,279.27, $4,684.22, $189.12, $7,839.14, $627.95, $1,474.27, $1,657.19. Calculate the accounts payable balance after these payments.

c. PROVING SUBTRACTION

The easiest way to prove the accuracy of subtraction is to add the remainder to the subtrahend. This total should equal the minuend.

ILLUSTRATIVE PROBLEM. Prove.

$$
\begin{array}{rl}
14 & \text{Minuend} \\
-\ 9 & \text{Subtrahend} \\
\hline
5 & \text{Remainder}
\end{array}
$$

SOLUTION: To prove: the remainder + the subtrahend = the minuend.

$$9 + 5 = 14 \quad \text{add from the remainder up:} \quad
\begin{array}{r}
14 \\
-\ 9 \\
\hline
5
\end{array}$$

1.12 SOLVE THESE PROBLEMS: Prove. Correct those that are wrong.

1.	376	2.	412	3.	829	4.	637
	−124		−263		−714		−524
	252		148		105		103

5.	1.263	6.	379.5	7.	18.62	8.	.9752
	− .126		− 12.74		− .268		−.87941
	1.037		356.74		18.352		.19579

Because the proof of subtraction is so simple, you should cultivate the habit of proving *every* subtraction example whether required or not.

As you have seen, the remainder plus the subtrahend equals the minuend. This can be rephrased as the minuend minus the remainder equals the subtrahend.

1.13 SOLVE THESE PROBLEMS:

1.	126	2.	378	3.	975	4.	186
	−		−		−		−
	75		9		876		147

5.	.375	6.	1.78	7.	.004	8.	18.2
	−		−		−		−
	.047		1.003		.0007		7.014

9.	.0047	10.	.3006	11.	.7875	12.	1.3704
	−		−		−		−
	.00379		.2784		.06752		.0067

Did you prove your work? You should have done so automatically.

d. HORIZONTAL SUBTRACTION

When numbers to be subtracted are presented horizontally, it is a waste of time to recopy them to subtract. The operation is almost as easy to perform horizontally. (Refer to page 12 for discussion on borrowing.)

ILLUSTRATIVE PROBLEM,

$$1375 - 688 = 687$$

1.14 SOLVE THESE PROBLEMS:

      1. $37 - 16 =$

      2. $128 - 75 =$

      3. $3648 - 2796 =$

      4. $13.52 - 6.75 =$

      5. $.1379 - .1072 =$

      6. $1.758 - 1.637 =$

      7. $144.6 - 137.8 =$

      8. $38495 - 26378 =$

e. MENTAL SUBTRACTION

When there are relatively few digits involved, mental subtraction is quite easy. The method, as we shall see, is to begin with the leftmost digit in the subtrahend, deduct that, and go on to the next leftmost digit, and so on.

ILLUSTRATIVE PROBLEM.

$$427 - 318 = 109$$

SOLUTION:

    1. Mentally deduct the leftmost digit of the subtrahend, 3̲ 1 8̲.
       Think: $427 - 300 = 127$

    2. Mentally deduct the next leftmost digit of the subtrahend, _ 1 8̲.
       Think: $127 - 10 = 117$

    3. Mentally deduct the next leftmost digit of the subtrahend, _ _ 8̲.
       Think: $117 - 8 = 109$

1.15 SOLVE THESE PROBLEMS MENTALLY:

      1. $63 - 24 =$

      2. $98 - 37 =$

      3. $114 - 85 =$

      4. $316 - 72 =$

      5. $488 - 279 =$

      6. $636 - 263 =$

      7. $749 - 680 =$

      8. $1347 - 1029 =$

3. MULTIPLICATION The arithmetic operation used to determine the product of two numbers is called multiplication. In essence, it is a shortcut method of addition. Thus $8 + 8 + 8 + 8 = 32$. This may be more simply performed as $4 \times 8 = 32$.

a. DEFINITIONS

$$
\begin{array}{r}
126 \quad \text{Multiplicand} \\
\times \quad 28 \quad \text{Multiplier} \\
\hline
1008 \\
252 \\
\hline
3528 \quad \text{Product}
\end{array}
$$

1008 ⎫
252 ⎬ Partial products

b. OPERATION—MENTAL MULTIPLICATION

Where the multiplier is represented by a one digit numeral, the operation of multiplication is so simple that it can be done mentally.

ILLUSTRATIVE PROBLEM.

$$1546 \times 7 =$$

SOLUTION:

$$1546 \times 7 = 10,822$$

The operation was performed in this manner:

Each digit in the multiplicand was multiplied by 7 starting with the rightmost.

1. Think: $7 \times 6 = 42$. Write 2 and carry 4.
2. Think: $7 \times 4 = 28 +$ carried $4 = 32$. Write 2 and carry 3.
3. Think: $7 \times 5 = 35 +$ carried $3 = 38$. Write 8 and carry 3.
4. Think: $7 \times 1 = 7 +$ carried $3 = 10$. Write 10.

1.16 SOLVE THESE PROBLEMS:

1. $467 \times 3 =$	7. $9263 \times 6 =$
2. $785 \times 5 =$	8. $15,237 \times 5 =$
3. $632 \times 9 =$	9. $27,985 \times 9 =$
4. $575 \times 8 =$	10. $36,883 \times 8 =$
5. $3726 \times 4 =$	11. $57,263 \times 7 =$
6. $5837 \times 7 =$	12. $365,237 \times 4 =$

c. OPERATION—LONG MULTIPLICATION

In multiplication, the multiplier and the multiplicand may be interchanged. That is, 4×8 will result in the same product as 8×4. For ease of operation, the number with the most digits is generally placed as the multiplicand. Thus, to multiply 36×127 you would write the example with 127 as the multiplicand and 36 as the multiplier. Having done this, the operation is as follows:

1. Multiply the multiplicand by the rightmost digit in the multiplier and write down the partial product.
2. Multiply the multiplicand by the second rightmost digit in the multiplier. Because the second rightmost digit is one column to the left of the first, the partial product must be written under the first partial product, one column to the left of it.
3. Continue until the multiplicand has been multiplied by each of the digits in the multiplier, writing the partial product of each digit in the multiplier column to the left of the partial product of the previous digit.
4. Add the partial products. The sum of the partial products is the product.

ILLUSTRATIVE PROBLEM.

$$
\begin{array}{rl}
368 & \\
132 & \\
\hline
736 & \text{Step 1} \\
1104 & \text{Step 2} \\
368 & \text{Step 3} \\
\hline
48,576 & \text{Step 4}
\end{array}
$$

1.17 SOLVE THESE PROBLEMS:

1.	326 $\times\ 37$	**2.**	416 $\times\ 28$	**3.**	875 $\times\ 66$	**4.**	129 $\times\ 94$
5.	378 $\times 163$	**6.**	647 $\times 518$	**7.**	928 $\times 767$	**8.**	735 $\times 914$
9.	1463 $\times 3795$	**10.**	2716 $\times 3829$	**11.**	7518 $\times 9836$	**12.**	2368 $\times 7459$

1.18 *SOLVE THESE PROBLEMS:*

1. The following are the hours worked for one week, and the rate per hour of each employee. Calculate the gross (total) payroll.

Employee	Hours Worked	Rate per Hour	Gross Payroll
1	36	$3.00	—
2	27	4.00	—
3	38	6.00	—
4	19	2.00	—
5	39	5.00	—

2. A dress manufacturer estimates that a particular style will require 2 yards of fabric per dress. If the goods cost $3.75 per yard, what will be the fabric cost for 788 dresses?

3. A furniture store received the following bill from a supplier. Determine the amount owed.

12 Chairs	@	$ 72 each
16 Sofas	@	115 each
36 Tables	@	63 each
18 Lamps	@	47 each

4. A stamping machine that produces 372 pieces per hour worked 167 hours during the month. How many pieces were produced?

d. MULTIPLICATION BY 10 OR POWERS OF 10

To multiply by 10, 100, 1,000, or any multiple of 10, move the decimal point in the multiplicand one place to the right for each zero to be found in the multiplier.

Illustrative Problem.

$$
\begin{array}{r}
784 \\
\times 100 \\
\hline
000 \\
000 \\
784 \\
\hline
78,400
\end{array}
$$

The same result could have been obtained by moving the decimal point in the multiplicand 2 places to the right (there are 2 zeros in the multiplier)

$$784 \times 100 = 78400$$

1.19   SOLVE THESE PROBLEMS:

1. 468 × 10 =   **5.** 926 × 10 =
2. 7,865 × 100 =   **6.** 3,752 × 100 =
3. 16 × 1,000 =   **7.** 295 × 1,000 =
4. 379 × 10,000 =   **8.** 462 × 10,000 =

**e. MULTIPLICATION WHEN ONE NUMERAL ENDS
IN ZERO**

When either the multiplicand or the multiplier end in zero, or both end in zero, it is not necessary to multiply by the zeros. Merely bring down the total number of ending zeros in either or both the multiplicand and the multiplier, and multiply as if there were no zeros.

ILLUSTRATIVE PROBLEMS.
   1. Where the multiplicand ends in zero:

```
    320          The same result could have been obtained
   ×42           this way:
   ────                              320
    640                             ×42│
   1280                             ───
  ──────                            64│
  13,440                           128 ↓
                                  ──────
                                  13,440
```

   2. Where the multiplier ends in zero:

```
    62           The same result could have been obtained
  ×  140         this way:
  ─────
    000                               62
    248                            ×  140
    62                            ──────
  ─────                            248│
   8680                            62 ↓
                                  ─────
                                   8680
```

   3. Where both the multiplier and the multiplicand end in zero:

```
    360          The same result could have been obtained
  ×1200          this way:
  ─────
    000                             360┐
    000                           ×1200│
    720                           ──── │
    360                            72││ │
  ───────                          36 ↓↓↓
  432,000                        ──────
                                 432000
```

1.20 SOLVE THESE PROBLEMS:

1. 3750 ×632	**2.** 6780 ×427	**3.** 63400 ×517	**4.** 83700 ×648
5. 4162 ×41560	**6.** 3783 ×16320	**7.** 9469 ×47800	**8.** 8173 ×92600
9. 37800 × 6340	**10.** 736000 × 12700	**11.** 41270 ×61000	**12.** 31700 ×420000

f. MULTIPLICATION WHEN ZEROS APPEAR WITHIN A NUMERAL

When a zero is found within the numeral representing the multiplier, it is not necessary to multiply the multiplicand by the zero. Instead, indent one extra column before multiplying by the next digit.

ILLUSTRATIVE PROBLEM.

$$
\begin{array}{r}
127 \\
\times 602 \\
\hline
254 \\
000 \\
762 \\
\hline
76454
\end{array}
$$

The same result could have been obtained this way:

$$
\begin{array}{r}
127 \\
\times 602 \\
\hline
254 \\
762 \\
\hline
76454
\end{array}
$$

Note that an extra column was indented before entering the second partial product.

1.21 SOLVE THESE PROBLEMS:

1. 316 ×104	**2.** 728 ×302	**3.** 898 ×407	**4.** 6752 × 809
5. 3718 ×5004	**6.** 6375 ×7008	**7.** 7918 ×6009	**8.** 3756 ×8007

g. MULTIPLICATION WITH DECIMALS

There is no difference in the operation of multiplication when there are decimals present. The only problem is the determination of the number of decimal places in the product. The rule is: *The number of decimal places in the product equals the sum of the decimal places in the multiplicand and the multiplier.*

ILLUSTRATIVE PROBLEM.

1.27
×.362
———
254
762
381
———
.45974

Because there are two decimal places in the multiplicand and three decimal places in the multiplier, there must be five decimal places in the product.

1.22   SOLVE THESE PROBLEMS:

1. 37.8	**2.** 3.62	**3.** .726	**4.** 986.1
× 126	×81.9	×.0047	×.0402
5. .175	**6.** .0762	**7.** .0401	**8.** .00067
×.364	×.0379	×.4007	×.00074
9. .0709	**10.** 3.727	**11.** 1426	**12.** .00673
×4.007	×.1077	×10.105	×.01047

1.23   SOLVE THESE PROBLEMS:

1. Fred worked 37 hours during the week. He is paid at the hourly rate of $3.7275. Calculate his earnings for the week.
2. Textile Mills, Inc., sold two pieces of fabric to a customer. The first was 63.875 yards at $8.275 per yard; the second was 74.125 yards at $7.625 per yard. What was the total amount of the bill?
3. Calculate the real estate tax due on a building assessed at $47,825.00, if the tax rate is $.02737.
4. Tom's earnings of $4,723.65 are subject to social security tax at the rate of .0585. Calculate his social security tax.
5. A metal casting that cost $3.727 to produce is sold for $5.2625. Determine the profit on 327 pieces.
6. The amount of lumber to be used to manufacture a table is 2.165 running feet. What is the lumber cost of the table if the lumber costs $.375 per running foot?

h. PROVING MULTIPLICATION

There are two common ways of proving the accuracy of multiplication: (1) by division, which we will discuss in the next unit; and (2) by interchanging the multiplier and multiplicand and multiplying. In other words, we can prove that 8 × 4 = 32 by multiplying 4 × 8.

ILLUSTRATIVE PROBLEM.

$$
\begin{array}{r}
127 \\
\times 312 \\
\hline
254 \\
127 \\
381 \\
\hline
39624
\end{array}
\qquad
\textit{Proof:}
\begin{array}{r}
312 \\
127 \\
\hline
2184 \\
624 \\
312 \\
\hline
39624
\end{array}
$$

1.24 SOLVE THESE PROBLEMS: Multiply and prove.

1. 675 ×327	**2.** 608 ×316	**3.** 279 ×360	**4.** 527 ×633
5. 607 ×309	**6.** 37.6 ×.124	**7.** 1.752 ×.0073	**8.** 19.65 ×.0105
9. .3706 ×1.0503	**10.** 793.7 ×128.4	**11.** 6.375 × 3792	**12.** .47305 × .0602

4. DIVISION

Division is the arithmetic operation that finds how many times one number goes into another. In essence, it is a short cut method of subtraction. Thus, $28 - 7 - 7 - 7 - 7 = 0$. This may be more simply performed as $28 \div 7 = 4$.

a. DEFINITIONS

$$
\begin{array}{r}
62 \quad \text{Quotient} \\
\text{Divisor} \quad 8\overline{)497} \quad \text{Dividend} \\
48 \\
\hline
17 \\
16 \\
\hline
1 \quad \text{Remainder}
\end{array}
$$

b. OPERATION—MENTAL DIVISION

When the divisor is less than 10, the operation can be performed mentally.

ILLUSTRATIVE PROBLEM.

$$2755 \div 6$$

SOLUTION:

$$\frac{459 \quad \text{Remainder 1 (or } 459\frac{1}{6}) \text{ Quotient}}{\text{Divisor} \quad 6\overline{)2755} \quad \text{Dividend}}$$

The operation was performed in this manner:

1. Think: 6 into 27 is 4 and 3 over, write the 4 and carry 3 in front of the 5, making 35.
2. Think: 6 into 35 is 5 and 5 over, write the 5 and carry 5 in front of the 5, making 55.
3. Think: 6 into 55 is 9 and 1 over, write the 9 and carry 1.
4. Think: 6 into 1 is 0 and 1 over. This is the remainder. In other words, 6 goes into 2755 four hundred and fifty-nine times and one over.

1.25 SOLVE THESE PROBLEMS: Determine the quotients mentally.

1.	$376 \div 4$	**7.**	$27,382 \div 3$
2.	$488 \div 8$	**8.**	$19,676 \div 5$
3.	$3,795 \div 6$	**9.**	$54,883 \div 9$
4.	$5,237 \div 7$	**10.**	$46,883 \div 8$
5.	$1,927 \div 9$	**11.**	$37,886 \div 8$
6.	$15,365 \div 4$	**12.**	$58,667 \div 7$

c. OPERATION—LONG DIVISION

When the divisor contains more than one digit, the operation becomes too complicated to be done mentally.

ILLUSTRATIVE PROBLEM.

$$4732 \div 27$$

SOLUTION:

$$
\begin{array}{r}
175\frac{7}{27} \\
27\overline{)4732} \\
\underline{27} \\
203 \\
\underline{189} \\
142 \\
\underline{135} \\
7
\end{array}
$$

The operation was performed in this manner:

1. Think: 27 into 47 is 1. Write 1 in the quotient over the 47. Then multiply 1 by 27, write the product under the 47 and deduct 47 − 27 = 20 and bring down the next digit (3) to arrive at 203.

2. Think: 27 into 203 is 7. Write the 7 in the quotient over the 3. Then multiply 7 by 27 (189) and write the product under the 203 and deduct 203 − 189 = 14 and bring down the next digit (2) and arrive at 142.

3. Think: 27 into 142 is 5. Write 5 in the quotient over the 2. Then multiply 5 by 27 and write the product under the 142 and deduct. Because there are no more digits in the dividend, 7 is the remainder. This may be expressed as $\frac{7}{27}$.

1.26 SOLVE THESE PROBLEMS:

1. 372 ÷ 12	**7.** 53,681 ÷ 321
2. 458 ÷ 27	**8.** 78,915 ÷ 572
3. 3,645 ÷ 35	**9.** 63,078 ÷ 468
4. 4,688 ÷ 46	**10.** 94,326 ÷ 512
5. 5,433 ÷ 97	**11.** 57,384 ÷ 631
6. 6,327 ÷ 84	**12.** 68,952 ÷ 478

d. DIVISION BY 10 OR POWERS OF 10

Division by 10, 100, 1,000, or any power of 10, can be simplified by moving the decimal point in the dividend to the left as many places as there are zeros in the divisor. Bear in mind that a whole number has an unwritten decimal point at the end. Thus, 7 is really 7., 5 is really 5., and so forth.

ILLUSTRATIVE PROBLEMS.

$$4750 \div 10 = 475 \qquad 3820 \div 100 = 38.20$$

SOLUTIONS: These problems were solved by moving the decimal point one place to the left for each zero in the divisor.

1.27 SOLVE THESE PROBLEMS:

1. 3,820 ÷ 10 =	**7.** .0638 ÷ 100 =
2. 47.58 ÷ 10 =	**8.** 75.37 ÷ 1000 =
3. .3750 ÷ 10 =	**9.** 763.8 ÷ 1000 =
4. 26,375 ÷ 100 =	**10.** .9426 ÷ 1000 =
5. 37.81 ÷ 100 =	**11.** 31 ÷ 1000 =
6. 4.639 ÷ 100 =	**12.** 2 ÷ 1000 =

e. DIVISION WHEN THE DIVISOR ENDS IN ZERO

In division, the quotient will remain the same if both the dividend and the divisor are divided by the same number. For example, $16 \div 4 = 4$. If we divide both the dividend and the divisor by 2, we get $8 \div 2 = 4$. Note that in either case, the quotient is 4. To simplify the operation of division when the divisor ends in one or more zeros, divide both numbers by an amount equal to the ending zeros in the divisor. That is, a divisor ending in two zeros would allow both the divisor and the dividend to be divided by 100. As we have seen, we can divide by 100 by moving the decimal two places to the left.

ILLUSTRATIVE PROBLEM.

$$
\begin{array}{r}
321 \\
1500\overline{)481500} \\
4500 \\
\hline
3150 \\
3000 \\
\hline
1500 \\
1500 \\
\hline
\end{array}
$$

The same result could have been obtained by moving the decimal point two places to the left in the divisor (one for each zero) and two places to the left in the dividend. Thus:

$481,500 \div 1500 = 481,500 \div 1500$

$$
\text{or} \quad
\begin{array}{r}
321 \\
15\overline{)4815} \\
45 \\
\hline
31 \\
30 \\
\hline
15 \\
15 \\
\hline
\end{array}
$$

1.28 SOLVE THESE PROBLEMS:

1. $463 \div 120$	**7.** $8,263 \div 350$
2. $579 \div 300$	**8.** $7,861 \div 4,800$
3. $2,785 \div 260$	**9.** $8,276 \div 3,600$
4. $3,796 \div 370$	**10.** $9,263 \div 9,400$
5. $4,826 \div 420$	**11.** $7,826 \div 7,800$
6. $9,412 \div 3,900$	**12.** $3,502 \div 2,700$

1.29 SOLVE THESE PROBLEMS:

1. An office building has 10,356 square feet of rental space for which it receives a gross annual rental of $25,890. What is the annual rent per square foot?

2. John received $98.10 for working 27 hours. Calculate his hourly rate of pay.

3. A factory buys 437 parts, paying $1,857.25 for the lot. Determine the cost per piece.

4. If the total cost of manufacture for the month was $37,685.12, and the total production was 7,827 units, what was the cost per unit to the nearest tenth of a cent?

5. A machine that produces 63 units per hour produced 525 units in one week. How many hours did it run?

6. Apex Motors produced 4,620 cars in October; 3,763 cars in November; and 5,268 cars in December. What was the average daily production for the quarter? (To find the average, total all of the production and divide by the number of months.)

f. DIVISION WHEN THERE ARE DECIMALS IN THE DIVISOR

Decimals in the divisor are cleared before the operation is performed. This is done by moving the decimal point in the divisor as many places to the right as is necessary to clear the decimal places. The decimals in the dividend must then be moved the same number of places to the right. Frequently, zeros must be added to the dividend to accomplish this. For example, $37.263 \div 12.6842$ should be restated as:

$$12.6842.\overline{)37.2630.}$$

Because we moved four places in the divisor, we had to move four places in the dividend. This required the placing of an additional zero in the dividend. What we are actually doing is multiplying both the divisor and the dividend by the same amount. This has no effect on the quotient. For example:

$$8 \div 2 = 4 \text{ is the same as } 80 \div 20 = 4$$

ILLUSTRATIVE PROBLEM.

$$.2556 \div 1.8 =$$

SOLUTION:

1. Set up the problem for long division and clear the decimals in the divisor.

$$1.8.\overline{)2.556}$$

Note that the decimals in the dividend are not cleared and that the decimal point in the quotient will appear above the newly positioned decimal point in the dividend.

2. Perform the operation.

$$
\begin{array}{r}
.142 \\
18\overline{)2.556} \\
\underline{1\ 8} \\
75 \\
\underline{72} \\
36 \\
\underline{36}
\end{array}
$$

1.30 SOLVE THESE PROBLEMS:

1. 327 ÷ 1.9   **7.** .0926 ÷ 37.5

2. 416 ÷ .23   **8.** .7520 ÷ .382

3. 41.7 ÷ 307   **9.** 92.56 ÷ 3.705

4. 4.98 ÷ .78   **10.** 8.763 ÷ 63.8

5. .826 ÷ 3.27   **11.** 295.7 ÷ .326

6. .947 ÷ 7.63   **12.** 7386 ÷ 42.04

g. DIVISION TO PROVE MULTIPLICATION

The product determined by multiplying two numbers can be proven by dividing either of the numbers multiplied and getting the other as a quotient.

ILLUSTRATIVE PROBLEM.

$$
\begin{array}{r}
37 \\
\times\ 26 \\
\hline
222 \\
74 \\
\hline
962
\end{array}
\qquad
Proof:\
\begin{array}{r}
26 \\
37\overline{)962} \\
74 \\
\hline
222 \\
222 \\
\hline
\end{array}
\quad or \quad
\begin{array}{r}
37 \\
26\overline{)962} \\
78 \\
\hline
182 \\
182 \\
\hline
\end{array}
$$

1.31 SOLVE THESE PROBLEMS: Multiply and prove.

1. 37 × 86 =   **7.** 362 × 129 =

2. 94 × 73 =   **8.** 785 × 317 =

3. 27 × 64 =   **9.** 539 × 462 =

4. 94 × 75 =   **10.** 926 × 785 =

5. 38 × 86 =   **11.** 847 × 736 =

6. 41 × 57 =   **12.** 236 × 927 =

h. PROVING DIVISION

To prove the accuracy of the quotient, multiply it by the divisor. The product should be the dividend. In other words, if 3 × 6 = 18, then 18 ÷ 3 = 6 (or 18 ÷ 6 = 3).

ILLUSTRATIVE PROBLEM. Divide and prove.

$$486 \div 18 =$$

SOLUTION:

$$
\begin{array}{r}
27 \\
18\overline{)486} \\
36 \\
\hline
126 \\
126 \\
\hline
\end{array}
\qquad
\textit{Proof:}
\begin{array}{r}
27 \\
\times\ 18 \\
\hline
216 \\
27 \\
\hline
486 \\
\end{array}
\quad \text{or} \quad
\begin{array}{r}
18 \\
27\overline{)486} \\
27 \\
\hline
216 \\
216 \\
\hline
\end{array}
$$

1.32 SOLVE THESE PROBLEMS:

1. $144 \div 12 =$ 7. $252 \div 18 =$
2. $323 \div 19 =$ 8. $552 \div 24 =$
3. $361 \div 19 =$ 9. $391 \div 23 =$
4. $462 \div 21 =$ 10. $575 \div 25 =$
5. $252 \div 36 =$ 11. $308 \div 22 =$
6. $625 \div 25 =$ 12. $306 \div 17 =$

**5. ROUNDING
OFF**

Frequently arithmetic solutions are more exact than is necessary or practical. In such cases, it is allowable to round off the number. In most business, numbers are generally rounded off to the nearest cent. The rules for rounding off are:

1. If the digits to be dropped begin with 5 or more add 1 to the rightmost digit retained.
2. If the digits to be dropped begin with less than 5, do not change the rightmost digit retained.

ILLUSTRATIVE PROBLEM. How much money, to the nearest cent, is needed to buy 17 units at $3.7525 per unit?

SOLUTION:

$$
\begin{array}{r}
\$3.7525 \\
\times\ 17 \\
\hline
262675 \\
37525 \\
\hline
\$63.7925 \\
\end{array}
$$

Answer: $63.79. If the product was $63.7951, the answer would be $63.80.

1.33 SOLVE THESE PROBLEMS: Round off the following numbers to the nearest cent.

1. $37.275
2.   1.47236
3.   .5865
4.   .0329

5. 16.759
6. 12.349
7.   .3749
8.   .684999

1.34 SOLVE THESE PROBLEMS:

1. Last year Prichard's, Inc., had sales of $12,637.48. What was the average monthly sales? (Round to nearest dollar.)
2. The payroll of the Olson Book Company was $27,632.14 for the month of July. During that month 327 people were employed. Calculate the average salary. (Round to nearest cent.)
3. The Brite Baking Company used 7,857 pounds of flour during one month to bake 15,623 loaves of bread. How much flour was used per loaf? (Round off to nearest thousandth.)
4. An oil tank has a capacity of 7,000 cubic feet. Each gallon of oil requires $7\frac{1}{2}$ cubic feet. How many gallons of oil are there in the tank? (Round off to the nearest gallon.)
5. The Blair Company is considering computerizing its payroll department. The computer has the capacity of processing 1,750 payroll checks per minute. Calculate the computer time necessary to process 27,636 employee checks. (Round to nearest minute.)
6. If the price of a 36 foot by 27 foot lot is $4,700, what is the cost per square foot? (Round to nearest dollar.)

6. ESTIMATING

A fairly close approximation of a solution may be obtained by rounding off the numbers to the nearest tens, hundreds, thousands, and so on, and then adding the rounded-off numbers. This can be done mentally.

ILLUSTRATIVE PROBLEMS.

1.	27 rounds off to	30	2.	362 rounds off to	400
	52 rounds off to	50		427 rounds off to	400
	36 rounds off to	40		912 rounds off to	900
	48 rounds off to	50		787 rounds off to	800
	68 rounds off to	70		362 rounds off to	400
	24 rounds off to	20		546 rounds off to	500
	12 rounds off to	10		257 rounds off to	300
	267	270		3,653	3,700
	Actual	Approximate		Actual	Approximate

This is an excellent method of checking the approximate correctness of any problem, particularly because it can be done mentally.

1.35   SOLVE THESE PROBLEMS: Add. Test the approximate correctness of your solution by mentally rounding off and adding.

1.	87		2.	36	
	22			21	
	36			17	
	94			12	
	24			79	
	19			13	
	Actual	Approximate		Actual	Approximate

3.	126		4.	378	
	375			129	
	264			471	
	129			812	
	574			943	
	315			629	
	Actual	Approximate		447	
				590	
				Actual	Approximate

5.	1,688		6.	2,798	
	1,356			8,316	
	2,971			4,681	
	5,161			5,416	
	9,263			2,937	
	4,877			5,116	
	7,368			3,718	
	2,706			7,341	
	Actual	Approximate		Actual	Approximate

7. THE METRIC SYSTEM

In most of the nations in the world, with the United States and the United Kingdom as exceptions, the metric system of measurement is the standardized system. From all indications, the United States will ultimately join the United Kingdom, which will switch to the metric system in 1975, as the last of the major nations to do so.

The metric system has, to a limited extent, been used in actual practice in the United States since it was legalized in 1866. It has been used until this time on a restrictive, voluntary basis by industrialists, engineers, and scientists.

Among the reasons given for the eventual conversion by the U.S. to such a system are the following:

1. It is the most widely used system of weights and measures in the world.

2. The present state and potential increase in international trade dictates that a universal system of measurement will be necessary for computational purposes.

Conversion to the metric system will necessitate familiarization and understanding by all citizens in the United States. In particular, business students, many of whom will be gainfully employed in marketing positions that involve transactions with foreign countries, will find it essential to understand the system.

The basic units of measurement in the metric system are linear, volume, and weight. Linear measurement is done in meters, weight in grams, and volume in liters.

Exploration of the arithmetic involved in metric measurement and conversions to and from the system presently used in the United States follows. The table, which represents approximate equivalents and conversions, is used in the solution of the problem material.

METRIC EQUIVALENTS AND CONVERSIONS

1 inch	= 25 millimeters
1 foot	= 0.3 meter
1 yard	= 0.9 meter
1 mile	= 1.6 kilometers
1 square inch	= 6.5 square centimeters
1 square foot	= 0.009 square meter
1 square yard	= 0.8 square meter
1 acre	= 0.4 hectare
1 cubic inch	= 16 cubic centimeters
1 cubic foot	= 0.003 cubic meter
1 cubic yard	= 0.8 cubic meter
1 quart	= 0.95 liter
1 gallon	= 0.004 cubic meter
1 gallon	= 3.785 liters
1 ounce	= 28 grams
1 pound	= 0.45 kilogram
1 millimeter	= 0.04 inch
1 meter	= 3.3 feet
1 meter	= 1.1 yards
1 kilometer	= 0.6 mile
1 square centimeter	= 0.16 square inch
1 square meter	= 11 square feet
1 square meter	= 1.2 yards
1 hectare	= 2.5 acres
1 cubic centimeter	= 0.006 cubic inch
1 cubic meter	= 35 cubic feet
1 cubic meter	= 1.3 cubic yards
1 liter	= 1.05 quarts
1 gram	= 0.035 ounce
1 kilogram	= 2.2 pounds

a. LINEAR MEASUREMENT

Both long and short distances can be easily measured by using the basic "meter." In our present system of measurement individuals are confronted with inches, feet, yards, and so forth.

ILLUSTRATIVE PROBLEM. The distance from the receiving room to the selling floor in Crowley's Supermarket is 35 yards, 2 feet in length. Express the distance in meters.

SOLUTION:

   1. Using the conversion table:

$$1 \text{ yard} = 0.9 \text{ meter}$$
$$1 \text{ foot} = 0.3 \text{ meter}$$

   2. 35 yards multiplied by 0.9 = 31.5 meters
   2 feet multiplied by 0.3 = .6 meter
   3. 31.5 added to .6 = 32.1

1.36   SOLVE THESE PROBLEMS:

   1. A television antenna is 84 feet high; what is the height in meters?
   2. Brown's Specialty Shops is opening a new branch that is located 127 miles from its nearest unit. How far away is the new location, expressed in kilometers?
   3. The store window in Cardell's Shoe Shop measures 9 feet by 4 feet. Express the area of the window in terms of square meters.
   4. Before merchandise is loaded on a ship headed for the United States it must travel 20 kilometers by truck from the factory. In terms of miles, how far must the goods travel?
   5. Relating to problem 4, what will be the cost of shipment if the trucking rate is $2.50 per mile?

b. WEIGHT

The gram is the term of measurement used in the metric system.

ILLUSTRATIVE PROBLEM. Tempty-Biscuits, a producer of cookies, plans to export its products to France and must use the metric system to specify weight. How should a box of cookies weighing 14 ounces be labeled?

SOLUTION:
> 1. Using the conversion table, 1 ounce is equal to 28 grams.
> 2. Multiply 28 by 14.
> 3. Answer: 392 grams.

1.37   *SOLVE THESE PROBLEMS:* Round off to the nearest tenth.
> 1. A butcher shop sells a customer 5 pounds of beef. How much does the meat weigh in kilograms?
> 2. Mrs. Jones purchases the following produce:
>
> > 10 pounds of potatoes
> > 2 pounds of tomatoes
> > 3 pounds of onions
>
> How much, in kilograms, does the produce total?
> 3. Using problem 2, if potatoes are 6¢ per kilogram, tomatoes 27¢, and onions 16¢, how much will the order cost?
> 4. Imported tea, amounting to 10,000 bags weighing 20 kilograms each, will be sold at retail for 35¢ per pound. How much will the entire shipment be marked for retail?

c. VOLUME MEASURE

Measurement of volume is expressed in liters and can be easily converted to and from our system of measurement.

ILLUSTRATIVE PROBLEM. A wine producer in France wants to sell his product, which contains 2 liters per bottle, to the U.S. In terms of our measurement system, how must he label the volume of each bottle?

SOLUTION:
> 1. Using the table, 1 liter = 1.05 quarts
> 2. Multiply 1.05 by 2
> 3. Answer: 2.1 quarts

1.38   *SOLVE THESE PROBLEMS:* Round off to the nearest tenth.
> 1. How many liters of milk are there in a 2-gallon jug?
> 2. Determine the total number of liters for the following paint order:
>
> > 1 gallon of red paint
> > 1 quart of white paint
> > $\frac{1}{2}$ quart of blue paint
>
> 3. A shipment of 365 liters of imported perfume totals how much in quarts?

1. The daily sales of a retail grocery store were: $216.54; $127.18; $206.47; $198.75; $312.63; $572.90. Calculate the sales for the week.

2. On June 1, the Blake Company owed its suppliers $6,375.18. During June it purchased on account $10,642.15 and paid its suppliers $8,826.19. What was the accounts payable on July 12?

3. The cost of a manufactured part is $1.367 per unit. The item sells for $2.237. Determine the profit on a sale of 3,712 pieces.

4. An item that cost $4.2736 per piece was increased by $.0464. Calculate the new cost on a purchase of 678 pieces.

5. If the total payroll for the week was $5,843.75 and the number of units produced was 1,375, what was the labor cost per unit?

6. The total cost of 6,375 tons is $198,900. Calculate the cost per ton.

7. Round off to the nearest cent: $12.372; $.0997; $6.376; $.005763.

8. Add horizontally: $16.3 + 42.1 + 27.8 + 38.7 + 96.4 =$

2

fractions and decimals

1. FRACTIONS
   a. Types of fractions
   b. Reducing fractions
   c. Raising fractions
   d. Converting mixed numbers to improper fractions
   e. Converting improper fractions to mixed numbers
   f. Lowest common denominator
   g. Addition of fractions
   h. Subtraction of fractions
   i. Multiplication of fractions
   j. Multiplication of fractions by cancellation
   k. Division of fractions

2. DECIMAL FRACTIONS
   a. Converting decimals to fractions
   b. Converting fractions to decimals
   1. Remainders and repeating decimals

1. FRACTIONS   A fraction is one or more equal parts of a whole number. It consists of two numerals, one above the other, separated by a line. The numeral above the line is called the numerator, the numeral below the line is called the denominator. In the fraction $\frac{3}{4}$, three is the numerator and four is the denominator.

The denominator indicates the number of parts the whole is divided into.

The numerator indicates the number of parts in the particular numeral.

Thus, the numeral $\frac{3}{4}$ indicates that the whole is divided into four parts and that three of the four parts are represented by the numeral $\frac{3}{4}$.

The bar in the fraction indicates *divided by*. $\frac{3}{4}$ can also be expressed as $3 \div 4$.

If a loaf of bread contains seven slices and five slices are eaten, the quantity eaten may be expressed as:

$\frac{5}{7}$ Numerator (Number of parts in this particular numeral)
   Denominator (Number of parts into which the whole is divided)

a. TYPES OF FRACTIONS

There are three types of fractions:

1. *Proper fractions* are fractions in which the numerator is less than the denominator, such as $\frac{1}{3}$, $\frac{4}{5}$, $\frac{5}{8}$. A proper fraction is less than one (the whole).

2. *Improper fractions* are fractions in which the numerator is greater than the denominator, such as $\frac{5}{4}$, $\frac{3}{2}$, $\frac{8}{5}$. An improper fraction is greater than one.

3. *Mixed numerals* combine units and fractions. For example, $1\frac{1}{2}$, $5\frac{5}{6}$, $6\frac{7}{8}$ are mixed numerals. They combine one or more whole numerals plus a part of a whole.

37

b. REDUCING FRACTIONS

The value of a fraction will not be changed if both the numerator and denominator are divided by the same number; this makes it possible to reduce fractions. As a general rule, fractions should be reduced to their lowest terms; that is, reduced to a point at which no whole number can be divided evenly (with no remainder) into both the numerator and the denominator. A common method of doing this is by the trial and error method in which both the numerator and denominator are first divided by a small number that divides into both evenly. The answer is then divided by another number which divides into both evenly, and so on until no number can be found that divides into both evenly.

ILLUSTRATIVE PROBLEM. Reduce the fraction $\frac{216}{288}$ to its lowest terms.

SOLUTION: Because both the numerator and the denominator end in even numbers, they can be divided by 2:

$$\frac{216 \div 2 = 108 \div 4 = 27 \div 9 = 3}{288 \div 2 = 144 \div 4 = 36 \div 9 = 4}$$

It was found, by trial and error, that both 108 and 144 were evenly divisible by 4. This resulted in $\frac{27}{36}$—both numbers that are evenly divisible by 9. The resulting fraction, $\frac{3}{4}$, is not evenly divisible by any whole number. It is the lowest term of the fraction $\frac{216}{288}$. This can be stated as $\frac{216}{288} = \frac{3}{4}$.

2.1 SOLVE THESE PROBLEMS: Using the trial and error method, reduce the following fractions to their lowest terms.

1. $\frac{125}{175} =$	**7.** $\frac{316}{752} =$
2. $\frac{81}{189} =$	**8.** $\frac{612}{848} =$
3. $\frac{288}{396} =$	**9.** $\frac{945}{963} =$
4. $\frac{504}{658} =$	**10.** $\frac{428}{844} =$
5. $\frac{365}{755} =$	**11.** $\frac{355}{1065} =$
6. $\frac{217}{434} =$	**12.** $\frac{255}{340} =$

Though the trial and error method is suitable for fractions containing few digits, as the number of digits in the fraction increases, the number of separate division problems becomes unwieldy. Finding the greatest common divisor is a method that will allow us to divide once, by a relatively large number, to find the lowest terms of a fraction.

The method is as follows:

1. Divide the larger number by the smaller.
2. Divide the divisor (smaller number) by remainder.
3. Continue this operation until there is no remainder.
4. The last divisor is the greatest common divisor. When this number is divided into the numerator and denominator of the fraction, the fraction will be reduced to its lowest terms.

ILLUSTRATIVE PROBLEM. Using the greatest common divisor method, reduce the fraction $\frac{216}{288}$ to its lowest terms.

SOLUTION:

1. Divide the numerator into the denominator

$$
\begin{array}{r}
1 \\
216\overline{)288} \\
216 \\
\hline
72
\end{array}
$$

2. Divide the numerator by the remainder

$$
\begin{array}{r}
3 \\
72\overline{)216} \\
216 \\
\hline
\end{array}
$$

3. $\dfrac{216 \div 72}{288 \div 72} = \dfrac{3}{4}$

2.2 SOLVE THESE PROBLEMS: Reduce the following fractions to their lowest terms by finding the greatest common divisor.

1. $\frac{126}{294} =$ 7. $\frac{189}{315} =$

2. $\frac{316}{948} =$ 8. $\frac{168}{352} =$

3. $\frac{108}{744} =$ 9. $\frac{132}{372} =$

4. $\frac{124}{217} =$ 10. $\frac{336}{496} =$

5. $\frac{342}{568} =$ 11. $\frac{558}{738} =$

6. $\frac{147}{224} =$ 12. $\frac{399}{589} =$

c. RAISING FRACTIONS

As we have seen, fractions can be reduced by dividing the numerator and the denominator by the same number; similarly, they may be raised by multiplying the numerator and the denominator by the same number. For example, $\frac{3}{8}$ can be raised to sixteenths by multiplying both terms by 2: $\frac{3}{8} \times \frac{2}{2} = \frac{6}{16}$. Then, $\frac{3}{8} = \frac{6}{16}$.

ILLUSTRATIVE PROBLEM.

$$\frac{3}{4} = \frac{}{12}$$

SOLUTION: Because the denominator 4 was multiplied by 3 to be raised to 12, the numerator must also be multiplied by 3: $\frac{3}{4} \times \frac{3}{3} = \frac{9}{12}$.

2.3   SOLVE THESE PROBLEMS:

1. $\dfrac{5}{6} = \dfrac{}{24}$

2. $\dfrac{3}{8} = \dfrac{}{40}$

3. $\dfrac{5}{9} = \dfrac{}{36}$

4. $\dfrac{6}{7} = \dfrac{}{77}$

5. $\dfrac{1}{8} = \dfrac{}{96}$

6. $\dfrac{7}{16} = \dfrac{}{96}$

7. $\dfrac{20}{25} = \dfrac{}{250}$

8. $\dfrac{5}{18} = \dfrac{}{126}$

9. $\dfrac{7}{11} = \dfrac{}{132}$

10. $\dfrac{9}{12} = \dfrac{}{180}$

11. $\dfrac{13}{17} = \dfrac{}{85}$

12. $\dfrac{20}{27} = \dfrac{}{216}$

**d. CONVERTING MIXED NUMBERS TO IMPROPER
FRACTIONS**

A mixed number is one that is made up of a whole number and a fraction such as $4\frac{1}{3}$, $7\frac{1}{2}$, $6\frac{3}{8}$. Any number can be expressed as a fraction with any denominator by multiplying it by the value of 1 expressed as a fraction. For example:

The number 1 can be expressed as $\dfrac{1}{1}, \dfrac{2}{2}, \dfrac{3}{3}, \cdots$

The number 3 can be expressed as $\dfrac{3}{1}, \dfrac{6}{2}, \dfrac{9}{3}, \cdots$

and to express the number 6 in ninths, multiply

$$\frac{6}{1} \times \frac{9}{9} = \frac{54}{9}$$

To convert a mixed number to a fraction, multiply the whole number by the denominator of the fraction, add the numerator of the fraction, and place the total over the original denominator.

ILLUSTRATIVE PROBLEM. Convert $7\frac{5}{8}$ to an improper fraction.

SOLUTION:

1. Convert the whole number 7 to a fraction with the denominator of 8.

$$7 \times \frac{8}{8} = \frac{56}{8}$$

2. Add the fraction,

$$\frac{56}{8} + \frac{5}{8} = \frac{61}{8} \quad \text{Answer}$$

This could have been done by multiplying the whole number by the denominator of the fraction and adding the numerator. Thus,

$$\frac{7 \times 8 + 5}{8} = \frac{61}{8}$$

2.4 SOLVE THESE PROBLEMS: Convert the following mixed numbers to improper fractions.

1. $6\frac{3}{8}$
2. $8\frac{5}{6}$
3. $10\frac{3}{16}$
4. $8\frac{5}{8}$
5. $12\frac{3}{7}$
6. $18\frac{4}{5}$

7. $11\frac{3}{16}$
8. $16\frac{11}{12}$
9. $1\frac{6}{37}$
10. $26\frac{5}{17}$
11. $48\frac{6}{19}$
12. $37\frac{2}{23}$

e. CONVERTING IMPROPER FRACTIONS TO MIXED NUMBERS

To convert an improper fraction to a mixed number use the following method:

1. Divide the numerator by the denominator. This results in the whole number part of the mixed number.
2. The remainder over the denominator is the fraction part of the mixed number.

ILLUSTRATIVE PROBLEM. Convert the fraction $\frac{127}{15}$ to a mixed number.

SOLUTION:

1. Divide the numerator by the denominator to get the whole number part of the mixed number:

$$15\overline{\smash{)}127}$$
$$\frac{120}{7} \quad 8$$

Whole number $= 8$

2. The remainder over the denominator is the fraction part of the mixed number.

$$\frac{7}{15}$$

Answer: $8\frac{7}{15}$

2.5 SOLVE THESE PROBLEMS: Convert the following fractions to mixed numbers.

1. $\frac{65}{2}$		**7.** $\frac{326}{8}$	
2. $\frac{78}{3}$		**8.** $\frac{427}{15}$	
3. $\frac{46}{5}$		**9.** $\frac{635}{18}$	
4. $\frac{99}{2}$		**10.** $\frac{726}{15}$	
5. $\frac{37}{4}$		**11.** $\frac{163}{23}$	
6. $\frac{86}{7}$		**12.** $\frac{764}{21}$	

f. LOWEST COMMON DENOMINATOR

The operations of addition and subtraction of fractions require us to convert all fractions in the example to fractions having the same denominators. To simplify the work as much as possible, we use the smallest denominator that can be divided evenly (with no remainder) by all of the denominators in the problem. This is called the lowest common denominator. Finding the lowest common denominator can frequently be done by inspection.

ILLUSTRATIVE PROBLEM. Find the lowest common denominator of the following fractions and convert each fraction to its equivalent with the lowest common denominator as its denominator.

$$\frac{1}{2}, \frac{3}{4}, \frac{5}{6}, \frac{1}{3}$$

SOLUTION: In this simple problem it can be seen that the smallest number into which each of the denominators can be divided is twelve. To convert each fraction to its equivalent with the denominator of twelve, it is necessary to recall the rule that the value of a fraction will not be changed if its numerator and denominator are both multiplied by the same number.

To convert $\frac{1}{2}$ to twelfths:

Because the denominator 2 must be multiplied by 6 to equal 12, then to change $\frac{1}{2}$ to twelfths without changing its value, both the numerator and the denominator must be multiplied by 6.

$$\frac{1}{2} \times \frac{6}{6} = \frac{6}{12}$$

Similarly:

$$\frac{3}{4} \times \frac{3}{3} = \frac{9}{12}$$

$$\frac{5}{6} \times \frac{2}{2} = \frac{10}{12}$$

$$\frac{1}{3} \times \frac{4}{4} = \frac{4}{12}$$

In each case we must determine the number that when multiplied by the denominator will equal 12, and then multiply that number by both the numerator and the denominator.

2.6 SOLVE THESE PROBLEMS: Find the lowest common denominator. Convert each fraction to its equivalent with the lowest common denominator as the denominator for each set of examples.

1. $\frac{1}{3}, \frac{5}{6}, \frac{3}{4}$

2. $\frac{4}{5}, \frac{3}{10}, \frac{3}{20}$

3. $\frac{1}{2}, \frac{2}{5}, \frac{3}{4}$

4. $\frac{3}{8}, \frac{1}{4}, \frac{2}{3}$

5. $\frac{1}{6}, \frac{2}{3}, \frac{3}{4}$

6. $\frac{1}{2}, \frac{5}{9}, \frac{5}{6}$

7. $\frac{2}{3}, \frac{3}{10}, \frac{4}{15}, \frac{5}{6}$

8. $\frac{1}{9}, \frac{5}{18}, \frac{5}{12}, \frac{1}{6}$

9. $\frac{3}{14}, \frac{1}{2}, \frac{2}{7}, \frac{25}{28}$

10. $\frac{2}{3}, \frac{8}{21}, \frac{6}{7}, \frac{5}{6}$

11. $\frac{2}{5}, \frac{5}{9}, \frac{2}{15}, \frac{1}{3}$

12. $\frac{5}{24}, \frac{10}{12}, \frac{3}{8}, \frac{1}{6}$

In some cases, the lowest common denominator cannot be determined by inspection. In such cases the procedure for determining the lowest common denominator is as follows:

1. Place the denominators horizontally across the page.

2. Divide each denominator by a prime number (one that can be divided only by itself or 1). Choose a prime number that can be divided evenly into as many of the denominators as possible.

3. Carry to the next line the quotients of those numbers that divided evenly, and the original denominator in cases where the quotient did not come out evenly.

4. Continue until all of the quotients equal 1.

5. The lowest common denominator is the product of all of the prime numbers.

ILLUSTRATIVE PROBLEM. Find the lowest common denominator of the following fractions and convert each fraction to its equivalent with the lowest common denominator as its denominator:

$$\frac{5}{8}, \frac{3}{15}, \frac{7}{10}, \frac{5}{12}, \frac{5}{6}$$

SOLUTION: The numbering of the steps in the solution conforms with the steps indicated in the explanation above.

1.	8	15	10	12	6
2.	2⌋8	2⌋15	2⌋10	2⌋12	2⌋6
3.	4	15	5	6	3
4a.	3⌋4	3⌋15	3⌋5	3⌋6	3⌋3
4b.	4	5	5	2	1
4c.	5⌋4	5⌋5	5⌋5	5⌋2	5⌋1
4d.	4	1	1	2	1
4e.	2⌋4	2⌋1	2⌋1	2⌋2	2⌋1
4f.	2	1	1	1	1
4g.	2⌋2	2⌋1	2⌋1	2⌋1	2⌋1
4h.	1	1	1	1	1

5. $2 \times 3 \times 5 \times 2 \times 2 = 120$ Lowest common denominator

Having determined that the lowest common denominator is 120, to change each fraction to a fraction of the same value, having 120 as the denominator, we must find what number, multiplied by the original denominator, yields a product of 120, and multiply that number by both the numerator and the denominator of the original fraction.

$$\frac{5}{8}: \quad 120 \div 8 \; = 15 \qquad \frac{5}{8} \times \frac{15}{15} = \frac{75}{120}$$

$$\frac{3}{15}: \quad 120 \div 15 = 8 \qquad \frac{3}{15} \times \frac{8}{8} \; = \frac{24}{120}$$

$$\frac{7}{10}: \quad 120 \div 10 = 12 \qquad \frac{7}{10} \times \frac{12}{12} = \frac{84}{120}$$

$$\frac{5}{12}: \quad 120 \div 12 = 10 \qquad \frac{5}{12} \times \frac{10}{10} = \frac{50}{120}$$

$$\frac{5}{6}: \quad 120 \div 6 \; = 20 \qquad \frac{5}{6} \times \frac{20}{20} = \frac{100}{120}$$

2.7 SOLVE THESE PROBLEMS: Find the lowest common denominator of the following fractions and convert each fraction to its equivalent with the lowest common denominator as its denominator.

1. $\frac{3}{8}, \frac{5}{6}, \frac{8}{15}$

2. $\frac{7}{18}, \frac{5}{27}, \frac{19}{36}$

3. $\frac{3}{8}, \frac{5}{12}, \frac{7}{20}$

4. $\frac{5}{8}, \frac{3}{10}, \frac{4}{15}$

5. $\frac{11}{42}, \frac{1}{6}, \frac{11}{15}$

6. $\frac{3}{5}, \frac{5}{6}, \frac{7}{8}$

7. $\frac{7}{16}, \frac{7}{24}, \frac{7}{8}, \frac{7}{32}$

8. $\frac{1}{3}, \frac{3}{4}, \frac{5}{6}, \frac{6}{7}$

9. $\frac{5}{12}, \frac{3}{20}, \frac{7}{15}, \frac{9}{10}$

10. $\frac{1}{6}, \frac{5}{12}, \frac{7}{18}, \frac{11}{20}$

11. $\frac{5}{32}, \frac{3}{16}, \frac{9}{64}, \frac{11}{20}$

12. $\frac{5}{6}, \frac{2}{9}, \frac{7}{12}, \frac{3}{16}$

g. ADDITION OF FRACTIONS

The addition of fractions (proper fractions, improper fractions, and mixed numbers) is done in the following manner:

1. Change all the fractions to their equivalent value with the lowest common denominator. This will result in all of the fractions having the same common denominator.

2. Add the numerators of each of the fractions, and make a new fraction with the total of the numerators as numerator and the lowest common denominator as denominator:

$$\frac{\text{Total of the numerators}}{\text{Lowest common denominator}}$$

3. Reduce to lowest terms.

ILLUSTRATIVE PROBLEM. Add.

$$\tfrac{2}{3} + \tfrac{3}{4} + \tfrac{5}{6} + \tfrac{3}{8}$$

SOLUTION:

1. Change each fraction to its equivalent value with the lowest common denominator as denominator. The lowest common denominator is 24.

$$\frac{2}{3} = \frac{16}{24}$$
$$\frac{3}{4} = \frac{18}{24}$$
$$\frac{5}{6} = \frac{20}{24}$$
$$\frac{3}{8} = \frac{9}{24}$$

2. Add the numerators.

$$16 + 18 + 20 + 9 = 63$$

Make a new fraction.

$$\frac{\text{Total of the numerator}}{\text{Lowest common denominator}} \quad \frac{63}{24}$$

3. Reduce to lowest terms.

$$\tfrac{63}{24} = 63 \div 24 = 2\tfrac{15}{24} = 2\tfrac{5}{8}$$

2.8   SOLVE THESE PROBLEMS: Add.

1. $\frac{1}{3} + \frac{1}{2} + \frac{3}{4}$

2. $\frac{5}{5} + \frac{7}{8} + \frac{5}{12}$

3. $\frac{2}{5} + \frac{3}{10} + \frac{1}{6}$

4. $\frac{2}{3} + \frac{5}{9} + \frac{4}{27}$

5. $\frac{3}{8} + \frac{5}{6} + \frac{7}{12} + \frac{1}{4}$

6. $\frac{7}{24} + \frac{1}{12} + \frac{5}{48} + \frac{3}{8}$

7. $\frac{5}{12} + \frac{3}{20} + \frac{8}{15} + \frac{1}{4}$

8. $\frac{2}{15} + \frac{3}{15} + \frac{6}{25} + \frac{2}{3}$

9. $\frac{5}{32} + \frac{7}{16} + \frac{3}{8} + \frac{1}{4}$

10. $\frac{5}{16} + \frac{3}{20} + \frac{2}{5} + \frac{7}{40}$

11. $\frac{5}{36} + \frac{7}{18} + \frac{4}{9} + \frac{19}{72}$

12. $\frac{1}{2} + \frac{7}{16} + \frac{1}{8} + \frac{3}{4}$

Where mixed numbers and improper fractions are to be added, the same rule still applies. That is, change all of the fractions to the lowest common denominator and add.

ILLUSTRATIVE PROBLEM. Add.

$$3\tfrac{1}{8} + \tfrac{19}{16} + 7\tfrac{1}{2} + \tfrac{7}{4}$$

SOLUTION: The least common denominator of the denominators 8, 16, 2, and 4 is 16. Therefore, the figures to be added must be changed to their value with the denominator 16, and added.

$$3\,\frac{1}{8} = 3\,\frac{2}{16}$$

$$\frac{19}{16} = \frac{19}{16}$$

$$7\,\frac{1}{2} = 7\,\frac{8}{16}$$

$$\frac{7}{4} = \frac{28}{16}$$

$$10\,\frac{57}{16} \quad \frac{\text{Total of the numerators}}{\text{Lowest common denominator}} \quad \frac{(2 + 19 + 8 + 28)}{}$$

Then reduce.

$$10\frac{57}{16} \qquad \left(\frac{57}{16} = 16\overline{)57} = 3\frac{9}{16}\right)$$

$$= 10 + 3\frac{9}{16}$$

$$= 13\frac{9}{16}$$

2.9 SOLVE THESE PROBLEMS: Add.

1. $5\frac{7}{8} + \frac{11}{8} + \frac{3}{4}$

2. $\frac{3}{2} + \frac{11}{20} + 1\frac{4}{5}$

3. $2\frac{1}{3} + 7\frac{1}{9} + \frac{35}{18}$

4. $\frac{10}{3} + \frac{15}{7} + 6\frac{11}{14}$

5. $3\frac{1}{8} + 4\frac{5}{36} + 7\frac{2}{9}$

6. $5\frac{3}{61} + 7\frac{5}{12} + 4\frac{17}{24}$

7. $3\frac{5}{6} + 7\frac{8}{5} + \frac{19}{15}$

8. $\frac{27}{6} + \frac{35}{18} + \frac{95}{54}$

9. $6\frac{1}{9} + 7\frac{3}{11} + 5\frac{8}{33}$

10. $14\frac{2}{7} + 16\frac{7}{15} + 14\frac{3}{35}$

11. $7\frac{7}{12} + 9\frac{7}{15} + \frac{8}{3}$

12. $8\frac{4}{16} + 7\frac{3}{15} + 18\frac{37}{30}$

2.10 SOLVE THESE PROBLEMS:

1. What is the perimeter of a lot whose sides measure $120\frac{1}{2}$ feet, $96\frac{3}{4}$ feet, $107\frac{1}{8}$ feet, and $90\frac{1}{6}$ feet?

2. The parts used to make a piece of furniture weigh $7\frac{1}{3}$ pounds, $5\frac{1}{6}$ pounds, $3\frac{7}{12}$ pounds, and $5\frac{3}{8}$ pounds. Calculate the total weight.

3. How many running feet of lumber are needed to build a rectangular box, one board high, whose sides are $4\frac{3}{8}$ feet and $6\frac{4}{7}$ feet?

4. Fred worked the following hours per day during one week: $4\frac{1}{4}$, $6\frac{1}{3}$, $7\frac{1}{2}$, $5\frac{1}{8}$, and $10\frac{3}{4}$. How many hours did he work that week?

5. Two lengths of metal are soldered together. One is $4\frac{1}{16}$ inches long, the other is $3\frac{7}{15}$ inches long. The solder joint is $\frac{1}{40}$ inch thick. Determine the total length of the soldered piece.

6. During the month of January, heating oil was purchased in the following amounts: $72\frac{3}{8}$ gallons, $46\frac{5}{6}$ gallons, $89\frac{7}{16}$ gallons, and $56\frac{2}{15}$ gallons. Calculate the total gallons purchased during the month.

h. SUBTRACTION OF FRACTIONS

The rules for subtracting fractions are very similar to those for adding fractions.

1. Change the fractions to their equivalent value with the lowest common denominator. This will result in the fractions having the same denominators.

2. Subtract the numerators and make a new fraction with the difference between the numerators as numerator and the lowest common denominator as denominator:

$$\frac{\text{Difference between the numerators}}{\text{Lowest common denominator}}$$

3. Reduce to lowest terms (if possible).

ILLUSTRATIVE PROBLEM. Subtract.

$$\tfrac{5}{6} - \tfrac{3}{4}$$

SOLUTION:

1. Change each fraction to its equivalent value with the lowest
common denominator as denominator. The lowest common
denominator is 12.

$$\tfrac{5}{6} = \tfrac{10}{12}$$
$$\tfrac{3}{4} = \tfrac{9}{12}$$

2. Subtract the numerators.

$$10 - 9 = 1$$

Make a new fraction.

$$\frac{\text{Difference between the numerators} = 1}{\text{Lowest common denominator} = 12}$$

2.11 SOLVE THESE PROBLEMS: Subtract.

1. $\tfrac{5}{6} - \tfrac{1}{3}$ 7. $\tfrac{5}{8} - \tfrac{3}{7}$

2. $\tfrac{4}{9} - \tfrac{5}{18}$ 8. $\tfrac{9}{16} - \tfrac{1}{3}$

3. $\tfrac{17}{36} - \tfrac{4}{9}$ 9. $\tfrac{7}{15} - \tfrac{8}{25}$

4. $\tfrac{7}{8} - \tfrac{2}{3}$ 10. $\tfrac{3}{5} - \tfrac{3}{16}$

5. $\tfrac{5}{9} - \tfrac{1}{6}$ 11. $\tfrac{17}{24} - \tfrac{7}{16}$

6. $\tfrac{9}{16} - \tfrac{2}{9}$ 12. $\tfrac{19}{36} - \tfrac{11}{24}$

In the event that the numbers to be subtracted are mixed numbers or improper fractions, the same method may be used.

ILLUSTRATIVE PROBLEM. Subtract.

$$6\tfrac{7}{8} - 4\tfrac{5}{12}$$

SOLUTION:

1. The lowest common denominator is 24.
2. $6\frac{7}{8} = 6\frac{21}{24}$
   $4\frac{5}{12} = 4\frac{10}{24}$
3. $6\frac{21}{24} - 4\frac{10}{24} = 2\frac{11}{24}$
4. Because $\frac{11}{24}$ cannot be reduced, the answer is $2\frac{11}{24}$.

ILLUSTRATIVE PROBLEM. Subtract.

$$7\frac{13}{8} - 6\frac{4}{3}$$

SOLUTION:

1. The lowest common denominator is 24.
2. $7\frac{13}{8} = 7\frac{39}{24}$
   $6\frac{4}{3} = 6\frac{32}{24}$
3. $7\frac{39}{24} - 6\frac{32}{24} = 1\frac{7}{24}$

ALTERNATE SOLUTION:

1. Reduce to lowest terms.

$$7\frac{13}{8} = 8\frac{5}{8}$$
$$6\frac{4}{3} = 7\frac{1}{3}$$

Then:

$$8\frac{5}{8} - 7\frac{1}{3}$$

2. The lowest common denominator is 24.
3. $8\frac{15}{24} - 7\frac{8}{24}$
4. $1\frac{7}{24}$

2.12 SOLVE THESE PROBLEMS: Subtract.

1. $3\frac{5}{6} - \frac{3}{4}$
2. $4\frac{3}{7} - 2\frac{1}{3}$
3. $14\frac{5}{6} - 8\frac{5}{9}$
4. $26\frac{3}{8} - 14\frac{1}{3}$
5. $375\frac{5}{9} - 263\frac{5}{18}$
6. $26\frac{8}{5} - 10\frac{3}{14}$

7. $\frac{111}{21} - \frac{23}{7}$
8. $\frac{127}{18} - \frac{4}{5}$
9. $16\frac{37}{8} - 4\frac{3}{16}$
10. $136\frac{3}{16} - 27\frac{1}{40}$
11. $329\frac{8}{7} - 127\frac{7}{8}$
12. $64\frac{5}{11} - 36\frac{2}{9}$

As is the case with all subtraction, it is often necessary to borrow. This is done when the numerator of the subtrahend is greater than the numerator of the minuend. Remember, the number 1 can be expressed as a fraction with any denominator. That is $1 = \frac{8}{8}, \frac{7}{7}, \frac{6}{6}$, and so on. Therefore, $3\frac{1}{8}$ can be expressed as $2\frac{9}{8}$. Then 1 borrowed from the 3 was changed to $\frac{8}{8}$ and added to $\frac{1}{8}$.

$$3\frac{1}{8} = 2\frac{8}{8} + \frac{1}{8} = 2\frac{9}{8}$$

ILLUSTRATIVE PROBLEM. Subtract.

$$8\frac{1}{8} - 6\frac{5}{6}$$

SOLUTION:
1. The least common denominator is 24.
2. $8\frac{1}{8} = 8\frac{3}{24}$
   $6\frac{5}{6} = 6\frac{20}{24}$
3. $8\frac{3}{24} - 6\frac{20}{24}$

Because $\frac{20}{24}$ cannot be deducted from $\frac{3}{24}$, it is necessary to borrow 1 from the 8 and convert it to $\frac{24}{24}$. The $8\frac{3}{24}$ then becomes $7\frac{24}{24} + \frac{3}{24} = 7\frac{27}{24}$. The problem can now be solved.

$$7\frac{27}{24} - 6\frac{20}{24} = 1\frac{7}{24}$$

2.13 SOLVE THESE PROBLEMS: Subtract.

1. $6\frac{1}{3} - \frac{4}{5}$
2. $14\frac{3}{8} - \frac{13}{12}$
3. $6\frac{1}{4} - 3\frac{2}{3}$
4. $5\frac{7}{8} - 2\frac{8}{7}$
5. $16\frac{1}{5} - 4\frac{5}{16}$
6. $326\frac{2}{9} - 127\frac{3}{4}$
7. $1\frac{5}{4} - \frac{13}{14}$
8. $26\frac{9}{8} - 13\frac{11}{6}$
9. $46\frac{1}{13} - 15\frac{7}{21}$
10. $28\frac{3}{40} - 16\frac{5}{16}$
11. $6\frac{7}{8} - 3\frac{19}{20}$
12. $12\frac{5}{36} - \frac{6}{5}$

2.14 SOLVE THESE PROBLEMS:
1. A $9\frac{3}{16}$-inch piece of wood consists of 3 lengths. Two of the pieces are $6\frac{3}{5}$ inches and $2\frac{1}{8}$ inches. How long is the third piece?
2. The Fromm Dress Shop has $326\frac{1}{2}$ square feet of floor space. There are three departments: dresses, sportswear, and lingerie. The dress department uses $127\frac{5}{8}$ square feet and the sportswear department uses $112\frac{3}{16}$ square feet. How many square feet are used by the lingerie department?
3. John worked 42 hours during one 5-day week. The following are his hours from Monday through Thursday: $8\frac{1}{4}$, $5\frac{7}{12}$, $7\frac{3}{16}$, $10\frac{5}{8}$. Calculate the number of hours he worked on Friday.
4. A freight car was $\frac{3}{16}$ full. Freight was added to bring the load to $\frac{14}{15}$ of capacity. What fraction of the car's capacity was added?

5. A four-sided lot has sides of $37\frac{3}{16}$ feet, $65\frac{5}{8}$ feet, and $40\frac{3}{8}$ feet. The perimeter is $206\frac{7}{8}$ feet. Calculate the length of the fourth side.

6. It took $4\frac{3}{4}$ days to erect a fence. During the first day, $\frac{7}{25}$ of the job was completed. During the second day another $\frac{7}{40}$ was completed. During the third day $\frac{7}{20}$ more was completed. What part of the job was unfinished at the end of the third day?

i. MULTIPLICATION OF FRACTIONS

The method of multiplying two fractions is as follows:

1. Multiply the numerators.
2. Multiply the denominators.
3. Reduce to lowest terms.

(It is not necessary to find the lowest common denominator.)

ILLUSTRATIVE PROBLEM. Multiply.

$$\tfrac{3}{8} \times \tfrac{5}{6}$$

SOLUTION:

$$\begin{matrix} \textbf{1.} \\ \textbf{2.} \end{matrix} \frac{3 \times 5}{8 \times 6} = \frac{15}{48}$$

$$\textbf{3. } \tfrac{15}{48} = \tfrac{5}{16}$$

2.15 SOLVE THESE PROBLEMS: Multiply.

1. $\frac{3}{4} \times \frac{5}{9}$
2. $\frac{5}{12} \times \frac{6}{7}$
3. $\frac{6}{15} \times \frac{3}{8}$
4. $\frac{3}{7} \times \frac{5}{8}$
5. $\frac{4}{17} \times \frac{6}{13}$
6. $\frac{17}{25} \times \frac{9}{13}$

7. $\frac{45}{137} \times \frac{6}{17}$
8. $\frac{12}{25} \times \frac{3}{5}$
9. $\frac{7}{12} \times \frac{3}{8} \times \frac{4}{7}$
10. $\frac{3}{15} \times \frac{7}{12} \times \frac{18}{21}$
11. $\frac{14}{27} \times \frac{26}{37} \times \frac{15}{17}$
12. $\frac{6}{13} \times \frac{4}{5} \times \frac{25}{36} \times \frac{2}{3}$

When one or more of the fractions is a mixed number, it is necessary to convert it into an improper fraction before multiplying.

ILLUSTRATIVE PROBLEM. Multiply.

$$1\tfrac{3}{8} \times 2\tfrac{2}{3} \times \tfrac{7}{6} \times \tfrac{1}{2}$$

SOLUTION:

$$1\tfrac{3}{8} = \tfrac{11}{8}$$
$$2\tfrac{2}{3} = \tfrac{8}{3}$$
$$\tfrac{7}{6} = \tfrac{7}{6} \quad \text{(Already an improper fraction)}$$
$$\tfrac{1}{2} = \tfrac{1}{2}$$

Then:

$$\frac{11 \times 8 \times 7 \times 1}{8 \times 3 \times 6 \times 2} = \frac{616}{288} = \frac{77}{36} = 2\frac{5}{36}$$

2.16 SOLVE THESE PROBLEMS: Multiply.

1. $1\tfrac{1}{4} \times 3\tfrac{1}{2} \times \tfrac{8}{3}$

2. $\tfrac{7}{6} \times 1\tfrac{9}{8} \times 3\tfrac{5}{12}$

3. $6\tfrac{1}{2} \times 7\tfrac{3}{8} \times 4\tfrac{5}{4}$

4. $\tfrac{14}{10} \times 3\tfrac{5}{6} \times 7\tfrac{2}{5}$

5. $8\tfrac{3}{16} \times 4\tfrac{3}{8} \times \tfrac{7}{4}$

6. $10\tfrac{1}{2} \times 6\tfrac{7}{5} \times \tfrac{42}{30}$

7. $6\tfrac{8}{7} \times 8\tfrac{16}{21} \times 14\tfrac{5}{6}$

8. $7\tfrac{6}{5} \times 4\tfrac{5}{8} \times \tfrac{7}{15}$

9. $\tfrac{7}{12} \times 1\tfrac{29}{30} \times 14\tfrac{2}{3}$

10. $1\tfrac{2}{18} \times 4\tfrac{5}{8} \times 7\tfrac{12}{9}$

11. $2\tfrac{3}{18} \times 5\tfrac{12}{36} \times 6\tfrac{2}{72}$

12. $5\tfrac{2}{16} \times \tfrac{7}{40} \times \tfrac{9}{8}$

j. MULTIPLICATION OF FRACTIONS BY CANCELLATION

The multiplication of fractions can be simplified by cancelling before multiplying. This procedure is based on the rule that the value of a fraction will not be changed if both the numerator and denominator are divided by the same number. We discussed this procedure earlier under the heading "Reducing to lowest terms." The difference between cancellation and reducing to lowest terms is that we reduce individual fractions to lowest terms, and we cancel groups of fractions that are to be multiplied. This permits us to divide any of the numerators in the group by any denominator that can be divided equally by the same number.

ILLUSTRATIVE PROBLEM. Multiply.

$$3\tfrac{4}{8} \times 2\tfrac{4}{6} \times \tfrac{3}{4}$$

SOLUTION:

$$3\tfrac{4}{8} = \tfrac{28}{8}$$
$$2\tfrac{4}{6} = \tfrac{16}{6}$$
$$\tfrac{3}{4} = \tfrac{3}{4}$$

Then:

$$\frac{^{1}\cancel{28}^{7}}{\cancel{28}_{1}}\times\frac{^{2}\cancel{16}^{1}}{\cancel{36}_{\cancel{12}}}\times\frac{^{3}\cancel{3}^{1}}{\cancel{14}_{1}}=\frac{^{5}7\times1\times1}{1\times1\times1}=7$$

The problem was solved as follows:

¹ The numerator 28 and the denominator 4 were both divided by 4, yielding 7 and 1.

² The numerator 16 and the denominator 8 were both divided by 8, yielding 2 and 1.

³ The numerator 3 and the denominator 6 were both divided by 3, yielding 1 and 2.

⁴ The numerator 2 and the denominator 2 were both divided by 2, yielding 1 and 1.

⁵ The remaining numerators and denominators were multiplied.

2.17 SOLVE THESE PROBLEMS: Multiply by the cancellation method.

1. $\frac{3}{8}\times\frac{4}{16}\times\frac{4}{9}$

2. $\frac{8}{12}\times\frac{5}{8}\times\frac{4}{15}$

3. $\frac{12}{18}\times\frac{6}{24}\times\frac{3}{4}$

4. $1\frac{2}{7}\times\frac{14}{30}\times\frac{2}{5}$

5. $2\frac{1}{16}\times3\frac{18}{26}\times\frac{7}{12}$

6. $4\frac{1}{20}\times2\frac{3}{32}\times3\frac{12}{18}$

7. $\frac{8}{5}\times\frac{16}{12}\times\frac{2}{3}$

8. $\frac{14}{21}\times\frac{16}{3}\times\frac{24}{7}$

9. $1\frac{3}{8}\times\frac{16}{5}\times2\frac{4}{7}$

10. $3\frac{17}{15}\times2\frac{8}{5}\times1\frac{7}{4}$

11. $6\frac{12}{5}\times8\frac{4}{3}\times3\frac{5}{8}$

12. $11\frac{16}{3}\times12\frac{5}{4}\times9\frac{13}{24}$

2.18 SOLVE THESE PROBLEMS:

1. A person who owns $\frac{5}{16}$ of a partnership sold $\frac{8}{25}$ of his interest to a new partner. What fraction of the partnership does the new man own?

2. John Gordon's old office was rectangular in shape, with sides of $16\frac{3}{7}$ feet and $11\frac{4}{5}$ feet. His new office measures $19\frac{3}{8}$ feet by $12\frac{4}{15}$ feet. How many more square feet of space does his new office contain?

3. A machine that can make $14\frac{4}{7}$ parts an hour was run for $3\frac{5}{12}$ hours. What was the production?

4. Frank's automobile runs $15\frac{5}{8}$ miles per gallon of gasoline. How far can it travel on $9\frac{8}{10}$ gallons?

5. A grocery store bought $37\frac{3}{8}$ pounds of butter at $46\frac{3}{16}$ cents a pound and $17\frac{5}{8}$ pounds of cream cheese at $37\frac{5}{16}$ cents a pound. Determine the total cost of the two items.

k. DIVISION OF FRACTIONS

The most widely used method of dividing fractions is to invert the divisor and multiply. To invert a fraction, place the denominator above the line and the numerator below the line. Thus: $\frac{7}{8}$ inverted $= \frac{8}{7}$; $\frac{2}{3} = \frac{3}{2}$; $\frac{5}{64} = \frac{64}{5}$. In multiplying the inverted divisor by the dividend, use the cancellation method.

ILLUSTRATIVE PROBLEM. Divide.

$$\frac{8}{9} \div \frac{2}{3}$$

SOLUTION: The divisor $\frac{2}{3}$ is inverted to $\frac{3}{2}$ and multiplied by the dividend.

$$\overset{4}{\underset{3}{\cancel{\frac{8}{9}}}} \times \overset{1}{\underset{1}{\cancel{\frac{3}{2}}}} = \frac{4}{3} = 1\frac{1}{3}$$

2.19 SOLVE THESE PROBLEMS: Divide.

1. $\frac{3}{8} \div \frac{3}{4}$
2. $\frac{7}{16} \div \frac{14}{24}$
3. $\frac{12}{25} \div \frac{8}{15}$
4. $\frac{2}{3} \div \frac{8}{9}$
5. $\frac{8}{9} \div \frac{2}{3}$
6. $\frac{15}{24} \div \frac{5}{18}$

7. $\frac{6}{7} \div \frac{5}{8}$
8. $\frac{13}{15} \div \frac{7}{9}$
9. $\frac{12}{52} \div \frac{3}{13}$
10. $\frac{125}{630} \div \frac{55}{350}$
11. $\frac{37}{82} \div \frac{15}{24}$
12. $\frac{65}{120} \div \frac{15}{36}$

Some other rules for dividing fractions are:

1. Where the numbers to be divided include whole numbers, use the number as the numerator and 1 as the denominator. The number 6 can be expressed as $\frac{6}{1}$.

2. Mixed numbers should be converted to improper fractions before dividing with them.

ILLUSTRATIVE PROBLEM. Divide.

$$8 \div \frac{4}{2}$$

SOLUTION:

$$\frac{\cancel{8}^{2}}{1} \times \frac{2}{\cancel{4}_{1}} = \frac{4}{1} = 4$$

2.20 SOLVE THESE PROBLEMS: Divide.

1. $5 \div \frac{5}{6}$

2. $7 \div \frac{14}{15}$

3. $\frac{9}{10} \div 6$

4. $\frac{7}{8} \div 14$

5. $\frac{3}{16} \div \frac{9}{8}$

6. $\frac{7}{15} \div \frac{14}{5}$

7. $\frac{10}{3} \div \frac{15}{6}$

8. $\frac{15}{12} \div \frac{5}{3}$

9. $3\frac{2}{5} \div 2\frac{3}{10}$

10. $2\frac{6}{15} \div 1\frac{5}{14}$

11. $3\frac{11}{18} \div 5\frac{9}{5}$

12. $4\frac{12}{9} \div 6\frac{3}{32}$

2.21 SOLVE THESE PROBLEMS:

1. How many pieces of $3\frac{3}{8}$ inches each can be cut from a steel rod 54 feet long?

2. A bolt of material 63 yards long is to be used by a dress manufacturer. Each dress requires $2\frac{5}{8}$ yards. How many dresses can be made?

3. A worker who produces $16\frac{2}{5}$ pieces an hour produced 164 pieces. How many hours did he work?

4. If $\frac{5}{16}$ of the amount of an invoice is $640, what is the total value of the invoice?

5. If $\frac{3}{16}$ ounce of nitric acid is used to produce one production unit, how many units can be made from a container with $16\frac{3}{8}$ ounces?

6. John's auto runs $16\frac{3}{10}$ miles per gallon of gasoline, which costs $38\frac{2}{5}$ cents per gallon. How far can he drive on a gasoline purchase of $3.84?

2. DECIMAL FRACTIONS

As you have seen, proper fractions express values less than a whole unit. The fraction $\frac{9}{10}$, for example, tells us that the whole is divided into 10 parts (the denominator) and that this particular fraction contains 9 of those parts (the numerator). Decimal fractions afford another method of indicating values less than the whole, and any fractional numeral can be converted to an equivalent decimal numeral. For example, $\frac{9}{10}$ can be recorded as .9, $\frac{27}{100}$ as .27, and $\frac{236}{1000}$ as .236.

Frequently, computational time can be saved by converting the fraction to a decimal before performing the arithmetic operation. Compare these two solutions of the problem $5\frac{1}{4} \times 5\frac{3}{10}$.

Fraction method:

$$5\frac{1}{4} \times 5\frac{3}{10} = \frac{21}{4} \times \frac{53}{10} = \frac{21 \times 53}{4 \times 10} = \frac{1113}{40} = 27\frac{33}{40}$$

Decimal method:

$$5\frac{1}{4} = 5.25; \quad 5\frac{3}{10} = 5.3$$
$$5.25 \times 5.3 = 27.825$$

An illustration similar to the one above could as easily have been set up to indicate that frequently the fraction method is easier to handle than the decimal. The choice of method to use in solving problems involving fractions must be based upon the particular problem involved.

a. CONVERTING DECIMALS TO FRACTIONS

In the decimal numbering system, all values less than one that are expressed as decimals are, in effect, fractions whose denominators are 10 or powers of 10. That is, 10, 100, 1,000, ... Thus $.1 = \frac{1}{10}$; $.01 = \frac{1}{100}$; $.001 = \frac{1}{1000}$.

To convert decimals to fractions:

1. Remove the decimal point.
2. The decimal number given becomes the numerator.
3. The denominator is 1 plus as many zeros as there are places in the given decimal.
4. Reduce to lowest terms.

ILLUSTRATIVE PROBLEM. Convert .6375 to its fractional equivalent.
1. Remove the decimal point .6375
2. Numerator $\overline{6375}$
3. Denominator $\overline{10000}$

Because there are four places in the decimal .6375, four zeros were added to the numeral 1 to obtain the correct denominator.

4. Reduce to lowest terms.

$$\frac{6375}{10000} = \frac{1275}{2000} = \frac{255}{400} = \frac{51}{80}$$
$$.6375 = \frac{51}{80}$$

When the decimal is part of a mixed decimal (a whole number and a decimal), the whole number is not affected. It becomes part of the mixed fraction in the same form as it appeared in the mixed decimal.

$$6.7 = 6\frac{7}{10} \quad \text{and} \quad 3.27 = 3\frac{27}{100}$$

2.22 SOLVE THESE PROBLEMS: Convert to fractional equivalents.

1.	.75	**7.** 26.35
2.	.37	**8.** 47.705
3.	.325	**9.** 19.3755
4.	.575	**10.** 26.47108
5.	1.64	**11.** 4.37350
6.	5.4	**12.** 10.67585

b. CONVERTING FRACTIONS TO DECIMALS

Converting fractions to decimals requires nothing more than dividing the denominator into the numerator. In other words:

1. The numerator of the fraction becomes the dividend. Place a decimal point after the numerator and add as many zeros as decimal places required.
2. Divide by the denominator.

ILLUSTRATIVE PROBLEM. Find the decimal equivalent of the fraction $\frac{7}{8}$. Limit your answer to three decimal places.

SOLUTION:

$$
\begin{array}{r}
.875 \\
8\overline{)7.000} \quad \frac{7}{8} = .875 \\
6\ 4 \\
\overline{60} \\
56 \\
\overline{40} \\
40 \\
\end{array}
$$

2.23 SOLVE THESE PROBLEMS: Find the decimal equivalent of the following fractions. Limit your answer to three decimal places.

1. $\frac{1}{8}$		**7.** $\frac{19}{40}$
2. $\frac{4}{5}$		**8.** $\frac{5}{12}$
3. $\frac{6}{50}$		**9.** $\frac{3}{8}$
4. $\frac{9}{25}$		**10.** $\frac{1}{12}$
5. $\frac{7}{12}$		**11.** $\frac{5}{8}$
6. $\frac{17}{20}$		**12.** $\frac{11}{12}$

As is the case with decimal to fraction conversion, the presence of a whole number has no effect on the conversion. It becomes part of the solution in the same form in which it appeared in the question. $12\frac{3}{4} = 12.75$.

Remainders and Repeating Decimals. In fraction to decimal conversion, the denominator will not always divide evenly into the numerator. In such cases, if required, the decimal may be carried to the desired number of places and the remainder put over the divisor to form a new fraction. The fraction may be reduced to its lowest terms.

ILLUSTRATIVE PROBLEM. Convert the fraction $\frac{11}{16}$ to its decimal equivalent. The decimal should be carried to three places.

SOLUTION:

$$
\begin{array}{r}
.687\frac{8}{16} = .687\frac{1}{2} \\
16\overline{)11.000} \\
9\,6 \\
\overline{1\,40} \\
1\,28 \\
\overline{120} \\
112 \\
\overline{8}
\end{array}
$$

If the problem required that the answer be rounded out at three places, the answer would be .688. (See page 29.)

Some fractions, when converted to decimals, result in constantly repeating figures. This can be shown by placing dots for each repeating decimal over the rightmost repeating digits in the decimal.

ILLUSTRATIVE PROBLEM. Find the decimal equivalent of $\frac{3}{11}$. Carry to four places.

SOLUTION:

$$
\begin{array}{r}
\overset{\cdot\ \ \cdot}{.2727} \\
11\overline{)3.0000} \\
2\,2 \\
\overline{80} \\
77 \\
\overline{30} \\
22 \\
\overline{80}
\end{array}
$$

2.24 SOLVE THESE PROBLEMS: Find the decimal equivalent of the following problems. Carry to four places.

1. $\frac{6}{11}$

2. $\frac{5}{9}$

3. $\frac{2}{3}$

4. $\frac{1}{6}$

5. $3\frac{5}{12}$

6. $5\frac{2}{7}$

7. $7\frac{3}{16}$

8. $5\frac{8}{19}$

9. $2\frac{6}{14}$

10. $12\frac{7}{15}$

11. $11\frac{6}{13}$

12. $9\frac{5}{22}$

Addition, subtraction, multiplication, and division of decimals have already been discussed in the previous chapter.

CHAPTER REVIEW

1. Add: $2\frac{1}{3} + 10\frac{7}{12} + 5\frac{1}{6} + 6\frac{5}{18} =$

2. Reduce: $\frac{636}{1296} =$ $\frac{525}{1525} =$ $\frac{488}{1264} =$

3. Raise: $\frac{5}{28} = \frac{}{56}$ $\frac{25}{36} = \frac{}{144}$ $\frac{7}{18} = \frac{}{180}$

4. Subtract: $28\frac{3}{8} - 14\frac{3}{12} =$ $6\frac{1}{9} - \frac{3}{8} =$

5. Multiply: $\frac{4}{15} \times \frac{1}{3} \times \frac{9}{24} =$ $\frac{3}{8} \times \frac{4}{9} \times \frac{5}{12} \times \frac{18}{25} =$

6. Divide: $8\frac{16}{25} \div 2\frac{2}{5} =$ $7\frac{7}{8} \div 10\frac{7}{24} =$

7. Convert to fractions: 10.25; 15.375; 1.1076; 1.6375

8. Convert to decimals: $\frac{15}{40}$; $\frac{9}{25}$; $\frac{8}{15}$; $\frac{3}{7}$

TWO

PERCENTAGES, ALIQUOT PARTS, AND INTEREST

For the most part, American business is done **on credit**. Instead of paying cash for goods and services, most businessmen satisfy their business needs by promising to pay their suppliers at some future time. Another widely used form of credit is the borrowing of money, which can be obtained from banks and finance companies. The charge for such credit is called interest. Although this text is primarily interested in business applications, understanding the calculation of interest is important to the consumer as well, because buying on time is a vital factor in the economic life of all persons.

The discussion of interest will center around two areas, simple interest and compound interest.

The arithmetic procedures involved in solving the various types of interest problems require a thorough understanding of percentages and aliquot parts. For this reason the discussion of interest will be preceded by discussion and drill on percentages and aliquot parts.

percentages and aliquot parts

1. PERCENTAGES
   a. Converting percents to fractions
   b. Converting percents to decimals
   c. Formulas
   d. Finding the percentage
   e. Finding the rate
   f. Finding the base
   g. Finding the amount
   h. Finding the difference

2. ALIQUOT PARTS
   a. Aliquot parts of 1.00
   b. Multiplication by aliquot parts
   c. Aliquot parts of multiples of 10
   d. Aliquot parts in combinations

1. PERCENTAGES   Now that we have reviewed fractions and decimals, we must turn our attention to a particular type of problem dealing with the business application of this knowledge. Percents are widely used in business and must be fully understood by businessmen. They are used to determine discounts, taxes, interest, and numerous comparisons. The balance of this textbook is based upon the assumption that your understanding of percents (as well as the other fundamental arithmetic processes) is complete.

Percents are fractions or decimals with the denominator of 100. In other words, the $\%$ sign means hundredths. To use percents in an arithmetic application, they must first be changed to a decimal or a fraction.

a. CONVERTING PERCENTS TO FRACTIONS

Because percents are fractions (or decimals) with the denominator of 100, to convert a percent to a decimal:

1. Remove the percent sign ($\%$).
2. Make a fraction with the percent as numerator and 100 as denominator.
3. Reduce to lowest terms.

ILLUSTRATIVE PROBLEM. What is the fractional equivalent of 80$\%$?

SOLUTION:

$$80\% = \tfrac{80}{100} = \tfrac{4}{5}$$

Percents may also be used to express values greater than one. In such cases, a percent may be converted to an equivalent mixed fractional numeral.

64

ILLUSTRATIVE PROBLEM. What is the fractional equivalent of 145%?

SOLUTION:

$$145\% = \tfrac{145}{100} = 1\tfrac{45}{100} - 1\tfrac{9}{20}$$

3.1 SOLVE THESE PROBLEMS: Find the fractional equivalents.

1. 42%	**7.** 260%
2. 78%	**8.** 346%
3. 86%	**9.** 750%
4. 25%	**10.** 96%
5. 125%	**11.** 425%
6. 148%	**12.** 370%

b. CONVERTING PERCENTS TO DECIMALS

Because percents can be converted to fractions by placing the percent as numerator over the denominator of 100, and because a fraction can be converted to a decimal by dividing the numerator by the denominator, we have this situation when we want to convert a percent to a decimal:

$$75\% = \tfrac{75}{100} = 75 \div 100 = .75$$

In effect, what is being illustrated above is that a percent can be changed to a decimal by removing the percent sign, and dividing by 100. As you have seen, to divide by 100, move the decimal point two places to the left.

$$75\% = .75 \qquad 125\% = 1.25$$

3.2 SOLVE THESE PROBLEMS: Convert to decimals.

1. 76%	**7.** 37%
2. 38%	**8.** 1%
3. 126%	**9.** 10%
4. 347%	**10.** .001%
5. 63%	**11.** .0004%
6. 248%	**12.** .0101%

3.3 *SOLVE THESE PROBLEMS:* Find the missing equivalent numerals.

	Fraction	Decimal	%
1.	$\frac{3}{4}$	.75	75
2.		.125	—
3.	2	23	75
4.	$\frac{5}{8}$	—	—
5.	—	.33$\frac{1}{3}$	—
6.	—	—	3.75
7.	$\frac{4}{5}$	—	—
8.	—	1.25	—
9.	$1\frac{2}{5}$	—	—
10.	$\frac{7}{4}$	—	—

c. FORMULAS

There are five different types of percentage problems. The formulas for solving these problems are listed below. The succeeding pages will explain, illustrate and provide drill on these formulas.

First, some simple definitions:

Base: The number upon which the percent is taken.

Rate: The % that is taken of the base.

Percentage: The product of the base multiplied by the rate.

Amount: The base plus the percentage.

Difference: The base minus the percentage.

The formula for finding the percentage:

$$\text{Percentage} = \text{Base} \times \text{Rate}$$

The formula for finding the base:

$$\text{Base} = \frac{\text{Percentage}}{\text{Rate}}$$

The formula for finding the rate:

$$\text{Rate} = \frac{\text{Percentage}}{\text{Base}}$$

The formula for finding the amount:

$$\text{Amount} = \text{Base} + \text{Percentage}$$

The formula for finding the difference:

$$\text{Difference} = \text{Base} - \text{Percentage}$$

d. FINDING THE PERCENTAGE

The most common type of percentage problem involves finding the percentage when both the base and the rate are known. As has been shown, the formula for solving such problems is:

$$\text{Percentage} = \text{Base} \times \text{Rate}$$

The problem can then be solved by substituting the known amounts for the words in the formula and multiplying. The rate is changed to a decimal or fraction before multiplying.

ILLUSTRATIVE PROBLEM. What is 30% of $520?

SOLUTION:

$$\text{Percentage} = \text{Base} \times \text{Rate}$$
$$\text{Percentage} = \$520 \times 30\%$$
$$\text{Percentage} = \$520 \times .30$$
$$\text{Percentage} = \$156$$

3.4 SOLVE THESE PROBLEMS: Calculate the percentages.

	Base	*Rate*	*Percentage*
1.	$1,200.00	5%	—
2.	360.00	6%	—
3.	12.00	7%	—
4.	6.00	4%	—
5.	412.38	2%	—
6.	563.14	$3\frac{1}{2}$%	—
7.	3,658.19	$4\frac{3}{4}$%	—
8.	7,426.35	$6\frac{1}{8}$%	—

3.5 SOLVE THESE PROBLEMS:

1. The Family Savings Bank pays 5% simple interest per annum. Calculate the annual interest on an account of $750.

2. A wholesaler allows customers 2% discount for payment within 30 days. How much cash will be received from a customer's bill of $246 paid within 20 days?

3. Tom Mason earned \$78.20 for one week. From his salary, 17% is deducted for payroll taxes. Calculate his net pay.

4. A bushel of apples weighs 36 pounds. It is estimated that 5% of the fruit will be damaged. How many pounds of usable fruit are there in the bushel?

5. Because of damages found in a shipment of goods, the Ace Furniture Company is permitted to deduct 32% of the bill of \$1,637.50. Determine the amount it must pay.

6. Each fall, the Clark Ladies Shop estimates that the summer goods still on hand are worth $33\frac{1}{3}$% less than cost. If the summer goods on hand cost \$1,675.25, calculate their present worth.

7. The Ace Dress Company determines the selling price of its dresses by adding 35% to the cost. Calculate the selling price of a garment that cost \$12.42.

8. The dyeing of woolens results in a $4\frac{1}{2}$% loss due to shrinkage. Calculate the number of lost yards resulting from the processing of $126\frac{1}{8}$ raw yards.

9. Of the gross sales of \$326,520, 12% were returned. Calculate the net sales. (Note: Gross Sales − Returns = Net Sales.)

10. A batch of goods that were damaged during production were sold at 23% below cost. What was the selling price if the cost was \$8,376.80?

11. A telephone bill reads as follows:

Cost of calls	\$12.50
Service charge	10%
Federal tax	15% (on calls plus service charge)

Calculate the total bill.

12. A commission salesman is paid as follows:

3% on the first \$1,000 of sales
$4\frac{1}{2}$% on the next \$3,000 of sales
$6\frac{1}{2}$% on all over \$4,000 of sales

Calculate his earnings on sales of \$10,325.00.

e. FINDING THE RATE

Many percentage problems require finding the rate when both the base and the percentage are known. To solve such a problem, you must divide the percentage by the base.

$$\text{Rate} = \frac{\text{Percentage}}{\text{Base}}$$

The problem is then solved by substituting the known amounts for the words in the formula and dividing.

ILLUSTRATIVE PROBLEM. $12 is what percent of $300?

SOLUTION:

$$\text{Rate} = \frac{\text{Percentage}}{\text{Base}}$$

$$\text{Rate} = \frac{12}{300}$$

$$\text{Rate} = \$12 \div 300 = .04 = 4\%$$

3.6 SOLVE THESE PROBLEMS: Find the rate. Round off to the nearest 1%.

	Base	*Rate*	*Percentage*
1.	$ 360.00	—	$ 6.00
2.	8.00	—	2.00
3.	412.00	—	3.20
4.	6.00	—	4.80
5.	527.15	—	10.24
6.	365.80	—	10.97
7.	1,427.14	—	21.41
8.	3,852.75	—	32.63

3.7 SOLVE THESE PROBLEMS: Find the rate. Round off to nearest 1%.

1. A wholesale fruit dealer bought a carload of apples weighing 2,758 lbs. After sorting, it was discovered that 217 pounds were spoiled. Find the percent of spoiled apples.

2. A bank account that had an average balance of $5,312 during the year received simple interest of $225.76. Calculate the interest rate.

3. A salesman receiving a flat commission rate was paid $926.38 for selling $18,527.50 worth of goods. What was the percent rate of his commission?

4. John earned $87.50 during the week. After payroll taxes were deducted, he received a net check of $71.75. What percent was deducted?

5. An alloy contains 372 pounds of copper and $15\frac{1}{2}$ pounds of nickel. What percent of the alloy is copper?

6. A manufacturer allows his customers a deduction for prompt payment. A sales of $127.75 was paid promptly with a check for $125.19. Determine the percent allowed.

7. The selling price of a manufactured part is $6.16. If the part costs $4.62, what is the percent of markup (selling price − cost) based on selling price?

8. A retail store was permitted to deduct $272 from an $850 invoice (bill) because of damaged merchandise. Calculate the percent of the allowance.

9. Included in the inventory that cost $12,752.70 are shopworn goods that cost $1,530.32 and are considered to be worth $800. What percent of the total inventory is shopworn?

10. Rent of $175 per month is paid by a family whose weekly earnings are $225. What percent of earnings is used to pay rent? (1 month = $4\frac{1}{3}$ weeks.)

11. The formula for determining net sale is: Net sales = Gross sales − Sales returns. If the gross sales were $327,526 and the net sales $320,975.48, what percent of gross sales were returned?

12. The Corwin family budget is as follows: rent $165; food $220; clothing $55; all other expenses $110. Calculate the percent that each expenditure bears to the total budget.

f. FINDING THE BASE

Problems in determining the base when the rate and the percentage are given can be solved by dividing the percentage by the rate.

$$\text{Base} = \frac{\text{Percentage}}{\text{Rate}}$$

The problem can then be solved by substituting the known amounts for the words in the formula and dividing.

ILLUSTRATIVE PROBLEM. What number multiplied by 6% equals $90?

SOLUTION:

$$\text{Base} = \frac{\text{Percentage}}{\text{Rate}}$$

$$\text{Base} = \frac{90}{.06}$$

$$\text{Base} = 90 \div .06 = \$150$$

In effect, this problem asks us to find 100% (the base) when we are given the information that 6% = $90. The formula provides for finding what 1% equals by dividing the rate into the percentage. Knowing 1% we can find 100% by multiplying by 100. The same problem might appear easier if it was stated as follows:

Find the cost of 100 chairs if 6 chairs cost $90.

Then you would find the cost of 1 chair $90 \div 6 = \$15$ and multiply by 100. $\$15 \times 100 = \$1,500$.

3.8 SOLVE THESE PROBLEMS: Calculate the base.

Base	Rate	Percentage
1. —	6%	$21.00
2. —	2%	.50
3. —	4%	32.16
4. —	5%	4.05
5. —	$4\frac{1}{2}\%$	9.90
6. —	3.2%	12.80
7. —	1.6%	8.08
8. —	$.5\%$	.01

3.9 SOLVE THESE PROBLEMS:

1. Calculate the amount of cash held in a savings bank that pays simple interest at $4\frac{1}{2}\%$ per annum if the amount of interest was $23.40.

2. In analyzing the sizes sold in the men's shoe department, a store found that 450 pairs of size $10\frac{1}{2}$ were sold. This was 9% of the total shoe sales. What was the total number of pairs sold?

3. Of Mr. Jameson's stock market holdings, 12% of his total investment was in common stock valued at $5,406.00. Determine the total value of his total investment.

4. A metal alloy contains 42.7 pounds of zinc. This is 7% of the total weight of the alloy. What is the total weight?

5. John's payroll deductions for one week came to $12.90, which was 15% of his total earnings. Calculate his gross pay.

6. The waste in a metal turning plant is 1.5% of the total metal used. During January the waste totaled 330.6 pounds. How much metal was worked in January?

7. If the sales returns of $450.72 equaled 6% of the total sales for the week, how much was sold during the week?

8. A waiter, whose tips average 15% of the total checks, earned $72 in tips during the week. What was the total of his week's checks?

9. Automobile prices were increased by $3\frac{1}{2}\%$ over last year. This increase averaged $63.07 per car sold. Calculate the average selling price of last year's models.

10. In one major U.S. city, sales tax is charged at the rate of 5% of sales. Calculate the amount of sales that resulted in sales tax collections of $125.15.

11. A monthly family budget allows 25% of income for rent, 20% for food, 10% for clothing, and the balance for other expenditures. The family spent $127.12, the exact amount budgeted, for clothing. Calculate the gross income.

12. Johnson, a commission salesman, was paid one month as follows:

$240.00 on sales at the rate of 4%
$330.00 on sales at the rate of $5\frac{1}{2}$%
$126.12 on sales at the rate of 6%

Determine the total that Johnson sold that month.

g. FINDING THE AMOUNT

Some percentage problems require the percentage to be added to the base to find the amount. The formula for this solution is:

$$\text{Amount} = \text{Base} + \text{Percentage}$$

ILLUSTRATIVE PROBLEM. This year's sales exceeded those of last year by 15%. Last year, $426,836 of goods were sold. Calculate this year's sales.

SOLUTION:

1. Because the percentage is not given, it must be calculated.

Percentage = Base × Rate
Percentage = $426,836 × .15
Percentage = $64,025.40

2. After the percentage has been determined we can apply the formula for the amount:

Amount = Base + Percentage
Amount = $426,836 + ($426,836 × .15)
Amount = $426,836 + $64,025.40
Amount = $490,861.40

Another way of solving this problem is to consider last year's sales (the base) to be 100%. Then this year's sales is 100% + 15% = 115% of last year's:

$$100\% + 15\% = 115\%$$
$$\$426,836 \times 1.15 = \$490,861.40$$

3.10 SOLVE THESE PROBLEMS: Calculate the percentage and the amount.

	Base	Rate	Percentage	Amount
1.	$ 450.00	6%	—	—
2.	320.00	5%	—	—
3.	576.00	2%	—	—
4.	8.00	$33\frac{1}{3}\%$	—	—
5.	.75	40%	—	—
6.	3.68	3.5%	—	—
7.	412.68	4.25%	—	—
8.	326.18	6.5%	—	—
9.	5,263.12	$7\frac{1}{2}\%$	—	—
10.	6,788.90	$4\frac{3}{8}\%$	—	—
11.	1,456.37	8.125%	—	—
12.	927.27	7.375%	—	—

3.11 SOLVE THESE PROBLEMS: Round out to the nearest hundredth.

1. A company sells its merchandise at 42% over cost. Determine total sales if the cost was $126,800.

2. A union contract provides pay raises of 17%. Calculate the new weekly salary of a person who earned $85 per week prior to the increase.

3. Securities, which were purchased some years ago at a cost of $3,216, have increased in value by 136%. Calculate the present value of the securities.

4. The cost of an automobile is $3,224.00. The cost of the same model will be increased next year by 13%. What will be next year's cost?

5. The total weight of a packaged article is $37\frac{1}{2}\%$ greater than its net weight of 6 pounds. Determine the total weight.

6. This year's sales were 110% of last year's sales of $68,475.16. How much was sold this year?

7. A sales tax of 5% is added on all sales. What is the total cost to a customer for an item selling for $7.25 before tax?

8. To make brass, zinc must be mixed with copper. If we begin with 140 pounds of copper and add zinc in amount of $12\frac{1}{2}\%$ of the copper, how much will the total alloy weigh?

9. Last year's rainfall was 28.32 inches. This year the rainfall increased by 16.372%. Calculate this year's rainfall.

10. Because of favorable market conditions, a house that cost $14,850 was sold for 41% above cost. What was the selling price?

11. It is expected that community college enrollment will increase by 56% during the next three years. Current enrollment is 1,426,312. Determine the projected enrollment three years from now.

h. FINDING THE DIFFERENCE

Certain percentage problems require the percentage to be deducted from the base to find the difference. The formula for solving such problems is:

$$\text{Difference} = \text{Base} - \text{Percentage}$$

In the event that the percentage is not given, it must be calculated before the formula for finding the difference can be used.

ILLUSTRATIVE PROBLEM. John's earnings are subject to 16% payroll deductions. Calculate his take-home pay for a week in which he earned $85 gross.

SOLUTION:
  1. Because the percentage is not given, it must be calculated.

$$\text{Percentage} = \text{Base} \times \text{Rate}$$
$$\text{Percentage} = \$85 \times .16$$
$$\text{Percentage} = \$13.60$$

  2. After the percentage has been determined we can apply the formula for the difference.

$$\text{Difference} = \text{Base} - \text{Percentage}$$
$$\text{Difference} = \$85 - \$13.60$$
$$\text{Difference} = \$71.40$$

An alternate solution would be to consider the base as 100%, deduct the payroll deductions, 16%, and multiply the difference by his salary, $85. This method uses the fact that his take-home pay is 84% of his salary.

$$100\% - 16\% = 84\%$$
$$\$85 \times .84 = \$71.40$$

3.12   SOLVE THESE PROBLEMS: Calculate percentage and difference. Round off to nearest hundredth.

	Base	Rate	Percentage	Difference
1.	$ 320.00	6%	—	—
2.	260.00	3%	—	—
3.	185.00	4%	—	—
4.	583.00	8%	—	—
5.	7.20	$33\frac{1}{3}\%$	—	—
6.	.38	60%	—	—
7.	12.16	55%	—	—
8.	825.36	38%	—	—
9.	1,426.80	$12\frac{1}{2}\%$	—	—
10.	1,739.27	$8\frac{1}{3}\%$	—	—
11.	2,638.12	$16\frac{2}{3}\%$	—	—
12.	5,716.40	8.125%	—	—

3.13   SOLVE THESE PROBLEMS:

1. A 120-pound ingot of brass, consisting of zinc and copper, contains 12% zinc. How many pounds of copper does the alloy contain?

2. Originally 126,312 persons, the population of a city declined by 12.635% during a 5-year period. Calculate the population at the end of the fifth year.

3. The costs of the Cagan Company are 37% less than selling price. Determine the cost of an item that sells for $12.75.

4. Tom Andrews bought 100 shares of stock at a total cost of $3,825. After 6 months, the stock declined in value by $16\frac{1}{8}\%$. What was the stock worth after the decline?

5. The manufacturing process of a wood-turning plant results in a 3.5% loss due to imperfections in the raw materials. Calculate the number of pounds of wood (after loss) produced by a production run of 2,612 pounds.

6. On sales of $412,632.15, there were returns of 2.361%. Determine the net sales.

7. Last year, the net income of the Schneider Corporation decreased by 6.251% from its previous high of $7,637,426.18. How much did the company earn last year?

8. A packaged article has a total weight of 11.63 pounds. Of this, 17.4% is the packaging, and the balance is the manufactured item. Calculate the net weight of the item to the nearest hundredth of a pound.

9. A and B are partners in a business worth $36,512.60. If A owns a 22% interest, how much is B's share worth in dollars?

10. A college has a student body of 3,625. Of these, 52% are boys. Determine the number of girls.

11. Bloomsburg is 12 miles from Richardville. The town of Culver, in between the two, is reached after traveling 37% of the distance to Bloomsburg. How far is Culver from Richardville?

2. ALIQUOT PARTS

Any number that can be divided into another number evenly (with no remainder) is an aliquot part of that number.

a. ALIQUOT PARTS OF 1.00

We shall be concerned here with aliquot parts of 1.00; that is, with numbers that can be divided evenly into 1.00. The understanding of the use of aliquot parts permits many shortcuts in arithmetic.

The following is a table of the most commonly used aliquot parts of 1.00. Those that you do not already know should be memorized:

$\frac{1}{2} = .50$	$\frac{5}{6} = .83\frac{1}{3}$
$\frac{1}{3} = .33\frac{1}{3}$	$\frac{1}{7} = .14\frac{2}{7}$
$\frac{2}{3} = .66\frac{2}{3}$	$\frac{1}{8} = .12\frac{1}{2}$ or .125
$\frac{1}{4} = .25$	$\frac{3}{8} = .37\frac{1}{2}$ or .375
$\frac{3}{4} = .75$	$\frac{5}{8} = .62\frac{1}{2}$ or .625
$\frac{1}{5} = .20$	$\frac{7}{8} = .87\frac{1}{2}$ or .875
$\frac{2}{5} = .40$	$\frac{1}{10} = .10$
$\frac{3}{5} = .60$	$\frac{1}{12} = .08\frac{1}{3}$
$\frac{4}{5} = .80$	$\frac{1}{15} = .06\frac{2}{3}$
$\frac{1}{6} = .16\frac{2}{3}$	$\frac{1}{16} = .06\frac{1}{4}$
	$\frac{1}{20} = .05$

b. MULTIPLICATION BY ALIQUOT PARTS

As we have seen, multiplication by 100 requires no more effort than moving the decimal point two places to the right. Those numbers that are aliquot parts of 100 are easily handled and simple to work with. We simply multiply by 100 by moving the decimal two places to the right, then multiply that product by the aliquot part of 100 given in the problem.

ILLUSTRATIVE PROBLEM. Multiply.

$$368 \times .25$$

SOLUTION WITHOUT ALIQUOT PARTS:

$$
\begin{array}{r}
368 \\
.25 \\
\hline
1840 \\
736 \\
\hline
92.00
\end{array}
$$

SOLUTION WITH ALIQUOT PARTS:

$$368 \times \tfrac{1}{4} = 92$$

The aliquot part solution could have been done mentally because .25 is $\tfrac{1}{4}$ of 1.

3.14 SOLVE THESE PROBLEMS: Multiply.

1. $394 \times .50 =$	**6.** $864 \times .875 =$	**11.** $964 \times .25 =$
2. $639 \times .33\tfrac{1}{3} =$	**7.** $330 \times .06\tfrac{2}{3} =$	**12.** $147 \times .14\tfrac{2}{7} =$
3. $264 \times .08\tfrac{1}{3} =$	**8.** $669 \times .66\tfrac{2}{3} =$	**13.** $660 \times .83\tfrac{1}{3} =$
4. $\ 96 \times .75 =$	**9.** $648 \times .37\tfrac{1}{2} =$	**14.** $456 \times .62\tfrac{1}{2} =$
5. $126 \times .16\tfrac{2}{3} =$	**10.** $320 \times .06\tfrac{1}{4} =$	**15.** $497 \times .28\tfrac{4}{7} =$

c. ALIQUOT PARTS OF MULTIPLES OF 10

If .25 is an aliquot part of 1.00, it follows that 2.5 is an aliquot part of 10, 25 is an aliquot part of 100, and so forth. The aliquot part table shown on page 76 can be used for any multiple of 10 by moving the decimal one place to the right for each zero following the 1. For example, the table shows that .20 is $\tfrac{1}{5}$ of 1. Therefore, the aliquot part of 10 equal to $\tfrac{1}{5}$ is 2, of 100 is 20, and so on.

Iᴌᴌᴜsᴛʀᴀᴛɪᴠᴇ Pʀᴏʙʟᴇᴍ. Multiply.

$$648 \times 125$$

SOLUTION WITHOUT ALIQUOT PARTS:

$$
\begin{array}{r}
648 \\
125 \\
\hline
3240 \\
1296 \\
648 \\
\hline
81,000
\end{array}
$$

SOLUTION WITH ALIQUOT PARTS:

$$648 \times 1{,}000 = 648{,}000$$
$$648{,}000 \times \tfrac{1}{8} = 81{,}000$$

Because 125 is $\tfrac{1}{8}$ of 1,000,

1. 648 was multiplied by 1,000 by adding 3 decimal places.
2. The product 648,000 was multiplied by $\tfrac{1}{8}$.

3.15 SOLVE THESE PROBLEMS:

1. $387 \times 333\tfrac{1}{3} =$	**6.** $396 \times 16\tfrac{2}{3} =$	**11.** $1{,}728 \times 62.5 =$
2. $412 \times 7.5 =$	**7.** $475 \times .75 =$	**12.** $987 \times 14\tfrac{2}{7} =$
3. $639 \times 66\tfrac{2}{3} =$	**8.** $864 \times 1.2\tfrac{1}{2} =$	**13.** $396 \times 6.6\tfrac{2}{3} =$
4. $492 \times 8\tfrac{1}{3} =$	**9.** $336 \times 6\tfrac{1}{4} =$	**14.** $816 \times .06\tfrac{1}{4} =$
5. $576 \times 37.5 =$	**10.** $20 \times .5 =$	**15.** $135 \times .6\tfrac{2}{3} =$

d. ALIQUOT PARTS IN COMBINATIONS

Frequently, aliquot parts are found in combination with other numbers. In such cases, the aliquot part should be multiplied separately and added to the product of the other numbers.

Illustrative Problem. Multiply.

$$416 \times 6.125$$

SOLUTION:

$$416 \times 6 = 2496$$
$$416 \times \tfrac{1}{8} = \underline{52}$$
$$2548$$

3.16 SOLVE THESE PROBLEMS:

1. $6{,}432 \times 6.75 =$	**6.** $72 \times 7.75 =$	**11.** $3{,}864 \times 6.16\tfrac{2}{3} =$
2. $412 \times 9.25 =$	**7.** $468 \times 7.16\tfrac{2}{3} =$	**12.** $5{,}962 \times 4.20 =$
3. $372 \times 6.3\tfrac{1}{3} =$	**8.** $465 \times 3.06\tfrac{2}{3} =$	**13.** $3{,}975 \times 8.4 =$
4. $4{,}920 \times 7.8\tfrac{1}{3} =$	**9.** $6{,}464 \times 2.0625 =$	**14.** $6{,}388 \times 1.25 =$
5. $1{,}456 \times 6.25 =$	**10.** $2{,}166 \times 8.83\tfrac{1}{3} =$	**15.** $5{,}712 \times 4.66\tfrac{2}{3} =$

1. Convert to fractional equivalents:

$$72\% = \qquad 64\% = \qquad 365\% = \qquad 236\% =$$

2. How much interest is earned on a savings account of $9,625 that draws interest at $6\frac{1}{4}\%$? $R = B \times R$

3. The purchaser of $7,565.25 worth of goods is permitted to deduct $7\frac{1}{2}\%$ for prompt payment. How much must be paid to settle the account within the discount period? $D = B - P$

4. A purchase of $8,947.23 was settled by a payment of $8,231.25. Calculate the rate of discount. $R = \frac{P}{B}$ Subtract

5. Last year's labor cost of $316,423.16 increased to $335,976.01 during the current year. Determine the percent of increase based on last year's sales. |

6. If the sales tax rate was 7% of sales and the amount of tax paid for the month was $612.93, calculate the month's sales. $B = \frac{P}{R}$

7. The amount of discount was $14.16. The discount rate was 3%. Find the amount of the invoice. $B \frac{Q}{R}$

8. An investment of $12,500.00 increased in value by 13% during the year. What is the value of the investment at the end of the year? $AB \times P$

9. In paying an invoice of $168 the buyer is entitled to deduct 20% for damaged merchandise and 20% of the balance for prompt payment. Calculate the cash required to settle the bill. 107.52

10. Solve these problems using aliquot parts:

$$368 \times .62\tfrac{1}{2} = \qquad 376 \times 14\tfrac{2}{7} = \qquad 128 \times 6.25 =$$

$$230 \qquad\qquad 537 \qquad\qquad 800$$

4

interest

1. SIMPLE INTEREST
   a. Time
   b. Cancellation method
   c. 6% 60-day method
   d. Using simple interest tables
   e. Finding the principal
   f. Finding the time
   g. Finding the rate

2. COMPOUND INTEREST
   a. Arithmetic computation
   b. Using compound interest tables

**1. SIMPLE
INTEREST**

The following formula is used to calculate simple interest.

$$\text{Interest} = \text{Principal} \times \text{Rate} \times \text{Time}$$

Where:

Interest = The amount charged for the loan

Principal = The amount borrowed

Rate = The percent applied to the principal to determine the interest charge. This is usually on an annual basis. Thus, an interest charge of 6% means 6% per year.

Time = The fraction of a year for which the loan is made.

ILLUSTRATIVE PROBLEM. What is the interest on a $1,500 loan for one year at an interest rate of 6%?

SOLUTION:

$$\begin{aligned}
\text{Interest} &= \text{Principal} \times \text{Rate} \times \text{Time} \\
&= \$1,500 \times 6\% \times 1 \\
&= \$90
\end{aligned}$$

4.1 SOLVE THESE PROBLEMS: Determine the interest.

	Principal	Rate	Time	Interest
1.	$ 400.00	6%	1 year	—
2.	750.00	5%	1 year	—
3.	645.00	3%	1 year	—
4.	726.00	$4\frac{1}{2}\%$	1 year	—
5.	836.45	3.375%	1 year	—
6.	1,462.18	6.4%	1 year	—
7.	3,527.40	$16\frac{2}{3}\%$	1 year	—
8.	5,289.63	$6\frac{1}{4}\%$	1 year	—

a. TIME

Because interest is charged at an annual rate, loans of less than a year must be calculated at a fraction of a full year. Thus, a $1,500 note at 6% for a year yields interest of $90. If the time were 6 months (half a year), the interest would be $\frac{1}{2}$ of $90 or $45.

1. In Months. When the time is given in months, time in the formula is represented by a fractional numeral with the numerator being the number of months considered and the denominator being 12, representative of the full year.

ILLUSTRATIVE PROBLEM. What is the interest on a $1,500 loan for 8 months at an interest rate of 6%?

SOLUTION:

$$
\begin{aligned}
\text{Interest} &= \text{Principal} \times \text{Rate} \times \text{Time} \\
&= \$1,500 \quad \times 6\% \quad \times \tfrac{8}{12} \\
&= \$90 \quad\quad \times \tfrac{2}{3} \\
&= \$60
\end{aligned}
$$

4.2   SOLVE THESE PROBLEMS: Calculate the interest.

	Principal	*Rate*	*Time*	*Interest*
1.	$ 600.00	4%	6 months	—
2.	420.00	3%	3 months	—
3.	640.00	6%	4 months	—
4.	8.00	$5\frac{1}{2}$%	9 months	—
5.	37.50	$33\frac{1}{3}$%	11 months	—
6.	128.75	8.2%	7 months	—
7.	936.84	$16\frac{2}{3}$%	5 months	—
8.	1,511.64	$8\frac{1}{3}$%	1 month	—

2. Thirty-Day-Month Ordinary Interest. When the time is given in days (60 days, 75 days) instead of months, it is necessary to represent the time as a fractional numeral with the numerator being the actual number of days considered and the denominator being 360, representative of the full year, for ease in calculation. Some long-term loans are made in which each month is considered to have 30 days and the year is considered to consist of 360 days. Under this method, to determine the time:

1. Find the number of months between the date the loan is made and the same date in the month the loan is due, and multiply by 30.
2. Add or deduct the number of days between the day the loan was made and the date it is due.
3. The time of the loan is written as a fractional numeral with the numerator the number of days calculated, and the denominator 360.

ILLUSTRATIVE PROBLEM. What is the ordinary interest on a $1,500 loan made on July 5, due September 17 of the same year with interest at 6%?

SOLUTION:

First find the time:

1. July 5 to September 5 = 2 months $\times$ 30 days = 60 days
2. The fifth day to the seventeenth day   = 12 days

                                    Total days $\overline{72}$

3. $\frac{72}{360}$ = Time

Then, find the ordinary interest:

$$\begin{aligned} \text{Ordinary Interest} &= \text{Principal} \times \text{Rate} \times \text{Time} \\ &= \$1,500 \quad \times 6\% \quad \times \tfrac{72}{360} \\ &= \$90 \qquad \times \tfrac{1}{5} \\ &= \$18 \end{aligned}$$

ILLUSTRATIVE PROBLEM. What is the ordinary interest on a $1,500 loan made on July 25 due on October 15 of the same year with interest at 6%?

SOLUTION:

First calculate the time:

1. July 25 to October 25 = 3 months $\times$ 30 days =   90 days
2. The twenty-fifth day back to the fifteenth day = -10 days

                                    Total days $\overline{80}$

Then, find the ordinary interest:

$$\begin{aligned}
\text{Ordinary Interest} &= \text{Principal} \times \text{Rate} \times \text{Time} \\
&= \$1,500 \quad \times 6\% \quad \times \tfrac{80}{360} \\
&= \$90 \qquad \times \tfrac{2}{9} \\
&= \$20
\end{aligned}$$

4.3 SOLVE THESE PROBLEMS: Determine the 30-day-month interest. Round off to the nearest cent.

	Principal	Rate	Period	Time	Ordinary Interest
1.	$1,200	6%	January 9–June 19	$\frac{}{360}$	—
2.	420	3%	March 24–May 9 45	$\frac{}{360}$	—
3.	720	5%	January 9–February 19 40	$\frac{}{360}$	—
4.	360	4.5%	May 12–June 6	$\frac{}{360}$	—
5.	520	$6\frac{1}{2}\%$	April 15–June 27	$\frac{}{360}$	—
6.	4,200	$8\frac{1}{3}\%$	October 10–January 28	$\frac{}{360}$	—
7.	1,500	$7\frac{3}{5}\%$	July 28–December 22	$\frac{}{360}$	—
8.	7,200	1.8%	August 13–October 7	$\frac{}{360}$	—

3. Exact Time—Exact Interest. Most loans require the calculation of the exact time. Unlike the 30-day-month method, the exact number of days in the interest period must be calculated and this used as numerator with 365 as denominator. For the purposes of this text, February will always be considered to have 28 days.

The method for counting the exact number of days is:

1. Deduct the day the loan is made from the total days in the month in which the loan was made.
2. Add the total days in each month up to the month before the note is due.
3. Add the date the note is due.

ILLUSTRATIVE PROBLEM. Calculate the exact number of days on which interest must be paid on a loan taken out on May 17 and due on October 25 of the same year.

SOLUTION:

a) Days in May: 31 − 17 =   14
b) Days in June   =   30
   Days in July   =   31
   Days in August   =   31
   Days in September   =   30
c) Days in October   =   25
   Total days of loan   161

4.4 SOLVE THESE PROBLEMS: Calculate the exact time of each loan.

	Date of Loan	Due Date	Exact Time in Days
1.	July 15	Oct. 28	105
2.	May 6	Nov. 23	201
3.	Aug. 28	Dec. 3	—
4.	Jan. 18	May 12	—
5.	Mar. 26	Sept. 1	—
6.	Feb. 4	Apr. 11	—
7.	June 21	Oct. 12	—
8.	Sept. 11	Dec. 3	—

4. Ordinary Interest at Exact Time. The interest on many business loans is based on a calculation in which the exact time is used as the numerator over the denominator of 360. In other words, the number of days the debt is outstanding is counted exactly and placed over 360 to determine the fraction of the year for which the loan is outstanding.

ILLUSTRATIVE PROBLEM. Calculate the fraction of a year on which interest must be paid on a loan taken out on June 5 and due on September 5. The interest method is ordinary interest at exact time.

SOLUTION:

Days in June: 30 − 5 = 25
Days in July   = 31
Days in August   = 31
Days in September = 5
Total days of loan 92

Fraction of a year based on ordinary interest at exact time: $\frac{92}{360}$.

4.5 SOLVE THESE PROBLEMS: Calculate the time fraction using the ordinary interest at exact time system.

Date of Loan	Due Date	Time Fraction
1. January 4	March 18	
2. May 27	July 5	
3. June 16	September 16	
4. March 5	July 27	
5. August 19	November 12	
6. September 23	December 6	
7. July 6	October 20	
8. November 16	December 27	

5. Determining Time by Use of a Table. To save time in calculating the number of days between two dates, business people often use the following chart:

	TO THE SAME DAY OF THE NEXT											
From Any Day of	*Jan.*	*Feb.*	*Mar.*	*Apr.*	*May*	*June*	*July*	*Aug.*	*Sept.*	*Oct.*	*Nov.*	*Dec.*
January	365	31	59	90	120	151	181	212	243	273	304	334
February	334	365	28	59	89	120	150	181	212	242	273	303
March	306	337	365	31	61	92	122	153	184	214	245	275
April	275	306	334	365	30	61	91	122	153	183	214	244
May	245	276	304	335	365	31	61	92	123	153	184	214
June	214	245	273	304	334	365	30	61	92	122	153	183
July	184	215	243	274	304	335	365	31	62	92	123	153
August	153	184	212	243	273	304	334	365	31	61	92	122
September	122	153	181	212	242	273	303	334	365	30	61	91
October	92	123	151	182	212	243	273	304	335	365	31	61
November	61	92	120	151	181	212	242	273	304	334	365	30
December	31	62	90	121	151	182	212	243	274	304	335	365

The chart indicates the number of days between any day in the month in the vertical column on the left to the same day in the horizontal columns across the top of the chart. Thus, to find the number of days from the 10th of April to the 10th of February:

1. Go down the left column, stopping at April.
2. Go across the page to the column headed February.
3. The number of days is given at the point at which the vertical and the horizontal paths meet. In this case, 306 days.

If the problem required the number of days between April 10 and February 15, the answer would be 311 days:

$$\begin{array}{ll} \text{April 10 to February 10} & = 306 \\ \text{February 10 to February 15} & = \underline{5} \\ \text{Total} & \overline{311} \end{array}$$

4.6 *SOLVE THESE PROBLEMS:* From the table, determine the exact time of each loan.

Date of Loan	Due Date	Exact Time in Days
1. January 14	April 16	118
2. May 11	November 5	
3. August 29	October 12	—
4. December 15	May 11	—
5. February 18	April 6	—
6. April 30	September 21	—
7. March 21	August 14	—
8. June 6	October 15	—

b. CANCELLATION METHOD

When the fractional numeral representing time is cumbersome to work with, the usual practice in working with the interest formula is to calculate the interest using the cancellation of fractions method. To cancel, you must first convert all of the numerals in the formula to fractional numerals.

1. Put the principal over 1.

2. Convert the percent to its fractional equivalent.

3. Include the time fraction.

4. Cancel.

ILLUSTRATIVE PROBLEM. Calculate the ordinary interest on a $720 loan at 5% for 45 days.

SOLUTION:

$$
\text{Interest} = \text{Principal} \times \text{Rate} \times \text{Time}
$$

$$
= 720 \times 5\% \times 45 \text{ days}
$$

$$
= \frac{720}{1} \times \frac{5}{100} \times \frac{45}{360}
$$

$$
= \frac{\cancel{720}^{9}}{1} \times \frac{\cancel{5}^{1}}{\cancel{100}_{20}^{} {}_{2}} \times \frac{\cancel{45}^{1}}{\cancel{360}}
$$

$$
= \frac{9}{2} = 4\frac{1}{2}
$$

$$
= \$4.50
$$

4.7 SOLVE THESE PROBLEMS: Calculate the ordinary interest by the cancellation method.

	Principal	Rate	Time	Ordinary Interest
1.	$1,000	6%	36 days	—
2.	540	8%	135 days	—
3.	120	5%	72 days	—
4.	1,800	8%	40 days	—
5.	864	3%	45 days	—
6.	639	4.5%	120 days	—
7.	480	$12\frac{1}{2}$%	30 days	—
8.	660	$16\frac{2}{3}$%	60 days	—

c. 6%, 60-DAY METHOD

The 6%, 60-day method of calculating interest is a widely used short cut for determining ordinary interest. This method is based on the fact that 60 days is approximately $\frac{1}{6}$ of a year, and 60 days at 6% equals $6\% \times \frac{1}{6}$ or 1%. Therefore, 6% for 60 days is the same as 1%. It is calculated by moving the decimal in the principal two places to the left.

ILLUSTRATIVE PROBLEM. Calculate the interest on $650 at 6% for 60 days.

SOLUTION:

$$
\begin{aligned}
\text{Interest} &= \text{Principal} \times \text{Rate} \times \text{Time} \\
&= \$650 \quad \times 6\% \times \frac{1}{6} \quad (6\% \times \frac{1}{6} = 1\%) \\
&= \$650 \quad \times 1\% \\
&= \$6.50
\end{aligned}
$$

Having determined the interest at 6% for 60 days, we can calculate the interest at 6% for any number of days.

ILLUSTRATIVE PROBLEMS. Calculate the interest on $720 at 6% for 95 days.

SOLUTION:

$720 at 6% for	60 days		= $ 7.20
If 60 days = $7.20 then	30 days = $\frac{1}{2}$ of $7.20		= 3.60
If 30 days = $3.60 then	5 days = $\frac{1}{6}$ of $3.60		= .60
	95 days	Total interest	$11.40

In other words, because 30 days is $\frac{1}{2}$ of 60 days, 30 days' interest will be $\frac{1}{2}$ of 60 days' interest. $7.20 \times \frac{1}{2} = $3.60.

Because 5 days is $\frac{1}{6}$ of 30 days, 5 days' interest will be $\frac{1}{6}$ of 30 days' interest. $3.60 \times \frac{1}{6} = $.60.

4.8 SOLVE THESE PROBLEMS: Calculate the interest using the 6%, 60-day method.

	Principal	Rate	Time	Interest
1.	$1,000.00	6%	60 days	—
2.	450.00	6%	36 days	—
3.	360.00	6%	90 days	—
4.	720.00	6%	120 days	—
5.	8.00	6%	15 days	—
6.	1,236.00	6%	12 days	—
7.	2,637.50	6%	48 days	—
8.	1,896.25	6%	50 days	—
9.	7,263.14	6%	84 days	—
10.	2,897.11	6%	48 days	—
11.	1,436.12	6%	54 days	—
12.	5,768.47	6%	67 days	—

As you have seen, the 6%, 60-day method can be used to calculate interest for time periods other than 60 days. Similarly, the method can be adjusted to interest rates other than 6%. For example, if the interest for a specific number of days at 6% equals $46.20, we can convert this to a 3% ($\frac{1}{2}$ of 6%) by taking $\frac{1}{2}$ of $46.20. Similarly, the interest at 4% can be calculated because 4% is $\frac{2}{3}$ of 6%, the interest would be $46.20 × $\frac{2}{3}$.

ILLUSTRATIVE PROBLEM. Using the 6%, 60-day method, find the interest on $720 at 5% for 82 days.

SOLUTION:

1. Find the interest at 6%:

60 days interest	= $7.20
20 days interest ($\frac{1}{3}$ of 60 days)	= 2.40
2 days interest ($\frac{1}{10}$ of 20 days) =	.24
82 days at 6%	= $9.84

2. Convert to 5%:

Because 5% is $\frac{5}{6}$ of 6%, the interest at 5% is $\frac{5}{6}$ of the interest at 6%.

$$\frac{5}{6} × \$9.84 = \$8.20 \text{ interest at } 5\%$$

or

$$6\% = \$9.84$$
$$\text{Less: } \tfrac{1}{6} = \underline{1.64}$$
$$5\% = \$8.20 \text{ interest at } 5\% \text{ for 82 days}$$

4.9 SOLVE THESE PROBLEMS: Calculate the interest using the 6%, 60-day method.

	Principal	Rate	Time	Interest
1.	$ 375.00	6%	60 days	—
2.	750.00	7%	36 days	—
3.	416.00	4%	54 days	—
4.	328.00	5%	9 days	—
5.	519.00	8%	23 days	—
6.	327.50	9%	85 days	—
7.	462.80	3%	75 days	—
8.	1,236.50	2%	96 days	—
9.	5,340.40	12%	16 days	—
10.	6,247.10	1%	42 days	—
11.	8,168.15	$6\frac{1}{2}$%	57 days	—
12.	3,627.18	$4\frac{1}{2}$%	67 days	—

d. USING SIMPLE INTEREST TABLES

There is a table of simple interest frequently used by businesses that are faced with many interest problems.

The table illustrated on page 91 gives the interest on $1 for 1 through 30 days at the rates indicated at the top of each column. The table is used as follows:

1. Go down the leftmost column to find the number of days for which the interest is to be computed.
2. Having found the number of days, move to the right to the column headed by the rate of interest required by the problem.
3. The intersection point states the amount that is the interest on $1 for the required number of days at the required rate of interest.
4. Multiply the principal by the interest on $1 that was determined in Step 3.
5. For time periods over 30 days, combine the amounts indicated on the table. For example, to find the interest on $1 for 73 days, add the interest for 30 days, 30 days, and 13 days.

ILLUSTRATIVE PROBLEM. Calculate the interest on $650 for 46 days at 5%.

SOLUTION: From the interest table it is found that the interest on $1 at 5% for:

$$30 \text{ days} = \$.00417$$
$$16 \text{ days} = \underline{\quad.00222}$$
$$\text{Interest on } \$1 \text{ for } 46 \text{ days} \quad \$.00639$$
$$\text{Principal} \qquad\qquad\qquad \$650.$$
$$\text{Interest on } \$1 \text{ for } 46 \text{ days} \times \underline{\quad.00639}$$
$$\text{Interest on } \$650 \text{ for } 46 \text{ days} \quad \$\ \ 4.1535 \text{ or } \$4.15$$

SIMPLE INTEREST ON PRINCIPAL OF $1.00 $P \times \ell \times T$

Days	1%	2%	3%	4%	5%	6%
1	.00003	.00006	.00008	.00011	.00014	.00017
2	.00006	.00011	.00017	.00022	.00028	.00033
3	.00008	.00017	.00025	.00033	.00042	.00050
4	.00011	.00022	.00033	.00044	.00056	.00067
5	.00014	.00028	.00042	.00056	.00069	.00083
6	.00017	.00033	.00050	.00067	.00083	.00100
7	.00019	.00039	.00058	.00078	.00097	.00117
8	.00022	.00044	.00067	.00089	.00111	.00133
9	.00025	.00050	.00075	.00100	.00125	.00150
10	.00028	.00056	.00083	.00111	.00139	.00167
11	.00031	.00061	.00092	.00122	.00153	.00183
12	.00033	.00067	.00100	.00133	.00167	.00200
13	.00036	.00072	.00108	.00144	.00181	.00217
14	.00039	.00078	.00117	.00156	.00194	.00233
15	.00042	.00083	.00125	.00167	.00208	.00250
16	.00044	.00089	.00133	.00178	.00222	.00267
17	.00047	.00094	.00142	.00189	.00236	.00283
18	.00050	.00100	.00150	.00200	.00250	.00300
19	.00053	.00106	.00158	.00211	.00264	.00317
20	.00056	.00111	.00167	.00222	.00278	.00333
21	.00058	.00117	.00175	.00233	.00292	.00350
22	.00061	.00122	.00183	.00244	.00306	.00367
23	.00064	.00128	.00192	.00256	.00319	.00383
24	.00067	.00133	.00200	.00267	.00333	.00400
25	.00069	.00139	.00208	.00278	.00347	.00417
26	.00072	.00144	.00217	.00289	.00361	.00433
27	.00075	.00150	.00225	.00300	.00375	.00450
28	.00078	.00156	.00233	.00311	.00389	.00467
29	.00081	.00161	.00242	.00322	.00403	.00483
30	.00083	.00167	.00250	.00333	.00417	.00500

4.10   SOLVE THESE PROBLEMS: Calculate the interest using the table above.

	Principal	Rate	Time	Interest
1.	$ 550.00	5%	12 days	—
2.	632.00	4%	27 days	—
3.	1,127.00	6%	36 days	—
4.	6,375.18	3%	57 days	—
5.	6,173.50	1%	68 days	—
6.	11.12	2%	95 days	—
7.	63.08	5%	81 days	—
8.	2.51	3%	76 days	—

e. FINDING THE PRINCIPAL

It is possible to find the principal when the interest, rate, and time are known. The method is as follows:

1. Find the interest of $1 at the known rate and time.
2. Divide the interest on $1 into the known interest. The quotient is the principal.

$$\text{The formula is: } \frac{\text{Total interest}}{\text{Interest on \$1}} = \text{Principal}$$

ILLUSTRATIVE PROBLEM. Determine the principal of a loan that costs $36 in interest at 6% for 90 days.

SOLUTION:

1. To find the interest on $1.

$$\text{Interest} = \text{Principal} \times \text{Rate} \times \text{Time}$$
$$= \quad \$1 \quad \times .06 \times \tfrac{90}{360}$$
$$= \quad .015$$

2. To find the principal.

$$\frac{\text{Total interest}}{\text{Interest on \$1}} = \frac{\$36}{.015} = \$2,400 \text{ Principal}$$

4.11 SOLVE THESE PROBLEMS: Determine the principal by using the formula

$$\frac{\text{Total interest}}{\text{Interest on \$1}}$$

	Principal	Time	Rate	Interest
1.	—	30 days	6%	$ 3.60
2.	—	45 days	5%	4.20
3.	—	60 days	3%	8.60
4.	—	72 days	8%	5.30
5.	—	4 months	2%	12.10
6.	—	90 days	4%	15.40
7.	—	3 months	$4\frac{1}{4}$%	23.80
8.	—	15 days	2.4%	.70

4.12 SOLVE THESE PROBLEMS:

1. Determine the amount of money in a bank account that earned $64 in 120 days at 4%.

2. Mr. Golden plans to make an investment in $4\frac{1}{4}\%$ corporate bonds that will yield an income of $120 every 90 days. How much must he invest?

3. A finance company earns $36,000 of interest every two months. It charges borrowers interest at the rate of 6%. What is the total amount owed the company?

4. The maximum amount of interest on a mortgage that a real estate owner can afford to pay is $3,200 per annum. If the mortgage interest will be calculated at the rate of 5%, determine the largest amount he can borrow.

5. The Dynamics Company made a loan, paying $62.50 in interest for 72 days. Calculate the amount of the loan if the interest rate was 4%.

6. A company that charges its customers 6% interest on invoices that are not paid in 30 days, received an interest check for $15.65 from a customer whose account was 75 days past due. How much did the customer owe?

f. FINDING THE TIME

When the principal, rate, and interest are known, the time can be determined by dividing the interest known by the interest for one year.

$$\text{The formula is: } \frac{\text{Interest known}}{\text{Interest for one year}}$$

When the answer is a decimal or fraction, the time may be determined by multiplying by 360 (or 365 if the interest was calculated on exact time).

ILLUSTRATIVE PROBLEM. In how many days will $1,640 produce $6.56 in interest at 4%?

SOLUTION:

1. Find the interest for one year:

$$\$1,640 \times 4\% = \$65.60$$

2. Find the decimal numeral that represents the part $6.56 is of $65.60.

$$\$6.56 \div \$65.60 = .10$$

3. Convert to days:

$$360 \text{ days} \times .10 = 36 \text{ days}$$

4.13 SOLVE THESE PROBLEMS: Determine the time (in days) of each loan.

	Principal	Rate	Time	Interest
1.	$ 720.	4%	—	$19.20
2.	360.	5%	—	4.50
3.	800.	6%	—	4.00
4.	240.	7%	—	4.20
5.	520.	6%	—	26.00
6.	1,560.	3%	—	11.70
7.	1,820.	8%	—	14.56
8.	3,720.	6%	—	27.90

4.14 SOLVE THESE PROBLEMS:

1. During the slow season, a furrier has excess cash of $10,500. U.S. Treasury Bonds paying interest at 4% are available for short-term investment. How long must the money be invested to earn $105?

2. A savings bank paying interest at 5% credits one of its depositors with $7 in interest. The amount in the account was $2,800. Calculate the number of days for which interest was paid.

3. An investment of $9,000 in 6% corporate bonds produced interest of $60. How long were the bonds held?

4. Interest of $58.50 was received on a $4,500, $6\frac{1}{2}$% note. Calculate the number of days in the term of the note.

5. A company was charged interest at the rate of 6% for delinquent taxes. The amount of taxes in arrears was $5,500 and the interest charge was $55. Calculate the number of days the taxes were in arrears.

6. Haskin's, Inc., borrowed $4,200 from a finance company paying interest at $6\frac{1}{2}$%. If the interest came to $9.10, what was the term of the loan?

g. FINDING THE RATE

When the principal, interest, and time are known, it is possible to find the rate as follows:

1. Find the interest at 1% for the principal and time known.
2. Divide the interest at 1% into the known interest. The quotient is the rate.

The formula is:

$$\frac{\text{Total interest}}{\text{Interest at } 1\%} = \text{Rate}$$

ILLUSTRATIVE PROBLEM. Determine the rate of interest that produces $12 on Principal of $1,200 in 90 days.

SOLUTION:

1. Find the interest at 1%.

$$\text{Interest} = \text{Principal} \times \text{Rate} \times \text{Time}$$
$$= \$1,200 \times 1\% \times \tfrac{90}{360}$$
$$= \$1,200 \times 1\% \times \tfrac{1}{4}$$
$$= \$3$$

2. Find the rate.

$$\frac{\text{Total interest}}{\text{Interest at } 1\%} = \frac{\$12}{\$3}$$
$$= 4\%$$

4.15   SOLVE THESE PROBLEMS: Determine the rate.

	Principal	Time	Rate	Interest
1.	$ 750	60 days	—	$ 3.75
2.	300	90 days	—	4.50
3.	1,200	45 days	—	3.00
4.	900	72 days	—	9.00
5.	450	80 days	—	10.00
6.	720	15 days	—	1.50
7.	1,440	10 days	—	2.80
8.	3,600	108 days	—	5.40

4.16   SOLVE THESE PROBLEMS:

1. A mortgage of $12,000 produces interest of $180 every 90 days. Calculate the interest rate charged.

2. The interest earned in a savings account is $12. The amount in the account is $2,000, and the period for which the interest was paid is 45 days. Determine the bank's interest rate.

3. An investor in corporate bonds received a semi-annual interest check of $640. The amount invested in the bonds was $16,000. What interest rate do the bonds pay?

4. The Croswell Company borrowed $6,000 from the bank for 30 days paying interest of $75 for the loan. At what rate was it charged?

5. The Frank Company charges interest on its customers' overdue accounts. A customer, owing $4,200, remitted an interest check of

96

*Percentages
and Aliquot
Parts*

$25.20 for being 72 days overdue. At what interest rate was he charged?

6. Interest in the amount of $30 was charged on a note of $2,250 for 96 days. Calculate the interest rate.

2. COMPOUND INTEREST

When interest is computed on the combined total of principal and prior interest, it is called compound interest.

a. ARITHMETIC COMPUTATION

To calculate compound interest, you must determine the simple interest, add it to the principal, determine the interest on the principal plus prior interest, add it on, and keep doing this for the required number of periods for the which interest is to be calculated. For the purposes of this text, all compound interest calculations should be rounded off to the nearest cent. In actual practice, compound interest calculations are not generally rounded off in this manner.

ILLUSTRATIVE PROBLEM. Calculate the amount of interest produced by $100 with interest at 6% compounded annually for four years.

SOLUTION:

$100 × 6% =	$	6.00	First year's interest
	+	100.00	Principal
		$106.00	Balance—end of first year
$106 × 6% =	+	6.36	Second year's interest
		$112.36	Balance—end of second year
$112.36 × 6% =	+	6.74	Third year's interest (rounded off)
		$119.10	Balance—end of third year
$119.10 × 6% =	+	7.15	Fourth year's interest (rounded off)
		$126.25	Balance—end of fourth year
	−	100.00	Balance at beginning
	$	26.25	Amount of compound interest

This solution could also be accomplished by multiplying the principal and each year's balance by 1.06.

4.17 SOLVE THESE PROBLEMS: Calculate the interest, compounded annually.

	Principal	Rate	Time	Compound Interest
1.	$600	2%	3 years	—
2.	200	3%	4 years	—
3.	300	6%	2 years	—
4.	100	5%	5 years	—
5.	500	4%	4 years	—

In the event that compound interest is to be computed quarterly or semi-annually, the problem is solved in the same manner. However, the interest is calculated for each interest period at $\frac{1}{4}$ or $\frac{1}{2}$ of the annual interest and added to the principal quarterly or semi-annually.

ILLUSTRATIVE PROBLEM. Calculate the amount of compound interest produced by $200 at 5% compounded semi-annually for one year.

SOLUTION:

$$\$200 \times 5\% \times \frac{1}{2} = \$ \ \ 5.00 \quad \text{First half-year interest}$$

$$\underline{200.00} \quad \text{Principal}$$
$$\$205.00 \quad \text{Balance—end of half-year}$$
$$\$205 \times 5\% \times \frac{1}{2} = \underline{5.13} \quad \text{Second half-year interest (rounded off)}$$

$$\$210.13 \quad \text{Balance—end of year}$$

$$\$210.13 \quad \text{Balance—end of year}$$
$$\underline{200.00} \quad \text{Balance at beginning}$$
$$\$ \ 10.13 \quad \text{Amount of compound interest}$$

4.18 SOLVE THESE PROBLEMS: Calculate the interest, compounded as noted.

	Principal	Rate	Time	Interest Period	Compound Interest
1.	$300	3%	1 year	Quarterly	—
2.	500	5%	2 years	Semi-annually	—
3.	200	2%	1 year	3 months	—
4.	700	6%	1½ years	Semi-annually	—
5.	400	4%	1½ years	Quarterly	—

b. USING COMPOUND INTEREST TABLES

Using tables to determine the amount of compound interest saves a great deal of computation, particularly where there are many periods involved. The table for compound interest is illustrated below:

COMPOUNDED AMOUNT ON PRINCIPAL OF $1.00
(amount of 1)

Periods (Yrs.)	1%	2%	3%	4%	5%	6%
1	1.0100000	1.0200000	1.0300000	1.0400000	1.0500000	1.0600000
2	1.0201000	1.0404000	1.0609000	1.0816000	1.1025000	1.1236000
3	1.0303010	1.0612080	1.0927270	1.1248640	1.1576250	1.1910160
4	1.0406040	1.0824322	1.1255088	1.1698586	1.2155062	1.2624770
5	1.0510100	1.1040808	1.1592741	1.2166529	1.2762816	1.3382256
6	1.0615202	1.1261624	1.1940523	1.2653190	1.3400956	1.4185191
7	1.0721354	1.1486857	1.2298739	1.3159318	1.4071004	1.5036303
8	1.0828567	1.1716594	1.2667701	1.3685690	1.4774554	1.5938481
9	1.0936853	1.1950926	1.3047732	1.4233118	1.5513282	1.6894790
10	1.1046221	1.2189944	1.3439164	1.4802443	1.6288946	1.7908477
11	1.1156684	1.2433743	1.3842339	1.5394541	1.7103394	1.8982986
12	1.1268250	1.2682418	1.4257609	1.6010322	1.7958563	2.0121965
13	1.1380933	1.2936066	1.4685337	1.6650735	1.8856491	2.1329283
14	1.1494742	1.3194788	1.5125897	1.7316764	1.9799316	2.2609040
15	1.1609690	1.3458683	1.5579674	1.8009435	2.0789282	2.3965582
16	1.1725786	1.3727857	1.6047064	1.8729812	2.1828746	2.5403517
17	1.1843044	1.4002414	1.6528476	1.9479005	2.2920183	2.6927728
18	1.1961475	1.4282462	1.7024331	2.0258165	2.4066192	2.8543392
19	1.2081090	1.4568112	1.7535061	2.1068492	2.5269502	3.0255995
20	1.2201900	1.4859474	1.8061112	2.1911231	2.6532977	3.2071355
21	1.2323919	1.5156663	1.8602946	2.2787681	2.7859626	3.3995636
22	1.2447159	1.5459797	1.9161034	2.3699188	2.9252607	3.6035374
23	1.2571630	1.5768993	1.9735865	2.4647155	3.0715238	3.8197497
24	1.2697346	1.6084372	2.0327941	2.5633042	3.2250999	4.0489346
25	1.2824320	1.6406060	2.0937779	2.6658363	3.3863549	4.2918707

The above table shows the amounts of $1 compounded at the rates of 1% through 6% for periods of 1 through 25 years. It is used as follows:

1. Find the required number of years in the column at the left.
2. Move horizontally across the page to the column headed by the required interest rate.
3. The point of intersection shows the value of $1 compounded at the required rate for the required number of years.
4. Multiply the compounded value of $1 by the principal to determine the compounded value of the principal.

5. Deduct the original principal from the compounded principal to determine the amount of compound interest.

ILLUSTRATIVE PROBLEM. Calculate the compound interest produced by $200 with interest at 4% compounded annually for 12 years.

SOLUTION:

1. In the left column, go to 12 years.

2. Go across the 12-year line to the column headed 4%.

3. Where the two columns meet, the amount shown $1.6010322 is the amount of $1 compounded at 4% for 12 years.

4. $200 × $1.6010322 = $320.20644 rounded off to $320.21, the value of $200 compounded at 4% for 12 years.

5. $320.21 − 200 = $120.21, the amount of compound interest.

4.19 SOLVE THESE PROBLEMS: Calculate the amount of compound interest, using tables.

	Principal	Rate	Time	Interest Period	Compound Interest
1.	$ 600.00	4%	5 years	Annual	—
2.	700.00	2%	9 years	Annual	—
3.	800.00	3%	12 years	Annual	—
4.	950.00	6%	26 years	Annual	—
5.	1,200.00	5%	13 years	Annual	—
6.	6,500.00	1%	17 years	Annual	—

The table can also be used to solve problems in which the interest is compounded for periods other than one year. To adjust the table to quarterly interest periods, take $\frac{1}{4}$ of the rate and 4 times the number of periods. To adjust to a semi-annual rate, take $\frac{1}{2}$ the rate and twice the number of periods.

ILLUSTRATIVE PROBLEM. Calculate the compound interest on $100 at 4% compounded quarterly for 4 years, using the table on page 98.

SOLUTION:

1. Because the interest period is quarterly, multiply the time (4 years) by 4: 4 × 4 = 16 periods. Find 16 periods in the leftmost column of the table.

2. Because the interest period is quarterly, take $\frac{1}{4}$ of the rate. 4% × $\frac{1}{4}$ = 1%. Go across the 16 period line to the 1% column. The amount $1.1725786 is the amount of $1 compounded quarterly for 4 years at 4%.

3. $100 \times \$1.1725786 = \$117.26$ (rounded off), the amount of $100 compounded quarterly at 4% for 4 years.

4. $117.26 - 100 = \$17.26$, the amount of compound interest.

4.20 SOLVE THESE PROBLEMS: Calculate the interest, using the table on page 98.

	Principal	Rate	Time	Interest Period	Compound Interest
1.	$ 700	4%	4 years	Quarterly	—
2.	300	6%	8 years	Semi-annually	—
3.	600	2%	10 years	Semi-annually	—
4.	500	4%	7 years	Semi-annually	—
5.	1,000	6%	9 years	Semi-annually	—

CHAPTER REVIEW

1. Find the simple interest for 1 year:

$650 - 3\% = \qquad \$712 - 4.12\% = \qquad \$6,316.24 - 12\frac{1}{2}\% =$

2. Find the simple interest on a monthly basis:

$600 - 3 \text{ mos} - 6\% = \qquad \$412 - 9 \text{ mos} - 5\% =$

3. Using the 30-day-month method, determine the interest on a $750 loan at 5%. The loan was taken out on March 15 and paid on May 26.

4. Find the exact time between the following dates:

March 10 to August 15 = \qquad July 27 to October 5 =

5. Find the exact time between the following dates by using the table on page 86 of the text:

January 16 to April 9 = \qquad June 21 to November 12 =

6. Calculate the ordinary interest by the cancellation method on a loan of $800 at 7% for 45 days.

7. Calculate the interest using the 6% 60-day method:

$1,240 - 7\% - 69 \text{ days} = \qquad \$648 - 4\% - 37 \text{ days} =$

8. A loan carrying interest at 6% requires a quarterly interest payment of $600. Determine the principal of the loan.

9. A note for $12,000 at 6% produced interest of $48. How long was the loan outstanding?

10. The interest on a $12,800 loan was $144 in a 90-day period. Calculate the interest rate.

11. Calculate the compound interest arithmetically:

$1,200 — 4% — 2 years — annually =
$ 825 — 8% — 1 year — quarterly =

12. Calculate the compound interest using the table on page 98 of the text:

$500 — 6% — 3 years — annual =
$600 — 4% — 2 years — semi-annual =

THREE
CONSUMER MATHEMATICS

The growing practice of buying on time, paying by check instead of cash, ownership of property rather than leasing, etc. confronts individuals daily with the solving of problems concerning, their household activities. With the understanding of the simple mathematics involved, consumers can reconcile their checking accounts, determine the excess they are spending on installment purchases as compared with cash purchases and that amount of interest that is being charged, determine the tax rates they are paying on real estate, the difference between annual and semi-annual payments on life insurance policies, decide which lending institution offers the lower interest rate, etc.

In the two following chapters, attention is paid to the mathematics needed by consumers, the necessary formulas, and their applications.

5

consumer loans

1. PERSONAL LOANS

2. INSTALLMENT BUYING

3. HOME MORTGAGES

4. LOAN REPAYMENT SCHEDULES

5. TABLES

| 1. PERSONAL LOANS | Individuals frequently borrow money to purchase such articles as automobiles, furniture, and clothing. One can borrow from banks, savings and loan associations, personal finance companies, insurance companies, credit unions, and individuals. The interest rates charged and the duration of time a loan may run are generally regulated by individual states. These rates and lending periods vary among the states. The lending institutions publish schedules listing the amounts of loans, the periods of repayment, and the amount per payment of each period. The Truth in Lending Law, technically called Regulation Z, requires that whenever money is borrowed, the lender must state, in writing, the true annual interest rate. To determine the rate of interest charged, the following formulas are used: |

1. Number of payments $\times$ Amount per payment = Amount to be paid

2. Amount to be paid $-$ Amount of loan = Total interest (including service charge)

3. $\dfrac{2 \times \text{No. of periods in 1 year*} \times \text{Interest (including service charge)}}{\text{Amount of loan} \times \text{(no. of payments} + 1)}$
= interest rate

ILLUSTRATIVE PROBLEM. Fred Parker borrowed $200 to be paid in ten monthly installments of $22.72 per month. Find the rate of interest paid by Parker.

SOLUTION:

1. Number of payments $\times$ Amount per payment = Total amount to be paid

| 10 | $\times$ | $22.72 | = | $227.20 |

* The number of periods in 1 year does not refer to the length of the loan. For example, the number of periods in 1 year for a loan that is to be paid in 6 months is 12 because there are 12 months in 1 year.

106

2. Total amount to be paid − Amount of loan =   Interest

      $227.20   − $200   = $27.20 Interest

3. Interest rate $= \dfrac{2 \times \text{No. of periods in 1 year} \times \text{service charge}}{\text{Amount of loan} \times (\text{No. of payments} + 1)}$

   Interest rate $= \dfrac{2 \times 12 \times \$27.20}{200(10 + 1)}$

   Interest rate $= \dfrac{652.80}{2200}$

   Interest rate $= .296$ or 29.6%

Although lending institutions must advertise their interest rates on personal loans, it is worthwhile for individuals to understand the mathematics needed to determine the rate. With this knowledge, one will understand the costs involved in borrowing. Generally, one can borrow at a lower interest rate from a bank than from a personal loan company.

5.1 SOLVE THESE PROBLEMS:

1. On the following loans, determine the total amounts to be paid and the interest rates.

	Amount of Loan	No. of Monthly Payments	Amount per Payment	Total Amount to be Paid	Interest Rate
a.	$ 100	4	$26.00	—	—
b.	150	8	22.50	—	—
c.	375	10	43.00	—	—
d.	225	12	23.00	—	—
e.	400	15	32.08	—	—
f.	600	18	39.76	—	—
g.	750	24	41.50	—	—
h.	1,500	30	61.12	—	—
i.	1,775	35	59.72	—	—
j.	1,900	42	53.28	—	—

2. Warren Cameron bought a motorboat for $500. He borrowed the total amount from the Goodfriend Personal Loan Company to be paid back in 15 equal monthly payments of $42.20 each. Determine the rate of interest he must pay.

3. In order to pay for a European trip, Pauline Smith borrowed $750 to be repaid in 26 equal weekly payments of $32.75 each. What rate of interest did Pauline pay for the loan?

4. John Fellows repaid a loan of $400 with 14 weekly payments of $29 and one of $29.50. At what rate of interest was the loan made?

2. INSTALLMENT BUYING For many years the conventional system of retail selling required that the consumer pay cash, in full, for the purchase of goods. At the time of purchase and payment, the sale was completed. In an effort to attract customers, retailers now offer credit terms to prospective buyers. This allows the customer to use the item before it is completely paid for. In addition to permitting customers to purchase merchandise before they accumulate the full cash amount needed to pay for it, this permits families to buy more merchandise—very often more expensive merchandise—than they could generally afford in an outright purchase. Retailers advertise by using such attractive phrases as "Easy Payment Plan," "Buy Now, Pay Later," etc. This purchase arrangement, called installment buying, allows the customer to select merchandise and pay for it over a period of time. The length of time for payments extends from a few weeks to years. Some stores require a small down payment while others advertise "No Down Payment." For the privilege of installment buying, a service charge or carrying charge is added to the cost of the purchase. This charge consists of interest and other changes to cover the cost incurred by the installment arrangement such as bookkeeping expenses, insurance against bad debt risks (customers not paying their installment), investigations of those applying for this plan, and making a profit. It is important for the customer to be able to make the following computations when purchasing on an installment plan:

1. The total cost of the installment plan.
2. The service or carrying charge (including interest).
3. The interest rate (including service charge).

These formulas are used in the above computations:

1. To determine the total cost under installment buying.

Total installment cost = Periodic payment × No. of payments

If there is a down payment, this formula is used:

Installment cost = Down payment
+ (Periodic payment × No. of payments)

2. To determine the service charge:

Service charge = Total installment cost
− Cash price (if bought outright)

3. To determine the interest rate:

$$\text{Interest rate} = \frac{2 \times \text{No. of periods in 1 year} \times \text{Service charge}}{\text{Amount of loan} \times (\text{No. of payments} + 1)}$$

ILLUSTRATIVE PROBLEM. A washing machine that sells for $200 can be purchased on the installment plan for $35 down and nine equal monthly payments of $20. Find the total cost under the installment plan, the service charge, and the interest rate.

SOLUTION:

To find the cost when purchased on the installment plan:

Total installment cost
$$= \text{Down payment} + (\text{periodic payment} \times \text{No. of payments})$$
$$= \$35 + (9 \times \$20)$$
$$= \$35 + \$180$$
$$= \$215$$

To find the service charge:

$$\text{Service charge} = \text{Installment cost} - \text{Cash price}$$
$$= \$215 - \$200$$
$$= \$15$$

To find the interest rate:

$$\text{Interest rate} = \frac{2 \times \text{No. of periods in year} \times \text{Service charge}}{\text{Amount of loan} \times (\text{No. of payments} + 1)}$$
$$= \frac{2 \times 12 \times \$15}{(\$200 - \$35) \times (9 + 1)}$$
$$= \frac{\$360}{\$1650} = \frac{36}{165} = \frac{12}{55}$$
$$= .218 \text{ or } 21.8\%$$

Note: If the payments are paid weekly, the formula for interest would substitute 52 (payments in year) in place of 12 (monthly payments).

5.2 SOLVE THESE PROBLEMS:

1. Jill Harmon purchased the following pieces of furniture from different companies on the installment plan. How much will each item actually cost her?

Item	Down Payment	No. of Payments	Each Payment
Sofa	None	8 monthly	$39.00
Chair	$15.00	6 monthly	25.00
Table	$20.00	12 monthly	10.00
Bar	None	45 weekly	6.50
Stereo unit	$22.50	26 weekly	10.25

2. Find the interest (service charges) on these items that were bought on the installment plan.

Item	Cash Price	No. of Payments	Each Payment
Washing machine	$150	6	$27.75
Dryer	185	8	25.00
TV set	129	52	2.85
Refrigerator	265	26	13.25
Dishwasher	225	20	12.35

3. The Rocklyn Department Store advertised a piano for $750. Mr. Warren decided to purchase the piano on the installment plan, agreeing to pay $75 down and make 18 equal monthly payments of $45. Determine the total cost of the piano under the installment plan, the interest (service charge), and the rate of interest.

4. Paul Fredericks purchased a color television set from Trade-Rite, Inc., on the installment plan. Mr. Fredericks was required to make a down payment of 10% and 30 monthly payments of $15. If the cash price was $425, how much additional did he pay for the set and what was the interest rate?

5. To furnish a studio apartment, Mr. Thomas bought the following merchandise from the Wainrite Department Store:

1 sofa bed	$350.00
1 table	125.00
4 chairs	24.50 each
2 lamps	17.25 each
1 recliner	69.50
1 stereo-television combination	450.00
1 rug	99.75

He agreed to pay 15% down and the balance in monthly installments of $97.50 for one year. How much was the total cost of furniture if purchased for cash? On the installment plan? What was the interest (service charge) and the interest rate?

3. HOME MORTGAGES

The purchase of a home is more than likely the largest single purchase for personal use that a household consumer will make in his lifetime. Because the amount of cash needed for an outright purchase is generally more than most individuals can afford, the great majority of homes are purchased with a down payment, the remainder to be paid in monthly installments. The mortgage is the balance of the purchase price to be financed. Commercial banks, savings banks, savings and loan associations, and insurance companies are the largest home mortgage lenders. The number of years for which a home is financed usually depends upon the age, physical condition, market value, etc. of the home. At present, a new home can usually be mortgaged for up to 30 years; an older home, for 5, through 30 years. The interest rate varies from time to time because of economic factors and is established and regulated by the government.

The monthly mortgage payments include interest on the unpaid balance and payment on the principal. Frequently miscellaneous payments such as taxes and insurance are included. With each monthly payment, the portion allocated for principal increases while the portion allocated for interest decreases. Typically, the portion paid for interest during the first years is extremely high and the portion for the principal is low. The following chart shows typical monthly mortgage payments and the apportionment of the payment for the last 6 months of the first year of a 30-year mortgage.

PAYMENTS

Month	*Total*	*Principal*	*Interest*	*Escrow (for taxes)*
July	$250	$27.32	$117.68	$105
August	250	27.45	117.55	105
September	250	27.58	117.42	105
October	250	27.71	117.29	105
November	250	27.85	117.15	105
December	250	27.98	117.02	105

Figure 5-1 is an example of a typical mortgage statement which homeowners receive to inform them of payments due and how the monies are

Figure 5-1
Mortgage Statement

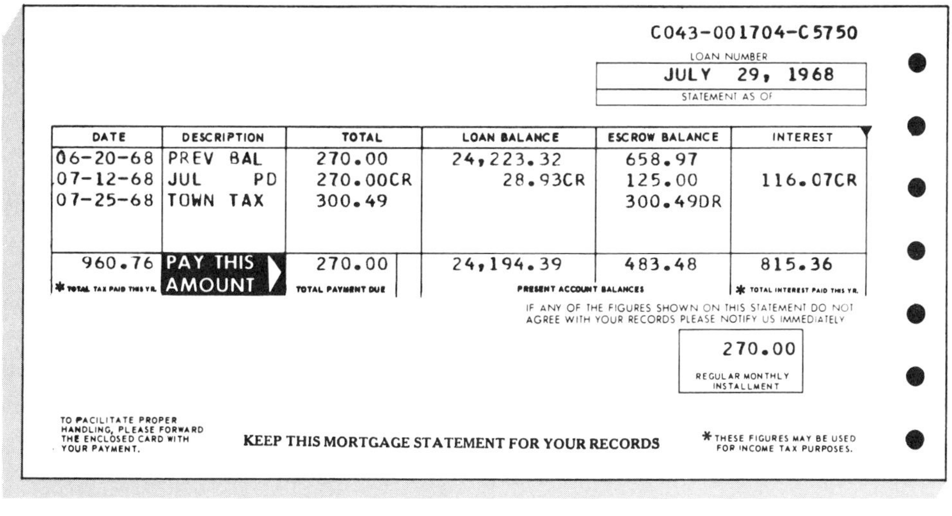
C043-001704-C5750
LOAN NUMBER
JULY 29, 1968
STATEMENT AS OF

DATE	DESCRIPTION	TOTAL	LOAN BALANCE	ESCROW BALANCE	INTEREST
06-20-68	PREV BAL	270.00	24,223.32	658.97	
07-12-68	JUL PD	270.00CR	28.93CR	125.00	116.07CR
07-25-68	TOWN TAX	300.49		300.49DR	
960.76	PAY THIS AMOUNT	270.00	24,194.39	483.48	815.36
* TOTAL TAX PAID THIS YR.		TOTAL PAYMENT DUE	PRESENT ACCOUNT BALANCES		* TOTAL INTEREST PAID THIS YR.

IF ANY OF THE FIGURES SHOWN ON THIS STATEMENT DO NOT AGREE WITH YOUR RECORDS PLEASE NOTIFY US IMMEDIATELY

270.00
REGULAR MONTHLY INSTALLMENT

TO FACILITATE PROPER HANDLING, PLEASE FORWARD THE ENCLOSED CARD WITH YOUR PAYMENT.

KEEP THIS MORTGAGE STATEMENT FOR YOUR RECORDS

* THESE FIGURES MAY BE USED FOR INCOME TAX PURPOSES.

apportioned. In the illustration on page 111, the regular monthly installment of $270 is divided in this manner:

1. *Loan balance*—$28.93 is the amount credited to the loan balance reducing the total to $24,194.39 from $24,223.32.
2. *Interest*—$116.07 is the amount of interest for the month on the loan. The total interest paid to date in this year is $815.36.
3. *Escrow balance*—$125 is the amount collected each month to pay for real estate taxes, such as the town tax and the school tax. This amount is added to the previous balance ($658.97) and is retained by the lending institution until taxes are due. In the illustrative statement, $300.49 was paid out of escrow funds for the town tax leaving a balance of $483.48.

Arithmetically:

$658.97   Previous escrow balance
+ 125.00   Last month's payment
─────
783.97   Total before this payment
− 300.49   Town tax
─────
$483.48   Escrow balance

The total tax paid thus far this year is $960.76, indicated at the extreme left side of the statement.

These figures are important to the homeowner for purposes of preparing income tax returns.

The various lending institutions inform their customers of the mortgage payments due in a number of ways. The statement used in the illustration is sent each month to the homeowner. Some mortgage holders send a booklet for an entire year with twelve payment statements; others send a booklet of statement for every payment due for the length of the mortgage.

Computation of the homeowner's monthly payment is based upon the tables entitled *Monthly Payment Necessary to Amortize a Loan* on pages 117–122. By finding the amount of the loan (mortgage), the total number of years, and the interest rate, the equal monthly payment is determined.

ILLUSTRATIVE PROBLEM. Find the amount of the monthly payments on a loan of $18,000 with interest at 8% for 25 years.

SOLUTION: On page 118 is a table listing amounts at 8% interest. In the leftmost column of the table, progress to $18,000. Follow that figure across to 25 years. The figure at this meeting point is $138.93. This is the amount that is paid each month for 25 years. This will pay the principal and all of the interest.

5.3 SOLVE THESE PROBLEMS:

1. Using the interest tables in the text, determine the equal monthly payments for each of the following mortgage loans.

Mortgage Loan	Interest	Term	Equal Monthly Payment
$12,000	8%	6 years	—
25,000	8%	30 years	—
21,000	8%	18 years	—
11,500	8%	8 years	—
12,700	8%	22 years	—

2. Sam Roberts purchased a home for $18,500. He made a down payment of $3,500 and agreed to repay the balance at 8% interest over 25 years. Find this monthly payment.

3. Carynshere Homes advertised houses selling for $20,000. The terms of the sale required a 10% down payment and the remainder to be amortized over 22 years at an interest rate of 8%. Find the monthly payment for purchasers of these homes.

4. LOAN REPAYMENT SCHEDULES

A schedule for the number of periods of a loan is usually prepared indicating the breakdown of each payment for the interest, the principal, and the balance of the principal. This can be determined after the amount of each monthly payment has been calculated. The formulas used are:

1. Amount of loan × Interest rate = Interest for one year

2. $\frac{\text{Interest for one year}}{12}$ = Interest for first month

3. Monthly payment − Interest for first month = Payment on principal

4. Amount of loan − Payment on principal − Balance of principal (to be used for calculating interest for the second month.)

ILLUSTRATIVE PROBLEM. Prepare the first monthly payment of a loan schedule for $15,000 at 8%, for 20 years.

SOLUTION:

Find the interest for one year:

$$\begin{array}{r} \$15,000 \\ \times \quad .08 \\ \hline \$1200.00 \end{array} \quad \text{Interest for one year}$$

Find the interest for one month:

$$\frac{\$1200}{12} = \$100$$

Find the payment on the principal:
(Monthly payment is $125.47, found in the table on page 119.)

$125.47
− 100.00
$ 25.47   Payment on principal

Find the balance of principal:

$15,000.00
−   25.47
$14,974.53   Balance of principal

Prepare the first payment of the loan payment schedule.

Loan—$15,000
Interest rate—8%
Term of loan—20 years
Monthly payment—$125.47

SCHEDULE			
Payment Number	*Interest Payment*	*Principal Payment*	*Balance of Principal*
1	$100	$25.47	$14,974.53

The entire schedule of payments can be completed using the same formulas with interest computed each time on the balance of the principal.

This is an example of a typical loan repayment schedule:

RATE % 6.00	PAYMENT $ 210.94	LOAN $ 19,000.00	TERM:	YEARS 10	MONTHS	PERIODS 120

Payment Number	Payment on Interest	Principal	Balance of Loan	Payment Number	Payment on Interest	Principal	Balance of Loan
1	95.00	115.94	18,884.06	61	54.55	156.39	10,754.48
2	94.42	116.52	18,767.54	62	53.77	157.17	10,597.31
3	93.84	117.10	18,650.44	63	52.99	157.95	10,439.36
4	93.25	117.69	18,532.75	64	52.20	158.74	10,280.62
5	92.66	118.28	18,414.47	65	51.40	159.54	10,121.08
6	92.07	118.87	18,295.60	66	50.61	160.33	9,960.75
7	91.48	119.46	18,176.14	67	49.80	161.14	9,799.61
8	90.88	120.06	18,056.08	68	49.00	161.94	9,637.67
9	90.28	120.66	17,935.42	69	48.19	162.75	9,474.92
10	89.68	121.26	17,814.16	70	47.37	163.57	9,311.35
11	89.07	121.87	17,692.29	71	46.56	164.38	9,146.97
12	88.46	122.48	17,569.81	72	45.73	165.21	8,981.76
13	87.85	123.09	17,446.72	73	44.91	166.03	8,815.73
14	87.23	123.71	17,323.01	74	44.08	166.86	8,648.87
15	86.62	124.32	17,198.69	75	43.24	167.70	8,481.17
16	85.99	124.95	17,073.74	76	42.41	168.53	8,312.64
17	85.37	125.57	16,948.17	77	41.56	169.38	8,143.26
18	84.74	126.20	16,821.97	78	40.72	170.22	7,973.04
19	84.11	126.83	16,695.14	79	39.87	171.07	7,801.97
20	83.48	127.46	16,567.68	80	39.01	171.93	7,630.04
21	82.84	128.10	16,439.58	81	38.15	172.79	7,457.25
22	82.20	128.74	16,310.84	82	37.29	173.65	7,283.60
23	81.55	129.39	16,181.45	83	36.42	174.52	7,109.08
24	80.91	130.03	16,051.42	84	35.55	175.39	6,933.69
25	80.26	130.68	15,920.74	85	34.67	176.27	6,757.42
26	79.60	131.34	15,789.40	86	33.79	177.15	6,580.27
27	78.95	131.99	15,657.41	87	32.90	178.04	6,402.23
28	78.29	132.65	15,524.76	88	32.01	178.93	6,223.30
29	77.62	133.32	15,391.44	89	31.12	179.82	6,043.48
30	76.96	133.98	15,257.46	90	30.22	180.72	5,862.76
31	76.29	134.65	15,122.81	91	29.31	181.63	5,681.13
32	75.61	135.33	14,987.48	92	28.41	182.53	5,498.60
33	74.94	136.00	14,851.48	93	27.49	183.45	5,315.15
34	74.26	136.68	14,714.80	94	26.58	184.36	5,130.79
35	73.57	137.37	14,577.43	95	25.65	185.29	4,945.50
36	72.89	138.05	14,439.38	96	24.73	186.21	4,759.29
37	72.20	138.74	14,300.64	97	23.80	187.14	4,572.15
38	71.50	139.44	14,161.20	98	22.86	188.08	4,384.07
39	70.81	140.13	14,021.07	99	21.92	189.02	4,195.05
40	70.11	140.83	13,880.24	100	20.98	189.96	4,005.09
41	69.40	141.54	13,738.70	101	20.03	190.91	3,814.18
42	68.69	142.25	13,596.45	102	19.07	191.87	3,622.31
43	67.98	142.96	13,453.49	103	18.11	192.83	3,429.48
44	67.27	143.67	13,309.82	104	17.15	193.79	3,235.69
45	66.55	144.39	13,165.43	105	16.18	194.76	3,040.93
46	65.83	145.11	13,020.32	106	15.20	195.74	2,845.19
47	65.10	145.84	12,874.48	107	14.23	196.71	2,648.48
48	64.37	146.57	12,727.91	108	13.24	197.70	2,450.78
49	63.64	147.30	12,580.61	109	12.25	198.69	2,252.09
50	62.90	148.04	12,432.57	110	11.26	199.68	2,052.41
51	62.16	148.78	12,283.79	111	10.26	200.68	1,851.73
52	61.42	149.52	12,134.27	112	9.26	201.68	1,650.05
53	60.67	150.27	11,984.00	113	8.25	202.69	1,447.36
54	59.92	151.02	11,832.98	114	7.24	203.70	1,243.66
55	59.16	151.78	11,681.20	115	6.22	204.72	1,038.94
56	58.41	152.53	11,528.67	116	5.19	205.75	833.19
57	57.64	153.30	11,375.37	117	4.17	206.77	626.42
58	56.88	154.06	11,221.31	118	3.13	207.81	418.61
59	56.11	154.83	11,066.48	119	2.09	208.85	209.76
60	55.33	155.61	10,910.87	120	1.05	209.76	210.81*

Prepared by Financial Publishing Company, Boston.
* The final payment is usually somewhat different from the regular payment, and is shown starred on the last line.

5.4 *SOLVE THIS PROBLEM:* John Williams purchased a house for $20,000. He put down 20% and agreed to pay the balance in 20 years with interest at 6%. Find his monthly payment. Prepare the first three payments on his loan payment schedule.

5. TABLES

The following tables (pages 117–122) are excerpts from tables entitled "*Monthly Payment Necessary to Amortize a Loan.*"

CHAPTER REVIEW

1. Calculate the interest on a personal loan of $500 which is to be repaid in 17 payments of $36.84 each.

2. A loan of $1,200 will be repaid in 15 equal payments of $83.50 per week. What is the interest rate on the loan?

3. A typewriter that can be purchased for $450 cash is bought on the installment plan for 10% down and 26 weekly payments of $17 each. What is the total cost? The service charge? The interest rate?

4. From the interest tables on page 118 in the text, determine the monthly mortgage payments on a mortgage loan of $28,000 at 8% for 30 years.

5. Prepare the first two monthly payments of a loan schedule on a mortgage of $20,000 at 8% for 30 years.

Term Amount	25 Years	26 Years	27 Years	28 Years	29 Years	30 Years	35 Years	40 Years
$11100	85.68	84.65	83.73	82.90	82.14	81.45	78.84	77.18
11200	86.45	85.42	84.48	83.64	82.88	82.19	79.55	77.88
11300	87.22	86.18	85.24	84.39	83.62	82.92	80.26	78.58
11400	87.99	86.94	85.99	85.14	84.36	83.65	80.97	79.27
11500	88.76	87.70	86.75	85.88	85.10	84.39	81.69	79.97
11600	89.54	88.47	87.50	86.63	85.84	85.12	82.40	80.66
11700	90.31	89.23	88.26	87.38	86.58	85.86	83.11	81.36
11800	91.08	89.99	89.01	88.12	87.32	86.59	83.82	82.05
11900	91.85	90.75	89.76	88.87	88.06	87.32	84.53	82.75
12000	92.62	91.52	90.52	89.62	88.80	88.06	85.24	83.44
12100	93.39	92.28	91.27	90.36	89.54	88.79	85.95	84.14
12200	94.17	93.04	92.03	91.11	90.28	89.52	86.66	84.83
12300	94.94	93.80	92.78	91.86	91.02	90.26	87.37	85.53
12400	95.71	94.57	93.54	92.60	91.76	90.99	88.08	86.22
12500	96.48	95.33	94.29	93.35	92.50	91.73	88.79	86.92
12600	97.25	96.09	95.04	94.10	93.24	92.46	89.50	87.61
12700	98.03	96.85	95.80	94.84	93.98	93.19	90.21	88.31
12800	98.80	97.62	96.55	95.59	94.72	93.93	90.92	89.00
12900	99.57	98.38	97.31	96.34	95.46	94.66	91.63	89.70
13000	100.34	99.14	98.06	97.08	96.20	95.39	92.34	90.40
13100	101.11	99.91	98.82	97.83	96.94	96.13	93.05	91.09
13200	101.88	100.67	99.57	98.58	97.68	96.86	93.76	91.79
13300	102.66	101.43	100.32	99.32	98.42	97.60	94.47	92.48
13400	103.43	102.19	101.08	100.07	99.16	98.33	95.18	93.18
13500	104.20	102.96	101.83	100.82	99.90	99.06	95.89	93.87
13600	104.97	103.72	102.59	101.56	100.64	99.80	96.60	94.57
13700	105.74	104.48	103.34	102.31	101.38	100.53	97.31	95.26
13800	106.52	105.24	104.10	103.06	102.12	101.26	98.02	95.96
13900	107.29	106.01	104.85	103.80	102.86	102.00	98.73	96.65
14000	108.06	106.77	105.60	104.55	103.60	102.73	99.44	97.35
14100	108.83	107.53	106.36	105.30	104.34	103.47	100.15	98.04
14200	109.60	108.29	107.11	106.04	105.08	104.20	100.86	98.74
14300	110.37	109.06	107.87	106.79	105.82	104.93	101.57	99.43
14400	111.15	109.82	108.62	107.54	106.56	105.67	102.28	100.13
14500	111.92	110.58	109.38	108.29	107.30	106.40	102.99	100.83
14600	112.69	111.34	110.13	109.03	108.04	107.13	103.70	101.52
14700	113.46	112.11	110.88	109.78	108.78	107.87	104.41	102.22
14800	114.23	112.87	111.64	110.53	109.52	108.60	105.12	102.91
14900	115.01	113.63	112.39	111.27	110.26	109.34	105.83	103.61
15000	115.78	114.39	113.15	112.02	111.00	110.07	106.54	104.30
15100	116.55	115.16	113.90	112.77	111.74	110.80	107.25	105.00
15200	117.32	115.92	114.66	113.51	112.48	111.54	107.96	105.69
15300	118.09	116.68	115.41	114.26	113.22	112.27	108.67	106.39
15400	118.86	117.45	116.16	115.01	113.96	113.00	109.39	107.08
15500	119.64	118.21	116.92	115.75	114.70	113.74	110.10	107.78
15600	120.41	118.97	117.67	116.50	115.44	114.47	110.81	108.47
15700	121.18	119.73	118.43	117.25	116.18	115.21	111.52	109.17
15800	121.95	120.50	119.18	117.99	116.92	115.94	112.23	109.86
15900	122.72	121.26	119.94	118.74	117.66	116.67	112.94	110.56
16000	123.50	122.02	120.69	119.49	118.40	117.41	113.65	111.25
16100	124.27	122.78	121.44	120.23	119.14	118.14	114.36	111.95
16200	125.04	123.55	122.20	120.98	119.88	118.87	115.07	112.65
16300	125.81	124.31	122.95	121.73	120.62	119.61	115.78	113.34
16400	126.58	125.07	123.71	122.47	121.36	120.34	116.49	114.04
16500	127.35	125.83	124.46	123.22	122.10	121.08	117.20	114.73

Term Amount	25 Years	26 Years	27 Years	28 Years	29 Years	30 Years	35 Years	40 Years
$16600	128.13	126.60	125.22	123.97	122.84	121.81	117.91	115.43
16700	128.90	127.36	125.97	124.71	123.58	122.54	118.62	116.12
16800	129.67	128.12	126.72	125.46	124.32	123.28	119.33	116.82
16900	130.44	128.88	127.48	126.21	125.06	124.01	120.04	117.51
17000	131.21	129.65	128.23	126.95	125.80	124.74	120.75	118.21
17100	131.99	130.41	128.99	127.70	126.54	125.48	121.46	118.90
17200	132.76	131.17	129.74	128.45	127.28	126.21	122.17	119.60
17300	133.53	131.93	130.50	129.19	128.02	126.95	122.88	120.29
17400	134.30	132.70	131.25	129.94	128.76	127.68	123.59	120.99
17500	135.07	133.46	132.00	130.69	129.50	128.41	124.30	121.68
17600	135.84	134.22	132.76	131.43	130.24	129.15	125.01	122.38
17700	136.62	134.98	133.51	132.18	130.98	129.88	125.72	123.08
17800	137.39	135.75	134.27	132.93	131.72	130.62	126.43	123.77
17900	138.16	136.51	135.02	133.67	132.46	131.35	127.14	124.47
18000	138.93	137.27	135.78	134.42	133.20	132.08	127.85	125.16
18100	139.70	138.04	136.53	135.17	133.94	132.82	128.56	125.86
18200	140.48	138.80	137.28	135.92	134.68	133.55	129.27	126.55
18300	141.25	139.56	138.04	136.66	135.42	134.28	129.98	127.25
18400	142.02	140.32	138.79	137.41	136.16	135.02	130.69	127.94
18500	142.79	141.09	139.55	138.16	136.89	135.75	131.40	128.64
18600	143.56	141.85	140.30	138.90	137.63	136.49	132.11	129.33
18700	144.33	142.61	141.06	139.65	138.37	137.22	132.82	130.03
18800	145.11	143.37	141.81	140.40	139.11	137.95	133.53	130.72
18900	145.88	144.14	142.56	141.14	139.85	138.69	134.24	131.42
19000	146.65	144.90	143.32	141.89	140.59	139.42	134.95	132.11
19100	147.42	145.66	144.07	142.64	141.33	140.15	135.66	132.81
19200	148.19	146.42	144.83	143.38	142.07	140.89	136.38	133.50
19300	148.97	147.19	145.58	144.13	142.81	141.62	137.09	134.20
19400	149.74	147.95	146.34	144.88	143.55	142.36	137.80	134.90
19500	150.51	148.71	147.09	145.62	144.29	143.09	138.51	135.59
19600	151.28	149.47	147.84	146.37	145.03	143.82	139.22	136.29
19700	152.05	150.24	148.60	147.12	145.77	144.56	139.93	136.98
19800	152.82	151.00	149.35	147.86	146.51	145.29	140.64	137.68
19900	153.60	151.76	150.11	148.61	147.25	146.02	141.35	138.37
20000	154.37	152.52	150.86	149.36	147.99	146.76	142.06	139.07
21000	162.09	160.15	158.40	156.82	155.39	154.10	149.16	146.02
22000	169.80	167.78	165.95	164.29	162.79	161.43	156.26	152.97
23000	177.52	175.40	173.49	171.76	170.19	168.77	163.37	159.93
24000	185.24	183.03	181.03	179.23	177.59	176.11	170.47	166.88
25000	192.96	190.65	188.57	186.69	184.99	183.45	177.57	173.83
26000	200.68	198.28	196.12	194.16	192.39	190.78	184.67	180.79
27000	208.40	205.91	203.66	201.63	199.79	198.12	191.78	187.74
28000	216.11	213.53	211.20	209.10	207.19	205.46	198.88	194.69
29000	223.83	221.16	218.75	216.57	214.59	212.80	205.98	201.65
30000	231.55	228.78	226.29	224.03	221.99	220.13	213.08	208.60
31000	239.27	236.41	233.83	231.50	229.39	227.47	220.19	215.55
32000	246.99	244.04	241.37	238.97	236.79	234.81	227.29	222.50
33000	254.70	251.66	248.92	246.44	244.19	242.15	234.39	229.46
34000	262.42	259.29	256.46	253.90	251.59	249.48	241.49	236.41
35000	270.14	266.91	264.00	261.37	258.99	256.82	248.60	243.36
36000	277.86	274.54	271.55	268.84	266.39	264.16	255.70	250.32
37000	285.58	282.17	279.09	276.31	273.78	271.50	262.80	257.27
38000	293.30	289.79	286.63	283.77	281.18	278.84	269.90	264.22
39000	301.01	297.42	294.17	291.24	288.58	286.17	277.01	271.18
40000	308.73	305.04	301.72	298.71	295.98	293.51	284.11	278.13

Term Amount	17 Years	18 Years	19 Years	20 Years	21 Years	22 Years	23 Years	24 Years
$11100	99.71	97.13	94.85	92.85	91.07	89.49	88.08	86.81
11200	100.61	98.00	95.71	93.69	91.89	90.30	88.87	87.60
11300	101.51	98.88	96.56	94.52	92.71	91.10	89.67	88.38
11400	102.41	99.75	97.42	95.36	93.53	91.01	90.46	89.16
11500	103.30	100.63	98.27	96.20	94.35	92.72	91.25	89.94
11600	104.20	101.50	99.13	97.03	95.17	93.52	92.05	90.72
11700	105.10	102.38	99.98	97.87	96.00	94.33	92.84	91.51
11800	106.00	103.25	100.84	98.70	96.82	95.13	93.63	92.29
11900	106.90	104.13	101.69	99.54	97.64	95.94	94.43	93.07
12000	107.80	105.00	102.55	100.38	98.46	96.75	95.22	93.85
12100	108.69	105.88	103.40	101.21	99.28	97.55	96.01	94.63
12200	109.59	106.75	104.25	102.05	100.10	98.36	96.81	95.42
12300	110.49	107.63	105.11	102.89	100.92	99.16	97.60	96.20
12400	111.39	108.50	105.96	103.72	101.74	99.97	98.39	96.98
12500	112.29	109.38	106.82	104.56	102.56	100.78	99.19	97.76
12600	113.19	110.25	107.67	105.40	103.38	101.58	99.98	98.54
12700	114.08	111.13	108.53	106.23	104.20	102.39	100.77	99.33
12800	114.98	112.00	109.38	107.07	105.02	103.20	101.57	100.11
12900	115.88	112.88	110.24	107.91	105.84	104.00	102.36	100.89
13000	116.78	113.75	111.09	108.74	106.66	104.81	103.15	101.67
13100	117.68	114.63	111.94	109.58	107.48	105.61	103.95	102.45
13200	118.57	115.50	112.80	110.42	108.30	106.42	104.74	103.24
13300	119.47	116.38	113.65	111.25	109.12	107.23	105.53	104.02
13400	120.37	117.25	114.51	112.09	109.94	108.03	106.33	104.80
13500	121.27	118.12	115.36	112.92	110.76	108.84	107.12	105.58
13600	122.17	119.00	116.22	113.76	111.58	109.65	107.91	106.36
13700	123.07	119.87	117.07	114.60	112.40	110.45	108.71	107.15
13800	123.96	120.75	117.93	115.43	113.22	111.26	109.50	107.93
13900	124.86	121.62	118.78	116.27	114.04	112.06	110.29	108.71
14000	125.76	122.50	119.64	117.11	114.86	112.87	111.09	109.49
14100	126.66	123.37	120.49	117.94	115.69	113.68	111.88	110.27
14200	127.56	124.25	121.34	118.78	116.51	114.48	112.68	111.06
14300	128.46	125.12	122.20	119.62	117.33	115.29	113.47	111.84
14400	129.35	126.00	123.05	120.45	118.15	116.09	114.26	112.62
14500	130.25	126.87	123.91	121.29	118.97	116.90	115.06	113.40
14600	131.15	127.75	124.76	122.13	119.79	117.71	115.85	114.18
14700	132.05	128.62	125.62	122.96	120.61	118.51	116.64	114.97
14800	132.95	129.50	126.47	123.80	121.43	119.32	117.44	115.75
14900	133.85	130.37	127.33	124.63	122.25	120.13	118.23	116.53
15000	134.74	131.25	128.18	125.47	123.07	120.93	119.02	117.31
15100	135.64	132.12	129.03	126.31	123.89	121.74	119.82	118.10
15200	136.54	133.00	129.89	127.14	124.71	122.54	120.61	118.88
15300	137.44	133.87	130.74	127.98	125.53	123.35	121.40	119.66
15400	138.34	134.75	131.60	128.82	126.35	124.16	122.20	120.44
15500	139.23	135.62	132.45	129.65	127.17	124.96	122.99	121.22
15600	140.13	136.50	133.31	130.49	127.99	125.77	123.78	122.01
15700	141.03	137.37	134.16	131.33	128.81	126.57	124.58	122.79
15800	141.93	138.25	135.02	132.16	129.63	127.38	125.37	123.57
15900	142.83	139.12	135.87	133.00	130.45	128.19	126.16	124.35
16000	143.73	140.00	136.73	133.84	131.27	128.99	126.96	125.13
16100	144.62	140.87	135.58	134.67	132.09	129.80	127.75	125.92
16200	145.52	141.75	138.43	135.51	132.91	130.61	128.54	126.70
16300	146.42	142.62	139.29	136.34	133.73	131.41	129.34	127.48
16400	147.32	143.50	140.14	137.18	134.56	132.22	130.13	128.26
16500	148.22	144.37	141.00	138.02	135.38	133.02	130.92	129.04

Term Amount	17 Years	18 Years	19 Years	20 Years	21 Years	22 Years	23 Years	24 Years
$16600	149.12	145.25	141.85	138.85	136.20	133.83	131.72	129.83
16700	150.01	146.12	142.71	139.69	137.02	134.64	132.51	130.61
16800	150.91	147.00	143.56	140.53	137.84	135.44	133.31	131.39
16900	151.81	147.87	144.42	141.36	138.66	136.25	134.10	132.17
17000	152.71	148.75	145.27	142.20	139.48	137.06	134.89	132.95
17100	153.61	149.62	146.12	143.04	140.30	137.86	135.69	133.74
17200	154.51	150.50	146.98	143.87	141.12	138.67	136.48	134.52
17300	155.40	151.37	147.83	144.71	141.94	139.47	137.27	135.30
17400	156.30	152.25	148.69	145.55	142.76	140.28	138.07	136.08
17500	157.20	153.12	149.54	146.38	143.58	141.09	138.86	136.86
17600	158.10	154.00	150.40	147.22	144.40	141.89	139.65	137.65
17700	159.00	154.87	151.25	148.05	145.22	142.70	140.45	138.43
17800	159.89	155.75	152.11	148.89	146.06	143.50	141.24	139.21
17900	160.79	156.62	152.96	149.73	146.86	144.31	142.03	139.99
18000	161.69	157.50	153.82	150.56	147.68	145.12	142.83	140.77
18100	162.59	158.37	154.67	151.40	148.50	145.92	143.62	141.56
18200	163.49	159.25	155.52	152.24	149.32	146.73	144.41	142.34
18300	164.39	160.12	156.38	153.07	150.14	147.54	145.21	143.12
18400	165.28	161.00	157.23	153.91	150.96	148.34	146.00	143.90
18500	166.18	161.87	158.09	154.75	151.78	149.15	146.79	144.69
18600	167.08	162.75	158.94	155.58	152.60	149.95	147.59	145.47
18700	167.98	163.62	159.80	156.42	153.43	150.76	148.38	146.25
18800	168.88	164.50	160.65	157.26	154.25	151.57	149.17	147.03
18900	169.78	165.37	161.51	158.09	155.07	152.37	149.97	147.81
19000	170.67	166.25	162.36	158.93	155.89	153.18	150.76	148.60
19100	171.57	167.12	163.21	159.77	156.71	153.98	151.55	149.38
19200	172.47	168.00	164.07	160.60	157.53	154.79	152.35	150.16
19300	173.37	168.87	164.92	161.44	158.35	155.60	153.14	150.94
19400	174.27	169.75	165.78	162.27	159.17	156.40	153.93	151.72
19500	175.17	170.62	166.63	163.11	159.99	157.21	154.73	152.51
19600	176.06	171.50	167.49	163.95	160.81	158.02	155.52	153.29
19700	176.96	172.37	168.34	164.78	161.63	158.82	156.32	154.07
19800	177.86	173.25	169.20	165.62	162.45	159.63	157.11	154.85
19900	178.76	174.12	170.05	166.46	163.27	160.43	157.90	155.63
20000	179.66	175.00	170.91	167.29	164.09	161.24	158.70	156.42
21000	188.64	183.75	179.45	175.66	172.29	169.30	166.63	164.24
22000	197.62	192.50	188.00	184.02	180.50	177.36	174.56	172.06
23000	206.60	201.25	196.54	192.39	188.70	185.43	182.50	179.88
24000	215.59	210.00	205.09	200.75	196.91	193.49	190.43	187.70
25000	224.57	218.75	213.63	209.12	205.11	201.55	198.37	195.52
26000	233.55	227.50	222.18	217.48	213.32	209.61	206.30	203.34
27000	242.53	236.24	230.72	225.84	221.52	217.67	214.24	211.16
28000	251.52	244.99	239.27	234.21	229.72	225.73	222.17	218.98
29000	260.50	253.74	247.81	242.57	237.93	233.80	230.11	226.80
30000	269.48	262.49	256.36	250.94	246.14	241.86	238.04	234.62
31000	278.46	271.24	264.90	259.30	254.34	249.92	245.98	242.44
32000	287.45	279.99	273.45	267.67	262.54	257.98	253.91	250.26
33000	296.43	288.74	281.99	276.03	270.75	266.04	261.84	258.08
34000	305.41	297.49	290.54	284.39	278.95	274.11	269.78	265.90
35000	314.39	306.24	299.08	292.76	287.15	282.17	277.71	273.72
36000	323.38	314.99	307.63	301.12	295.36	290.23	285.65	281.54
37000	332.36	323.74	316.17	309.49	303.56	298.29	293.58	289.37
38000	341.34	332.49	324.72	317.85	311.77	306.35	301.52	297.19
39000	350.33	341.24	333.26	326.22	319.97	314.41	309.45	305.01
40000	359.31	349.99	341.81	334.58	328.18	322.48	317.39	312.83

8%   Necessary to Amortize a Loan   8%

Term / Amount	1 Year	2 Years	3 Years	4 Years	5 Years	6 Years	7 Years	8 Years
$11100	965.58	502.03	347.84	270.99	225.07	194.62	173.01	156.92
11200	974.28	506.55	350.97	273.43	227.10	196.38	174.57	158.34
11300	982.97	511.07	354.11	275.87	229.13	198.13	176.13	159.75
11400	991.67	515.60	357.24	278.31	231.16	199.88	177.69	161.16
11500	1000.37	520.12	360.37	280.75	233.18	201.64	179.25	162.58
11600	1009.07	524.64	363.51	283.19	235.21	203.39	180.81	163.99
11700	1017.77	529.16	366.64	285.64	237.24	205.14	182.36	165.40
11800	1026.47	533.69	369.77	288.08	239.27	206.90	183.92	166.82
11900	1035.17	538.21	372.91	290.52	241.29	208.65	185.48	168.23
12000	1043.87	542.73	376.04	292.96	243.32	210.40	187.04	169.65
12100	1052.56	547.25	379.18	295.40	245.35	212.16	188.60	171.06
12200	1061.26	551.78	382.31	297.84	247.38	213.91	190.16	172.47
12300	1069.96	556.30	385.44	300.28	249.40	215.66	191.72	173.89
12400	1078.66	560.82	388.58	302.73	251.43	217.42	193.27	175.30
12500	1087.36	565.35	391.71	305.17	253.46	219.17	194.83	176.71
12600	1096.06	569.87	394.84	307.61	255.49	220.92	196.39	178.13
12700	1104.76	574.39	397.98	310.05	257.52	222.68	197.95	179.54
12800	1113.46	578.91	401.11	312.49	259.54	224.43	199.51	180.95
12900	1122.16	583.44	404.24	314.93	261.57	226.18	201.07	182.37
13000	1130.85	587.96	407.38	317.37	263.60	227.94	202.63	183.78
13100	1139.55	592.48	410.51	319.81	265.63	229.69	204.18	185.20
13200	1148.25	597.01	413.65	322.26	267.65	231.44	205.74	186.61
13300	1156.95	601.53	416.78	324.70	269.68	233.20	207.30	188.02
13400	1165.65	606.05	419.91	327.14	271.71	234.95	208.86	189.44
13500	1174.35	610.57	423.05	329.58	273.74	236.70	210.42	190.85
13600	1183.05	615.10	426.18	332.02	275.76	238.46	211.98	192.26
13700	1191.75	619.62	429.31	334.46	277.79	240.21	213.54	193.68
13800	1200.45	624.14	432.45	336.90	279.82	241.96	215.09	195.09
13900	1209.14	628.66	435.58	339.34	281.85	243.72	216.65	196.50
14000	1217.84	633.19	438.71	341.79	283.87	245.47	218.21	197.92
14100	1226.54	637.71	441.85	344.23	285.90	247.22	219.77	199.33
14200	1235.24	642.23	444.98	346.67	287.93	248.98	221.33	200.75
14300	1243.94	646.76	448.12	349.11	289.96	250.73	222.89	202.16
14400	1252.64	651.28	451.25	351.55	291.99	252.48	224.45	203.57
14500	1261.34	655.80	454.38	353.99	294.01	254.24	226.01	204.99
14600	1270.04	660.32	457.52	356.43	296.04	255.99	227.56	206.40
14700	1278.73	664.85	460.65	358.87	298.07	257.74	229.12	207.81
14800	1287.43	669.37	463.78	361.32	300.10	259.50	230.68	209.23
14900	1296.13	673.89	466.92	363.76	302.12	261.25	232.24	210.64
15000	1304.83	678.41	470.05	366.20	304.15	263.00	233.80	212.06
15100	1313.53	682.94	473.18	368.64	306.18	264.76	235.36	213.47
15200	1322.23	687.46	476.32	371.08	308.21	266.51	236.92	214.88
15300	1330.93	691.98	479.45	373.52	310.23	268.26	238.47	216.30
15400	1339.63	696.51	482.59	375.96	312.26	270.02	240.03	217.71
15500	1348.33	701.03	485.72	378.41	314.29	271.77	241.59	219.12
15600	1357.02	705.55	488.85	380.85	316.32	273.52	243.15	220.54
15700	1365.72	710.07	491.99	383.29	318.34	275.28	244.71	221.95
15800	1374.42	714.60	495.12	385.73	320.37	277.03	246.27	223.36
15900	1383.12	719.12	498.25	388.17	322.40	278.78	247.83	224.78
16000	1391.82	723.64	501.39	390.61	324.43	280.54	249.38	226.19
16100	1400.52	728.16	504.52	393.05	326.45	282.29	250.94	277.61
16200	1409.22	732.69	507.65	395.49	328.48	284.04	252.50	229.02
16300	1417.92	737.21	510.79	397.94	330.51	285.80	254.06	230.43
16400	1426.62	741.73	513.92	400.38	322.54	287.55	255.62	231.85
16500	1435.31	746.26	517.06	402.82	334.57	289.30	257.18	233.26

Term Amount	1 Year	2 Years	3 Years	4 Years	5 Years	6 Years	7 Years	8 Years
$16600	1444.01	750.78	520.19	405.26	336.59	291.06	258.74	234.67
16700	1452.17	755.30	523.32	407.70	338.62	292.81	260.29	236.09
16800	1461.41	759.82	526.46	410.14	340.65	294.56	261.85	237.50
16900	1470.11	764.35	529.59	412.58	342.68	296.32	263.41	238.91
17000	1478.81	768.87	532.72	415.02	344.70	298.07	264.97	240.33
17100	1487.51	773.39	535.86	417.47	346.73	299.82	266.53	241.74
17200	1496.21	777.91	538.99	419.91	348.76	301.68	268.09	243.16
17300	1504.90	782.44	542.12	422.35	350.79	303.33	269.65	244.57
17400	1513.60	786.96	545.26	424.79	352.81	305.08	271.21	245.98
17500	1522.30	791.48	548.39	427.23	354.84	306.84	272.76	247.40
17600	1531.00	796.01	551.53	429.67	356.87	308.59	274.32	248.81
17700	1539.70	800.53	554.66	432.11	358.90	310.34	275.88	250.22
17800	1548.40	805.05	557.79	434.56	360.92	312.10	277.44	251.64
17900	1557.10	809.57	560.93	437.00	362.95	313.85	279.00	253.05
18000	1565.80	814.10	564.06	439.44	364.98	315.60	280.56	254.47
18100	1574.50	818.62	567.19	441.88	367.01	317.36	282.12	255.88
18200	1583.19	823.14	570.33	444.32	369.04	319.11	283.67	257.29
18300	1591.89	827.66	573.46	446.76	371 06	320.86	285.23	258.71
18400	1600.59	832.19	576.59	449.20	373.09	322.62	286.79	260.12
18500	1609.29	836.71	579.73	451.64	375.12	324.37	288.35	261.53
18600	1617.99	841.23	582.86	454.09	377.15	326.12	289.91	262.95
18700	1626.69	845.76	586.00	456.53	379.17	327.88	291.47	264.36
18800	1635.39	850.28	589.13	458.97	381.20	329.63	293.03	265.77
18900	1644.09	854.80	592.26	461.41	383.23	331.38	294.58	267.19
19000	1652.79	859.32	595.40	463.85	385.26	333.14	296.14	268.60
19100	1661.48	863.85	598.53	466.29	387.28	334.89	297.70	270.02
19200	1670.18	868.37	601.66	468.73	389.31	336.64	299.26	271.43
19300	1678.88	827.89	604.80	471.17	391.34	338.40	300.82	272.84
19400	1687.58	877.41	607.93	473.62	393.37	340.15	302.38	274.26
19500	1696.28	881.94	611.06	476.06	395.39	341.90	303.94	275.67
19600	1704.98	886.46	614.20	478.50	397.42	343.66	305.49	277.08
19700	1713.68	890.98	617.33	480.94	399.45	345.41	307.05	278.50
19800	1722.38	895.51	620.47	483.38	401.48	347.16	308.61	279.91
19900	1731.07	900.03	623.60	485.82	403.51	348.92	310.17	281.32
20000	1739.77	904.55	626.73	488.26	405.53	350.67	311.73	282.74
21000	1826.76	949.78	658.07	512.68	425.81	368.20	327.32	296.88
22000	1913.75	995.01	689.41	537.09	446.09	385.74	342.90	311.01
23000	2000.74	1040.23	720.74	561.50	466.36	403.27	358.49	325.15
24000	2087.73	1085.46	752.08	585.92	486.64	420.80	374.07	339.29
25000	2174.72	1130.69	783.41	610.33	506.91	438.34	389.66	353.42
26000	2261.70	1175.91	814.75	634.74	527.19	455.87	405.25	367.56
27000	2348.69	1221.14	846.09	659.15	547.47	473.40	420.83	381.70
28000	2435.68	1266.37	877.42	683.57	567.74	490.94	436.42	395.83
29000	2522.67	1311.60	908.76	707.98	588.02	508.47	452.01	409.97
30000	2609.66	1356.82	940.10	732.39	608.30	526.00	467.59	424.11
31000	2696.65	1402.05	971.43	756.81	628.57	543.54	483.18	438.24
32000	2783.63	1447.28	1002.77	781.22	648.85	561.07	498.76	452.38
33000	2870.62	1492.51	1034.11	805.63	669.13	578.60	514.35	466.52
34000	2957.61	1537.73	1065.44	830.04	689.40	596.14	529.94	480.65
35000	3044.60	1582.96	1096.78	854.46	709.68	613.67	545.52	494.79
36000	3131.59	1628.19	1128.11	878.87	729.96	631.20	561.11	508.93
37000	3218.58	1673.41	1159.45	903.28	750.23	648.73	576.69	523.06
38000	3305.57	1718.64	1190.79	927.70	770.51	666.27	592.28	537.20
39000	3392.55	1763.87	1222.12	952.11	790.78	683.80	607.87	551.34
40000	3479.54	1809.10	1253.46	976.52	811.06	701.33	623.45	565.47

6

other consumer computations

1. REAL ESTATE TAXES
   a. Tax
   b. Assessed valuation
   c. Tax rate

2. LIFE INSURANCE
   a. Types of policies
   b. Cash surrender value

3. BANK RECONCILIATION

1. REAL ESTATE TAXES

Real estate taxes are those taxes which are levied against land and buildings. They may be imposed by the state, county, town, city, etc., the levies varying from one locale to another. Generally, these taxes are charged annually.

The recipients of real estate taxes and the reasons for the levies are as follows:

State—To provide additional funds necessary to carry out the operation of the state government. The limited amount collected through the personal income taxes, sales taxes, and auto taxes is not usually sufficient for state needs.

County—To provide the revenue needed for welfare cases, road development, operation of corrective institutions, etc.

Town—To provide for the operation of the local government buildings, collection of refuse, parks maintenance, etc.

School Districts—To provide for educational needs. This tax is frequently separate and apart from other real estate taxes and very often is the greatest single tax, based on property ownership, paid by the property owner.

City—To provide for educational systems, maintenance of police, fire, and sanitation departments, the courts, etc.

The number of real estate taxes imposed upon property owners vary; some pay one all-inclusive tax while others are taxed separately by several groups.

The terms with which property owners should be familiar so that they may solve problems relating to real estate taxes are:

1. *Tax*—The amount of money necessary to carry out the programs of the locality.
2. *Assessed valuation*—The value of the property (either the true market value or a percentage of the market value) as determined

by a representative of the taxing body upon examination and appraisal of the real property.

3. *Tax rate*—The percent charged the property owner which has been determined by dividing the taxes to be collected by the total assessed valuation of taxable community.

The mathematics of real estate taxes includes the computation of the tax rate, the assessed valuation, and the tax to be collected.

1. Finding the Tax Rate. To determine this rate, the following formula is used:

$$\text{Tax rate} = \frac{\text{Amount of taxes required}}{\text{Total assessed valuation}}$$

ILLUSTRATIVE PROBLEM. The total assessed valuation in Selwin County is $12,000,000. In order to carry out their programs, a total of $650,400 must be collected. Find the tax rate.

SOLUTION:

$$\text{Tax rate} = \frac{\$650,400}{\$12,000,000}$$

$$\text{Tax rate} = 12,000,000 \overline{).650,400.}^{.054200}$$

Tax rate = $.0542

The tax rate is generally expressed on one hundred or one thousand dollars. Thus,

$.0542 = $5.42 per hundred
$.0542 = $54.20 per thousand

6.1 SOLVE THESE PROBLEMS:

1. John Peters, reading the local newspaper, learned that the town in which he lives needs $48,500 in property taxes. If the assessed valuation on property for the town is $4,300,000, how much is the tax rate?

2. The annual budget for the Oceandale School District is:

Teacher's salaries	$2.6,328.50
Building maintenance	18,472.50
Books and supplies	4,210.35
Miscellaneous expenses	12,000.65

The total assessed valuation of the property involved for tax purposes is $14,000,000. Find the tax rate (per hundred).

3. The true market value of property in Bayville County is $846,-000,000. The county, for tax purposes, appraises property at 60% of its true value. If the tax to be raised is $5,642,086, what is the tax rate per thousand?

2. Finding the Assessed Valuation. The following formula is used when the total budget needed and the tax rate are known.

$$\text{Assessed valuation} = \frac{\text{Tax (budget needed)}}{\text{Tax rate}}$$

ILLUSTRATIVE PROBLEM. The budget requirements for the town of Plattsholm are $287,514. The tax rate is .0315. Find the assessed valuation.

SOLUTION:

$$\text{Assessed valuation} = \frac{\$287,514}{.0315}$$

$$\text{Assessed valuation} = 315\overline{)287514.0000}^{\,9127428.57}$$

$$\text{Assessed valuation} = \$9,127,428.57$$

6.2 SOLVE THESE PROBLEMS:
1. If the tax rate is .0742 and the revenue needed to operate the Elliotville School District is $148,420, what is the assessed valuation of the taxable property?
2. The tax rate is $8.16 per hundred; the total budget requirement for the taxing body is $3,426,525. What is the total assessed valuation?
3. The town of Anderson has a school tax rate of $12.52 per thousand and a town tax of $3.40 per thousand. If the total budget is $6,842,-750, what is the total assessed valuation?

3. Finding the Tax to be Collected. To determine the total tax to be collected when the tax rate is established and the assessed valuation is known, the following formula is used:

$$\text{Tax} = \text{Tax rate} \times \text{Assessed valuation}$$

ILLUSTRATIVE PROBLEM. If the assessed valuation of Mr. Smith's property is $8,648 and the tax rate is .0624, what is Mr. Smith's real estate tax?

SOLUTION:

$$\text{Tax} = \text{Tax rate} \times \text{Assessed valuation}$$
$$\text{Tax} = .0624 \times \$8,648$$
$$\text{Tax} = \$539.6352 = \$539.64$$

6.3   SOLVE THESE PROBLEMS:

1. Sam Cooper's land and home were assessed for $16,439. The county tax rate was .0231. How much was his tax bill?

2. Elliot Smith had to pay a village tax of $.27 per hundred and a school tax of $4.28 per hundred. What was his total tax bill if his property had an assessed valuation of $21,628?

3. George McCan bought a home for $27,000. The property is appraised, for tax purposes, at two-thirds of its cost by the town assessor. If the tax rate is $47.40 per thousand, what is McCan's tax bill?

2. LIFE INSURANCE

a. TYPES OF POLICIES

The primary purpose of life insurance is to provide money for an individual's survivors after his death. It is purchased to replace a portion of the family income that was contributed by the deceased. Other reasons for the purchase of life insurance are to provide for an individual's final medical expenses, to pay for dependents' education, to complete payment of a home mortgage, etc. The types of policies (contracts) available to individuals vary according to need and also from one company to another. The most common classifications of life insurance policies are:

1. Term Insurance. This policy provides the individual with protection for a specified period of time. Typically, policies are written for terms of up to 20 years, but some companies offer terms of up to 50 years with an age limit of 65 or occasionally 70. The policy expires at the end of the stated term. Conversion to another type of policy, at this point, is often possible, but at higher premiums (amount paid by the insured). Normally, the policy has no cash surrender value.

2. Straight Life (Ordinary Life). Among the most widely purchased, this policy requires the payment of the premium each year until the death of the insured. At that time, the beneficiary (individual to whom the policy is payable upon death of insured) collects the proceeds of the policy. This policy has a cash surrender value (amount paid to policyholder if he stops paying premiums and elects to cash in the policy).

3. Limited Payment Life. Lifetime protection is guaranteed but rather than constant payments until death, as in straight life, the insured pays for 10, 20, or 30 years or up until a specified age. Because the number of payments is limited, the premiums and cash surrender value are higher than straight life.

4. Endowment. This type of policy enables the insured to accumulate money which becomes available at maturity of the policy. Maturity dates generally run from 10 to 30 years. In the event of death prior to the maturity date, the beneficiary collects the face (the amount provided by the policy) of the policy.

The computational work involved in life insurance requires nothing more than the use of the fundamental arithmetic processes and their application to the variety of tables published by insurance companies.

The following table has been constructed from portions of the annual premium tables of an insurance company:

	ANNUAL PREMIUM RATES PER $1,000*			
Age	*10-Year Term*	*Straight Life*	*20-Payment Life*	*20-Year Endowment*
20	8.44	16.06	26.30	47.08
21	8.66	16.44	26.78	47.15
22	8.87	16.83	27.28	47.23
23	9.09	17.23	27.78	47.31
24	9.31	17.66	28.31	47.40
25	9.53	18.10	28.85	47.49
26	9.75	18.57	29.40	47.60
27	9.97	19.06	29.98	47.71
28	10.18	19.57	30.57	47.84
29	10.51	20.10	31.18	47.98
30	10.73	20.67	31.82	48.14
35	12.47	23.95	35.34	49.20
40	14.87	28.19	39.60	50.92
45	17.93	33.68	44.75	53.54
50		40.85	51.18	57.58
55		50.33	59.54	63.82
60		63.06	70.84	73.39

Note: Semi-annual rate .51 times annual; quarterly .26; monthly .0875.

* These are rates for males; to determine rates for females use 3 years younger than actual age.

ILLUSTRATIVE PROBLEM. Fred O'Rourke is 28 years old and wants to purchase a straight life policy for $10,000. Find the annual premium for this policy.

SOLUTION:

1. From the annual premium table on page 128 locate age 28 and move across to that position under the column headed straight life. The number is $19.57.

2. Because $19.57 is the amount for $1,000, you must multiply by 10 to find premium for $10,000.

$$\$19.57 \times 10 = \$195.70 \quad \text{Annual premium}$$

ILLUSTRATIVE PROBLEM. If a 20-payment life policy for $5,000 is purchased at age 30, how much will each payment be if payments are made semi-annually?

SOLUTION:

At the bottom of the table on annual premiums, it is noted that semi-annual rates are .51 times annual. Thus, to find the semi-annual rate:

1. First find the annual rate for age 30 on the table—31.82.

2. Multiply 31.82 by .51

$$
\begin{array}{r}
31.82 \\
.51 \\
\hline
3182 \\
15910 \\
\hline
16.2282 \\
\end{array}
\quad \text{Semi-annual premium per \$1,000}
$$

3. $16.2282 \times 5 = 81.1410$

4. \$81.14 Semi-annual payment for \$5,000 policy.

6.4   SOLVE THESE PROBLEMS:

1. Find the annual premium for Jack Gordon, age 40, on a 20-payment life policy for \$8,000.

2. What is the monthly payment on 10-year term insurance for a man age 22, on a policy of \$15,000?

3. Roger Smith is planning to purchase a straight life policy. He is 26 years old. How much would he save a year by making annual payments rather than quarterly payments?

4. Mr. Scott, 22 years old, purchased a 20-year endowment policy of \$6,000. If he paid the premiums quarterly, how much was each payment?

b. CASH SURRENDER VALUE

The cash surrender value is the amount of money paid to the insured if he decides to no longer retain the policy. This amount is paid in a lump sum.

The tables on page 130 have been constructed from the actual tables of an insurance company. Because term insurance does not generally provide for cash surrender values, the term insurance category was not included.

ILLUSTRATIVE PROBLEM. John Arnold wishes to surrender the \$8,000 straight life policy that he purchased at age 25. He has had the policy for 5 years. What is the cash surrender value?

SOLUTION:

1. Using the straight life cash value table on page 130, locate age 25. Move across to column headed "End of 5 years." The number is 34. This is the cash value for \$1,000.

CASH VALUES PER $1,000—MALE AND FEMALE

STRAIGHT LIFE

Age	1	2	3	End of Year 5	10	15	20
20			3	26	87	158	239
25			8	34	106	187	277
30			15	45	127	218	318
35		5	22	57	151	253	361
40		11	30	70	176	289	406
45		17	39	85	204	376	451
50		23	49	101	233	365	494
55	1	31	60	118	263	401	533
60	5	38	71	136	291	433	570

CASH VALUES PER $1,000—MALE AND FEMALE

20-PAYMENT LIFE

Age	1	2	3	End of Year 5	10	15	20
20		10	29	70	183	315	468
25		14	35	81	206	351	518
30		18	42	93	231	390	571
35		24	50	106	257	429	625
40		29	58	118	282	467	679
45	3	34	66	131	307	503	731
50	5	39	73	143	329	534	779
55	8	44	80	154	347	559	822
60	10	49	87	164	360	573	860

CASH VALUES PER $1,000—MALE AND FEMALE

ENDOWMENT AT 65

Age	1	2	3	End of Year 5	10	15	20
20			14	44	127	223	333
25		5	22	58	157	270	399
30		12	33	76	195	329	481
35		21	47	99	243	405	590
40	2	33	65	130	308	510	746
45	11	51	91	175	405	672	1000
50	25	81	138	257	591	1000	
55	53	143	235	430	1000		

2. Because the policy is for $8,000, multiply 34 × 8.

34 × 8 = $272 cash value after 5 years.

6.5 *SOLVE THESE PROBLEMS:*

1. Determine the cash surrender value on a $5,000, 20-payment life policy, taken out at age 40 at the end of 3 years. At the end of 5 years. At the end of 10 years.

2. Tom Mannix presently owns two life insurance policies. One is a straight life policy taken out at age 20 for $10,000; the other is an endowment at 65 policy for $6,000 taken out at age 30. Today he is 35 years old and wishes to surrender both policies so that he can invest in a business. How much total cash will he receive from both policies?

3. The Atlas Company purchased 20-payment, $10,000 life insurance policies for their salesmen after one full year of employment. The company went out of business and each salesman decided to cash in his policy. What was the cash surrender value of each policy (holding time determined by length of employment)?

Salesmen	Age at Purchase of Policy	Years of Employment
A	20	16
B	25	21
C	30	11
D	35	6
E	40	4

3. BANK RECONCILIATION

At a regular period during the month, all depositors receive statements from their banks. These statements list the deposits added to their accounts, the amounts deducted from their accounts—including checks and service charges, the opening balance at the beginning of the period, and the closing balance at the end of the period.

Although it seems reasonable that the depositor's balance should agree with the bank's balance, it is possible that they might not for the following reasons:

1. A delay, by either side, in recording all the transactions.

2. Service charges for insufficient funds, overdrawn accounts, etc. are deducted by the bank but not by the depositor.

3. Arithmetic errors by either party.

For these reasons, it is important that individuals compare the bank's records with their own. This comparison is known as a bank statement reconciliation.

The bank statement on page 133 was sent for the period August 20 through September 17.

The bank statement shows a detailed analysis of the month's transactions in the account. The first three columns labeled "checks and debits" are a daily list of all of the deductions from the bank account. The fourth column is a list of the items that increased the account. Finally, the rightmost column indicates the balance after each day's transactions. These transactions are summarized across the top of the statement. At the top, the balance at the beginning of the month, the total increases, total decreases, and balance at the end of the month ($77.40) are given.

In addition to the itemized list of transactions shown on the bank statement, there is also available an itemized list kept by the depositor in his checkbook. Generally, if the checkbook balance does not agree with the bank statement balance it is for one of the reasons mentioned above. To prove the accuracy of the two balances, it is necessary to adjust each balance to a point at which the adjusted balances are equal.

The most common adjustments to the bank statement balance are:

1. Add to the balance shown on the bank statement any additions made by the depositor which are not on the bank statement. For example, a deposit made on the afternoon of the last day of the month would not be included in that month's bank statement. Because such a deposit would be added to the checkbook balance, it will be necessary to add it to the bank statement's balance to reconcile the two balances.

2. Deduct from the bank statement balance any deductions made in the checkbook that are not reflected on the bank statement. For example, because of a time lag, checks that were deducted from the checkbook balance might not have been paid out by the bank during the month. Because such checks have been deducted from the checkbook balance, they must be deducted from the bank statement balance to reconcile the two balances.

The most common adjustments to the checkbook balance are:

1. Add to the checkbook balance those items collected by the bank but not recorded in the checkbook.

2. Deduct, from the depositor's checkbook balance, charges made by the bank, which were unrecorded in the checkbook. The adjusted bank statement balance and the adjusted checkbook balance should be in agreement.

ILLUSTRATIVE PROBLEM. After comparing the bank statement on page 133 with the checkbook and the returned canceled checks, the following differences were noted:

Statement balance	$77.40
Checkbook balance	57.62
These checks were issued but did not reach bank	12.48
	10.70
There was a service charge of	3.40

Prepare a bank reconciliation statement for this period.

Figure 6-1
Checking Account Statement

PREVIOUS STATEMENT DATE	PREVIOUS STATEMENT BALANCE	DEPOSITS & OTHER CREDITS NO.	DEPOSITS & OTHER CREDITS AMOUNT	CHECKS & OTHER DEBITS NO.	CHECKS & OTHER DEBITS AMOUNT
8-20	209.56	5	1,040.00	29	1,168.76

CHECKING ACCOUNT STATEMENT

AS OF THIS DATE → 9/ 17/ 68

YOUR BALANCE IS $ 77.40

CHECKS & DEBITS	CHECKS & DEBITS	CHECKS & DEBITS	DEPOSITS & CREDITS	DATE	BALANCE
8940				821	12016
2500				822	9516
1500	3000			823	5016
			10000	826	15016
3500				827	11516
5930			50000	830	55586
793	2478	3000		903	49315
408	1500	3271		904	44136
395	2701	3182		905	
3417	9300			905	25141
816	2200			906	22125
10000				909	12125
3327				910	8798
1000	1168		30000	912	36630
2500				913	34130
1700			12000	916	44430
800	3146	7404	2000	917	
27000	340S			917	7740

540/177 5/68

B - BANCARDCHEK M - MEMO (DEBIT)
C - CERTIFIED CHECK R - RETURN ITEM
S - SERVICE CHARGE L - LIST POSTING

M - MEMO (CREDIT)
OD - OVERDRAWN

SOLUTION:

Bank balance (shown on bank statement)		$77.40
Less: Outstanding checks	$12.48	
	10.70	23.18
Adjusted bank balance		$54.22
Bank balance (in checkbook)	$57.62	
Less: service charge	3.40	
Adjusted checkbook balance	$54.22	

6.6 *SOLVE THESE PROBLEMS:*

1. Using the following information, reconcile the bank balance:

Checkbook balance		$840.26
Outstanding checks:	No. 17	$15.50
	No. 22	23.45
	No. 29	82.50
Service charge	$2.00	

The bank statement balance for the period is $959.71.

2. John Peters received his statement from the Crowley Exchange Bank showing a balance of $620.45. His checkbook balance, for that period, was $587.77. The checks outstanding were:

No. 237	$12.47
No. 239	22.18
No. 257	11.53
No. 258	9.12
No. 259	26.08

The bank returned an uncollectible check deposited to his account for $45.20 and also deducted a service charge of $3.50. Reconcile the balances.

3. The bank statement dated June 30 showed a balance of $1,248.52 for Mr. Parks. The deposit on June 29 amounting to $112.06 was not recorded on the statement. These checks were outstanding: No. 804, $14.38; No. 808, $25.30; No. 810, $30.45; and No. 811, $125. A service charge of $4.25 was on the bank's statement. In addition, the bank returned an uncollectible check amounting to $58.25 which Mr. Parks deposited. The checkbook balance was $1,227.95. Reconcile the balances.

4. Prepare a bank statement from the following information:

Service charge	$ 4.96
Checkbook balance	627.18
Collection of customer's note by the bank that was not entered in the checkbook	700.00
Interest earned on the above note	7.00
Erroneous deduction from account by bank	90.00

Balance per bank statement	1,000.00
Outstanding checks	627.15
Error in checkbook, failure to deduct check	450.00
Deposit not credited to account by the bank	416.37

CHAPTER REVIEW

1. The budget for a rural school district is $67,200. Determine the real estate tax rate per thousand if the total assessed valuation is $10,500,000.

2. Compute the assessed valuation on a home that has an annual real estate tax of $1,135.31 and a tax rate of $.02615.

3. John Ford's home is assessed at $53,064.34. If the town tax rate is .0369, what was his annual tax?

4. Mary Apley, age 27, has purchased a 20-payment life policy of $16,000. What will the premium be if she pays annually? Quarterly? Monthly? (Use tables on page 128 of the text.)

5. Calculate the cash surrender value of a straight life policy of $40,000 taken out at the age of 20 at the end of 3 years; 5 years; 10 years. (Use tables on page 130 of text.)

6. Reconcile these balances:

    Checkbook balance: $1,390.00
    Outstanding checks: No. 42, $75.00; No. 47, $150.00; No. 53, $125.00
    Bank statement balance: $1,784.50
    Deposit included in checkbook, not listed in bank statement: $145.00
    Note collected by bank, not included in checkbook: $200.00
    Bank charges: $10.50

FOUR

RETAILING AND MARKETING MATHEMATICS

Persons involved in the area of marketing are faced with certain mathematical problems necessary to the proper functioning of a business enterprise. For example, in the retail field, buyers and merchandisers must pay strict attention to markup (the difference between the amount one pays for goods and the price for which he hopes to sell the goods to the consumer) and make certain that it is sufficiently high to cover reductions in price (markdowns) that might occur due to changes in fashion, poor planning, soiled merchandise, etc. It is vital that the gross profit (the difference between the cost of goods and the actual selling price) is large enough to cover operating expenses and provide the required profit. In addition, control of inventories, selling prices, discounts, etc. require specialized mathematical procedures.

Many students entering this field are very often aware only of the area of marketing that includes research procedures, advertising and sales techniques, and product planning. They are less familiar, or in some cases unfamiliar, with the important part mathematics plays in the field. This section of the book will concentrate on applying mathematics to marketing with emphasis on the retail field.

7

markup and markdown

1. MARKUP
   a. Individual markup
   b. Markup percent based on retail
   c. Markup percent based on cost
   d. Buyer's wheel
   e. Average markup
   f. Cumulative markup

2. MARKDOWN

1. MARKUP

a. INDIVIDUAL MARKUP

Markup is the difference between the amount one pays for the goods and the price for which he hopes to sell the goods to the consumer. The markup on a single item is called individual markup.

ILLUSTRATIVE PROBLEM. A buyer purchased a dress for $10 and offered it for sale for $15. His markup, or the difference between the cost and the selling price, was $5.

SOLUTION: Mathematically we would state this as follows:

$$
\begin{array}{lr}
\text{(Retail: selling price)} & \$15 \\
\text{(Cost)} & -\ \underline{10} \\
\text{(Markup)} & \$\ 5
\end{array}
$$

These are the basic equations:

$$
\begin{aligned}
\text{Markup} &= \text{Retail} - \text{Cost} \\
\text{Cost} &= \text{Retail} - \text{Markup} \\
\text{Retail} &= \text{Cost} + \text{Markup}
\end{aligned}
$$

Although it is important to know the dollar markup, buyers and merchandisers, whose responsibility it is to set markup, are more concerned with markup in terms of percent.

The markup percent can be based either on cost or retail (selling price). Markup expressed as a percent of cost is used primarily by retailers of perishables and hardware lines. Department stores and fashion merchandisers usually figure markup as a percent of retail. We will illustrate both methods.

140

b. MARKUP PERCENT BASED ON RETAIL

To find the markup percent based on retail, divide the dollar markup (the difference between the cost and the retail price) by the retail price.

ILLUSTRATIVE PROBLEM. A dress that cost $13 retails for $20. Find the markup percent based on retail.

SOLUTION: To find the markup:

$$Markup = Retail - Cost$$
$$= \$20 - \$13$$
$$= \$7$$

To find the markup percent based on retail:

$$\frac{Markup}{Retail} = Markup \% \text{ on retail}$$

$$\frac{\$7}{\$20} = 35\% \text{ Markup on retail}$$

ILLUSTRATIVE PROBLEM. A retail store buyer purchases a dress for $35 and sells it for $42. What is the dollar markup? What is the markup percent based on retail?

SOLUTION: To find the markup:

$$Markup = Retail - Cost$$
$$= \$42 - \$35$$
$$= \$7$$

To find the markup percent based on retail:

$$\frac{Markup}{Retail} = Markup \% \text{ on retail}$$

$$\frac{\$7}{\$42} = 16\frac{2}{3}\% \text{ Markup on retail}$$

If we compare the markups in both illustrative problems, we find they have the same dollar markup. By computing the percent and comparing them, we see the importance of markup percent to the retailer. The first markup percent, 35%, was certainly better than the second, $16\frac{2}{3}\%$.

7.1 SOLVE THESE PROBLEMS:

1. A clock costs $8 and retails for $12. What is the markup percent on retail?

2. What markup percent on retail will the buyer derive from a card table costing $30 and retailing for $50?

3. A poker table and four chairs cost $95. If the buyer retails it for $150, what markup percent on retail will he achieve?

4. Lamps which cost $25 retail for $45 at the Atlas Furniture Shop. What is the store's markup percent on retail?

5. Blouses costing $36 per dozen retail for $5 each at Higgin's Department Store. What markup percent on retail is achieved on each blouse?

6. A retailer purchased an automobile stereo system for $90 and sold it installed for $180. In order to charge that retail price, however, it was necessary for the retailer to have the stereo installed in the customer's auto at a cost of $10. What was the markup percent on retail? Round off to the nearest percent.

In addition to being able to figure the markup when the retail price and the cost are known, the retailer is very often concerned with the following:

1. Determining the cost when both the retail price and the markup percent on retail are known.

2. Determining the retail price when the cost and markup percent on retail are known.

ILLUSTRATIVE PROBLEM. Find the cost of a camera retailing at $40 with a markup of 40% on retail.

SOLUTION:

$$\text{Cost} = \text{Retail} - \text{Markup}$$

then: $\text{Cost} \% = \text{Retail} \% - \text{Markup} \%$

ALTERNATE SOLUTION:

$$\text{Retail price} \times 70\% = \$42$$

$$\text{Retail price} = \frac{42}{.7}$$

$$\text{Retail price} = \$60$$

If the retail price equals 100%, then

$$\text{Cost} \% = 100\% - 40\%$$
$$\text{Cost} \% = 60\%$$
$$\text{Cost} = 60\% \times \$40 \text{ (retail price)}$$
$$\text{Cost} = \$24$$

ILLUSTRATIVE PROBLEM. Find the retail price for a typewriter costing $42 and marked up 30% on retail.

SOLUTION:

$$\text{Retail} = \text{Cost} + \text{Markup}$$

then:

$$\text{Retail } \% = \text{Cost } \% + \text{Markup } \%$$
$$100\% = 70\% + 30\%$$
$$70\% = \text{Cost}$$
$$(\text{Cost}) \ 70\% = \$42$$
$$1\% = \frac{\$42}{70}$$
$$1\% = \$ \qquad .60$$
$$(\text{Retail}) \ 100\% = \$60$$

7.2 SOLVE THESE PROBLEMS:

1. A surfboard retails for $80. The markup on the item is 30% on retail. Find the cost.
2. A furniture buyer selects a rocking chair for $105 and marks it up 40% on retail. Find the retail price.
3. The retail price of a phonograph is $60 and it is marked up $33\frac{1}{3}\%$ on retail. What is the cost?
4. A dress buyer retails a bridal gown for $135. If the markup on retail is 42%, what is the cost of the gown?
5. A buyer chooses a group of blouses which cost $66 per dozen. Find the retail price of one blouse if there is a markup of 45% on retail.

c. MARKUP PERCENT BASED ON COST

To find the markup on cost, divide the dollar markup by the cost.

ILLUSTRATIVE PROBLEM. A camera cost the retailer $33 and sells for $44. Find the markup percent based on the cost.

SOLUTION: To find the markup:

$$\text{Markup} = \text{Retail} - \text{Cost}$$
$$= \$44 - \$33$$
$$= \$11$$

To find the markup percent:

$$\frac{\text{Markup}}{\text{Cost}} = \text{Markup percent on cost}$$

$$\frac{\$11}{\$33} = 33\frac{1}{3}\% \text{ Markup on cost}$$

7.3 SOLVE THESE PROBLEMS:

1. If a raincoat costs $16 and retails for $24, what is the markup percent on cost?
2. What is the markup percent on cost for a transistor radio which costs $15 and retails for $25?
3. A hardware buyer purchases electric coffeemakers at $19 apiece and retails them at $35. What is the markup percent based on cost? Round off to nearest percent.
4. Stereo speakers which cost $240 per dozen retail at $40 each. What is the percent of markup on cost?
5. If drinking glasses cost $144 a gross (12 dozen) and retail for $18 per dozen, what is the markup percent on cost per dozen?

As has been previously discussed in the section on markup percent based on retail, buyers are required to determine the following computations when markup percent is based on cost:

1. Determining the cost when both the retail price and the markup percent on cost are available.
2. Determining the retail price when the cost and the markup percent on cost are known.

ILLUSTRATIVE PROBLEM. A sport coat that retails for $50 has a markup of 60% on cost. Find the cost.

SOLUTION:

$$\text{Cost} + \text{Markup} = \text{Retail}$$
$$100\% + 60\% = \$50$$
$$160\% = \$50$$
$$1\% = \quad .3125$$
$$100\% = \$31.25$$

ILLUSTRATIVE PROBLEM. A buyer purchases a dress for $20 and marks it up 40% on cost. Find the retail price.

SOLUTION:

$$Cost + Markup = Retail$$
$$100\% + 40\% = 140\%$$
$$140\% \text{ of } \$20 = \$28 \text{ (Retail)}$$

7.4 SOLVE THESE PROBLEMS:

1. If a rug retails for $100 and is marked up 50% of cost, what is the actual cost?

2. When visiting the furniture market a buyer purchases a table for $80 and plans to mark it up 40% of cost. What should the retail price be?

3. Find the cost of a lamp which retails for $60 and is marked up $33\frac{1}{3}\%$ of cost.

4. The swimsuit buyer for Brandt's Specialty Shop buys a dozen swimsuits for $156. If the suits are marked up 48% of cost, what would each suit retail for?

5. A supermarket purchasing agent buys a gross of potted plants for $432. At what price should each plant be retailed if the agent wants a markup of 35% of cost?

6. The buyer at Jane's Specialty Shop purchased swimsuits for the summer season. At the end of the season, one white suit which had been marked $20 had to be sold for $15 because it was soiled. If the suit was supposed to bring a markup of 40%, what percent of the cost did it actually gain for the store?

d. BUYER'S WHEEL

When visiting the market to purchase goods for his department, the buyer very often must quickly calculate the individual markup on merchandise. The *Profit Calculator* in Figure 7-1 and the *Buyer's Markup Calculator* in Figure 7-2 are examples of devices that are available to help the buyer perform these calculations quickly. Although these are valuable tools, it is beneficial to be able to calculate markup mathematically. For the problems a buyer must solve in determining average markup or cumulative markup, knowledge of the actual calculations involved is necessary.

The profit calculator is used as follows: By setting the arrow at the proper cost (opposite the cost of the merchandise) the selling price sought is the figure opposite the desired percentage. This device quickly calculates the profit on selling price and the profit on cost. The buyer selects the one he needs.

As the profit calculator indicates in Figure 7-1, an item costing $100 and marked up 40% on retail will sell for $167. In the same diagram, an item costing $337.50 and marked up 60% on cost will sell for $540.

Figure 7-1
Profit Calculator

7.5 *SOLVE THESE PROBLEMS:* Complete the blank spaces, rounding off to the nearest percent.

	MARKUP ON RETAIL		
	Retail	*Cost*	*Markup* %
1.	—	$130	30%
2.	$260	—	36%
3.	$320	$173	—
4.	$1.75	$1.00	—
5.	—	$2.60	42%
6.	$5.50	—	38%
7.	—	$35	45%
8.	$76	—	35%
9.	$23	$12	—
10.	$348	—	40%

	MARKUP ON COST		
	Retail	*Cost*	*Markup* %
1.	—	$175	60%
2.	$235	—	50%
3.	$1.90	$1.10	—
4.	—	$2.65	42%
5.	$760	$430	—
6.	$3.75	—	36%
7.	—	$155	40%
8.	$25	—	38%
9.	—	$63.75	45%
10.	$65	$35	—

The buyer's markup calculator works on the same principle as the profit calculator. The buyer's markup calculator differs from the profit calculator in that it offers only the markup based on the selling price (retail). Only those buyers in an industry calculating markup based on retail will find the buyer's markup calculator useful.

Figure 7-2
Buyer's Markup Calculator

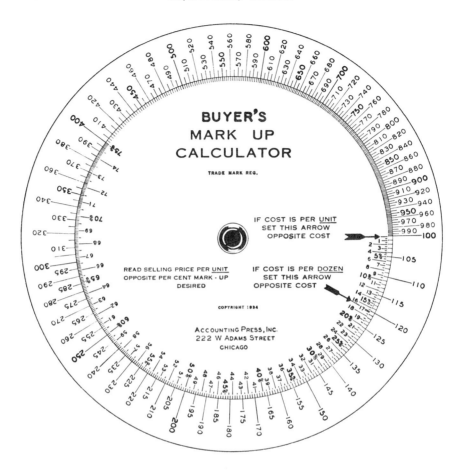

e. AVERAGE MARKUP

Up to this point, we have considered the markup on single items. This is called the *individual markup*. In retailing, it is unusual for buyers to price each piece of merchandise in the department with a common markup. The nature of some merchandise is such that it warrants a higher than usual markup; similarly, other merchandise requires a lower markup. For example, high fashion merchandise and precious jewelry are typically marked up higher than merchandise that is carried as an accommodation for customers or must meet competitor's prices.

To cover expenses and realize a profit, buyers must make certain that their departments are maintaining an adequate *average markup* on the merchandise.

ILLUSTRATIVE PROBLEM. A buyer plans to purchase $1,500 worth of toys to be marked up 40% on retail. Of this planned total amount, one item is bought to attract customers to his store; this merchandise costs $200 for 100 units and will retail at $250, or $2.50 per unit. If he is to maintain the desired 40% markup on retail on the *total* purchase, what markup % is needed on the balance of the purchases?

SOLUTION:

1. Determine the total planned purchases at retail.

$$\text{Retail } \% = \text{Cost } \% + \text{Markup } \%$$
$$100\% = 60\% + 40\%$$
$$60\% = \text{Cost}$$
$$(\text{cost}) \; 60\% = \$1,500$$
$$1\% = \frac{\$1,500}{60}$$
$$1\% = \$25$$
$$100\% = \$2,500 \text{ (retail)}$$

2. Subtract from the total planned purchases the purchases already made.

	Cost	Retail	Markup %
Total planned purchases	$1500	$2500	40%
Purchases made	− 200	− 250	
Balance needed	$1300	$2250	42.22%

The balance of the planned purchase—$1,300—should be marked up to retail for $2,250—a dollar markup of $950. To achieve an overall markup of 40%, the remaining $1,300 of purchases must be marked up 42.22% on retail.

$$\frac{\text{Markup}}{\text{Retail}} = \text{Markup } \% \text{ on retail}$$

$$\frac{\$950}{\$2250} = 42.22\%$$

7.6 SOLVE THESE PROBLEMS:

1. A suit buyer visits the New York market to purchase $25,000 worth of merchandise to be marked up 50% on retail. After three days of purchasing, he tallies his orders and discovers he already purchased $20,000 worth of goods which will retail for $35,000. How much should his remaining purchases be marked up on retail to achieve an average markup of 50% on retail for the $25,000?

2. The merchandise manager of fashion apparel for Holme's Department Store checks the purchase orders of new buyers to make cer-

tain that they are obtaining the correct average markups on their beginning of the season purchases. Determine the markup that Holme's new coat and suit buyer must realize on the remaining planned purchases of $45,000 to achieve an average markup of 40% on retail. His purchases to date are:

		Cost	Retail
January 1	100 coats	$10,000	$18,000
January 10	175 suits	$14,000	$23,000
January 15	50 ensembles	$ 6,000	$ 8,000

Round off your answer to the nearest percent.

3. A textiles buyer made the following purchases:

Quantity	Description	Cost (per yard)	Retail (per yard)
500 yards	Sail cloth	$ .40	$ .75
1000 yards	Silk shantung	1.50	2.25
800 yards	Wool jersey	2.25	3.25
1200 yards	Cotton lace	.80	1.50

His planned total amount of purchases for the period is $7,000 at cost. If he is to achieve an average markup of 38% on retail, how much must the remainder of his purchases be marked up? Round off your answer to the nearest percent.

f. CUMULATIVE MARKUP

The buyer, in addition to being concerned with the individual markup on merchandise and the average markup for groups of goods purchased, is interested in the total merchandise handled (the goods he is about to purchase plus his inventory). The markup arrived at by considering both factors is called *cumulative markup*.

ILLUSTRATIVE PROBLEM. Mr. Simms operates a high fashion boutique and is planning his purchases for the fall–winter season. He requires a 40% markup on retail to realize a satisfactory profit. He plans to purchase merchandise to retail at $20,000 to add to an opening inventory (merchandise carried over from a previous season) of $8,000 that cost $5,000. His purchases to date cost $6,000 to retail at $10,000. At what percent must the rest of his purchases be marked up so that he can achieve a cumulative markup of 40%?

SOLUTION:
   1. Determine the total amount of goods to be handled.

Opening inventory $ 8,000 (retail)
Planned purchases   20,000 (retail)
Total goods to be handled $28,000

2. Determine cost of goods to be handled.

Cost = Retail − Markup % (desired cumulative markup)
Cost = 100% − 40%
Cost = 60% × $28,000
Cost = $16,800

3. Determine balance to be purchased.

			Cost		Retail
	Total planned purchases		$16,800		$28,000
Less {	Opening inventory	$5000		$ 8,000	
	Purchases already made	6000	11,000	10,000	18,000
			$ 5,800		$10,000

4. Determine markup needed on balance of purchases so that the desired cumulative markup can be achieved.

Retail − Cost = Markup
$10,000 − $ 5,800 = Markup
$ 4,200 = Markup

$$\frac{\$ 4,200}{\$10,000} = \text{Markup on retail}$$

42% = Markup % on retail for balance of purchases

7.7   *SOLVE THESE PROBLEMS:* Round off to the nearest percent.

1. The opening inventory for a glove department for the period beginning February 1 and ending April 30 is $6,000 retail and $4,800 at cost. The total amount of merchandise at retail to be handled for this period is $25,000 at a 45% markup on retail. What markup % would be required on the purchases yet to be made to maintain a cumulative markup of 45% for the period?

2. The haberdashery buyer for Esquire, Ltd., has purchased $20,000 worth of merchandise to retail for $32,000. His opening inventory, including merchandise with various individual markups, has an average markup of 38% and a retail value of $63,000. How much must the buyer's additional purchases be marked up to achieve a cumulative markup of 40% and a grand total of $125,000 at retail?

3. During the month of June a swimsuit buyer tries to bring his cumulative markup to 40% for the first six months of the year. It is possible at this time for him to purchase odd lots of merchandise and mark them sufficiently high to reach this overall markup. The following are figures for his department's first five months:

	Cost	*Retail*
January	$ 8,000	$12,000
February	7,000	12,000
March	14,000	22,000
April	20,000	31,000
May	23,000	35,000

If the total amount of goods to be purchased is $120,000 for the six-month period, what must the remainder be marked to achieve the desired cumulative markup?

2. MARKDOWN

Although it is desirable to sell goods at the decided retail price, the buyer is very often unable to sell everything at this price. The most common reasons for not being able to obtain the original markup on merchandise is summarized as follows:

1. Poor planning, which might lead to buying more merchandise than needed.
2. Buying the wrong sizes, colors, styles.
3. Changes in fashion.
4. Soiled or damaged merchandise.
5. Uncontrollable happenings such as bad weather or economic recessions.
6. Even if the original estimates are correct one can't plan so perfectly that every last piece is sold.

Any of the above reasons might require the buyer to reduce his prices. This difference between the original retail price and the new selling price is the *markdown*.

An important consideration of markdown is the markdown percent, based on actual sales when the markdown from the original retail (selling price) is known. Because markup is generally thought of in terms of a percent of retail, markdown must be thought of in these terms as well.

ILLUSTRATIVE PROBLEM. A retail store buyer decides to reduce his entire inventory by 15%. His inventory is $5,000 at retail. What is the markdown percent based on sales, assuming he sells his entire inventory?

SOLUTION:

1. Determine the dollar markdown

Original retail × Reduction percent = $ Markdown
$5000 × .15 = $750

2. Determine the actual sales

Original retail − Reduction = Sales (New retail)
$5000 − $750 = $4250

3. Determine the markdown percentage on sales

$$\text{Markdown } \% = \frac{\$ \text{ Markdown}}{\$ \text{ Sales}}$$

$$= \frac{\$750}{\$4250}$$

$$= 17.6\%$$

7.8 SOLVE THESE PROBLEMS:

1. If a buyer reduces the entire stock in a sweater department 25 % and sells it out completely, what is his markdown percent on actual sales? Assume the original retail value to be $1,000.

2. Smoke from a nearby fire soiled a $26,000 inventory of the Gotham Fabric Shop. To dispose of the merchandise the buyer reduced the entire stock 20 %. Assuming it was all sold, what was his markdown percent?

3. The Bel-Air Sweater Shop reduces its remaining winter inventory of $38,000 by 30 %. If all the merchandise is sold during this period, what is the markdown percent based on sales?

4. The budget and the moderate-price dress departments are planning to close out portions of their inventory to make room for new merchandise. The former reduces $7,000 worth of stock by 20 % and the latter reduces $12,000 worth of goods by $33\frac{1}{3}\%$. What is the markdown percent for each department, assuming both lots of merchandise are sold?

5. Wilkin's Department Store is going out of business and must dispose of its entire inventory within one month. Because each department's original markup on merchandise varies, the markdowns will vary as well. Assuming all merchandise is disposed of, determine the markdown percent for these departments using the following information:

Department	Inventory	Reduction	Markdown percent
Accessories	$ 39,000	30 %	—
Coats and suits	140,000	$33\frac{1}{3}\%$	—
Children's wear	62,000	25 %	—
Appliances	155,000	40 %	—
Precious jewelry	225,000	45 %	

153

1. Determine the markup percent on retail of a pair of shoes that costs $15 and sells for $25.

2. If a case of cookies costs $12 and retails for $18, find the markup percent based on cost.

3. How much does a guitar cost the retailer if it retails at $50 and has been marked up 50% on retail?

4. Mr. Jones purchases a set of tools to sell in his hardware store that costs $36 and is to be marked up 40% on retail. How much should he mark the tools?

5. A florist purchases a shipment of orchids that retail for $10 apiece based on a markup of 70% on cost. Find the florist's cost per orchid.

6. At what price should a chair be marked if it costs $40 and is marked up 60% on cost?

7. After careful evaluation, the menswear buyer at Roran's Department Store determines that his fall model stock necessitates a total purchase of $84,000 to be marked up 50% on retail. His first three purchases cost a total of $30,000 to retail at $58,000. In order to achieve his desired average markup, how much must the remainder of his purchases be marked up on retail? Round off to the nearest percent.

8. Harris Blum, jewelry buyer for Rubin's Department Store, has an opening inventory for the month of April that cost $70,000 and retails for $120,000. In addition, he has purchased $20,000 worth of merchandise to retail at $36,000. What is his cumulative markup, on retail, for the period?

9. Because of unusually warm weather, the proprietor of a ski shop decides to reduce his $35,000 inventory (at retail) 30%. Assuming that he completely sells his stock, what is the markdown percent based on sales?

8

merchandise and profit

1. GROSS PROFIT (GROSS MARGIN)
   a. Gross profit (margin) on sales
   b. Gross profit (margin) percentage
   c. Gross profit method of estimating inventories

2. MERCHANDISE INVENTORY (STOCK) TURNOVER

3. THE RETAIL METHOD OF ESTIMATING INVENTORY

4. OPEN TO BUY

1. GROSS PROFIT
(GROSS MARGIN)

a. GROSS PROFIT (MARGIN) ON SALES

To make a profit, retailers add an amount to the cost of an article. As indicated in Chapter 7, this amount is called markup and it is often an anticipated profit rather than a certain one. After the sale has actually been made, the difference between the cost and actual selling price is called the gross profit or the gross margin.

ILLUSTRATIVE PROBLEM. A pair of men's shoes that cost $8 is sold for $10. What is the gross profit?

SOLUTION:

Selling price	$10.00
Cost	8.00
Gross profit	2.00

8.1 SOLVE THESE PROBLEMS:
   1. Last year John's Jewelry Shop had sales of $327,168.12. The cost of goods sold was $170,216.12. Find the gross profit.
   2. An appliance store pays $179.50 for a dishwasher and offers it for sale for $280.00. Several weeks later, during a storewide sale, the dishwasher is sold for $249.95. Find (1) the markup and (2) the gross profit.
   3. Harvey's radio and television shop had sales of $90,638 and sales returns of $4,238 for the first quarter of the year. The cost of goods sold for that period was $51,318. Find the gross profit.
   4. A menswear buyer has sales of $12,400 and sales returns of $1,400 for one month. The sales consisted of merchandise from inventory costing $4,000 plus purchases of $3,000. What is the cost of goods sold? What is the gross profit?

155

5. Assuming that all the goods are sold, determine the gross profit, given the following conditions:

	Cost	Retail	Markup % on Retail
Inventory	$10,000	$18,000	—
Purchases		26,000	40%
Net sales		30,000	—

b. GROSS PROFIT PERCENT

The percentage of gross profit to sales is important to businessmen because it may be used to estimate gross profit, net profit, and merchandise inventory when the information necessary to prepare actual information is not available. It may be used as a test of efficiency. Comparisons of this year's gross profit percentage with that of last year's, or with that of similar businesses often reveal important information.

The formula for finding the gross profit percent is

$$\frac{\text{Gross profit}}{\text{Sales}} = \text{Gross profit percent}$$

ILLUSTRATIVE PROBLEM. Given the gross profit and the selling price, find the gross profit percent.

A retailer pays $10 for a ladies sweater. The sweater was sold for $15. What was the gross profit percent based on sales?

SOLUTION:

$$\begin{array}{ll}
\text{Selling price} & \$15 \\
\text{Cost} & \underline{10} \\
\text{Gross profit} & \$\ 5
\end{array}$$

$$\frac{\text{Gross profit }\$5}{\text{Selling price }\$15} = 33\tfrac{1}{3}\% \text{ Gross profit based on sales}$$

ILLUSTRATIVE PROBLEM. Given the cost and gross profit, find the gross profit percent.

A radio that cost $8 was sold at a price that included a gross profit of $2. What was the percent of gross profit based on sales?

SOLUTION:

$$\begin{array}{lll}
\text{Cost} + \text{Gross profit} &=& \text{Selling price} \\
\$8 \ + \ \ \ \ \ \$2 &=& \$10.00
\end{array}$$

$$\frac{\text{Gross profit }\ \$2}{\text{Sales}\ \ \ \ \ \ \ \ \$10} = 20\% \text{ Gross profit based on sales}$$

ILLUSTRATIVE PROBLEM. Given the percent of gross profit and the gross profit (in dollars), find the cost.

The gross profit percent on a television set was 40%. If the gross profit was $80, what was the cost of the set?

SOLUTION:

$$40\% = \$80$$

$$1\% = \frac{\$80}{40} = \$2$$

100% = $200 (Selling price)
Selling price $200 − Gross profit $80 = Cost $120

ILLUSTRATIVE PROBLEM. Given the percent of gross profit and the selling price, find the cost.

An article was sold for $24, which included a gross profit of 25%. What was the cost of the article?

SOLUTION:

Sales	$24
Gross profit $24 × 25%	6
Cost	$18

8.2 SOLVE THESE PROBLEMS: Round all percents off to one decimal place.

1. A buyer purchases a table for $65 and sells it for $100. What is the gross profit percent based on sales?

2. Determine the gross profit percent based on sales of twelve sweaters costing $84 per dozen and selling for $12 each.

3. If a set of chinaware cost $125 and was sold at a retail price which included a gross profit of $80, what was the percent of gross profit based on sales?

4. A gross profit of $25 was included in the selling price of a watch that cost $50. What was the percent of gross profit based on sales?

5. If the gross profit on a surfboard is $45 and the gross profit percent is $33\frac{1}{3}\%$, what is the cost of the board?

6. Find the cost of a dozen bicycles if the gross profit is $42 on each and the gross profit percent is 20%.

7. Determine the cost of a sofa that was sold for $350 and made a gross profit of 40% based on sales.

8. Slippers selling for $6 a pair made a gross profit of $33\frac{1}{3}\%$. How much does a buyer have to pay for every dozen pairs he purchases for his department?

9. Determine the gross profit percent for a department with net sales, $60,000; gross cost of goods sold, $38,000; and allowances on purchases, $1,000.

10. A music department, for the month of December, had gross sales of $78,000 and sales returns of $3,000. The merchandise sold cost $45,000, less an allowance of 2%. What was the gross profit percent based on sales?

11. Find the gross profit percent based on sales for a dress department that has net sales of $62,500, alteration expenses of $5,500, total merchandise costs of $38,000, and allowances on sales of 2.5%.

c. GROSS PROFIT METHOD OF ESTIMATING INVENTORIES

It is vital to the successful operation of a business that the profits be calculated periodically during the year. This poses a problem, because the amount of merchandise on hand—the closing inventory—is expensive and time-consuming to count and calculate. This can be overcome by estimating the closing inventory. Many businesses use the gross profit method to estimate their closing inventory.

As we have seen in the previous problems, the gross profit percent can be determined as follows:

$$\frac{\text{Gross profit}}{\text{Sales}} = \text{Gross profit percent}$$

The formula for estimating the closing inventory, using the gross profit method is:

Opening inventory $+$ Purchase $=$ Merchandise available for sale

Less: Sales $-$ Gross profit $= \dfrac{\text{Cost of goods sold}}{\text{Closing inventory}}$

ILLUSTRATIVE PROBLEM. Estimate the closing inventory from the following information:

Opening inventory	$10,000
Purchases	30,000
Sales	35,000
Gross profit percent	40%

SOLUTION:

1. Calculate the merchandise available for sale:

Opening inventory	$10,000
Purchases	30,000
Merchandise available for sale	$40,000

2. Calculate the cost of goods sold:

Sales	$35,000
Less: Gross profit 40%	14,000
Cost of goods sold	$21,000

3. Subtract the cost of goods sold from the merchandise available for sale:

Merchandise available for sale	$40,000
Less: cost of goods sold	21,000
Closing inventory	$19,000

8.3 SOLVE THESE PROBLEMS:

1. From the following information, estimate the closing inventory by using the gross profit method: gross profit percent 35%; sales $60,000; purchases $40,000; opening inventory $10,000.

2. During the first three years of operation the Clark Company sold a total of $450,000, which yielded a gross profit of $189,000. The opening inventory for the current year was $112,000. By June 30 of this year, purchases were $120,000 and sales were $260,000. Calculate the estimated inventory.

3. The inventory of Apex, Inc. was totally destroyed by fire. From their accounting records the following information was available: opening inventory, $100,000; purchases, $250,000; sales, $400,000; gross profit percent, 52%. Calculate the fire loss.

2. MERCHANDISE INVENTORY (STOCK) TURNOVER

In most retail enterprises, merchandise inventory (stock) requires a large part of the total capital of the organization. In addition, it is expensive to maintain because space, insurance, obsolescence, and handling are expensive. This creates a problem because the inventory must be large enough to ensure sufficient sales but not so large as to cause excessive expenses. By using the merchandise inventory turnover ratio, a businessman can test the efficiency with which he is handling the merchandise inventory. This ratio indicates the number of times per year the average dollar-value of inventory was sold. By comparing the turnover with the ratio of prior years, or with the turnover of similar businesses, decisions may be made as to the effectiveness of the inventory management.

The formulas for merchandise inventory turnover are:

$$\frac{\text{Cost of goods sold}}{\text{Average inventory}} = \text{Merchandise inventory turnover at cost}$$

$$\frac{\text{Sales}}{\text{Average inventory at retail}} = \text{Merchandise inventory turnover at retail}$$

1. Cost of goods sold is the cost of all of the merchandise sold during a period.
2. Sales is the total of the retail sales for a period.
3. Average inventory is usually determined by adding the inventory at the beginning of the period to the inventory at the end of the period and dividing by 2. A more accurate average for the year can be obtained by adding the beginning inventories of each of the 12 months and the ending inventory for the 12th month and dividing by 13.

The merchandise inventory turnover rate indicates the number of times the average inventory has been sold during the year.

ILLUSTRATIVE PROBLEM. Find the merchandise inventory turnover at cost:

Sales		$300,000
Cost of goods sold		
Merchandise inventory, January 1, 1970	$ 40,000	
Add: Purchases	220,000	
Merchandise available for sale	260,000	
Less: Merchandise inventory, December 31, 1970	20,000	
Cost of goods sold		240,000
Gross profit on sales		$ 60,000

SOLUTION:

1. Find the cost of goods sold = $240,000
2. Find the average inventory—Inventory at beginning $40,000
   Inventory at end   20,000
       $60,000

$$\frac{\$60,000}{2} = \$30,000 \text{ Average inventory}$$

3. Find the turnover.

$$\frac{\text{Cost of goods sold } \$240,000}{\text{Average inventory } \$30,000} = 8 \text{ Merchandise inventory turnover}$$

ILLUSTRATIVE PROBLEM. Sales at Herrick's Hosiery Shop were $24,000 for the first quarter of the year. Inventory at retail was $8,000 on January 1 and $4,000 on March 31. What was the turnover at retail for the period?

SOLUTION:

1. Find the average inventory.

$$\begin{array}{ll}
\text{Jan. 1 inventory} & \$\ 8,000 \\
\text{March 31 inventory} & \underline{\ \ 4,000} \\
 & \overline{\$12,000}
\end{array}$$

$$\frac{\$12,000}{2} = \$6,000 \text{ Average inventory}$$

2. Find the turnover.

$$\frac{\text{Sales}}{\text{Average inventory at retail}} = \text{Merchandise inventory turnover}$$

$$\frac{\$24,000}{6,000} = 4 \text{ Merchandise inventory turnover}$$

8.4 SOLVE THESE PROBLEMS:

1. From the following information, find the merchandise inventory turnover at cost: purchases, $340,000; sales, $400,000; gross profit, $100,000; merchandise inventory at end of period, $100,000; cost of goods sold, $300,000; merchandise inventory at beginning of period, $60,000; merchandise available for sale, $400,000.

2. Find the ratio of merchandise inventory (stock) turnover at cost.

	Cost of Goods Sold	*Merchandise Inventory Beginning of Period*	*Merchandise Inventory End of Period*	*Turn-over*
1.	$ 42,000	$12,400	$ 7,600	
2.	65,000	17,250	8,750	
3.	130,000	65,000	35,000	
4.	92,000	32,635	7,365	
5.	78,000	29,000	10,000	

3. Determine the merchandise inventory turnover at cost for Alcart's Specialty Shoppe for this 6-month period.

	Inventory at Cost	*Cost of Goods Sold for Month*
July 1	$17,000	$16,000
August 1	32,000	18,000
September 1	40,000	23,000
October 1	42,000	25,000
November 1	36,000	20,000
December 1	35,500	19,000
December 31	9,250	

4. Sales for the first six months at the Menken Carpet Company were:

January	$17,095
February	15,655
March	30,200
April	46,319
May	48,626
June	36,680

The retail inventory figures for the corresponding periods were:

January 1	$26,530
February 1	23,465
March 1	48,075
April 1	72,644
May 1	77,019
June 1	52,212
June 30	43,055

What was the stock turnover at retail for the six-month period? Round off to one decimal place.

5. Find the merchandise inventory (stock) turnover at retail and at cost for the final quarter of the year at the Jayson Shoe Shop.

MERCHANDISE INVENTORY

	Cost	Retail
October 1	$ 7,000	$12,625
November 1	8,200	14,126
December 1	11,000	18,321
December 31	8,000	13,328

SALES

	Cost	Retail
October	$5,735	$ 8,350
November	6,370	9,622
December	7,895	11,228

a. THE RETAIL METHOD OF ESTIMATING INVENTORY

To supply management with accounting statements that indicate the success of a business enterprise, it is necessary to know the *cost* of the merchandise inventory (merchandise on hand). For this reason, at least once a year, all of the merchandise is counted, its cost determined, and the total cost of the inventory calculated. This procedure is expensive, time-consuming, and disrupts the normal operation of the business. Because the accounting state-ments based upon the cost of the inventory are vital to managerial decision making, they must be provided more often than once a year. For this reason there are several methods of estimating the cost of the inventory. Retail establishments frequently use the retail method. It works this way:

1. Calculate the stock on hand by adding the opening inventory and purchases at both cost and retail.

2. The relationship (percent) of the cost of the merchandise to the selling price of the merchandise is determined by dividing the total merchandise at retail into the total merchandise at cost as deter-mined above.

3. From the original amount offered for sale (available) at selling price, deduct the amount sold. The remainder is that which is unsold (the inventory) at selling price.

4. The inventory at selling price is converted to inventory at cost by applying the percent found in the second step.

Simply stated, once we know the percent that cost is of retail selling price (step 2) and the amount of inventory at retail selling price (step 3), we can determine the inventory at cost by multiplying (step 4).

ILLUSTRATIVE PROBLEM. At the close of the prior year, the Acme Department Store had an inventory that cost $100,000 and had a retail value of $200,000. During the current year they bought merchandise costing $200,000 that was marked to sell for $300,000. The year's sales totaled $200,000. Find the cost of the inventory at the end of this year.

SOLUTION:

		Cost	Retail
1.	Opening inventory	100,000	200,000
	Purchases	200,000	300,000
	Gross Average for Sale	300,000	500,000

2. To determine the percent of the cost of the merchandise to its selling price:

$$\frac{\text{Cost} \quad 300,000}{\text{Selling price } 500,000} = 60\%$$

We have found that the cost is 60% of the selling price. Now if we find the inventory at selling price, we can convert it to cost by determining 60% of it.

3. To determine the inventory at selling price:

The total amount of merchandise available for sale had a selling price of	$500,000
Of this, the amount sold was	200,000
The amount left on hand (inventory) at selling price	$300,000

4. To convert the inventory at selling price to inventory at cost: We have already determined that cost is 60% of selling price. Therefore, if the inventory at selling price is $300,000, 60% of it, or $180,000, is the inventory at cost.

8.5   SOLVE THESE PROBLEMS:

1. If the merchandise available for sale has a selling price of $200,000 and cost $150,000, what is the relationship of cost of selling price expressed as a percent?

2. If the merchandise available for sale is $200,000 at selling price and sales were $50,000, what is the inventory at selling price?

3. If the cost is 75% of selling price and the inventory at selling price is $160,000, what is the inventory at cost?

4. The total purchases of Jones and Company cost $160,000 and were marked up to sell for $240,000. If the sales were $90,000, what was the inventory at cost?

5. A hosiery buyer purchases merchandise which costs $80,000 and retails for $120,000. If sales are $60,000, what is the inventory at retail?

6. Roberts and Company had an opening inventory of $50,000 to retail for $74,000. He made additional purchases of $40,000 which he planned to retail for $70,000. If his net sales were $60,000, what was the inventory at cost and at retail?

7. Find the closing inventory at retail and cost using the following information:

	Cost	Retail
Opening inventory	$36,000	$65,000
Purchases	42,000	85,000
Gross sales		95,000
Sales returns and allowances		4,000

8. Roger's Bootery grossed $120,000 and had sales returns of $6,000. Its opening inventory was $65,000 at cost and $100,000 at retail. To this amount $90,000 was purchased, to retail at $150,000. What was the inventory at cost and retail?

9. A sporting-goods buyer had an inventory of $25,000 which was marked to retail at $42,000. To this, he added purchases of $30,000

to be marked up 40% of retail. If sales were $18,000, what was his inventory at cost? At selling price?

b. OPEN-TO-BUY

Buyers, in order to effectively control their inventories, must carefully plan the amount of merchandise they are going to purchase at a given time. Because inventory needs vary from month to month, depending upon the season, sale periods, holidays, etc. the buyer must always adjust the amounts of merchandise needed to the particular situation. The amount of merchandise that can be ordered at any time during a period is the difference between the total purchases planned by the buyer and the commitments already made. The amount of this difference is called *open-to-buy* or, as it is referred to in practice, the O.T.B. The formula used is:

Merchandise needed for period — merchandise available = O.T.B.

ILLUSTRATIVE PROBLEM. The retail inventory for dresses in the budget department of Haring's Department Store figured at $42,000 on September 1 with a planned inventory of $36,000 for September 30. Planned sales, based upon last year's figures, were $22,000, including markdowns of $2,000, for the entire month. The commitments for September were $6,000 at retail. What was the open-to-buy?

SOLUTION:

Merchandise needed
— Merchandise available
―――――――――――――
Open-to-buy

Merchandise needed (Sept. 1–30)		
End-of-month inventory (planned)	$36,000	
Planned sales (Sept. 1–30)	22,000	
Planned markdowns	2,000	
Total merchandise needed		$60,000
Merchandise available (Sept. 1)		
Opening inventory	$42,000	
Commitments	6,000	
Total merchandise available		48,000
Open-to-buy (Sept. 1)		$12,000

The above illustration indicates how a buyer can determine his open-to-buy for a period of a month. Very often, buyers must determine their needs within the monthly period. By slightly adjusting the procedure outlined to include the sales actually recorded and the goods actually marked down, the open-to-buy for any specific date may be obtained.

ILLUSTRATIVE PROBLEM. On March 14 the blouse buyer for Kent's Specialty Shop decided to determine her open-to-buy. The following figures were available:

Present inventory at retail (March 14)	$12,000
Inventory commitments (March 14)	3,000
Planned end-of-month inventory (March 31)	15,000
Planned sales	6,000
Actual sales	3,000
Planned markdowns	500
Actual markdowns	200

What is the buyer's open-to-buy?

SOLUTION:

Merchandise needed
— Merchandise available
———————————
Open-to-buy

Merchandise needed (March 14–31)				
End-of-month inventory (planned)			$15,000	
Planned sales	$6,000			
Less: actual sales	3,000			
Balance of planned sales			3,000	
Planned markdowns	$ 500			
Less: actual markdowns	200			
Balance of planned markdowns			300	
Total merchandise needed				$18,300
Merchandise available (March 14)				
Present inventory		$12,000		
Commitments		3,000		
Total merchandise available			15,000	
Open-to-buy, March 14				$3,300

8.6 *SOLVE THESE PROBLEMS:*

1. A sweater buyer estimates sales for the month of December to be $62,000 at retail. His December 1 inventory is $110,000 at retail. He plans to have an end-of-the-month retail inventory of $100,000. If he has merchandise on order for $20,000 and expects to have markdowns of $2,000 for the month, what is his December 1 open-to-buy?

2. The accessories buyer of the Chic Specialty Shop is responsible for the purchase of handbags, costume jewelry, and hosiery. Determine the buyer's open-to-buy for each merchandise classification:

Hosiery Department

Estimated sales	$ 5,000
Beginning inventory	8,000
End-of-month inventory	10,000
Merchandise on order	1,500
Markdowns (estimated)	200

Costume Jewelry Department

Beginning inventory	$17,000
Planned sales	8,000
Markdowns (estimated)	600
Merchandise on order	1,100
End-of-month inventory	16,000

Handbag Department

Merchandise on order	$ 2,000
Planned sales	12,000
Markdowns (estimated)	900
Beginning inventory	30,000
End-of-month inventory	32,000

3. Chester's Men's Shop decided to participate in a special events sales promotion that is being conducted. His original estimate of sales must be adjusted to include the extra business from this event. His estimated sales have now increased to $36,000 for the month of May, which is now in its fifth day. Using the following figures, determine his open-to-buy as of May 5.

Actual sales (May 1–5)	$ 5,000
Merchandise on hand (May 5)	65,000
Planned end-of-month inventory	70,000
Merchandise on order (May 5)	23,000
Planned markdowns (May 1–31)	1,200
Actual markdowns (May 1–5)	100

4. Find the open-to-buy as of June 22 using the following figures:

Inventory on hand (June 22)	$38,000
Merchandise on order	2,000
Planned sales (June 1–30)	15,000
Actual sales (June 1–22)	11,000
Planned markdowns (June 1–30)	600
Actual markdowns (June 1–22)	400
Planned end-of-month inventory	42,000

5. Determine the open-to-buy for a record department as of February 10 whose inventory at that date is $9,000 at retail; planned end-of-month stock is $12,000; merchandise on order is $2,000; planned sales and actual sales are $4,500 and $1,000, respectively; and planned markdowns are $100. No merchandise has been marked down as yet.

CHAPTER REVIEW

1. Sales for the following departments were as follows for the month of January:

Sporting goods	$12,642.53
Toys	7,329.41
Appliances	76,141.72

If the cost of the goods was $48,732.19, what was the gross profit for the period?

2. What is the gross profit percent on a banjo that cost $25 and sells for $45? Round off to the nearest percent.

3. The gross profit percent on an electric typewriter was 30%. What was the cost of the typewriter if the gross profit was $90?

4. A chair that sold for $60 included a gross profit of 40%. How much did the chair cost?

5. The Rona Boutique had for the month of June an opening inventory of $68,000, a closing inventory of $42,000, purchases of $26,000, and sales of $104,000. What was the merchandise inventory turnover at cost?

6. Given the following figures, find the turnover rate, at retail for the Toby Shoppe:

Sales		Retail Inventory	
January	$23,000	January 1	$45,000
February	18,000	February 1	52,000
March	26,500	March 1	54,500
April	39,400	April 1	68,750
May	45,725	May 1	83,250
June	62,775	June 1	97,500
		July 1	89,000

Round off to the nearest tenth of a percent.

7. For its tenth year of business, the Mr. Martin Shop bought merchandise that cost $110,000 and marked it to retail at $220,000. If that year's sales were $80,000, what was the cost of the inventory at the end of the year?

8. A toy buyer estimates sales of $126,000 for the month of December. His inventory on December 1 is $180,000 and his planned end-of-the-month inventory is to be $145,000. If he has $30,000 worth of goods on order, what is his open-to-buy on December 1?

FIVE

MATHEMATICS IN OFFICE PROCEDURES

Although the world of business has enormous variety, the type of work done in the offices of the various enterprises is relatively similar. For example, all businesses that require payrolls to be prepared use methods that are nearly the same.

Office management mathematical procedures consist of simple arithmetic operations that are used to solve problems which are unique to the working business office, regardless of the type or purpose of the commercial enterprise. The more common office arithmetical procedures such as preparing payrolls and calculating commissions and discounts will be discussed in this unit.

salaries and wages

1. SOCIAL SECURITY NUMBERS

2. METHODS OF REMUNERATION
   a. Hourly wage
   b. Piecework
   c. Differential piecework

3. PAYROLL DEDUCTIONS
   a. FICA
   b. Federal income taxes
   c. Illustration of the completed payroll

4. CHANGE MEMO AND CHANGE TALLY

5. EMPLOYER'S PAYROLL TAXES
   a. FICA and withholding taxes

6. EMPLOYER'S PAYROLL RECORDS

The last 40 years has seen a considerable growth in the complexity of payroll accounting. New taxes, labor laws, and requirements for managerial control have made the computing and accounting of payrolls one of the most important and time-consuming of office functions. A well-trained office worker must be able to prepare a payroll and understand all the elements that make up payroll records.

1. SOCIAL SECURITY NUMBERS

Every employee must have a social security identification number; this is generally obtained by young people before taking their first job. The number may be obtained by filling out the following form supplied by the Internal Revenue Service.

The completed form is mailed to the nearest social security administration office, and the following card is sent to the applicant, indicating his social security account number.

Because the number assigned will be used many times in the life of the worker, it is generally a good policy to make copies of it and to keep the card in a safe place.

Each worker is required by his employer to fill out Form W-4.

Note that included in the information required on the form is the worker's social security number and the number of withholding exemptions he claims. The number of exemptions listed on Form W-4 provides the basis for determining the amount of the payroll deduction for income taxes. This will be discussed in detail in a later unit.

2. METHODS OF REMUNERATION

Although there are many methods of reimbursing a worker for his efforts, among those most frequently used are:

1. Hourly wage—A method in which the number of hours worked is multiplied by an agreed rate per hour to determine the gross (total) pay.

Figure 9-1

Application for Social Security Number

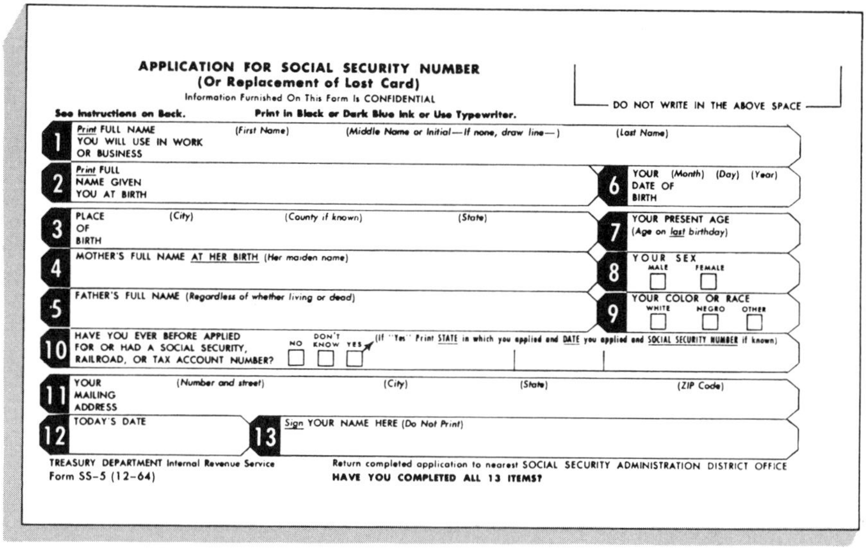

APPLICATION FOR SOCIAL SECURITY NUMBER
(Or Replacement of Lost Card)
Information Furnished On This Form Is CONFIDENTIAL

DO NOT WRITE IN THE ABOVE SPACE

See Instructions on Back.   Print in Black or Dark Blue Ink or Use Typewriter.

1 Print FULL NAME YOU WILL USE IN WORK OR BUSINESS — (First Name) (Middle Name or Initial—If none, draw line—) (Last Name)

2 Print FULL NAME GIVEN YOU AT BIRTH

6 YOUR DATE OF BIRTH (Month) (Day) (Year)

3 PLACE OF BIRTH (City) (County if known) (State)

7 YOUR PRESENT AGE (Age on last birthday)

4 MOTHER'S FULL NAME AT HER BIRTH (Her maiden name)

8 YOUR SEX MALE FEMALE

5 FATHER'S FULL NAME (Regardless of whether living or dead)

9 YOUR COLOR OR RACE WHITE NEGRO OTHER

10 HAVE YOU EVER BEFORE APPLIED FOR OR HAD A SOCIAL SECURITY, RAILROAD, OR TAX ACCOUNT NUMBER? NO DON'T KNOW YES (If "Yes" Print STATE in which you applied and DATE you applied and SOCIAL SECURITY NUMBER if known)

11 YOUR MAILING ADDRESS (Number and street) (City) (State) (ZIP Code)

12 TODAY'S DATE

13 Sign YOUR NAME HERE (Do Not Print)

TREASURY DEPARTMENT Internal Revenue Service
Form SS-5 (12-64)

Return completed application to nearest SOCIAL SECURITY ADMINISTRATION DISTRICT OFFICE
HAVE YOU COMPLETED ALL 13 ITEMS?

2. Piecework—A method in which the number of pieces completed is multiplied by a fixed rate per piece to determine the gross pay.

3. Differential piecework—A piecework method in which the rate per piece varies with the number of pieces completed.

We shall discuss the mathematics involved in figuring payrolls with each of these methods.

Figure 9-2

Social Security Card

SOCIAL SECURITY
ACCOUNT NUMBER
U.S.A.

499-14-8529

HAS BEEN ESTABLISHED FOR

JOSEPH K. JOHNSON

SIGNATURE Joseph K Johnson

FOR SOCIAL SECURITY PURPOSES • NOT FOR IDENTIFICATION

Figure 9-3

Form W-4

Form W-4
(Rev. Aug. 1972)
Department of the Treasury
Internal Revenue Service

Employee's Withholding Allowance Certificate
(This certificate is for income tax withholding purposes
only; it will remain in effect until you change it.)

Type or print your full name	Your social security number
Home address (Number and street or rural route)	Marital status ☐ Single ☐ Married
City or town, State and ZIP code	(If married but legally separated, or wife (husband) is a nonresident alien, check the single block.)

1 Total number of allowances you are claiming . . . .

2 Additional amount, if any, you want deducted from each pay (If your employer agrees) . . . . | $

I certify that to the best of my knowledge and belief, the number of withholding allowances claimed on this certificate does not exceed the number to which I am entitled.

Signature ▶ .... Date ▶ .... 19..........

a. HOURLY WAGE

In using the hourly method to determine salary, daily records are kept of the number of hours each employee works. At the end of each week, the work hours are totaled and this sum multiplied by the employee's rate per hour to determine his gross pay. The most common device for keeping records of the number of hours worked is the payroll time card on page 175. Note that the time card must be punched in and out before lunch and in and out after lunch. By calculating the time elapsed between each in and out punch, the number of hours worked can be determined. Payroll cards can be kept by hand or by machine (time clock).

The number of hours worked is transferred from the time cards to a payroll (a summary of periodic earnings for all employees). There, the number of total hours worked for each employee is multiplied by the hourly rate for each employee to determine his gross pay. The formula for determining gross pay is:

Gross pay = Total hours worked × Rate per hour

ILLUSTRATIVE PROBLEM. John Black, who is paid at the rate of $2.00 per hour, worked $37\frac{1}{2}$ hours during the week. Determine his gross pay for the week.

SOLUTION:

$$\text{Gross Pay} = \text{Total hours worked} \times \text{Rate per hour}$$
$$= 37\tfrac{1}{2} \times \$2$$
$$= \$75$$

174

Figure 9-4
Payroll Time Card

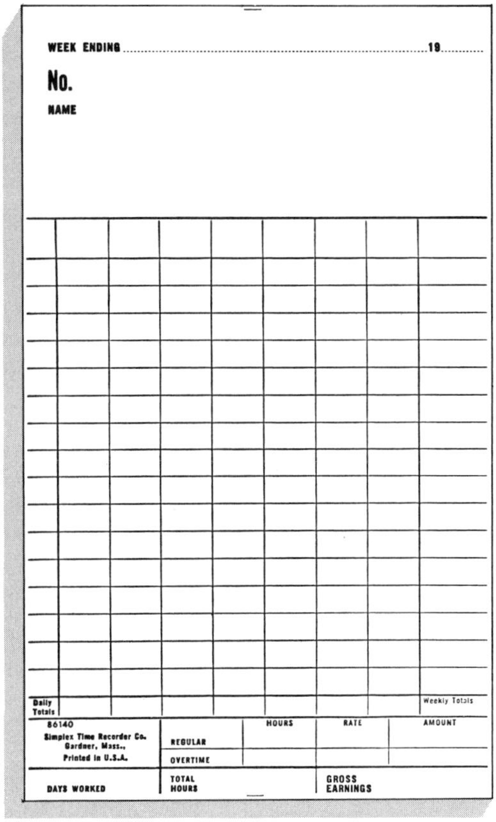

WEEK ENDING .... 19.......

No.

NAME

| Daily Totals | | | | | | | | | | Weekly Totals |

86140
Simplex Time Recorder Co.
Gardner, Mass.,
Printed in U.S.A.

	HOURS	RATE	AMOUNT
REGULAR			
OVERTIME			

| DAYS WORKED | TOTAL HOURS | | GROSS EARNINGS | |

9.1 SOLVE THIS PROBLEM:

If Tom Edwards worked $38\frac{1}{4}$ hours for the week, and his rate per hour is $1.625, what is his gross pay?

The following is an example of a section of a payroll:

WEEK ENDING APRIL 10, 197__

Name	Hours by Day M T W Th F					Total Hours	Rate per Hour	Gross Pay
R. Asher	6	7	7	8	4	32	3.00	$ 96.00
T. Blake	8	7	8	7	8	38	2.25	85.50
L. Jones	8	8	8	8	8	40	3.75	150.00
A. Simms	8	7	7	8	6	36	3.10	111.60
N. Thomas	7	6	8	8	8	37	3.90	144.30
P. Wade	7	7	7	7	7	35	2.80	98.00
L. Zinn	8	8	8	–	6	30	2.45	73.50
								$758.90

Information about the hours worked each day was obtained from each employee's time card. The daily hours were totaled; the total time that each person worked during the week was recorded. The total number of hours were then multiplied by the agreed rate per hour, and the gross pay (the total earnings before deductions) was determined. The total of the gross pay column ($572.90) is the total of the wages that the employer must pay for the week.

The provisions of the Fair Labor Standards Act of 1938 provide that time and a half must be paid to workers for all hours worked for one company in any one week in excess of 40. To determine gross pay for an employee who worked more than 40 hours in a week, two steps are necessary; determine the gross pay for 40 hours at the regular rate, and add to that the gross pay for the hours worked in excess of 40 at the overtime rate (regular rate $+ \frac{1}{2}$ regular rate).

The formula for determining gross pay when overtime is involved is:

Gross pay = Regular time hours worked $\times$ Rate per hour
$+$ Overtime hours worked $\times$ $1\frac{1}{2}$ rate per hour

ILLUSTRATIVE PROBLEM. Tom Murdock's rate of pay is $2.00 per hour. What is his gross pay if he works 46 hours in one week?

SOLUTION:

Regular pay—40 hours $\times$ $2.00 $\quad\quad\quad$ = $80
Overtime pay—6 hours $\times$ $3.00 (2.00 + 1.00) = $\underline{\ 18}$
$\quad\quad\quad$ Gross pay $\quad\quad\quad\quad\quad\quad\quad\quad\quad$ $98

His overtime pay could have been computed by increasing the overtime hours by one-half and multiplying by the regular rate of pay, thus:

Overtime pay = 9 hours (6 + 3) $\times$ $2 = $18

9.2 SOLVE THESE PROBLEMS:
1. Jones earns $3 per hour. Compute his gross pay if his total hours for the week are 48.
2. What is the gross pay for a worker who earns $1.25 per hour and worked 44 hours during the week? (In this case it will be easier to add $\frac{1}{2}$ to the overtime hours rather than to the hourly rate).

Including overtime in the calculation of gross pay requires an expansion of the payroll previously illustrated. The following is a portion of such a payroll:

WEEK ENDING APRIL 17, 19__

| Name | *Hours by Day* | | | | | *Hours Worked* | | *Rate of Pay* | | Gross Pay |
	M	T	W	Th	F	Regular	Over-time	Regular	Over-time	
J. Black	8	9	6	10	8	40	1	4.00	6.00	$166.00
T. Grimes	8	8	8	10	9	40	3	2.50	3.75	111.25
R. Johnson	0	0	6	12	12	30	0	3.00	4.50	90.00
L. Sweeney	9	9	10	8	11	40	7	2.68	4.02	135.34
N. Thompson	4	12	12	12	6	40	6	3.25	4.875	159.25
V. Garni	7	9	9	7	8	40	0	8.00	12.00	320.00
										$981.84

In some industries, overtime is calculated on a daily basis. Thus the hours worked in excess of 8 per day will be paid at the overtime rate without regard to the total hours worked during the week.

ILLUSTRATIVE PROBLEM. Determine the gross pay of a worker earning $2 per hour, when his daily hours were: Monday, 9; Tuesday, 10; Wednesday, 0; Thursday, 6; Friday, 11.

SOLUTION:

Total hours (9 + 10 + 6 + 11)   36
Overtime hours (hours in excess of 8 in any day 1 + 2 + 3)   −6
Regular hours   30

Gross pay = Regular time hours worked (30) × Regular rate ($2)
          + Overtime hours worked (6) × Overtime rate ($3 [2 + 1])
      = (30 × $2) + (6 × $3)
      = $78

9.3 SOLVE THESE PROBLEMS:

1. Jones and Company pays overtime on all hours worked over 40. Fill in the regular hours, the overtime hours, the overtime rate, and the gross pay for each employee.

| Name | *Hours by Day* | | | | | *Hours Worked* | | Regular Rate | *Over-time Rate* | Gross Pay |
	M	T	W	Th	F	Regular	Over-time			
R. Gold	8	7	9	11	6	4 ͦ	/	4.00		/66
S. Block ׳/ ²ˉ	3	14	6	10	8	↵ 0	/	2.80		/50 /56 ͯ
T. Jordan ׳²͜ͻ	9	9	8	9	11	4 ͦ	6	3.20		/56 ͯ
U. Smith 9͜	8	9	10	6	8	ι ͦ	/	2.40		99.6
V. Arons ι∠⁸	9	7	4	11	10	↵ ͦ	,	3.20		/32͜⁸ ͦ

2. Acme, Inc., pays overtime for all hours worked over 8 in any one day. Fill in the regular hours, the overtime hours, the overtime rate and the gross pay for each employee.

Name	Hours by Day					Hours Worked Regular	Over-time	Regular Rate	Over-time Rate	Gross Pay
	M	T	W	Th	F					
M. Meyer	10	0	5	3	9			3.50		
N. Dolan	10	8	8	7	9			5.60		
E. Shea	4	2	3	6	9			3.40		
N. Allen	8	8	10	8	8			2.10		
C. Gable	0	0	0	6	9			3.60		

b. PIECEWORK

With this method of determining gross pay, the number of pieces an employee completes during a payroll period is multiplied by a fixed rate per piece.

The formula for determining gross pay using the piecework method is:

$$\text{Gross pay} = \text{Number of pieces} \times \text{Rate per piece}$$

ILLUSTRATIVE PROBLEM. Ellen Archer earns $.10 each for sewing zippers into dresses. During the week she sews zippers on 1,000 dresses. Determine her gross pay.

SOLUTION:

$$\begin{aligned}
\text{Gross pay} &= \text{Number of pieces} \times \text{Rate per piece} \\
&= 1{,}000 \times \$.10 \\
&= \$100
\end{aligned}$$

9.4 SOLVE THIS PROBLEM: John Black completed the upholstering on 20 sofas during the week. If he is paid at the rate of $4.50 per piece, what was his gross pay?

The following is a section of a payroll calculated on the piecework basis.

Name	Pieces Completed					Total Pieces	Rate	Gross Pay
	M	T	W	Th	F			
R. Cross	20	14	27	16	18	95	$ .90	$ 85.50
T. Betts	36	27	40	19	28	150	1.25	187.50
L. Ross	127	131	119	152	126	655	.20	131.00
								$404.00

c. DIFFERENTIAL PIECEWORK

As a means of increasing production, businessmen frequently employ a piecework scale in which the rate per piece increases as the number of pieces completed increases. For example:

$$
\begin{array}{lll}
\text{1–100 pieces @} & \text{\$.30} \\
\text{101–200 pieces @} & \text{.32} \\
\text{201–300 pieces @} & \text{.35}
\end{array}
$$

ILLUSTRATIVE PROBLEM. Based on the above table, determine the gross pay of a person completing 270 pieces.

SOLUTION:

$$
\begin{array}{lll}
\text{100 pieces @} & \text{\$.30} = & \text{\$30.00} \\
\text{100 pieces @} & \text{.32} = & \text{32.00} \\
\text{70 pieces @} & \text{.35} = & \underline{\text{24.50}} \\
& & \overline{\text{\$86.50}}
\end{array}
$$

9.5 SOLVE THESE PROBLEMS:

1. Apex Furniture Corp. pays finishers $4 for painting style 103; $6 for style 108; and $8 for style 216. At the end of the week Ed Jones, a finisher, had painted 6 pieces of style 103; 8 pieces of style 108; and 4 pieces of style 216. What was his gross pay?

2. The differential piecework rates at Beacon Novelty Company were as follows:

$$
\begin{array}{lll}
\text{1–50 pieces @} & \text{\$.30} \\
\text{51–100 pieces @} & \text{.35} \\
\text{Over 100 pieces @} & \text{.45}
\end{array}
$$

What was Charlie Johnson's gross pay if he completed 142 pieces during the week?

3. Complete.

Name	M	T	W	Th	F	Total Pieces	Rate	Gross Pay
J. Berland	36	96	27	84	12	_____	$.50	$_____
S. Sorgen	42	85	36	97	78	_____	.63	_____
F. Timoni	18	73	127	88	90	_____	.48	_____
R. Jonas	86	64	90	78	74	_____	.36	_____
Totals	—	—	—	—	—	_____		$_____

4. The Kenneth Lawrence Company pays pieceworkers on the following differential basis:

$$
\begin{array}{ll}
1\text{--}250 \ @ & \$.30 \\
251\text{--}400 \ @ & .40 \\
401\text{--}500 \ @ & .52 \\
\text{Over } 500 \ @ & .65
\end{array}
$$

Complete the chart.

Name	M	T	W	Th	F	Total Pieces	Gross Pay
L. Tierney	112	79	95	86	55	427	$_____
J. Swarth	76	84	68	114	96	438	
E. Shea	88	112	38	84	90	_____	_____
M. Donovan	96	75	83	128	64	_____	_____
C. Olsen	14	79	91	88	96	_____	_____
Totals	—	—	—	—	—	_____	$_____

3. PAYROLL DEDUCTIONS

After having calculated the employee's gross pay, various deductions must be made before the net pay (the cash actually paid the employees) can be determined. Some of these deductions, such as FICA (social security) and withholding taxes, are required by law. Some, such as union dues, are withheld by contractual agreement; others, such as hospitalization and U.S. Savings Bonds, may be deducted at the request of the employee. In each case, the employer deducts an amount from gross pay, accumulates it over several payroll periods, and then sends it to the appropriate agency.

a. FICA (FEDERAL INSURANCE CONTRIBUTIONS ACT)

One of the provisions of the Social Security Act requires the employer to deduct from the first $10,800 of an employee's earnings, during any one year, an amount equal to 5.85% of his gross pay. The tax rate and the maximum salary subject to the tax are frequently changed. The purpose of the tax is to provide for a worker's old age retirement, for his survivors in case of death, for disability insurance, and for hospitalization.

ILLUSTRATIVE PROBLEM. Determine the FICA deduction for Henry Baker, whose gross pay for this week totaled $150. His earnings from January 1 until the beginning of this week were $6,000.

SOLUTION: Because this week's earnings ($150) added to his previous earnings for the year ($6,000) is less than the maximum on which tax must be deducted ($10,800), his salary is fully taxable.

$$\$150 \times 5.85\% = \$8.78$$

ILLUSTRATIVE PROBLEM. Bob Haines has earned $10,700 so far this year. His gross pay for this week is $250. What is his FICA deduction?

SOLUTION: Because no tax is deducted above a maximum of $10,800 of annual wages and deductions have already been made on $10,700, only $100 of his salary is taxable.

$10,000 (maximum table) — $10,700 (already taxed)

= $100 taxable this pay period

$100 × 5.85% = $5.85 FICA deduction

9.6   SOLVE THESE PROBLEMS:
   1. From January 1 to the beginning of this week, Gene Peter's gross pay totaled $10,550. This week he worked 40 hours at $5.25 per hour. How much is the FICA deduction for this week?
   2. Warren Jones has earned $10,700 from January 1 to the beginning of the week. This week he worked $37\frac{1}{2}$ hours at $4 per hour. Determine his FICA deduction.

For rapid determination of FICA deductions, the Internal Revenue Department provides charts. (See pages 182–83).

The social security tax table is used in the following fashion:

   1. In one of the four columns headed "wages," find the line on which the salary in question fits.
   2. The column immediately to the right of that range indicates the amount of FICA to be withheld.

ILLUSTRATIVE PROBLEM. Determine the FICA deduction on a salary of $92.50.

SOLUTION: The amount of $92.50 is found in the fourth wages column in the range "at least" $92.40, but "less than" $92.57. The FICA tax to be withheld, $5.41, is found in the column to the right of the appropriate wages range.

9.7   SOLVE THIS PROBLEM: Using the Social Security Employee Tax Table provided, determine the FICA deduction on the following amounts:

   1. $91.18
   2. $105.16
   3. $123.80

SOCIAL SECURITY EMPLOYEE TAX TABLE

5.85 percent employee tax deductions

| WAGES | | | WAGES | | | WAGES | | | WAGES | | |
At Least	But Less Than	Tax to Be Withheld	At Least	But Less Than	Tax to Be Withheld	At Least	But Less Than	Tax to Be Withheld	At Least	But Less Than	Tax to Be Withheld
$88.81	$88.98	$5.20	$99.92	$100.09	$5.85	$111.03	$111.20	$6.50	$122.14	$122.31	$7.15
88.98	89.15	5.21	100.09	100.26	5.86	111.20	111.37	6.51	122.31	122.48	7.16
89.15	89.32	5.22	100.26	100.43	5.87	111.37	111.54	6.52	122.48	122.65	7.17
89.32	89.49	5.23	100.43	100.60	5.88	111.54	111.71	6.53	122.65	122.83	7.18
89.49	89.66	5.24	100.60	100.77	5.89	111.71	111.89	6.54	122.83	123.00	7.19
89.66	89.83	5.25	100.77	100.95	5.90	111.89	112.06	6.55	123.00	123.17	7.20
89.83	90.00	5.26	100.95	101.12	5.91	112.06	112.23	6.56	123.17	123.34	7.21
90.00	90.18	5.27	101.12	101.29	5.92	112.23	112.40	6.57	123.34	123.51	7.22
90.18	90.35	5.28	101.29	101.46	5.93	112.40	112.57	6.58	123.51	123.68	7.23
90.35	90.52	5.29	101.46	101.63	5.94	112.57	112.74	6.59	123.68	123.85	7.24
90.52	90.69	5.30	101.63	101.80	5.95	112.74	112.91	6.60	123.85	124.02	7.25
90.69	90.86	5.31	101.80	101.97	5.96	112.91	113.08	6.61	124.02	124.19	7.26
90.86	91.03	5.32	101.97	102.14	5.97	113.08	113.25	6.62	124.19	124.36	7.27
91.03	91.20	5.33	102.14	102.31	5.98	113.25	113.42	6.63	124.36	124.53	7.28
91.20	91.37	5.34	102.31	102.48	5.99	113.42	113.59	6.64	124.53	124.71	7.29
91.37	91.54	5.35	102.48	102.65	6.00	113.59	113.77	6.65	124.71	124.88	7.30
91.54	91.71	5.36	102.65	102.83	6.01	113.77	113.94	6.66	124.88	125.05	7.31
91.71	91.89	5.37	102.83	103.00	6.02	113.94	114.11	6.67	125.05	125.22	7.32
91.89	92.06	5.38	103.00	103.17	6.03	114.11	114.28	6.68	125.22	125.39	7.33
92.06	92.23	5.39	103.17	103.34	6.04	114.28	114.45	6.69	125.39	125.56	7.34
92.23	92.40	5.40	103.34	103.51	6.05	114.45	114.62	6.70	125.56	125.73	7.35
92.40	92.57	5.41	103.51	103.68	6.06	114.62	114.79	6.71	125.73	125.90	7.36
92.57	92.74	5.42	103.68	103.85	6.07	114.79	114.96	6.72	125.90	126.07	7.37
92.74	92.91	5.43	103.85	104.02	6.08	114.96	115.13	6.73	126.07	126.24	7.38
92.91	93.08	5.44	104.02	104.19	6.09	115.13	115.30	6.74	126.24	126.42	7.39
93.08	93.25	5.45	104.19	104.36	6.10	115.30	115.48	6.75	126.42	126.59	7.40
93.25	93.42	5.46	104.36	104.53	6.11	115.48	115.65	6.76	126.59	126.76	7.41
93.42	93.59	5.47	104.53	104.71	6.12	115.65	115.82	6.77	126.76	126.93	7.42
93.59	93.77	5.48	104.71	104.88	6.13	115.82	115.99	6.78	126.93	127.10	7.43
93.77	93.94	5.49	104.88	105.05	6.14	115.99	116.16	6.79	127.10	127.27	7.44

$93.94	$94.11	$5.50	$105.05	$105.22	$6.15	$116.16	$116.33	$6.80	$127.27	$127.44	$7.45
94.11	94.28	5.51	105.22	105.39	6.16	116.33	116.50	6.81	127.44	127.61	7.46
94.28	94.45	5.52	105.39	105.56	6.17	116.50	116.67	6.82	127.61	127.78	7.47
94.45	94.62	5.53	105.56	105.73	6.18	116.67	116.84	6.83	127.78	127.95	7.48
94.62	94.79	5.54	105.73	105.90	6.19	116.84	117.01	6.84	127.95	128.12	7.49
94.79	94.96	5.55	105.90	106.07	6.20	117.01	117.18	6.85	128.12	128.30	7.50
94.96	95.13	5.56	106.07	106.24	6.21	117.18	117.36	6.86	128.30	128.47	7.51
95.13	95.30	5.57	106.24	106.42	6.22	117.36	117.53	6.87	128.47	128.64	7.52
95.30	95.48	5.58	106.42	106.59	6.23	117.53	117.70	6.88	128.64	128.81	7.53
95.48	95.65	5.59	106.59	106.76	6.24	117.70	117.87	6.89	128.81	128.98	7.54
95.65	95.82	5.60	106.76	106.93	6.25	117.87	118.04	6.90	128.98	129.15	7.55
95.82	95.99	5.61	106.93	107.10	6.26	118.04	118.21	6.91	129.15	129.32	7.56
95.99	96.16	5.62	107.10	107.27	6.27	118.21	118.38	6.92	129.32	129.49	7.57
96.16	96.33	5.63	107.27	107.44	6.28	118.38	118.55	6.93	129.49	129.66	7.58
96.33	96.50	5.64	107.44	107.61	6.29	118.55	118.72	6.94	129.66	129.83	7.59
96.50	96.67	5.65	107.61	107.78	6.30	118.72	118.89	6.95	129.83	130.00	7.60
96.67	96.84	5.66	107.78	107.95	6.31	118.89	119.06	6.96	130.00	130.18	7.61
96.84	97.01	5.67	107.95	108.12	6.32	119.06	119.24	6.97	130.18	130.35	7.62
97.01	97.18	5.68	108.12	108.30	6.33	119.24	119.41	6.98	130.35	130.52	7.63
97.18	97.36	5.69	108.30	108.47	6.34	119.41	119.58	6.99	130.52	130.69	7.64
97.36	97.53	5.70	108.47	108.64	6.35	119.58	119.75	7.00	130.69	130.86	7.65
97.53	97.70	5.71	108.64	108.81	6.36	119.75	119.92	7.01	130.86	131.03	7.66
97.70	97.87	5.72	108.81	108.98	6.37	119.92	120.09	7.02	131.03	131.20	7.67
97.87	98.04	5.73	108.98	109.15	6.38	120.09	120.26	7.03	131.20	131.37	7.68
98.04	98.21	5.74	109.15	109.32	6.39	120.26	120.43	7.04	131.37	131.54	7.69
98.21	98.38	5.75	109.32	109.49	6.40	120.43	120.60	7.05	131.54	131.71	7.70
98.38	98.55	5.76	109.49	109.66	6.41	120.60	120.77	7.06	131.71	131.89	7.71
98.55	98.72	5.77	109.66	109.83	6.42	120.77	120.95	7.07	131.89	132.06	7.72
98.72	98.89	5.78	109.83	110.00	6.43	120.95	121.12	7.08	132.06	132.23	7.73
98.89	99.06	5.79	110.00	110.18	6.44	121.12	121.29	7.09	132.23	132.40	7.74
99.06	99.24	5.80	110.18	110.35	6.45	121.29	121.46	7.10	132.40	132.57	7.75
99.24	99.41	5.81	110.35	110.52	6.46	121.46	121.63	7.11	132.57	132.74	7.76
99.41	99.58	5.82	110.52	110.69	6.47	121.63	121.80	7.12	132.74	132.91	7.77
99.58	99.75	5.83	110.69	110.86	6.48	121.80	121.97	7.13	132.91	133.08	7.78
99.75	99.92	5.84	110.86	111.03	6.49	121.97	122.14	7.14	133.08	133.25	7.79

b. FEDERAL INCOME TAXES

The federal income tax laws of the United States require that taxpayers "pay as they go." Employers are required to deduct a specified amount from their employees for the current year's income taxes, accumulate it for a number of payroll periods, and then send it to the government. Although the amount of the deduction can be determined arithmetically, most employers use charts provided by the Director of Internal Revenue. There are charts for a variety of payroll periods (weekly, semi-monthly, monthly) and for single or married taxpayers.

Because the amount of earnings and the number of exemptions a taxpaper claims are important in the determination of his income tax, withholding charts (see pages 186–187) are set up to indicate varying withholding deductions for different earning levels and numbers of dependents. An illustration of Form W-4, the employee's withholding exemption certificate, is on page 174. Because Form W-4 indicates the number of exemptions claimed by the employee, it provides the employer with the information necessary to determine the amount of the withholding tax deduction.

The employee is entitled to one exemption for himself plus one for each of his dependents. Thus a married person with two children would be entitled to four exemptions, one for himself and one each for his wife and children.

The following (pages 186–87) is a page taken from the charts provided by the Director of Internal Revenue for determining withholding tax deductions. It applies to a worker who is married and whose payroll period is weekly.

A withholding tax chart is used in the following manner:

1. In the two leftmost columns, determine the range into which the salary in question falls.
2. Move to the right of the column headed by the number equal to the number of exemptions the employee claims.
3. The number that falls at the junction of the salary range horizontal column, and the number of dependents vertical column, is the amount of the withholding tax deduction.

ILLUSTRATIVE PROBLEM. Jackson is married, has three children, and his gross pay for one week is $147.12. Determine his withholding tax deduction if the number of his exemptions is five (himself, his wife, and three children).

SOLUTION: At the left side of the chart, it is determined that his salary falls in the range of "at least" $145 but "less than" $150. Move along the chart to the right to the column marked five exemptions. His withholding deduction is $9.80. (If he had six dependents, his deduction would have been $7.50.)

9.8 SOLVE THESE PROBLEMS:

1. Sam Mayer earned $227.50 this week. He is married but does not have any children. Using the withholding tax chart, determine the amount of his deduction.

2. Frank O'Neal worked 40 hours this week. His hourly rate is $3.75. If Frank is married and has one child, how much is his withholding tax deduction?

3. Paul Henry is a shoe salesman who receives a weekly salary of $125 and 2% commission on all sales. This past week he sold $1,400 worth of merchandise. What is Paul Henry's tax deduction for the past week? Paul is married and has four children.

c. ILLUSTRATION OF THE COMPLETED PAYROLL

All the elements of the payroll function have now been described. The following (page 188) is an illustration of a completed payroll. Overtime is paid on all hours over 40 per week, at the rate of time and a half.

Note that the sum of the total deductions column is equal to the totals of the FICA and withholding tax columns and that total net pay plus total deductions equals total gross pay. This is called cross-footing, and is a method used by office personnel to check the accuracy of their arithmetic.

4. CHANGE MEMO AND CHANGE TALLY

Those firms that pay their employees in cash rather than by check must put the exact amount of net pay into each pay envelope. If care is not taken in this operation, a situation such as the following may arise. The last three pay envelopes require a net pay of $7 each: The $21 left to be distributed is in the form of two $10 bills and a $1 bill, which cannot be evenly distributed among the three envelopes.

To avoid such situations, a form called the change memo is used. The rule is: *Always use the largest denomination possible;* i.e., use a $20 bill instead of two $10 bills, or a quarter instead of two dimes and a nickel.

ILLUSTRATIVE PROBLEM. Prepare a change memo.

J. Black	$ 26.14
T. Ryan	73.08
L. Bryan	97.18
D. Grey	16.40
S. Blake	37.73
	$250.53

MARRIED PERSONS—WEEKLY PAYROLL PERIOD

AND THE NUMBER OF WITHHOLDING ALLOWANCES CLAIMED IS—

AND THE WAGES ARE—		0	1	2	3	4	5	6	7	8	9	10 or more
At least	But less than					The amount of income tax to be withheld shall be—						
$100	$105	$14.10	$11.80	$9.50	$7.20	$4.90	$2.80	$.80	$0	$0	$0	$0
105	110	14.90	12.60	10.30	8.00	5.70	3.50	1.50	0	0	0	0
110	115	15.70	13.40	11.10	8.80	6.50	4.20	2.20	.10	0	0	0
115	120	16.50	14.20	11.90	9.60	7.30	5.00	2.90	.80	0	0	0
120	125	17.30	15.00	12.70	10.40	8.10	5.80	3.60	1.50	0	0	0
125	130	18.10	15.80	13.50	11.20	8.90	6.60	4.30	2.20	.20	0	0
130	135	18.90	16.60	14.30	12.00	9.70	7.40	5.10	2.90	.90	0	0
135	140	19.70	17.40	15.10	12.80	10.50	8.20	5.90	3.60	1.60	0	0
140	145	20.50	18.20	15.90	13.60	11.30	9.00	6.70	4.40	2.30	.30	0
145	150	21.30	19.00	16.70	14.40	12.10	9.80	7.50	5.20	3.00	1.00	0
150	160	22.50	20.20	17.90	15.60	13.30	11.00	8.70	6.40	4.10	2.00	0
160	170	24.10	21.80	19.50	17.20	14.90	12.60	10.30	8.00	5.70	3.40	1.40
170	180	26.00	23.40	21.10	18.80	16.50	14.20	11.90	9.60	7.30	5.00	2.80
180	190	28.00	25.20	22.70	20.40	18.10	15.80	13.50	11.20	8.90	6.60	4.30
190	200	30.00	27.20	24.30	22.00	19.70	17.40	15.10	12.80	10.50	8.20	5.90
200	210	32.00	29.20	26.30	23.60	21.30	19.00	16.70	14.40	12.10	9.80	7.50
210	220	34.40	31.20	28.30	25.40	22.90	20.60	18.30	16.00	13.70	11.40	9.10
220	230	36.80	33.30	30.30	27.40	24.50	22.20	19.90	17.60	15.30	13.00	10.70
230	240	39.20	35.70	32.30	29.40	26.50	23.80	21.50	19.20	16.90	14.60	12.30
240	250	41.60	38.10	34.60	31.40	28.50	25.60	23.10	20.80	18.50	16.20	13.90
250	260	44.00	40.50	37.00	33.60	30.50	27.60	24.70	22.40	20.10	17.80	15.50
260	270	46.40	42.90	39.40	36.00	32.50	29.60	26.70	24.00	21.70	19.40	17.10
270	280	48.80	45.30	41.80	38.40	34.90	31.60	28.70	25.80	23.30	21.00	18.70
280	290	51.20	47.70	44.20	40.80	37.30	33.90	30.70	27.80	25.00	22.60	20.30
290	300	53.60	50.10	46.60	43.20	39.70	36.30	32.80	29.80	27.00	24.20	21.90
300	310	56.00	52.50	49.00	45.60	42.10	38.70	35.20	31.80	29.00	26.10	23.50
310	320	58.40	54.90	51.40	48.00	44.50	41.10	37.60	34.10	31.00	28.10	25.20
320	330	60.80	57.30	53.80	50.40	46.90	43.50	40.00	36.50	33.10	30.10	27.20
330	340	63.60	59.70	56.20	52.80	49.30	45.90	42.40	38.90	35.50	32.10	29.20
340	350	66.40	62.40	58.60	55.20	51.70	48.30	44.80	41.30	37.90	34.40	31.20

At least	But less than											
$350	360	$ 33.40	$ 36.80	$ 40.30	$ 43.70	$ 47.20	$ 50.70	$ 54.10	$ 57.60	$ 61.10	$ 65.20	$ 69.20
360	370	35.80	39.20	42.70	46.10	49.60	53.10	56.50	60.00	63.90	68.00	72.00
370	380	38.20	41.60	45.10	48.50	52.00	55.50	58.90	62.70	66.70	70.80	74.80
380	390	40.60	44.00	47.50	50.90	54.40	57.90	61.50	65.50	69.50	73.60	77.60
390	400	43.00	46.40	49.90	53.30	56.80	60.30	64.30	68.30	72.30	76.40	80.40
400	410	45.40	48.80	52.30	55.70	59.20	63.00	67.10	71.10	75.10	79.20	83.20
410	420	47.80	51.20	54.70	58.10	61.80	65.80	69.90	73.90	77.90	82.00	86.30
420	430	50.20	53.60	57.10	60.50	64.60	68.60	72.70	76.70	80.70	84.80	89.50
430	440	52.60	56.00	59.50	63.30	67.40	71.40	75.50	79.50	83.50	88.00	92.70
440	450	55.00	58.40	62.10	66.10	70.20	74.20	78.30	82.30	86.60	91.20	95.90
450	460	57.40	60.90	64.90	68.90	73.00	77.00	81.10	85.20	89.80	94.40	99.10
460	470	59.80	63.70	67.70	71.70	75.80	79.80	83.90	88.40	93.00	97.60	102.30
470	480	62.40	66.50	70.50	74.50	78.60	82.60	87.00	91.60	96.20	100.80	105.50
480	490	65.20	69.30	73.30	77.30	81.40	85.60	90.20	94.80	99.40	104.00	108.70
490	500	68.00	72.10	76.10	80.10	84.20	88.80	93.40	98.00	102.60	107.20	112.20
500	510	70.80	74.90	78.90	82.90	87.40	92.00	96.60	101.20	105.80	110.60	115.80
510	520	73.60	77.70	81.70	86.00	90.60	95.20	99.80	104.40	109.10	114.20	119.40
520	530	76.40	80.50	84.50	89.20	93.80	98.40	103.00	107.60	112.70	117.80	123.00
530	540	79.20	83.30	87.70	92.40	97.00	101.60	106.20	111.10	116.30	121.40	126.60
540	550	82.00	86.30	90.90	95.60	100.20	104.80	109.50	114.70	119.90	125.00	130.20
550	560	84.90	89.50	94.10	98.80	103.40	108.00	113.10	118.30	123.50	128.60	133.80
560	570	88.10	92.70	97.30	102.00	106.60	111.50	116.70	121.90	127.10	132.20	137.40
570	580	91.30	95.90	100.50	105.20	109.90	115.10	120.30	125.50	130.70	135.80	141.00
580	590	94.50	99.10	103.70	108.40	113.50	118.70	123.90	129.10	134.30	139.40	144.60
590	600	97.70	102.30	106.90	111.90	117.10	122.30	127.50	132.70	137.90	143.00	148.20
600	610	100.90	105.50	110.30	115.50	120.70	125.90	131.10	136.30	141.50	146.60	151.80
610	620	104.10	108.70	113.90	119.10	124.30	129.50	134.70	139.90	145.10	150.20	155.40
620	630	107.30	112.30	117.50	122.70	127.90	133.10	138.30	143.50	148.70	153.80	159.00
630	640	110.70	115.90	121.10	126.30	131.50	136.70	141.90	147.10	152.30	157.40	162.60
$640 and over		112.50	117.70	122.90	128.10	133.30	138.50	143.70	148.90	154.10	159.20	164.40

36 percent of the excess over $640 plus—

187

| Name | Marital Status | Exemptions | Hours by Day | | | | | Hours Reg. | Hours O.T. | Reg. Rate | O.T. Rate | Gross Pay | FICA | With. Tax | Total Deduc. | Net Pay |
			M	T	W	Th	F									
H. Olds	M	1	8	9	7	6	10	40	—	$3.00		$120.00	$7.02	$15.00	$22.02	$ 97.98
C. Baum	M	3	8	11	8	11	8	40	6	2.60	$3.90	127.40	7.45	11.20	18.65	108.75
L. Mott	M	4	3	9	16	10	8	40	6	2.10	3.15	102.90	6.02	4.90	10.92	91.98
B. Gann	M	2	10	8	10	8	6	40	2	2.50	3.75	107.50	6.29	10.30	16.59	90.91
												457.80	26.78	41.40	68.18	389.62

9.9 SOLVE THESE PROBLEMS:

1. Complete the payroll.

Name	Marital Status	Exemptions	Hours by Day M	T	W	Th	F	Hours Reg.	Worked O.T.	Reg. Rate	O.T. Rate	Gross Pay	FICA	With. Tax	Total Deductions	Net Pay
W. Abel	M	3	8	9	10	6	7			3.10						
C. Clare	M	2	8	8	10	9	11			2.20						
L. Baum	M	1	8	6	3	0	4			6.16						
M. Johns	M	4	9	9	9	10	9			2.28						
R. Simms	M	0	7	10	8	9	8			2.43						
Totals																

2. Complete the payroll.

Name	Marital Status	Exemptions	Hours by Day M	T	W	Th	F	Hours Reg.	Worked O.T.	Reg. Rate	O.T. Rate	Gross Pay	FICA	With. Tax	Total Deductions	Net Pay
L. Blair	M	0	8	7	9	8	8	46		2.62		104.80	6.13	14.10	20.23	84.57
C. Farr	M	3	10	11	8	6	9	47	4	2.26	3.37	106.96	6.00	7.20	13.28	90.68
R. Dunn	M	4	7	7	9	7	8	38		3.12		115.55	6.78	6.78	14.41	101.52
C. Holm	M	2	4	2	0	1	0			16.00						
L. Watts	M	1	9	9	10	9	10			2.60						
Totals																

189

SOLUTION:

Name	Net Pay	$20	$10	$5	$1	50¢	25¢	10¢	5¢	1¢
		Bills				Coins				
J. Black	$ 26.14	1		1	1			1		4
T. Ryan	73.08	3	1		3				1	3
L. Bryan	97.18	4	1	1	2			1	1	3
D. Grey	16.40		1	1	1		1	1	1	
S. Blake	37.73	1	1	1	2	1		2		3
	$250.53	9	4	4	9	1	1	5	3	13

To prove the accuracy of the change memo, and arrange it in the form required by banks, the change tally is prepared. A sample change tally follows:

CHANGE TALLY

Number	Denomination	Amount
9	$20	$180.00
4	10	40.00
4	5	20.00
9	1	9.00
1	Halves	.50
1	Quarters	.25
5	Dimes	.50
3	Nickels	.15
13	Pennies	.13
		$250.53

9.10   SOLVE THIS PROBLEM: The following is the net payroll for the Atlas Shoe Shop. Prepare a change memo for the company.

M. Thomson	$ 89.50
P. Avery	76.42
R. Johnson	83.11
S. Egert	55.78
T. Paul	92.25
	$397.06

**5. EMPLOYER'S
PAYROLL TAXES**

The employer's responsibility for payroll goes beyond the determination of salaries and disbursement of net pay. He is also required to send to the appropriate agency the money he withheld from his employee's wages, plus amounts that are his own rather than his worker's expense.

a. FICA AND WITHHOLDING TAXES

As has been indicated, the employer deducts a certain amount of money from each employee for FICA and withholding taxes. To this he must add an equal amount to FICA deducted. The total is sent to the director of Internal Revenue every three months. Thus the payment includes the FICA deducted from each employee, the employer's share of FICA (an amount equal to the total employee's deduction), and the withholding tax deduction. Form 941, illustrated on page 192, is provided by the Internal Revenue Service for this purpose.

Note that the lower half of the form requires the employee's social security number, name, and amount of earnings for the quarter (three-month period). The Social Security Administration transfers this amount to the employee's account. The amount of social security benefits an employee receives upon retirement are dependent, in part, upon the amount in his account.

The law provides that when the total amount of the employee's share of FICA, the employer's share of FICA, and the withholding tax deducted from employee's pay exceeds a total of $100 in any one month, this total must be paid by the fifteenth day of the following month. The depositary receipt on page 193 is used for such a purpose.

At the end of the quarter, the total due is calculated on Form 941. From this is deducted the amount paid by depositary receipt. A check for the balance due is sent along with Form 941 to the director of Internal Revenue.

9.11 SOLVE THIS PROBLEM: The following payroll data was taken from the payroll records of Acme, Inc., for the quarter ending June 30, 1968:

Payroll subject to FICA	$8,000.00
FICA deducted from employees	468.00
Withholding tax deducted	1,016.20
Amount paid by Depositary Receipt	1,767.10

Complete the following section of Form 941.

6. EMPLOYER'S PAYROLL RECORDS

Another governmental regulation regarding payrolls is that the employer must prepare Form W-2 annually for each employee. The form is illustrated on page 194.

Form W-2 is made out in quadruplicate. Two copies go to the employee, one for his personal records, and one to be attached to his income tax return. A third form is sent to the director of Internal Revenue to be checked against the employee's tax return, and the last form is kept by the employer.

In order to accumulate the data throughout the year so that Form W-2

Figure 9-5
Form 941

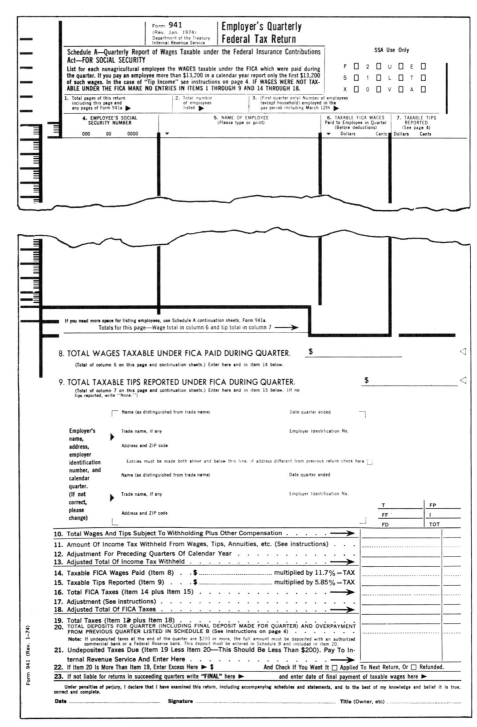

Figure 9-6
Federal Depositary Receipt

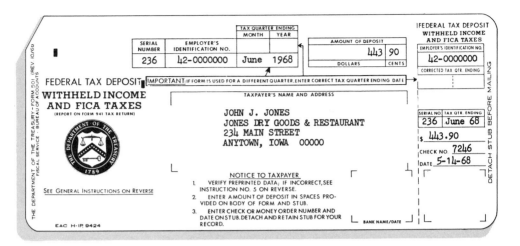

can be prepared on December 31, the employer must transfer the data from each payroll to a payroll ledger which consists of a page for each employee.

The following (page 194) is an illustration of an employee's payroll account as it would appear in the payroll ledger. Each line has been posted from the payroll of the date indicated.

Figure 9-7
Form 941

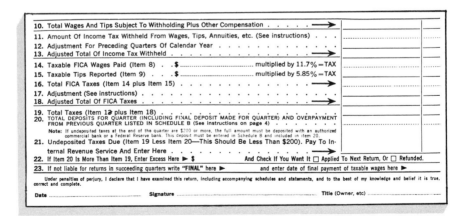

Figure 9-8
Form W-2

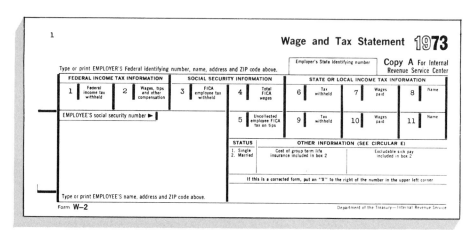

| THOMAS BENTLEY |
| 127 AMHERST ST., NEW YORK, N.Y. 12076 |

086-14-4948 *Gross Pay*	*MARRIED* *FICA*	*2 DEPENDENTS* *Withholding Tax*	*MILLING DEPT.* *Net Pay*
1st Quarter			
Totals 1267.18	74.13	122.20	1070.85
2nd Quarter			
Totals 1416.19	82.85	136.40	1196.94
3rd Quarter			
Totals 1063.13	62.19	100.30	900.64

4th Quarter

Oct 7	100.00	5.85	10.60	83.55
13	98.12	5.74	10.00	82.38
20	87.50	5.12	8.20	74.18
27	116.10	6.79	12.90	96.41
Nov 3	92.14	5.39	9.10	77.65
10	78.27	4.58	7.00	66.69
17	98.40	5.76	10.00	82.64
24	79.60	4.66	7.00	67.94
Dec 1	100.00	5.85	10.60	83.55
8	98.14	5.74	10.00	82.40
15	85.60	5.01	7.90	72.69
22	98.40	5.76	10.00	82.64
29	116.28	6.80	12.90	96.58

Fourth Quarter Totals

Totals for Year

9.12 SOLVE THIS PROBLEM: Complete the earnings record of Thomas Bentley and fill out his W-2 form for the year 1973. The employer is the Best Company, 127 East 17th St., New York, N.Y. 11603. The employer's identification number is 13-1767321. (Thomas Bentley's Payroll Account is on page 194).

Figure 9-9

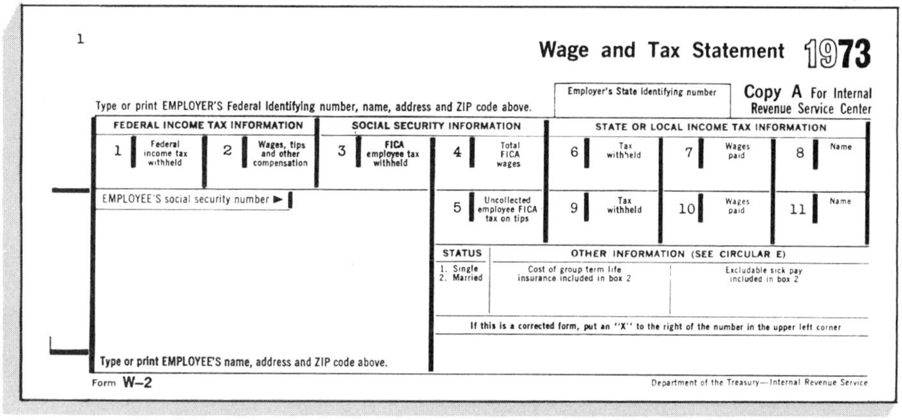
1

Wage and Tax Statement 1973

Employer's State identifying number

Copy A For Internal Revenue Service Center

Type or print EMPLOYER'S Federal identifying number, name, address and ZIP code above.

FEDERAL INCOME TAX INFORMATION — 1 Federal income tax withheld; 2 Wages, tips and other compensation

SOCIAL SECURITY INFORMATION — 3 FICA employee tax withheld; 4 Total FICA wages; 5 Uncollected employee FICA tax on tips

STATE OR LOCAL INCOME TAX INFORMATION — 6 Tax withheld; 7 Wages paid; 8 Name; 9 Tax withheld; 10 Wages paid; 11 Name

EMPLOYEE'S social security number ►

STATUS: 1. Single 2. Married

OTHER INFORMATION (SEE CIRCULAR E) — Cost of group term life insurance included in box 2; Excludable sick pay included in box 2

If this is a corrected form, put an "X" to the right of the number in the upper left corner

Type or print EMPLOYEE'S name, address and ZIP code above.

Form W–2

Department of the Treasury—Internal Revenue Service

CHAPTER REVIEW

1. Martin Epstein worked $37\frac{1}{2}$ hours last week at the rate of \$3.50 per hour. What was his gross pay?
2. If Harris Blum works 45 hours in one week at the rate of \$2.80 per hour, what is his gross pay?
3. What was the gross pay of Gerald Weinstein for the past week if he is paid at the rate of \$6 per hour?

Monday	7
Tuesday	10
Wednesday	12
Thursday	8
Friday	11

4. Determine the gross pay of Caroline Blum for sewing 800 sleeves into garments last week if she earns \$.25 for each sleeve.
5. The Electro Assembly Plant pays its assemblers on the following basis:

1–300 pieces	\$.42 each
301–500 pieces	\$.45 each
501–800 pieces	\$.50 each

Find the gross pay for the following people:

1. Stanley Roban   390 pieces
2. Edward Funk   275 pieces
3. Bernie Carlin   714 pieces
4. Joe Reihing   500 pieces
5. Milton Shuch   600 pieces

6. Find the FICA deduction this week for the following workers:

	Earnings from Jan. 1	*Earnings This Week*	*FICA Deduction*
Sam	$10,900	$250	
Ted	8,700	300	
Billy	10,800	175	
Jack	10,000	225	
Henry	10,700	200	

7. Using the FICA charts on pages 182–83 determine the FICA deduction on salaries of:

1. $ 99.07
2. 110.40
3. 120.43
4. 126.00
5. 133.06

8. Mr. Thomas Hastings worked 42 hours this week at an hourly rate of $3.12. Determine his withholding deduction, if he is married but hasn't any children.

9. Prepare a change memo for this net payroll:

Helen Tuzin $126.53
Blanche Adinolfi   121.14
Shirley Simon   114.75

10

commissions and discounts

1. COMMISSIONS
   a. Straight commission
   b. Sliding scale commission
   c. Straight salary plus commission
   d. Quota bonus commission

2. DISCOUNTS
   a. Cash discounts
   b. Trade discounts
   c. Series of trade discounts
   d. Equivalent trade discounts
   e. Anticipation

1. COMMISSIONS Commission is a method of compensation for services such as selling, leasing, and buying of merchandise, insurance, real estate, etc. It is a type of payment which is usually associated with salesmen, agent middlemen, or brokers whose responsibilities are selling merchandise, furnishing marketing information, and negotiating the terms of sales for manufacturers. It is used as an incentive to increase the individual's effort, because the amount of compensation increases as performance improves.

a. STRAIGHT COMMISSION

Salesmen are often paid on a straight commission basis. Their total earnings are computed as a percent of sales. The formula used is:

$$\text{Amount sold} \times \text{Commission rate} = \text{Commission}$$

ILLUSTRATIVE PROBLEM. A dress salesman sold $10,000 worth of merchandise in April. His commission rate is 5%. What was his commission for that month?

SOLUTION:

$$\text{Amount sold} \times \text{Commission rate} = \text{Commission}$$
$$\$10,000 \quad \times \qquad .05 \qquad = \text{Commission}$$
$$\$500 = \text{Commission for April}$$

It is significant to note that not all of the merchandise sold to customers is kept by them. Occasionally, customers return merchandise that is not up to specification, damaged, etc. The salesman is paid a commission only on the goods the customer retains. Returns are subtracted from the amount of merchandise sold to determine the amount on which commissions will be paid. The formula used is:

198

(Amount sold − Returns) × Commission rate = Commission

ILLUSTRATIVE PROBLEM. Howard Ogden sold $730 worth of men's sweaters to the Clyde Men's Shop. Upon inspecting the shipment, Clyde discovered three damaged sweaters, costing $30, and returned them to Ogden's company. If Ogden's rate of commission is 5%, how much commission did he receive?

SOLUTION:

$$
\begin{aligned}
(\text{Amount sold} - \text{Returns}) \times \text{Commission rate} &= \text{Commission} \\
(\$730 - \$30) \qquad \times \qquad .05 \quad\; &= \text{Commission} \\
\$700 \qquad\quad \times \qquad .05 \quad\; &= \text{Commission} \\
\$35 &= \text{Commission}
\end{aligned}
$$

In industry, many salesmen are paid a "draw against commission" to provide them with a steady income. Management advances an amount to each salesman based on the individual's expected commission. At the end of a predetermined period (once every month, every three months, etc.) the salesman's commission is computed, his "draw" is subtracted from that amount, and he is paid the excess. If his "draw" is more than his commission, he owes the difference. In cases where the "draw" is frequently greater than the actual commission, the draw may be decreased. To determine the amount due to the salesman, the following formula is used:

Amount sold × Commission rate = Commission

Then, find the difference between the draw and the commission. The difference is the amount owed to the salesman or the company.

ILLUSTRATIVE PROBLEM. Johnson draws $150 per week from The Rialto Company, manufacturers of office supplies. His rate of commission is 4% of all sales. At the end of each ten-week period he is sent a statement showing his current financial situation with the company. Find the difference between Johnson's draw and his commission for a ten-week period in which he sold $45,000 worth of merchandise.

SOLUTION:

$$
\begin{aligned}
\text{Amount sold} \times \text{Commission rate} &= \text{Commission} \\
\$45,000 \quad \times \qquad .04 \quad\; &= \text{Commission} \\
\$1,800 &= \text{Commission} \\[6pt]
\text{Draw} \times \text{Number of weeks} &= \text{Total draw} \\
\$150 \times \qquad 10 \qquad\; &= \text{Total draw} \\
\$1,500 &= \text{Total draw (10 weeks)}
\end{aligned}
$$

$1800   Commission
− 1500   Draw
$ 300   Owed to Johnson

10.1   *SOLVE THESE PROBLEMS:*

1. If Tom Avery's commission rate is 6% and he sells $8,465 worth of merchandise, how much are his earnings?

2. John Fallo, a wholesale shoe salesman, sold:

> 600 pairs of shoes at $6.75 per pair
> 150 pairs of shoes at $10.75 per pair
> 300 pairs of slippers at $2.50 per pair

If his commission rate is $4\frac{1}{2}$%, how much does he receive in earnings?

3. Stanley Smith sold $1,285 worth of ladies' slacks to the Century Shop. When unpacking the merchandise, the store manager discovered that some slacks in the shipment, amounting in value to $114, had not been ordered. He returned them to Smith's company. How much commission did Smith receive for this order if his rate was $5\frac{1}{2}$%?

4. In a shipment of 12 individual sets of chinaware that Hughes, a salesman, sold to the A-1 China Shop at $149.50 per set, one set was damaged in shipping. If Hughes receives a $6\frac{1}{2}$% commission, how much did he receive from the transaction?

5. At the end of each month, John Mason receives a statement from the Harmony Paper and Twine Company listing his sales for that month. Mr. Mason receives a 3% commission on all sales and a draw of $440 per month. If his sales for the month are $23,185, how much does the company owe him?

6. The following is a three-month statement received by Philip Borg indicating his monthly sales figures on which he is paid a 7% commission:

> January $17,842
> February   14,621
> March   18,597

If his monthly draw is $600, how much is due him in commissions?

7. Ralph Carter draws $225 per week against a commission of 4% as a dress salesman for the Fit-Rite Company. Every six months the company computes Ralph's sales and determines the amount due him or the company. Using the following figures, ascertain (1) which party is paid the difference between the draw and the commission; and (2) the amount of the difference.

Month	Sales	Sales Returns
July	$29,726	$1,270
August	28,413	2,019
September	32,011	3,115
October	31,927	1,894
November	27,426	1,426
December	22,747	812

To find the commission rate when the commission and the amount sold are known, this formula is used:

$$\text{Commission rate} = \frac{\text{Amount of commission}}{\text{Amount sold}}$$

ILLUSTRATIVE PROBLEM. A coat salesman received $450 in commissions for $15,000 of sales. What commission rate did he receive?

SOLUTION:

$$\text{Commission rate} = \frac{\text{Amount of commission}}{\text{Amount sold}}$$

$$\text{Commission rate} = \frac{\$450}{\$15,000}$$

$$\text{Commission rate} = 3\%$$

10.2 SOLVE THESE PROBLEMS:

1. What is Todd's commission rate on $800 in commissions for sales of $32,000?

2. If Regan's sales statement indicated these figures, how much of a commission rate did he receive?

	Sales	Commissions
January	$17,500	$510.22
February	22,745	763.33
March	24,632	997.15

3. Brown had sales of $68,350. Despite sales returns of $4,350 he received $6,000 in commissions. What was his commission rate?

4. At the end of four weeks, Fields, Ltd., owed Petri a commission of $600 after deducting his weekly draw of $150 from his total commissions for the period. His sales, on which the commissions were paid, were $48,000. What was Petri's commission rate?

To find the amount sold (sales) when the commission and the commission rate are known, this formula is used:

$$\text{Amount sold (sales)} = \frac{\text{Amount of commission}}{\text{Commission rate}}$$

ILLUSTRATIVE PROBLEM. Drucker receives $500 in commissions based on a commission rate of 5%. How much merchandise did he sell?

SOLUTION:

$$\text{Amount sold} = \frac{\text{Amount of commission}}{\text{Commission rate}}$$

$$\text{Amount sold} = \frac{500}{.05}$$

$$\text{Amount sold} = \$10,000$$

10.3 SOLVE THESE PROBLEMS:

1. Determine the amount of goods sold when a commission of $814, based on a rate of 6%, has been paid.

2. Penrod received a 4% commission rate. The following were his commissions for each of these months:

January	$ 765
February	842
March	945
April	1,065
May	1,250
June	972

(1) How much merchandise did he sell each month?

(2) How much were his total sales?

10.4 SOLVE THESE PROBLEMS: Complete.

	Amount Sold (Sales)	Commission Rate	Commission
1.	$ 8,635.00	4%	—
2.	4,764.32	5%	—
3.	12,641.55	$4\frac{1}{2}\%$	—
4.	19,426.00	6%	—
5.	23,742.29	7%	—
6.	9,000.00	—	$ 300.00
7.	12,708.00	—	635.40
8.	14,641.73	—	878.50
9.	22,740.00	—	795.90
10.	25,628.19	—	1,089.92
11.	—	3%	412.00
12.	—	5%	963.15
13.	—	4%	1,245.50
14.	—	$4\frac{1}{2}\%$	878.00
15.	—	$6\frac{1}{2}\%$	1,472.65

10.5 SOLVE THESE PROBLEMS: Complete.

Amount Sold	Sales Returns	Commission Rate	Commission
1. $ 876.00	$ 42.00	4%	—
2. 1,243.70	115.00	$3\frac{1}{2}$%	—
3. 2,781.60	214.10	5%	—
4. 95 pieces @ $6.75 each	13.50	6%	—
5. 12 sets @ $125 each	1 set	$5\frac{1}{2}$%	—

10.6 SOLVE THESE PROBLEMS: Complete.

Amount Sold	Commission Rate	Draw Against Commission	Due Salesman or Company
1. $15,000.00	5%	$600	—
2. 22,500.00	4%	750	—
3. 25,615.75	6%	800	—
4. 18,452.30	$5\frac{1}{2}$%	675	—
5. 24,750.00	7%	$325 per week for 4 weeks	—

10.7 SOLVE THESE PROBLEMS: Complete.

Amount Sold	Sales Returns	Commission Rate	Draw Against Commission	Due Salesman or Company
1. $14,000.00	$1,000.00	3%	$ 250	—
2. 36,500.50	2,500.76	5%	1,200	—
3. 18,450.23	675.00	$4\frac{1}{2}$%	950	—
4. 50 tables @ 239.50 each	3 tables	6%	425	—
5. 28,431.55	92 items @ $23 each	4%	800	—

b. SLIDING SCALE COMMISSION

Some companies find that a variation on the straight commission plan motivates salesmen to perform more effectively. Instead of awarding a fixed commission rate on total sales, management very often increases the commission rate after certain goals are reached. For example, a salesman, during a one-month period, receives 3% on the first $10,000 in sales; 4% on the next $10,000; and 5% on any sales over $20,000. This is known as sliding scale commission. The formula used is:

The sum of the commissions on each quota = Total commission

ILLUSTRATIVE PROBLEM. A toy salesman sold merchandise amounting to $37,000 during January. He receives 5% on the first $15,000; 6% on the next $15,000; and 7% on the remainder. What was his commission for the month?

SOLUTION: Find the commission for each quota.

$$\$15,000 \times .05 = \$750$$
$$\$15,000 \times .06 = \$900$$
$$\$\ 7,000 \times .07 = \$490$$

Sum of commission on each quota = $2,140 Commission for January

10.8   SOLVE THESE PROBLEMS:

1. The Gambit Company, manufacturers of swimsuits, pay their salesmen 3% commission for the first $10,000 sold each month; 3.5% for the next $12,000 sold; and 4% on the excess sold. How much did each salesman earn for the month of March?

Salesmen	March Sales	Earnings
1. Jack Harris	$19,000	$_____
2. John Philips	36,400	_____
3. Frank Jordan	12,650	_____
4. Phil Sens	46,000	_____
5. George Morris	27,890	_____
6. Sam Cohen	14,775	_____
7. Al Fuller	29,000	_____
8. Joe Kelly	32,545	_____
9. Herb Rose	28,427	_____
10. Bill Jenkins	42,725	_____

2. Find the commission due Fred Armor for sales of $46,463.70 for a month when his monthly commission rates are $4\frac{1}{2}$% on the first $20,000; 5% on the next $15,000; and 6% on the remainder. The merchandise returns, during this period, were $2,625.41.

3. Gregg Selwin draws $225 per week against commissions as a salesman for the Double-Knit Sweater Corp. on total sales for each ten-week period, Selwin earns 5% on the first $30,000; 6% on the next $25,000; and 7% on the balance. If his sales for the ten-week period ending April 15 are $87,479.41, how much is still owed to Selwin?

c. STRAIGHT SALARY PLUS COMMISSION

The larger retail stores have found that a straight salary to insure a regular income, plus a small commission as an incentive feature, is a wage payment plan that is satisfactory to employers and employees. The commission rate usually ranges from $\frac{1}{2}$% to $2\frac{1}{2}$%. Straight salary plus commission differs from draw against commission in that the former is a guaranteed amount and the latter is a loan against future commission earnings. To find the total earnings for straight salary plus commission, these formulas are used:

Amount sold × Commission rate = Commission
Commission + Straight salary = Total earnings

ILLUSTRATIVE PROBLEM. Mary Rogers receives a salary of $65 per week plus 1% commission on her total sales. What were her total earnings for the week ending May 18 on sales of $900?

SOLUTION:

Amount sold × Commission rate = Commission
$900   ×   .01   = $9

Commission + Straight salary = Total earnings
$9   + $65   = $74 Total earnings

10.9 SOLVE THESE PROBLEMS:

1. Amanda Edgar, a salesgirl in a Specialty Shop, regularly receives a weekly salary of $50. To this is added a $2\frac{1}{2}$% commission on her sales. Find her total earnings for a week in which she sells $840 worth of goods.

2. The Ritz Boutique ran a competition in its main store in which the person with the highest total earnings for the week of the contest would win a trip to the West Indies. Because each salesgirl's regular salary differs, it was necessary to compute her salary plus the uniform commission of $1\frac{1}{2}$%.

    (a) Find each girl's commission.
    (b) Find each girl's total earnings.
    (c) Who was the winner?

Name	Regular Salary	Amount Sold	Commission	Total Earnings
Joan Sharp	$57.50	$500.00	7.50	6450
Alice Pine	63.75	490.00	—	—
Caryn Joy	62.50	716.00	—	—
Ellen Frances	65.00	509.56	—	—
Sheri Beth	61.50	894.52	—	—

d. QUOTA BONUS COMMISSION

Retail store managers, sales managers, and salesmen are frequently paid bonuses on the amount of sales that their staffs produce over the regular quota set by management. The quota established is that amount which management expects to realize in an average period.

Managers receive these bonuses in the form of commissions. For example, a store manager will receive a bonus if the total sales of all of his sales personnel is greater than the designated quota. This bonus is arranged as an incentive for managers to effectively motivate their personnel. To determine quota bonus commission, this formula is used:

Quota bonus commission = Total sales − Quota × Commission rate

ILLUSTRATIVE PROBLEM. Joseph Halle is a sales manager for a suit manufacturer who employs fifteen salesmen. His quota for the first six months of the year is $1,300,000. On sales over this amount Mr. Halle receives a bonus commission of 1%. If his staff produces sales of $1,800,000, how much commission will Halle receive?

SOLUTION:

Quota bonus commission = (Total sales − Quota) × Commission percent
= ($1,800,000 − $1,300,000) × .01
= $500,000 × .01
= $5,000

10.10 SOLVE THESE PROBLEMS:

1. Cheers, a retail sportswear shop, pays its store manager a bonus of $2\frac{1}{2}$% commission on all sales exceeding $12,000 per month. How much commission did the manager receive for April sales of $14,955?

2. On yearly sales exceeding $1,675,000, Mr. Davids, sales manager for the Nu-Vogue Dress Corp., receives a bonus of 3%. From the following figures indicating the amounts sold by individual salesmen, determine if Mr. Adams will receive a bonus and, if so, how much it will be.

Salesmen	Sales
Eric Johns	$283,495.11
Scott Adams	395,062.38
Melvin Edwards	408,792.14
Mike Hellon	384,466.82
Moni Stevens	526,073.75

2. DISCOUNTS a. CASH DISCOUNTS

As an incentive to encourage prompt payment, many companies allow their customers a discount for bills paid within a specified number of days. The terms (the amount of discount and the number of days) are clearly stated on the invoice. The terms 2/10, n/30 indicate that 2% may be deducted if the bill is paid within 10 days, and that the full price must be paid in 30 days.

The formula for discount is:

$$\text{Discount} = \text{Amount of the sale} \times \text{Rate of discount}$$

ILLUSTRATIVE PROBLEM. Find the amount of the discount on a bill of $200 dated March 10, terms 2/10, n/30, if it is paid on March 15.

SOLUTION:

$$\text{Amount due} \times \text{Rate of discount} = \text{Amount of discount}$$
$$\$200 \quad \times \quad 2\% \quad = \$4$$

Where the amount of discount and the rate of discount are known, the amount of the payment may be determined. The formula for finding the amount due when the discount and the rate are known is:

$$\frac{\text{Amount of discount}}{\text{Rate of discount}} \times C = \text{Amount due before discount}$$

ILLUSTRATIVE PROBLEM. The Concord Company allows a 3% discount on payments made within 10 days. What was the amount due if the allowable discount was $6?

SOLUTION:

$$\frac{\text{(Amount of discount) }\$6}{\text{(Rate of discount) }.03} \times C = \$200$$

To state this another way:

$$
\begin{array}{ll}
\text{If} & \$6 = 3\% \\
\text{Then} & \$2 = 1\% \\
\text{And} & \$200 = 100\%
\end{array}
$$

Where the amount of the discount and the amount due before discount are known, the rate of discount may be determined by this formula:

$$\frac{\text{Amount of discount}}{\text{Amount due before discount}} = \text{Rate of discount}$$

ILLUSTRATIVE PROBLEM. A check for $72 was received from a customer in payment of an invoice of $80. What was the rate of discount?

SOLUTION:

1. Find the amount of the discount $80 — $72 = $8
2. $\dfrac{\text{(Amount of discount) \$8}}{\text{(Amount due) \$80}} = 10\%$ (Rate of discount)

10.11   SOLVE THESE PROBLEMS:

1. Determine the amount of discount on an invoice total of $535.20 that is dated January 5 and is paid on January 12, if the terms are 2/10, n/30.
2. Find the discount on the following bill dated October 20 with terms of 2/10, n/30, if it is paid on October 28:

      12 chairs @ $29.75 each
      3 tables @ $49.50 each
      3 lamps @ $14.90 each

3. What was the amount due the Edgemere Company, which allows an 8% discount, if the discount amounted to $64?
4. The Fashionette Manufacturing Corp. allows discounts of 2% on lingerie purchases paid within 10 days and 8% on sportswear purchases paid within the same time period. How much was due in each category if the allowable discounts were $80 and $40, respectively?
5. What was the rate of discount on a payment of $900 on an invoice of $960?
6. A check of $2,935.68 was received by the Perma Corp. in settlement of the following invoice:

      200 yards of sailcloth @ $1.79 per yard
      150 yards of wool knit @ $6.50 per yard
       50 yards of muslin @ $.50 per yard
      300 yards of silk shantung @ $3.00 per yard
      100 yards of wool tweed @ $8.00 per yard

   What was the discount rate?

Naturally, the discount is allowed only on the actual amount of the sale. Where part of the merchandise has been returned, the amount of the return must be deducted before the discount is calculated. Similarly, if freight charges have been included in the invoice, such charges must be deducted before calculating the discount. To summarize, the discount is taken on the invoice amount, less returns and freight charges.

ILLUSTRATIVE PROBLEM. Find the amount of cash necessary to settle the following transactions within the discount period. A bill was received for $312, consisting of $300 of merchandise and $12 of freight charges. Upon unpacking the merchandise, $20 worth was found to be defective, and was returned. The discount rate is 2%.

SOLUTION:

Amount of invoice	$312
Less returns	20
Net amount of invoice	292
Less freight charges	12
Amount on which discount is allowed	280
Discount $280 \times 2\% =$	$ 5.60
Amount of check: $292 - \$5.60 = \$286.40$	

10.12 *SOLVE THESE PROBLEMS:*

1. An invoice bearing terms of 2/10, n/30, was dated September 15. It listed $450 for merchandise and $5 for shipping costs. Upon examining the goods, it was discovered to include $45 of damaged merchandise that was returned. How much should the amount of the check be if the bill is paid on September 20?

2. The following is an invoice dated February 20 with terms of 3/10, n/30:

>   8 fruit bowls @ $8.50 each
>   144 drinking glasses @ $20 per dozen
>   4 salad bowls @ $12 each

In this shipment, one fruit bowl and one salad bowl were cracked and returned to the sender. Freight charges were $8. If the bill was paid on February 24, how much should the amount be?

3. Gordon and Arnold offer their customers terms of 2/10 n/30. Last week they received a check for $178.35 from Rubin Ltd. in payment of a bill. If the invoice was dated January 10 and payment was made on January 15, how much of a discount did the customer take? Round off to nearest cent.

4. Rona's Boutique purchased a dozen sweaters from Cheshire, Inc. The merchandise was subject to terms of 8/10 n/30. If the store

paid within 7 days and sent a check to cover the amount for $327.52, how much was the discount?

Frequently, partial payment is made on invoices. If such partial payment is made within the discount period, the customer is entitled to credit for the discount. The formula for this is:

$$100\% - \text{Discount rate} = \% \text{ paid}$$

$$\frac{\text{Payment}}{\% \text{ paid}} = \text{Amount of credit the customer receives}$$

ILLUSTRATIVE PROBLEM. Archer, Inc., pays $190 on account of a $270 purchase within the discount period. The discount rate is 5%. How much does Archer, Inc., still owe?

SOLUTION:

$$100\% - 5\% \text{ (Discount rate)} = 95\% \text{ Paid}$$

$$\frac{\$190 \text{ Payment}}{95\% \text{ Paid}} = \text{Amount of credit the customer receives}$$

$$= \$200 \text{ amount of credit the customer receives}$$

Amount still due = Original invoice $270
                 Less paid on account   200
                 Remaining balance $ 70

10.13 SOLVE THESE PROBLEMS:

1. On November 14, Sam Irwin pays one half of an invoice of $375 dated November 7 with terms of 2/10, n/30. How much does Irwin still owe?

2. Frank Tanen owes payment on the following invoices:

> 20 chairs @ $40 each
> 3 sofas @ $120 each
> 6 desks @ $52 each

He decided to pay $800 on account within the discount period. The discount rate is 4%. How much does Frank Tanen still owe?

b. OTHER CASH DISCOUNT TERMS

In addition to the common cash discounts already discussed, cash discounts may be given in other forms. Some of these are:

1. E.O.M.—This term indicates that the discount days are counted from the end of the month of the invoice. Thus, a bill dated January 15 bearing the terms 8/10 E.O.M. entitles the buyer to an 8% discount if paid by February 10.

2. R.O.G.—This term indicates that the discount period begins with the receipt of the goods rather than the date of the invoice.

c. TRADE DISCOUNTS

Businesses that sell to different types of customers frequently charge different prices to each class. For example, a retail buyer purchasing a single item would be charged list price, while a wholesaler buying in lots of 100 would be allowed a trade discount. A trade discount is a reduction in selling price used to differentiate between types of customers. Unlike cash discounts, which are deductions for prompt payment, trade discounts are reductions in the selling price. Business firms that invest heavily in selling through catalogs frequently use trade discounts because changes in the selling price can be effected much more inexpensively by adjusting the trade discount than by reprinting the catalog.

The formula for finding the net cost when the list price and the trade discount are known is:

1. List price × Rate of trade discount = Trade discount
2. List price − Trade discount = Net cost

ILLUSTRATIVE PROBLEM. Find the cost to the buyer of a television set listed at $90 less a trade discount of 40%.

SOLUTION:

List price ($90) × Rate of trade discount (40%) = Trade discount ($36)
List price ($90) − Trade discount ($36) = Net cost ($54)

10.14 SOLVE THESE PROBLEMS:

1. Bill Jordan, a retailer, purchased a color television set with a list price of $720. The trade discount to retailers was 45%. How much did Jordan pay for the set?

2. The Major Electronics Company sells electrical supplies to wholesalers, retailers, and industrial purchasers. Each purchaser receives a different discount according to the nature of his business—retailers, 40%; wholesalers, 43%; and industrial purchasers, 48%. How much did each of the following purchasers pay for stereo components listing at $32.50 each?

a. The retailer bought 8 pieces.
b. The wholesaler bought 50 pieces.
c. The industrial purchaser bought 85 pieces.

d. SERIES OF TRADE DISCOUNTS

Frequently, trade discounts are listed in series. That is, the list price is quoted less several trade discounts. For example, list price $100 less 20%, 10%, and 5%. The method for determining the net cost in this case is to take each discount separately *after* deducting the amount of prior discount from the net cost.

The formula for finding the net cost when the list price and a series of trade discounts is known follows:

1. List price $\times$ Rate of first trade discount = First trade discount
2. List price $-$ First trade discount = First remainder
3. First remainder $\times$ Rate of second trade discount = Second trade discount
4. First remainder $-$ Second trade discount = Second remainder and so on, until all of the trade discounts have been taken.

The order in which the discounts are taken has no bearing on the result. Therefore, the discounts should be taken in the order that offers the greatest arithmetic convenience.

ILLUSTRATIVE PROBLEM. What is the net cost of a refrigerator listed at $80 less 20%, 10% and 5%?

SOLUTION:

$80 $\times$ 20% = $16 First discount
$80 $-$ $16 = $64 First remainder
$64 $\times$ 10% = $6.40 Second discount
$64 $-$ $6.40 = $57.60 Second remainder
$57.60 $\times$ 5% = $2.88 Third discount
$57.60 $-$ $2.88 = $54.72 Net cost

10.15 SOLVE THESE PROBLEMS:

1. Frank Smith, owner of a retail paper goods shop, purchases all his supplies from a wholesaler who uses a list price system and allows discounts of 40%, 20%, and 2% to his customers. What is Smith's net cost on the following order?

   75 packages of cups @ $.59 per package
   125 packages of 7 inch plates @ $.89 per package

100 packages of 8 inch plates @ $.98 per package

150 packages of napkins @ $.65 per package

2. Piere and Company allows discounts of 35%, 10%, and 2% to retailers, and 40%, 10%, and 5% to wholesalers. What is the net cost
to a retailer and a wholesaler each purchasing an identical order of
156 sets of crystal glassware listing at $96 per dozen sets?

3. Determine amount of discount and net cost.

	List price	Percent of trade discount allowed	Amount of discount	Net cost
1.	$ 100.00	5, 10	—	—
2.	125.00	5, 10, 5	—	—
3.	375.00	10, 20, 3	—	—
4.	526.37	5, 15, 6	—	—
5.	339.14	8, 25, 12	—	—
6.	826.12	2, 16, 37	—	—
7.	1,247.00	10, 40, 25	—	—
8.	1,362.40	10, 10, 5	—	—
9.	2,795.68	5, 25, 30	—	—
10.	12,478.00	5, 15, 25	—	—

e. EQUIVALENT TRADE DISCOUNTS

It is possible to convert a series of discounts into a single discount which is
the same as the whole series. The equivalent discount of the series given in
the previous problem (20%, 10%, 5%) can be determined for an $80 refrig-
erator as follows, using $1.00 as a base (because $1.00 is the same as 100%):

$$1.00 \times 20\% = .20 \text{ First discount}$$
$$1.00 - .20 = .80 \text{ First remainder}$$
$$.80 \times 10\% = .08 \text{ Second discount}$$
$$.80 - .08 = .72 \text{ Second remainder}$$
$$.72 \times 5\% = .036 \text{ Third discount}$$
$$.72 - .036 = .684 \text{ Third remainder}$$
$$1.00 - .684 = .316 \text{ Equivalent discount}$$
$$\$80 \times .684 = \$54.72 \text{ Net cost or } \$80 - (\$80 \times .316) = \$54.72$$

In other words, 68.4% of an amount will give the same answer as the amount
less 20%, 10%, and 5%.

This same answer could have been calculated by deducting each discount from 1.00 and multiplying the answers.

Thus:

$$1.00 - .20 = .80$$
$$1.00 - .10 = .90$$
$$1.00 - .05 = .95$$

Then:
$$.80 \times .90 \times .95 = .684$$

A simple method for determining the equivalent trade discount of a series of two discounts is:

> Add the two discounts.
> Deduct the product of the two discounts.

ILLUSTRATIVE PROBLEM. Find the net cost of an item costing $120 less 30% and 20%.

SOLUTION:

Add: the two discounts 30% + 20% = 50%
Deduct: the product of the two discounts .30 × .20 = 6%
Equivalent trade discount 44%

(Cost) $120 × (Equivalent discount) 44% = $52.80 Trade discount
(Cost) $120 less (Trade discount) $52.80 = $67.20 Net cost

10.16 SOLVE THESE PROBLEMS:

List	Trade Discounts	Equivalent Rate of Discount	Amount of Trade Discount	Net Cost
1. 400	30% and 10%	—	—	—
2. 750	25% and 5%	—	—	—
3. 1,250	40% and 20%	—	—	—
4. 1,360	40%, 20% and 8%	—	—	—
5. 127.16	30%, 10% and 10%	—	—	—

10.17 SOLVE THESE PROBLEMS:

1. The Spiral Record Company allows a 40% trade discount to their retail customers and terms of 2/10, n/30 for prompt payment. How much must the Hi-Lo Record Shop pay on a bill of $425 dated May 20 and paid on May 28?

2. How much is due on the following invoice if the trade discount is 38%, the cash discount allowance is 3/10, n/30, and it is paid on June 25?

INVOICE

DATE: JUNE 19, 19—

Quantity	Item	Unit Price
8	Broiler	$39.50 —
6	Pressure cooker	14.90 —
12	Teflon pot	3.75 —
8	Electric coffee pot	29.50 —

3. What amount does Paul Williams owe on a piano he purchased that listed at $1,750 with trade discounts of 50%, 15%, and 5% and cash terms of 3% if he pays the bill promptly?

4. Philip Decker, a wholesaler, purchased the following order on September 8 from Brandt's, Inc., an office equipment manufacturer:

> 6 desks @ $129.75 each
> 24 desk lamps @ $25.50 each
> 6 chairs @ $52.80 each

Brandt's allows discounts of 45%, 8%, and 3% to wholesalers and cash terms of 2/10, n/30. If Decker pays this bill on September 12, how much will the net cost be?

5. Peters, a retailer, and Jenkins, a wholesaler, each bought 6 washing machines, listing at $295.50 each, from the Hamrod Manufacturing Company on October 4. Hamrod offers discounts of 40%, 7%, and 2% to retailers and 50%, 10%, and 3% to wholesalers with cash terms of 3/10, n/30 to both. What is the net cost of their purchases if Peters pays on October 20, and Jenkins pays on October 9?

f. ANTICIPATION

Some firms offer a bonus discount called anticipation to encourage their customers to pay their bills before they are due. Anticipation is usually at the rate of 6% and is in addition to the cash discount. Thus terms of 2/20, n/60 would permit a discount of 2% if paid within twenty days, plus anticipation at the rate of 6% for the number of days left in the 60-day net period. The formula for anticipation is the same as the one used to determine simple interest:

> Amount of the bill due × Rate of anticipation × Days prepaid
>
> or: Principal × Rate × Time = Amount of anticipation

ILLUSTRATIVE PROBLEM. A bill for $100 subject to terms of 2/10, n/60, dated March 1, is to be paid on March 7. If anticipation is allowed at the rate of 6%, what is the amount of the check required to pay this invoice?

SOLUTION:

1. Find the amount of the bill due.

Because the bill is paid within 10 days, the buyer is entitled to a 2% cash discount.

> $100 × 2% = $2
> $100 − $2 = $98   Amount of the bill due

2. Find the days in the anticipation period.

The bill had 60 days in which to be paid; it was paid in 6 days (March 1 to March 7). Therefore, it was prepaid by:

$$60 - 6 = 54 \text{ days}$$

At this point we use the formula for anticipation: Amount of bill due ($98) × Rate of anticipation (6%) × Days prepaid $\frac{54}{360}$ = Amount of anticipation

$$\$98 \times .06 \times \tfrac{54}{360} = 5.88 \times \tfrac{3}{20} = \$.88$$

Amount of the bill due	$98.00
Less anticipation	.88
Amount of check	$97.12

10.18 *SOLVE THESE PROBLEMS:*

1. Marbet Corp. owes a bill with terms of 6/10, n/30 and an anticipation allowance of 6% for goods invoiced on November 17. How much must be paid if this bill is settled on November 22?

> 10 transistor radios @ $12.95 each
> 15 portable phonographs @ $39.50 each
> 22 tape decks @ $56.75 each

2. How much does Charles and Company owe on a total purchase of merchandise listing for $6,500 with discounts of 42%, 8%, and 3%, cash terms of 2/10, n/30, and anticipation at the rate of 6%, if the purchase was made on April 4 and paid on April 5?

3. Calculate the amount of cash needed to pay the following bills.

    a. Amount of bill $125.60
        Date of purchase   Aug. 10
        Date of payment   Aug. 19
        Cash terms   3/10, n/30
        Rate of anticipation none
    b. Amount of bill $3,763.18
        Date of purchase   Sept. 6
        Date of payment   Sept. 26
        Cash terms   3/10, 1/20, n/60
        Rate of anticipation 6%
    c. Amount of bill $2,796.18
        Date of purchase   July 4
        Date of payment   Aug. 1
        Cash terms   4/10, 2/20, 1/30, n/60
        Rate of anticipation 5%
    d. Amount of bill $3,680.47

Date of purchase	June 5
Date of payment	July 7
Cash terms	2/10, 1/30, n/60
Rate of anticipation	$6\frac{1}{2}\%$

CHAPTER REVIEW

1. Charles sold $25,000 worth of pants last month. If his commission rate was 6%, how much did he earn?

2. Henry's sales for last month amounted to $38,200. Of that total $1,200 was returned because of late delivery. If his commission was 5%, how much did Henry earn?

3. Stan draws a weekly amount of $200 per week. He earns 7% commission on sales. For the first eight weeks at the Endico Company Stan had sales of $62,000. How much does the company owe Stan?

4. Determine Marty's rate of commission if he sold $40,000 worth of goods and received $1,600.

5. Peter works on a commission rate of 6%. If he earned $1,200 last month, how much did he sell?

6. David sold $62,000 worth of calculators last month. He is paid on the following basis:

   6% on the first $30,000
   7% on the second $30,000
   8% over $60,000

   How much did he earn last month?

7. Elaine Carlin receives $110 per week and 3% commission on all sales. If her sales amounted to $600 last week, how much did she earn?

8. At Piedmont, Inc., sales managers are paid a bonus in the amount of 2% if total sales exceed $1,500,000. Last year, Mr. Weinstein's division had sales of $2,300,000. How much was Weinstein's bonus?

9. Find the discount on an invoice of $325 dated January 1 and paid on January 8, if the terms are 2/10, n/30.

10. If the allowable discount was $20 and the discount rate was 5%, what was the amount due?

11. What was the discount rate if the invoice was for $150 and the check was for $145?

12. Samantha, Inc. received a shipment of toys amounting to $425. Two airplanes costing $8.50 each were damaged and had to be returned. Freight charges (included in the total invoice) amounted to $7. If the discount rate was 20%, how much did Samantha have to send to the vendor in settlement of its account?

13. Alan Rubin purchased an electronic calculator that listed at $420. Because he was a retailer, he was entitled to a trade discount of 40%. How much did he pay for the merchandise?

14. How much does an electric lighting track cost if it lists at $120 and has discounts of 40%, 10%, and 20%?

15. An invoice of $500 has terms of 2/10, n/30. If it is dated June 5 and is paid on June 11 and it provides for anticipation at the rate of 6%, how much must be paid to settle the account?

SIX

MATHEMATICS FOR ACCOUNTING

The function of the accountant to a business enterprise is to provide information. For this reason, accounting has been described as the "language of business." The information supplied may be historical (as in the case of financial results of prior periods), prognostic (as in predicting future financial events), or analytical (as in intensive studies for the control of costs). The end product of the accountant's efforts is the statement, which is a formal presentation of the informational material described above. Based upon these statements, prepared for management by the accountant, business decisions are made which are of enormous importance to the business enterprise involved, as well as to its employees.

Although the body of knowledge required of an accountant is enormous and complicated, through it all runs the thread of arithmetic procedures which are basic to the understanding of accounting principles. In this section of the text we will turn our attention to some of the more common arithmetic operations required of accountants.

11

basic accounting mathematics

1. DEPRECIATION
   a. Straight line
   b. Units of production
   c. Sum-of-years digits
   d. Declining balance

2. MERCHANDISE INVENTORY VALUATION
   a. FIFO
   b. LIFO
   c. Weighted average

3. DIVISION OF PARTNERSHIP INCOME
   a. Absence of partnership agreement
   b. Services of the partners
   c. Investment of the partners

1. DEPRECIATION Among the information reports that an accountant prepares for management are income statements. These reports show the profits or losses that an institution has made during a specific period of time. Calculating profits is a matter of deducting the expenses from the income. The remaining balance, the excess of income over expenses, is the profit. In the event the expenses exceed the income, such excess is a loss.

Some expenses are easily determined. For example, rent expense for the year is the total of the rent paid each month. However, the determination of other expenses is more complicated. The case of an expenditure that will benefit a business for more than one year—a delivery truck, for example—requires estimates of the amount of expense that should be charged to each of the years of the life of the truck. The truck loses value each year through wear and tear, obsolescence, and so forth. The yearly estimate of the amount of this loss is called depreciation. Depreciation is computed by multiplying a base by a rate. Because there are many acceptable methods of calculating depreciation, the accountant must decide the method best suited to each case. This decision is generally based on such estimates as the expected profits of the business during its early years, the availability of funds for income taxes, the amount of the depreciation involved, and so forth. Four different methods of calculating depreciation will be discussed in this chapter.

a. STRAIGHT LINE

The straight-line method of depreciation is based on the assumption that the cost of an item will be spread equally over its useful life. The formula for straight-line depreciation is:

$$\frac{\text{Cost} - \text{Salvage value}}{\text{Estimated years of life}} = \text{Annual depreciation}$$

222

223

Basic Accounting
Mathematics

ILLUSTRATIVE PROBLEM. On January 1, 1964, Stead and Company purchased a delivery truck for $4,000. It is estimated that the truck will have a useful life of four years and that at the end of that time it will have a salvage value (resale value) of $400. Find the depreciation per year using the straight-line method.

SOLUTION: First it is necessary to determine the actual amount to be depreciated. This is the base.

Cost of truck	$4,000
Salvage value	− 400
Actual amount to be depreciated	$3,600

Then the actual amount to be depreciated must be divided equally over the estimated life of the truck.

$$\frac{\text{Actual amount to be depreciated}}{\text{Estimated life of the truck}} \quad \frac{\$3,600}{4 \text{ years}} = \$900 \text{ depreciation per year}$$

To restate the solution:

$$\frac{\text{(Cost) } \$4,000 - \text{(Salvage value) } \$400}{\text{(Estimated years of life) } 4} = \frac{\$3,600}{4} = \$900 \text{ depreciation per year}$$

Total depreciation = $900 per year × 4 years = $3,600

11.1 SOLVE THESE PROBLEMS:

1. The Reliance Company purchased a machine for $400. The estimated life of the asset is four years. If there is no resale value, what is the amount of the depreciation for the third year? Use the straight-line method.

2. Using the straight-line method, find the annual depreciation of an asset that cost $5,300 and has an estimated life of six years. It will be worth $600 at the end of six years.

3. Blair and Company bought a piece of equipment for $2,600 on January 1, 1974. It had a salvage value of $500 and an estimated useful life of seven years. If the asset was sold on December 18, 1976 (round out to nearest full month), what was the total depreciation at the time of sale? Use the straight-line method of depreciation.

4. On September 3, 1974, an asset was purchased for $6,000. The estimated life was five years, and the salvage value was $800; the straight-line method of depreciation was employed. Depreciation is calculated annually on December 31. Find the depreciation for the income statements of 1974 and 1975.

b. UNITS OF PRODUCTION

A depreciation method that attempts to apply the cost of the asset to its actual use is the units-of-production method. With this method, the estimated life of the asset is computed in terms of its productive capacities rather than its years of life. By dividing the amount to be depreciated by the estimated number of units the asset has as potential, the depreciation per unit is determined. The depreciation for a particular period is determined by multiplying the number of units produced in that period by the depreciation per unit.

The formula is:

$$\frac{\text{Cost} - \text{Scrap value}}{\text{Estimated units of production}} = \text{Depreciation per unit}$$

Depreciation per unit $\times$ Number of units in period
$$= \text{Depreciation for the period}$$

ILLUSTRATIVE PROBLEM. On January 1, 1964, Stead and Company purchased a delivery truck for $4,000. It is estimated that the truck will have a useful life of four years, and that at the end of that time it will have a salvage value (resale value) of $400. It is expected that the truck will be used for 72,000 miles. Find the depreciation per year if the truck was used for 20,000 miles during the first year, 25,000 miles during the second year, 18,000 miles during the third year, and 9,000 miles during the fourth year. Use the units of production method for determining depreciation.

SOLUTION: To calculate the depreciation per unit:

$$\frac{\text{(Cost) \$4,000} - \text{(Scrap) \$400} = \$3,600}{\text{(Estimated units of production) 72,000 miles}} = \$.05 \text{ depreciation per mile}$$

To calculate the depreciation:

First year	20,000 miles $\times$ .05 Depreciation per mile =	$1,000.00
Second year	25,000 miles $\times$ .05 Depreciation per mile =	1,250.00
Third year	18,000 miles $\times$ .05 Depreciation per mile =	900.00
Fourth year	9,000 miles $\times$ .05 Depreciation per mile =	450.00
	72,000 miles	$3,600.00

11.2 SOLVE THESE PROBLEMS:

1. A truck with a useful life of 120,000 miles and a salvage value of $1,000 was purchased for $13,000. During the month of May 1974 it traveled 7,800 miles. Determine by use of the units of production the depreciation for May, 1974.

2. An electric generator that cost $70,000 has a useful life of 13,000 hours and a scrap value of $5,000. During the year it was operated for 6,000 hours. What was the amount of depreciation determined by the units of production method?

3. A punch press capable of punching 10,000 units cost $4,000 and had a residual value of $500. Using the units of production method, determine the amount of depreciation for each of the following years:
   a. First year's production 4,000 units.
   b. Second year's production 5,000 units.
   c. Third year's production 3,000 units.

c. SUM-OF-THE-YEARS DIGITS

Although the straight-line method of depreciation has the advantage of simplicity and ease of calculation, it ignores the fact that most assets do not depreciate equally over their lives. Anyone who has ever bought a new car knows that the depreciation in the early years exceeds the later years' depreciation. The sum-of-the-years digits method takes this into account and provides for the highest depreciation in the early years and the lowest in the final years. It does this by providing for each year a series of fractions to be multiplied by the cost less salvage. The largest fraction is that representing the first year, with each year's fraction smaller than that of the previous year. For comparative purposes, the same illustrative problem will be used for each depreciation method.

The formula for sum-of-the-years digits depreciation is:

$$\frac{(\text{Cost} - \text{Salvage value}) \times \text{Each year's digit}}{\text{Total digits}} = \text{Depreciation}$$

ILLUSTRATIVE PROBLEM. On January 1, 1964, Stead and Company purchased a delivery truck for $4,000. It is estimated that the truck will have a useful life of four years, and at the end of that time it will have a salvage value (resale value) of $400. Find the depreciation per year using the sum-of-the-years digits method.

SOLUTION: To find the amount to be depreciated:

(Cost) $4,000 − (Scrap value) $400 = $3,600 amount to be depreciated.

To set up the fractions:

Find the sum-of-the-years digits

If the estimated life is four years, then:

The first year's digit is	4
The second year's digit is	3
The third year's digit is	2
The fourth year's digit is	1
The sum-of-the-years digit is	10

The fractions are determined by using each year's digit as numerator and the sum of the years' digits as denominator. The depreciation is: Each year's fraction × (cost − scrap).

Thus:

$$1\text{st year depreciation} = \tfrac{4}{10} \times 3600 = \$1440$$
$$2\text{nd year depreciation} = \tfrac{3}{10} \times 3600 = 1080$$
$$3\text{rd year depreciation} = \tfrac{2}{10} \times 3600 = 720$$
$$4\text{th year depreciation} = \tfrac{1}{10} \times 3600 = 360$$
$$\text{Total depreciation} \quad \$3600$$

11.3 SOLVE THESE PROBLEMS:

1. Find the depreciation using the sum-of-the-years digit method for an asset costing $8,000 which has an estimated life of five years and no scrap value.

2. Anderson, a traveling salesman, purchased an automobile for $3,500. He estimated that he will use it for five years at which time it will be worth $500 as a trade-in for a new car. Determine the amount of depreciation for each of the five years Anderson will own the car using the sum-of-the-years digits method.

3. Using the sum-of-the-years digits method, determine depreciation.

	Cost	Scrap Value	Estimated Life	Depreciation for the Third Year
1.	$4,000	$1,000	3 years	—
2.	6,200	200	5 years	—
3.	5,500	500	4 years	—
4.	268	25	8 years	—
5.	3,726	400	6 years	—
6.	8,638	750	7 years	—
7.	7,516	800	5 years	—
8.	3,677	700	10 years	—

d. DECLINING BALANCE

Another method for determining depreciation, which provides for high depreciation in the early years and less in later years, is the declining-balance method. The sum-of-the-years digits method produces fractions, decreasing in value, which are applied to the same base each year; the declining-balance method uses the same fraction or rate (in terms of a percent) for each year, but the base consistently decreases. Another difference is that salvage value is *not* taken into account in the annual depreciation computation in the declining-balance method. The method requires the base to be decreased by the amount of all prior depreciation before the rate is applied to determine the current year's depreciation.

At twice the straight-line rate (straight-line rate × 2) the formula for declining balance depreciation is:

$$(\text{Cost} - \text{Prior depreciation}) \times \text{Straight line rate} \times 2 = \text{Depreciation}$$

ILLUSTRATIVE PROBLEM. On January 1, 1964, Stead and Company purchased a delivery truck for $4,000. It is estimated that the truck will have a useful life of four years, and at the end of that time it will have a salvage value of $400. Find the depreciation per year using the declining-balance method at twice the straight-line rate.

SOLUTION: Because salvage is not taken into account in the annual depreciation computation, the base is the same as the cost ($4,000).

To determine the rate:

Find the straight-line rate

4 years = $\frac{1}{4}$ = 25% per year
Twice the straight-line rate = $\frac{1}{4}$ × 2 = $\frac{1}{2}$ or 25% × 2 = 50%
Twice the straight-line rate = $\frac{1}{2}$ = 50%

Multiply rate and base

$4000 × 50% = $2000 First-year depreciation

Base ($4000) less prior depreciation ($2000)
= $2000 × 50%
= $1000 Second-year depreciation

Base ($4000) less prior depreciation ($2000 + $1000)
= $1000 × 50%
= $500 Third-year depreciation

Base ($4000) less prior depreciation ($2000 + $1000 + $500)
= $500 × 50%
= $250

Because the actual amount to be depreciated ($3600) is cost minus scrap ($4000 − $400) that amount is the maximum depreciation allowed. Therefore, the maximum amount of depreciation allowed for the fourth year is $100. Remember that, though salvage is not taken into account in computing annual depreciation, it must be used to determine maximum depreciation.

Amount to be depreciated		$3600
First-year depreciation	$2000	
Second-year depreciation	1000	
Third-year depreciation	500	
Total depreciation for three years		3500
Depreciation allowable for fourth year		$ 100

11.4 SOLVE THESE PROBLEMS:

1. Using the declining-balance method at twice the straight-line rate, determine the yearly depreciation over the life of a truck that cost $4,000 if it had a residual value of $1,000 and an estimated life of five years.

2. Find the depreciation for the first three years on a printing press that cost $6,000, has an estimated life of five years, and a salvage value of $1,000. Use the declining-balance method at $1\frac{1}{2}$ times the straight-line rate.

3. Using the declining balance at twice the straight-line rate method, determine depreciation.

	Cost	*Estimated Life*	*Depreciation for the Third Year*
1.	$1,500	4 years	—
2.	3,600	5 years	—
3.	2,800	10 years	—
4.	4,680	6 years	—
5.	3,790	8 years	—
6.	5,285	20 years	—
7.	6,396	40 years	—
8.	3,795	8 years	—

11.5 REVIEW PROBLEM ON DEPRECIATION: The cost of a new piece of equipment was $5,200. Its useful life was estimated at five years during which time it was expected to be capable of producing 10,000 units. The scrap value was $200.

Determine the depreciation for each year of the life of the equipment using the following methods:

a. Straight line
b. Sum-of-the-years digits
c. Declining balance at twice the straight-line rate
d. Units of production. Production units for the first 5 years were 3,215; 2,763; 4,890; 1,268; 647.

2. MERCHANDISE INVENTORY VALUATION

In a mercantile concern, the term "merchandise inventory" may be defined as the amount of goods being offered for sale at a particular time. Because the value of the inventory is usually important in relation to the total worth of the business, the calculation of its value requires great care. To determine the number of units on hand, a physical inventory (actual count of the number of units on hand) is taken. By multiplying the units counted in the physical inventory by the cost per unit, the value of the inventory may be determined. However, the method of calculating the cost per unit requires explanation.

ILLUSTRATIVE PROBLEM. During one year, a furniture store made the following purchases of bridge chairs:

> February 10   100 chairs @ $10
> June 20   200 chairs @ $12
> September 14   60 chairs @ $ 8
> December 12   100 chairs @ $14

On December 31, the date on which the inventory was determined, there were 120 bridge chairs on hand. Because it is the policy of the store to stock all bridge chairs together, it was impossible to ascertain the specific purchase lots from which the 120 chairs came. Calculate the value of the 120 chairs in the merchandise inventory.

SOLUTION: To solve this problem we must first make certain assumptions concerning the merchandising policy of the store. If the store is operated in such fashion that the first merchandise to come in is the first to be sold, then the inventory at December 31 must be valued at the cost of the last purchases. If the reverse is true, and the last goods to come in are the first to be sold, then the merchandise remaining on hand as of December 31 must be valued at the cost of the earliest purchases. Another method of valuing the inventory would be to use an average cost per chair. We shall solve the above problem using all three of these methods.

a. FIFO

FIFO is an abbreviation for the first-in-first-out method of pricing inventories. It assumes that the first chairs purchased by the store were the first that were sold. That is, that the first chairs to be sold were those purchased on February 10, the next sold were those purchased on June 20, and so on. Therefore, the 120 chairs remaining on hand on December 31 consisted of the last chairs purchased and the inventory should be valued as follows:

100 chairs @ $14 = $1400
20 chairs @ $ 8 = $ 160
‾‾‾   ‾‾‾‾‾
120                 $1560 FIFO inventory value

b. LIFO

LIFO is an abbreviation for last-in-first-out. It is the opposite of the first-in-first-out method. That is, it assumes that the last chairs purchased were the first to be sold. Therefore, the first chairs sold were those bought December 12, the next sales were the chairs purchased on September 14, and so on. Using the LIFO method, the chairs left on hand on December 31 were from the earliest purchased, thus,

100 chairs @ $10 = $1000
20 chairs @ $12 =   240
‾‾‾   ‾‾‾‾‾
120                 $1240 LIFO inventory value

c. WEIGHTED AVERAGE

Another method of determining the value of the inventory is the weighted-average method. This method assigns the average of all of the costs of all of all of the purchases to the units remaining in the inventory. It is necessary to use a weighted average—one that takes the number of units of each purchase into account—because in a simple average, the purchase of one unit would have as important an effect as the purchases of 1,000 units. The 120 chairs in the above problem would be valued as follows under the weighted-average method:

1. Find the weighted-average cost per unit.

February 10   100 chairs @ $10 = $1000
June 20   200 chairs @ $12 = $2400
September 12   60 chairs @ $ 8 = $ 480
December 12   100 chairs @ $14 = $1400
               ‾‾‾   ‾‾‾‾‾
               460               $5280

$\dfrac{\$5280}{460}$ = $11.48 weighted average cost per unit

2. Multiply the weighted-average cost per unit by the number of units in the inventory.

Units in inventory on December 31   120
Weighted average cost per unit $11.48
Weighted average inventory value   ‾‾‾‾‾‾‾‾
                                     $1377.60

A comparison of the three inventory methods discloses the following:

FIFO inventory	$1560.00
LIFO inventory	1240.00
Weighted-average inventory	1377.60

Because such important business considerations as the amount of net profit and the amount of income taxes are directly related to the value of the inventory, it is easy to understand that the method of evaluating inventory is of great importance to businessmen.

11.6 SOLVE THESE PROBLEMS:

1. The following are the purchases of commodity A during the year.

1st purchase	40 units at $39.00
2nd purchase	60 units at $42.00
3rd purchase	32 units at $41.00
4th purchase	28 units at $44.00

A count of the units on hand at the end of the year revealed that 42 units were unsold. Determine the cost of the closing inventory by the following methods:
   a. LIFO
   b. FIFO
   c. Weighted average

2. At the beginning of the year the Jones Furniture Company had four units of model 211 on hand that cost $33 each. During the year they purchased 8 units at $34.50, and 4 units at $36. The closing inventory consisted of three units. Find the cost of the closing inventory using the following methods of determining inventory value.
   a. LIFO
   b. FIFO
   c. Weighted average

3. DIVISION OF PARTNERSHIP INCOME

The Uniform Partnership Act defines a partnership as "an association of two or more persons to carry on as co-owners of a business for profit." This form of business organization is extensively used, particularly for enterprises with relatively few owners, and those that do not require large amounts of capital. A partnership is generally formed by a contract between the partners that clearly defines the rights and responsibilities of each partner. This contract is called the articles of co-partnership and may be verbal. Included in the agreement is the specific method of dividing among the partners, the profits and the losses of the concern. This division of income and losses raises some interesting mathematical problems.

a. ABSENCE OF PARTNERSHIP AGREEMENT

Occasionally a partnership is formed that represents an agreement for the sharing of profits and losses. In such cases, profits and losses are *always* divided equally.

ILLUSTRATIVE PROBLEM. Allen and Blake form a partnership to operate a restaurant. The articles of co-partnership contain no provision for the division of profit and loss. Allen's investment is $10,000 and Jones' investment is $2,000. At the end of the first year's operation the partnership showed a profit of $20,000. How should the profit be divided between the partners?

SOLUTION: Because there was no provision in the co-partnership agreement concerning the division of profits and losses, the $20,000 profit must be divided equally—$10,000 each.

11.7   SOLVE THESE PROBLEMS:

1. The following is pertinent information taken from the articles of co-partnership of Collins and Dunn: Collins is to invest $40,000; Dunn is to invest $20,000. Collins is to work 40 hours per week; Dunn is to work 20 hours per week. How should the first year's profits of $12,000 be divided?

2. Edwards, Frank, and Gold formed a partnership. Being old friends, they felt that no formal partnership agreement was necessary. Because of the illness of Edwards, the partnership lost $3,000 during the year. How shall this loss be divided among the partners?

b. SERVICES OF THE PARTNERS

In recognition of the fact that some partners bring unique skills to the organization or will work more hours per week, articles of co-partnership frequently provide for a salary allowance for each partner.

ILLUSTRATIVE PROBLEM. Harris, Ingalls, and Jones are partners. It is agreed that Harris should receive a salary of $10,000, Ingalls $5,000, Jones $2,000, and that the balance of profits should be divided equally. During the first two years of operations the profits were $20,000 and $14,000 respectively. How much would each man receive during (a) the first year, and (b) the second year?

SOLUTION:

a. $20,000 profit

	Harris	*Ingalls*	*Jones*	*Total*
Salary allowance	$10,000	$5,000	$2,000	$17,000
Balance equally	1,000	1,000	1,000	3,000
Partner's share	$11,000	$6,000	$3,000	$20,000

Because the total profit is $20,000, and the total salary allowance is $17,000, there is a remaining balance of $3,000. The partnership agreement provides that this balance should be divided equally. Therefore, each partner receives his agreed salary allowance plus $1,000 ($\frac{1}{3}$ of the remainder of $3,000).

b. $14,000 profit

	Harris	*Ingalls*	*Jones*	*Total*
Salary allowance	$10,000	$5,000	$2,000	$17,000
Balance equally	− 1,000	− 1,000	− 1,000	− 3,000
Partner's share	$ 9,000	$4,000	$1,000	$14,000

In this case, the total profit of $14,000 was less than the salary allowance of $17,000, resulting in a loss of $3,000 ($17,000 − $14,000). In accordance with the agreement, this loss was divided equally—$1,000 each.

11.8 *SOLVE THESE PROBLEMS:*

1. It is agreed that the partners Kalmus, Long, and Miller are to receive salary allowances of $10,000, $7,000, and $3,000 annually and that all profits in excess of their salary allowance are to be divided equally. How will they share profits of (a) $20,000, (b) $26,000, (c) $15,500?

2. Nolan, Olson, and Parker are partners. Their agreement provides that Nolan is to receive a salary allowance of $9,000 plus $\frac{1}{6}$ of the balance of profits after all salary allowances are deducted; Olson and Parker are to receive salary allowances of $6,000 each and share equally in the remaining $\frac{5}{6}$ of the profits after all salary allowances. How much will each partner receive of profits of (a) $30,000, (b) $18,000?

3. The articles of co-partnership of Quinn, Ross, and Siegal provide for the following salary allowances: $12,000 for Quinn; $6,000 for Ross; and $3,000 for Siegal. It is further provided that profits and losses in excess of salary allowances be shared equally. Determine each partner's share in profits of (a) $30,000, (b) $15,000.

c. INVESTMENT OF THE PARTNERS

Frequently, partners invest different amounts in the company. To compensate for this differential, many partnership agreements provide for interest to be paid on the investment as part of the profit-and-loss sharing agreement. In this manner, the partner with the larger investment would be given a larger share of the profits.

ILLUSTRATIVE PROBLEM. Turner and Victor form a partnership. Turner is to invest $10,000 and Victor $5,000. The articles of co-partnership specify that profits and losses are to be divided as follows: each partner is to receive 10% of his original investment plus one-half of the remaining profit or loss. Determine each partner's share in (a) a profit of $10,000, (b) a loss of $6,000.

SOLUTION:
  a. Profit of $10,000

	Turner	*Victor*	*Total*
10% of original investment	$1000	$ 500	$ 1500
Balance equally	4250	4250	8500
Partner's share	$5250	$4750	$10,000

  b. Loss of $6,000

	Turner	*Victor*	*Total*
10% of original investment	$1000	$ 500	$1500
Balance equally	− 3750	− 3750	− 7500
Partner's share	− 2750	− 3250	− 6000

REMEMBER:
  1. The specification in the partnership agreement that the balance is to be shared equally refers to either a profit or a loss.
  2. The final figure in the total column must equal the amount of profit or loss to be divided.

11.9 SOLVE THIS PROBLEM: The partnership contract of Collins, Duane, Edwards, and Fisher provides for profit sharing as follows:

  a. 12 percent on original investment
  b. Balance of profits and losses equally

Collins invested $10,000; Duane $6,000; Edwards $30,000; and Fisher had no original investment. Determine (a) each partner's share in a profit of $16,000, (b) each partner's share in a loss of $12,000.

Another method of dividing partnership profits based on the investment of each partner is to find the ratio of each partner's capital to the total capital. By applying these ratios to the profit, each partner's share can be determined.

ILLUSTRATIVE PROBLEM. Jones, Kelly, and Levine formed a partnership with investments of $10,000, $20,000, and $30,000, respectively. It was decided that each partner's share of profits and losses would be based on the ratio of his investment to the total amount invested. Determine each partner's share of $12,000 of profits.

SOLUTION:

1. To determine the ratio of each partner's investment to the total investment:

Jones' investment	$10,000
Kelly's investment	20,000
Levine's investment	30,000
Total investment	$60,000

$$\text{Jones' ratio} = \frac{\$10,000}{\$60,000} = \frac{1}{6}$$

$$\text{Kelly's ratio} = \frac{\$20,000}{\$60,000} = \frac{2}{6} \quad \text{This can be stated as a ratio of } 1:2:3$$

$$\text{Levine's ratio} = \frac{\$30,000}{\$60,000} = \frac{3}{6}$$

2. To determine the partner's share of the profits:

$$\text{Jones' share} = \tfrac{1}{6} \times \$12,000 = \$2,000$$
$$\text{Kelly's share} = \tfrac{2}{6} \times \$12,000 = \$4,000$$
$$\text{Levine's share} = \tfrac{3}{6} \times \$12,000 = \$6,000$$

11.10 SOLVE THESE PROBLEMS:

1. Lewis, Morris, and Neun have invested $10,000, $4,000, and $6,000, respectively, in a partnership. It is decided that profits and losses will be divided in the ratio of their original investments. Determine each partner's share in (a) profit of $12,000, (b) loss of $6,000.

2. The partnership agreement of O'Brien, Parker, and Ross specifies that profits and losses are to be divided in the ratio of 2:2:1. Determine each partner's share in profits of $25,000.

11.11 *ADDITIONAL PARTNERSHIP PROBLEMS:*

1. The partnership of Gibson and Hubbs made $36,000 profit during their first year of operation and $12,000 during the second. The articles of co-partnership provide that Gibson is to receive a salary allowance of $6,000 and Hubbs $5,000. It is further provided that each man is to receive interest at 6% on his investment (Gibson invested $10,000 and Hubbs $12,000). All additional profits or losses are to be shared equally. Determine the partner's share of the profits during the first two years.

2. Iffert, James, and Kearns invested $20,000, $6,000, and 0, respectively, in a partnership with the understanding that they are to receive 7% on their original investment. It is further understood that Kearns is to receive a salary allowance of $600 per month, James $400 per month, and Iffert is to receive no salary allowance. All remaining profits or losses are to be shared equally. Determine each partner's share of profits of (a) $40,000, (b) $10,000.

3. Lomars, Morris, and Nolan, partners, decided to divide profits and losses as follows: Lomars, who invested $10,000, is to receive 7% on his investment; Morris, who invested $12,000, is to receive 8% on his investment; Nolan, who invested $8,000, is to receive 4% on his investment. In addition Lomars is to receive a salary allowance of $500 per month, Morris $300 per month, and Nolan $700 per month. All profits and losses in excess of the amounts on investment and salary allowance are to be divided in the ratio of the partners' original investment. Determine each partner's share in profits of (a) $36,000, (b) $15,000.

CHAPTER REVIEW

1. The cost of a piece of equipment was $12,000. It was estimated that the asset would have a useful life of four years, at which time it would be worth $2,000. It was further estimated that the equipment would be capable of 100,000 hours of use. Complete the following chart. (The machine was used for 12,000, 26,500, 32,500, and 46,000 hours during the four-year period.)

DEPRECIATION PER YEAR

	Straight Line	Sum-of-the-Years Digits	Declining Balance Twice Straight-Line Rate	Units of Production
Year 1				
Year 2				
Year 3				
Year 4				

2. The inventory records of the Ace Novelty Company reveal:

Style	Inventory Jan. 1	First Purchase	Second Purchase	Third Purchase	On Hand Dec. 31
112	14 at $250	12 at $250	10 at $259	14 at $265	10
375	2 at $182	9 at $194	4 at $194	4 at $200	8
416	14 at $125	12 at $125	10 at $124.50	14 at $132.50	9
827	4 at $84	8 at $87	12 at $89		7

Determine the inventory value at December 31 using the following methods:

    a. FIFO
    b. LIFO
    c. Weighted average

3. Arnold, Blake, and Carter, partners, began a business with investments of $14,000, $28,000, and $42,000, respectively. They agree to the following division of profits and losses:

    a. 10% interest allowance on original investment.
    b. Weekly salary allowance: Arnold $200, Blake $300, Carter $150.
    c. Balance divided equally.

Divide up profits of (a) $30,200, (b) $45,200.

12

individual income taxes and other accounting computations

1. INDIVIDUAL INCOME TAXES
   a. Gross taxable income
   b. Adjustments to income
   c. Adjusted gross income
   d. Deductions
   e. Standard deductions
   f. Personal exemptions
   g. Calculating the tax
   h. Paying the tax

2. DISCOUNTING NOTES
   a. Promissory notes
   b. Interest on notes
   c. Days in discount period
   d. Maturity value
   e. Discounting notes receivable

3. BUSINESS INSURANCE
   a. Finding the premium
   b. Cancellation and short-term rates
   c. Co-Insurance

1. INDIVIDUAL
INCOME TAXES

Each year some 75 million Americans pay income taxes. The funds provided in this manner support the services we expect from our government. Although a considerable portion of federal income tax receipts are paid by corporations, our discussion will be confined to individual income taxes. However, the laws governing such payments are usually very similar to those set forth by federal regulation. Our discussion then, although limited to federal tax laws, may be applicable to nonfederal income tax regulations as well.

Although our tax laws are very complicated and subject to constant revision, certain basic definitions and calculations are relatively stable. For example, the formula for determining taxable income has remained unchanged for many years.

Gross taxable income		$10,000
Less adjustments to income		1,000
Adjusted gross income		9,000
Less deductions	$1,200	
(or Standard deduction)		
Personal exemption	1,500	
		2,700
Taxable income		$ 6,300

The amount of income tax is calculated by multiplying the taxable income by a particular tax rate.

a. GROSS TAXABLE INCOME

Tax regulations provide that certain types of income are exempt from income taxes. The starting point for determining the amount of income taxes owed is the separation of taxable and nontaxable income. Taxable income includes wages, tips, interest income, dividends, rents, and income from many other sources. Among the nontaxable types of income that are not included in tax calculations are social security payments, gifts, life insurance proceeds, certain tax-free interest, and inheritances.

239

b. ADJUSTMENTS TO INCOME

Having computed the gross taxable income, certain deductions may be made in arriving at the adjusted gross income. These adjustments include sick pay, certain moving expenses, certain employees' travel and customer entertainment expenses, and employees' educational expenses under certain conditions.

c. ADJUSTED GROSS INCOME

As previously indicated, gross taxable income less adjustments to income equals adjusted gross income. This is an important item because certain decisions concerning the manner in which the tax return will be filed are dependent upon the amount of adjusted gross income.

ILLUSTRATIVE PROBLEM. Frank Mason, a salesman, had the following income and expenses: wages, $15,000; includable dividend income, $1,000; taxable interest, $200; tax-free interest, $100; allowable moving expenses, $1,500; and allowable traveling and entertaining expense, $800. Calculate his adjusted gross income.

SOLUTION:

Gross taxable income		
Wages	$15,000	
Includable dividends	1,000	
Taxable interest	200	
		$16,200
Adjustments to income		
Moving expenses	$ 1,500	
Traveling and		
entertaining expenses	800	2,300
Adjusted gross income		$13,900

d. DEDUCTIONS

There are two types of deductions from adjusted gross income: personal deductions and exemptions. Personal deductions include medical and dental expenses, certain tax payments, contributions of cash and property, interest expense, and certain allowable miscellaneous deductions.

Medical and Dental Expenses. Medical and dental expenses that are not reimbursed are deductible, subject to certain limitations. The deduction is calculated in the following manner: one-half the amount paid for medical insurance is calculated (this amount may not exceed $150). The cost of medicines and drugs is deductible to the extent that they exceed 1% of adjusted gross income. To the medicines and drug deduction (exceeding 1% of adjusted gross income) add the costs of all medical expenses such as payments to physicians, dentists, hospitals, nurses, and the remainder of the medical insurance payments. This total is reduced by 3% of adjusted gross income. The medical expense deduction is the total of the amount calculated plus the one-half of the medical insurance premiums deducted at the beginning of the computation.

ILLUSTRATIVE PROBLEM. Tom Watson had an adjusted gross income of $10,000. Calculate his medical expense deduction from the following information: health insurance, $400; medicines and drugs, $150; other medical expenses, $800.

SOLUTION:

Medical insurance $400 \times \frac{1}{2}$	150 (Maximum)
Medicines and drugs	150
Less 1% of adjusted gross income $10,000	100
Deductible	50
Other medical expenses $800 + 250$	
(Balance of medical insurance)	1050
Total	1100
Less 3% of adjusted gross income $10,000	300
Balance	800
Add: Medical insurance from line 1	150
Allowable deduction	950

Taxes. Not all taxes paid are deductible. Those that are include state and local income taxes, real estate taxes, sales taxes, and gasoline taxes.

Contributions. Contributions to qualified organizations are deductible to the total of up to 50% of adjusted gross income. Qualified organizations include churches, educational institutions, and charitable organizations.

Interest Expense. Interest paid on loans and installment purchases are among the most common types of interest that are deductible from adjusted gross income.

Miscellaneous and Other Deductions. Among the other types of personal deductions allowable for income tax purposes are child and dependent care expenses, casualty or theft losses, union dues, and the cost and maintenance of uniforms.

e. STANDARD DEDUCTION

In the area of personal deductions, the taxpayer is given a choice. He may either list all the deductions discussed above or elect the alternative of taking a standard deduction. The standard deduction is 15% of adjusted gross income but may not exceed $2,000. The choice is made by adding up all the personal deductions, comparing the total with the standard deduction, and choosing the larger amount.

ILLUSTRATIVE PROBLEM. Sam Thomas, whose adjusted gross income is $18,000, has the following personal deductions: contributions, $900; interest expense, $600; allowable medical and dental expenses, $800; and union dues, $100. What amount of personal deductions should he take on his tax return?

SOLUTION:

$$\$900 + \$600 + \$800 + \$100 = \$2,400$$
$$\text{Standard deduction } \$18,000 \times 15\% = \$2,000 \text{ (Maximum)}$$

He should elect to itemize his deductions.

f. PERSONAL EXEMPTIONS

Each taxpayer is allowed one exemption for himself plus another if he or his wife is over 65 years of age or blind. Thus, a husband and wife filing a joint return may claim six exemptions if both are blind and over 65. (A joint return is one in which husband and wife combine their income and deductions and file a single return.) A taxpayer may deduct $750 for each exemption.

g. CALCULATING THE TAX

After calculating the taxable income by deducting the personal deductions (or standard deduction) and personal exemptions from the adjusted gross income, a tax table is required to calculate the amount of tax due. The table illustrated on page 243 is the one used by single taxpayers. (There are other tables for other classes of taxpayers.)

Other tables are provided for persons with incomes under $10,000 who elect to use a standard deduction. No calculation is required beyond adjusted gross income for those using these tables. The tables are calculated with the number of personal exemptions and the standard deduction taken into account.

**1972 TAX RATE SCHEDULES
SCHEDULE X—SINGLE TAXPAYERS NOT
QUALIFYING FOR RATES IN SCHEDULE
Y OR Z.**

*IF THE AMOUNT ON
FORM 1040,
LINE 55, IS:*

*ENTER ON
FORM 1040,
LINE 18:*

Not over $500
14% of the amount on line 55.

Over—	*But not over—*		*of excess over—*
$500	$1,000	$70+15%	$500
$1,000	$1,500	$145+16%	$1,000
$1,500	$2,000	$225+17%	$1,500
$2,000	$4,000	$310+19%	$2,000
$4,000	$6,000	$690+21%	$4,000
$6,000	$8,000	$1,110+24%	$6,000
$8,000	$10,000	$1,590+25%	$8,000
$10,000	$12,000	$2,090+27%	$10,000
$12,000	$14,000	$2,630+29%	$12,000
$14,000	$16,000	$3,210+31%	$14,000
$16,000	$18,000	$3,830+34%	$16,000
$18,000	$20,000	$4,510+36%	$18,000
$20,000	$22,000	$5,230+38%	$20,000
$22,000	$26,000	$5,990+40%	$22,000
$26,000	$32,000	$7,590+45%	$26,000
$32,000	$38,000	$10,290+50%	$32,000
$38,000	$44,000	$13,290+55%	$38,000
$44,000	$50,000	$16,590+60%	$44,000
$50,000	$60,000	$20,190+62%	$50,000
$60,000	$70,000	$26,390+64%	$60,000
$70,000	$80,000	$32,790+66%	$70,000
$80,000	$90,000	$39,390+68%	$80,000
$90,000	$100,000	$46,190+69%	$90,000
$100,000	—	$53,090+70%	$100,000

The table is used as follows:

1. Using the taxable income, find the appropriate columns on the left. A taxable income of $11,000 would fit on the line headed over $10,000 but not over $12,000.

2. The tax on $10,000 equals $2,090. Add to this 27% of the amount in excess over $10,000.

Tax on $10,000 = $2,090

Add:

$11,000 − $10,000
= $1,000 × 27% = <u>270</u>
Tax due <u>$2,360</u>

h. PAYING THE TAX

Ours is a pay-as-you-go tax system. In other words, the current year's taxes are paid by withholding deductions from employees' salaries and estimated taxes from self-employed individuals. After the tax has been calculated by using the appropriate table, the amount already paid in by withholding or estimated tax is compared with it. If tax is still due, a check must accompany the tax return. In case of overpayment, a refund is due.

12.1 SOLVE THESE PROBLEMS:

1. Calculate the taxable income.

Adjustments to income $ 1,000
Itemized deduction   1,500
Personal exemptions   1,500
Gross taxable income   11,000

2. Calculate the adjusted gross income.

Salaries $20,000
Interest income $4,000
Allowable moving expenses $1,000
Taxable dividends $2,000
Entertaining customers $4,000
Sick pay $3,000

3. Calculate the medical and dental deduction.

Health insurance $400   Adjusted gross income $10,000
Paid to dentist $200   Paid to physicians $600
Medicines and drugs $300   Hospital bills $200

4. Compute the tax for single taxpayers whose taxable incomes are: $8,000; $13,000; $28,000.

5. Tom Burke is single, over 65 years of age, and the sole support of his aged mother. He is a salesman whose salary is $16,000. His other income consists of taxable interest of $4,000 and nontaxable interest of $2,000. His expenses are as follows: traveling related to business, $1,000; contributions, $200; health insurance, $200; medicines and drugs, $200; other medical expenses, $1,400; allowable taxes, $800. Using the tax table on page 243, calculate Tom's income tax.

2. DISCOUNTING NOTES

a. PROMISSORY NOTES

Certain loans are supported by written documents called promissory notes. These are credit instruments that verify the information in a loan agreement such as the amount of the debt, the due date, and so forth. Many such notes are negotiable (transferable from one owner to another). To be negotiable, a promissory note must satisfy certain conditions set forth by the Uniform Commercial Code. These are:

1. The note must be in writing.

2. The note must contain an unconditional promise to pay a specific sum of money on demand, or at a definite time.

3. The note must be signed by the maker (borrower) and the amount must be payable to a specific person or bearer.

Figure 12-1
An Example of a Promissory Note

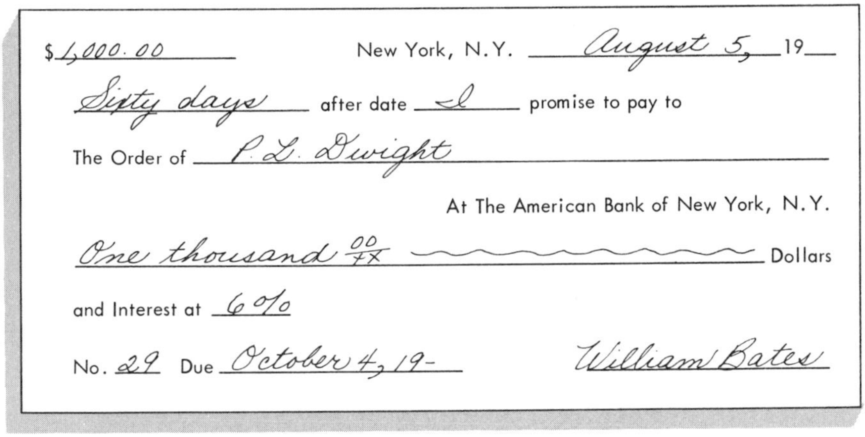

$1,000.00   New York, N.Y. _____ *August 5,* 19___

Sixty days _____ after date __*I*__ promise to pay to

The Order of __*P. L. Dwight*_____

At The American Bank of New York, N.Y.

One thousand 00/xx ~~~~~~~~~~~~~ Dollars

and Interest at __*6 %*__

No. *29* Due *October 4, 19-*   *William Bates*

Certain definitions concerning notes must be understood.

1. The maker (borrower) of the note is William Bates. He is also referred to as the payer.
2. The payee (person to be paid) is P. L. Dwight.
3. The face or principal of the note is $1,000.00.
4. The interest rate is 6%.

b. INTEREST ON NOTES

To calculate the interest due on a note, the interest formula:

$$\text{Principal} \times \text{Rate} \times \text{Time} = \text{Interest}$$

is used. Because of its simplicity, the 6%, 60-day method (see Chapter 4) is generally used to compute interest on notes. The interest on the above note is $10.

$$\begin{array}{ccccc} \text{Principal} & \times & \text{Rate} & \times & \text{Time} & = & \text{Interest} \\ \$1,000 & \times & 6\% & \times & 60 \text{ days} & = & \$10 \end{array}$$

c. DAYS IN THE INTEREST PERIOD

In some instances, the number of days to be used in computing the interest may not be specifically stated. In such cases, it is necessary to determine the number of days before the interest formula can be used.

ILLUSTRATIVE PROBLEM. A note that is due on July 20 was drawn on May 17. How many days will be used in calculating the interest?

SOLUTION:

Number of days in May	31
Date of the note	17
Number of interest days in May	14
Interest days in June	30
Interest days in July to due date	20
Number of interest days in loan	64

When the time of a note is given in months, the exact number of days is disregarded; the due day is the day of issue in the month due. Thus a 3-month note issued January 10 is due April 10.

12.2 SOLVE THESE PROBLEMS:

1. Determine the number of days between the following dates:

From	To	Number of Days
1. January 10	March 18	—
2. April 23	June 25	—
3. June 18	August 4	—
4. September 20	November 12	—
5. November 16	January 2	—
6. December 12	February 14	—

2. Determine the dates at which the following notes mature (become due).

Date of Issue	Number of Days	Due Date
1. January 15	60	—
2. March 6	90	—
3. May 12	1 month	—
4. June 4	70	—
5. July 27	2 months	—
6. September 9	90	—
7. November 15	60	—
8. December 8	3 months	—

d. MATURITY VALUE

The maturity value of a note is the amount that must be paid when a note falls due. In the case of a non-interest-bearing note, the maturity value will be equal to the principal. For an interest-bearing note, the maturity value is the principal plus the interest.

ILLUSTRATIVE PROBLEM. Find the maturity value of a 60-day note for $350 bearing interest at 6%.

SOLUTION: To find the interest:

$$\text{Principal} \times \text{Rate} \times \text{Time} = \text{Interest}$$
$$\$350 \times 6\% \times 60 \text{ days} = \$3.50$$

To find the maturity value:

$$\text{Principal} + \text{Interest} = \text{Maturity value}$$
$$\$350 + \$3.50 = \$353.50$$

12.3 SOLVE THESE PROBLEMS: Find the maturity value of the following notes.

1. Face of note—$1,500
   Time—60 days
   Interest—6%
2. Face of note—$1,462
   Time—90 days
   Interest—4%
3. Face of note—$1,000
   Date of issue—May 3
   Due date—July 2
   Interest—6%
4. Face of note—$1,260
   Date of issue—May 6
   Due date—June 5
   Interest—$5\frac{1}{2}$%
5. Face of note—$1,512
   Time—3 months
   Interest—5%
6. Face of note—$1,738
   Time—4 months
   Interest—2%

e. DISCOUNTING NOTES RECEIVABLE

A note receivable is a promissory note that is held by the payee. It is evidence that a debt is owed to him. Many such notes are negotiable; that is, their ownership may be transferred by the payee to another person. This is very important in business because it permits a lender to transfer a note in his possession to a third party, usually a bank; the payee receives the amount due on the note immediately, less a service charge called a discount. Many businesses need immediate cash and are willing to discount a note (pay the charge) so that they may have use of the money before the due date of the note. Discounting notes receivable is actually deducting interest in advance.

The calculations involved in discounting notes receivable require nothing more than the application of the simple interest formula of *Principal ✕ Rate ✕ Time = Interest*. However, because discount is interest deducted in advance, the net proceeds (amount of money received) is found by deducting the interest from the maturity value of the note. In essence, the bank is lending money to the holder of the note and deducting the interest on the loan in advance.

There are four simple steps involved in the discounting of notes receivable:

1. Find the maturity value.

   As has been stated, the bank lends the amount of money that it will receive when the note becomes due. This is the maturity value of the note, and it must be calculated to determine the amount of money the bank is lending. Then the maturity value of the note will be used as the principal for the formula Principal ✕ Rate ✕ Time = Interest.

2. Find the number of days in the discount period.

   Having found in the maturity value, the amount of the bank loan, it is necessary to know the number of days for which the bank is making the loan. This is simply a matter of counting the days between the date that the note is brought to the bank and the due date (the date on which the bank will be paid).

3. Find the amount of the discount.

   Having determined the amount of bank's loan (maturity value) and the time the loan has left to run (discount period), the determination of the discount (interest) requires the application of the simple interest formula Principal ✕ Rate ✕ Time = Interest.

4. Find the net proceeds.

   The net proceeds is the maturity value determined in Step 1 less the discount determined in Step 3.

ILLUSTRATIVE PROBLEM. On April 1, Blair and Company received an $800, 90-day, 6% note from a customer. On May 1, the note was discounted at the American Bank at a discount rate of 6%. How much cash did Blair and Company receive?

SOLUTION:

1. To find the maturity value

$$\text{Principal} \times \text{Rate} \times \text{Time} = \text{Interest}$$
$$\$800 \times 6\% \times 90 \text{ days} = \$12$$

Maturity Value = Principal + Interest
$812   = $800   + $12

2. To find the days in the discount period

Due date = 90 days after April 1

$$
\begin{array}{ll}
\text{April} & 30 \\
& -\ 1 \\ \hline
& 29 \\
\text{May} & 31 \\
\text{June} & 30 \quad \text{Due date} \\ \hline
& 90
\end{array}
$$

The note will be due, and the bank paid, on June 30. Because it loaned the money on May 1, the discount period (days of bank loan) is the number of days between May 1 and June 30.

$$
\begin{array}{ll}
\text{May} & 31 \\
& -\ 1 \\ \hline
& 30 \\
\text{June} & 30 \\ \hline
& 60 \quad \text{Days in discount period}
\end{array}
$$

3. To find the amount of the discount

Principal × Rate × Time = Interest (discount)
$812   × 6% × 60 days = $8.12

4. To find the net proceeds

Maturity value − Discount = Net proceeds
$812   − $8.12   = $803.88

12.4 *SOLVE THESE PROBLEMS:*

1. Each of the following non-interest-bearing notes were discounted at the bank. For each note, find (a) maturity value, (b) days in the discount period, (c) amount of bank discount, (d) net proceeds:

Date of Note	Face	Time	Rate of Discount	Date of Discount
January 15	$1000	90 days	6%	February 14
April 6	400	60 days	4%	April 26
June 12	800	45 days	5%	July 12
July 23	900	72 days	$6\frac{1}{2}$%	August 16

2. Blake, Inc., holds a 6%, 60-day note with a face value of $800 which it received on May 20. On June 19 the note was discounted at the bank at the rate of 6%. Find the maturity value, the days in the discount period, the amount of the discount, and the net proceeds.

3. The payee of a $2,000, 90-day, 6% note discounted the note at his bank at the discount rate of 7%. The note was dated April 5 and the discount date was June 4. What was the amount of the bank's discount? How much did the payee receive?

4. The following notes were discounted at a bank at the discount rate of 7%:

Date	Face	Term	Interest Rate	Date of Discount
May 3	$1000	60 days	6%	May 9
May 21	2000	30 days	7%	June 3
November 10	480	90 days	5%	December 2
April 20	1800	30 days	5%	May 10

Determine the following for each note:
a. maturity value
b. discount period
c. discount
d. net proceeds.

3. BUSINESS INSURANCE

Insurance is a means by which businesses protect themselves against certain types of unusual financial loss. The payment for this protection is called the premium. From the total premiums paid by many concerns, a large pool of money is set aside from which individual losses are paid out. In essence, insurance is a method of sharing unusual losses among many businesses. Thus all covered firms pay premiums for which they are protected against risks. Those concerns that actually sustain losses are reimbursed for such losses. Fire losses are typical of the types of risks that businesses insure themselves against.

The formula for determining the annual premium is:

Face of the policy × Rate = Annual premium

a. FINDING THE PREMIUM

To determine the premium for insuring an asset against possible fire loss, rates are established on an annual basis for specific types of possible losses. These rates are then multiplied by the amount to be insured. All insurance premiums are paid in advance of the period covered.

ILLUSTRATIVE PROBLEM. The rate for insuring a brick building against fire for one year is $3.64 per thousand. Determine the annual premium for a building to be insured for $12,500.

SOLUTION:

$12,500 = 12.5$ thousands

$12.5 \times \$3.64 = \$45.50$ annual premium

12.5 SOLVE THESE PROBLEMS:
1. Determine the annual premium on a building to be insured for $18,000 if the rate is quoted at $.594 per hundred.
2. The rate per hundred on a particular building is $.690. Determine the annual premium on insurance coverage of $13,500.
3. The annual premium of $126.40 was paid on a building that is rated at $.632 per hundred. What was the amount of the insurance coverage?
4. Determine the amount of insurance carried if the rate is $7.53 per thousand and the annual premium is $3,765.
5. If a $10,000 policy has an annual premium of $13.56 per hundred, what is the rate per hundred?

As an incentive to encourage businesses to insure themselves for more than one year at a time, insurance companies offer discounts for coverage in excess of one year. The following discounts are available:

2-year policies at $1.85 \times$ Annual premium
3-year policies at $2.7 \ \ \times$ Annual premium
4-year policies at $3.55 \times$ Annual premium
5-year policies at $4.4 \ \ \times$ Annual premium

In practice, most insurance is written for either one or three years.

ILLUSTRATIVE PROBLEM. The fire insurance rate on a particular building is $8.15 per thousand. The building is to be insured for $10,000. Calculate the premium if the building is to be insured for (a) 1 year, (b) 2 years, (c) 3 years, (d) 4 years, (e) 5 years.

SOLUTION:

$10,000 = 10$ thousands

$10 \times \$8.15 = \$81.50$ Annual premium

81.50 Annual premium $\times 1.85 = \$150.78$ Premium for 2-year policy
81.50 Annual premium $\times 2.7 \ = \$220.05$ Premium for 3-year policy
81.50 Annual premium $\times 3.55 = \$289.33$ Premium for 4-year policy
81.50 Annual premium $\times 4.4 \ = \$358.60$ Premium for 5-year policy

12.6 SOLVE THESE PROBLEMS:
1. If the annual premium on a fire insurance policy is $35.36, what would be the cost of a 2-year policy?

2. Determine the cost of a 5-year policy if the 1-year premium is $58.44.

3. The 2-year premium on a building is $42.55. Determine the annual premium.

4. Blake's premium is $92.40 for five years. What is the annual premium?

5. A building to be insured for $13,500 has an annual rate of $.878 per hundred. Determine the cost if the insured elects to purchase a 4-year contract.

6. What is the 5-year premium on a building insured for $17,000 rated at $.638 per hundred?

b. CANCELLATION AND SHORT-TERM POLICIES

1. Cancellation by the Insured. Insurance policies are frequently cancelled by the insured. This may be the result of the sale of the asset, its obsolescence, or other reasons. In such cases, because premiums are paid in advance, it becomes necessary to calculate the refund due for the unexpired portion of the premium.

The refund may be determined by using the table illustrated on the following page. The table may also be used for policies that are to be in force for less than one year.

The table is used as follows:

1. The exact number of days the policy has been in effect must be calculated.

2. The number of days in force must be found on the leftmost column of the table.

3. Having found the applicable leftmost column, move horizontally to the column in which the proper term of the policy is indicated (1 year, 2 years, 3 years, 4 years, 5 years).

4. The number indicated at the junction of the number of days in force and the term of the policy is the percentage of the premium earned by the insurance company.

5. Multiplying the percent earned by the insurance company and the amount of premium paid yields the dollar amount of the premium earned by the insurance company.

6. To determine the amount of the refund, deduct the amount earned by the insurance company from the total premium.

ILLUSTRATIVE PROBLEM. The Arnold Realty Corporation insured an apartment house for three years for a premium of $4,312. The term of the policy was from January 6, 1968 (inception) to January 6, 1971 (expiration). On

FIRE INSURANCE

CANCELLATION OR SHORT RATE TABLE SHOWING PERCENT OF PREMIUM EARNED

Policy in Force Days	1 Yr.	2 Yrs. Percent of Premium Earned	3 Yrs.	Policy in Force Days	1 Yr.	2 Yrs. Percent of Premium Earned	3 Yrs.
1	5	2.7	1.9	161–164	55	29.7	20.4
2	6	3.2	2.2	165–167	56	30.3	20.7
3–4	7	3.8	2.6	168–171	57	30.8	21.1
5–6	8	4.3	3.	172–175	58	31.4	21.5
7–8	9	4.9	3.3	176–178	59	31.9	21.9
9–10	10	5.4	3.7	179–182	60	32.4	22.2
11–12	11	5.9	4.1	183–187	61	33.	22.6
13–14	12	6.5	4.4	188–191	62	33.5	23.
15–16	13	7.0	4.8	192–196	63	34.1	23.3
17–18	14	7.6	5.2	197–200	64	34.6	23.7
19–20	15	8.1	5.6	201–205	65	35.1	24.1
21–22	16	8.6	5.9	206–209	66	35.7	24.4
23–25	17	9.2	6.3	210–214	67	36.2	24.8
26–29	18	9.7	6.7	215–218	68	36.8	25.2
30–32	19	10.3	7.	219–223	69	37.3	25.6
33–36	20	10.8	7.4	224–228	70	37.8	25.9
37–40	21	11.4	7.8	229–232	71	38.4	26.3
41–43	22	11.9	8.1	233–237	72	38.9	26.7
44–47	23	12.4	8.5	238–241	73	39.5	27.
48–51	24	13.	8.9	242–246	74	40.	27.4
52–54	25	13.5	9.3	247–250	75	40.5	27.8
55–58	26	14.1	9.6	251–255	76	41.1	28.1
59–62	27	14.6	10.	256–260	77	41.6	28.5
63–65	28	15.1	10.4	261–264	78	42.2	28.9
66–69	29	15.7	10.7	265–269	79	42.7	29.3
70–73	30	16.2	11.1	270–273	80	43.2	29.6
74–76	31	16.8	11.5	274–278	81	43.8	30.
77–80	32	17.3	11.9	279–282	82	44.3	30.4
81–83	33	17.8	12.2	283–287	83	44.9	30.7
84–87	34	18.4	12.6	288–291	84	45.4	31.1
88–91	35	18.9	13.	292–296	85	45.9	31.5
92–94	36	19.5	13.3	297–301	86	46.5	31.9
95–98	37	20.	13.7	302–305	87	47.	32.2
99–102	38	20.5	14.1	306–310	88	47.6	32.6
103–105	39	21.1	14.4	311–314	89	48.1	33.
106–109	40	21.6	14.8	315–319	90	48.6	33.3
110–113	41	22.2	15.2	320–323	91	49.2	33.7
114–116	42	22.7	15.6	324–328	92	49.7	34.1
117–120	43	23.2	15.9	329–332	93	50.3	34.4
121–124	44	23.8	16.3	333–337	94	50.8	34.8
125–127	45	24.3	16.7	338–342	95	51.4	35.2
128–131	46	24.9	17.	343–346	96	51.9	35.6
132–135	47	25.4	17.4	347–351	97	52.4	35.9
136–138	48	25.9	17.8	352–355	98	53.	36.3
139–142	49	26.5	18.1	356–360	99	53.5	36.7
143–146	50	27.	18.5	361–365	100	54.1	37.
147–149	51	27.6	18.9				
150–153	52	28.1	19.3				
154–156	53	28.6	19.6				
157–160	54	29.2	20.				

April 12, 1968 the building was sold and Arnold canceled the policy. Determine the amount of refund due.

SOLUTION:

    1. To determine the exact number of days the policy was in force:

January	31
	− 6
Days in January	25
Days in February	28
Days in March	31
Days in April	12
	96 days in force

    2. Using the chart, it is found that on a 3-year policy in force for 96 days the insurance company earns 13.7 percent of the premium.

    3. To determine the dollar amount of the premium earned by the insurance company:

(Total Premium) $4,312
    × (percent earned by insurance company) 13.7%
    = (Dollar amount of premium earned by the insurance company) $590.74

    4. To determine the amount of the refund:

Total amount of the premium	$4312.00
Less: Amount earned by insurance company	590.74
Refund (Amount of premium *not* earned by insurance company)	$3721.26

12.7 SOLVE THESE PROBLEMS:

    1. On January 10, Robinson canceled a 1-year fire insurance policy, the premium for which was $120. If the policy was dated November 5, find (a) the amount earned by the insurance company, (b) the refund due Robinson.

    2. The premium for a 3-year fire insurance policy dated March 3 was $365. How much will the insurance company earn if the policy is canceled by the customer on June 10 of the same year? What will the amount of the refund be?

    3. On May 1, Riley purchased $10,000 worth of fire insurance on his building for one year. The premium was based on a rate of $7.75 per thousand. On September 10 the building was sold and the policy was canceled. Determine (a) the amount of the refund, (b) the portion of the premium earned by the insurance company.

4. For one insurance policy the cost per thousand is $22.35; the amount to be insured is $12,500; the term is three years commencing March 5; and the cancelation date is September 9 of the same year. Determine the amount of the refund.

5. Calculate the return premium from the following information:

Face of the policy	$14,500
Term of the policy	3 years
Date of the policy	September 9, 1967
Cancelation date	January 10, 1968
Premium rate per thousand	$16.85

2. Cancelation by the Insurance Company. Fire insurance policies are written in such a fashion that either the insured or the insurance company has the right to cancel. In the event the insurance company decides to cancel, most state laws provide that the company must pro-rate the premium, keeping the earned portion and refunding the unused portion to the insured. Thus the insurance company is entitled to the part of the premium applicable to the days the policy was in force, and the insured is refunded the balance.

The formula is:

$$\frac{\text{Number of days policy was in force}}{\text{Total number of days in term of the policy}} \times \text{Premium}$$

$$= \text{Insurance company's share}$$

$$\text{Total premium} - \text{Insurance company's share} = \text{Amount of refund}$$

ILLUSTRATIVE PROBLEM. A 3-year fire insurance policy bearing the premium of $280 was dated March 15. Determine (a) the insurance company's share of the premium if the policy was canceled by the insurance company on March 30 of the second year; (b) the amount of the refund.

SOLUTION:

Number of days the policy was in force $= 365 + 15$

$= 380$ Insurance company's share

Total number of days in the insurance term $= 3 \times 365$

$\frac{380}{1095} \times \$280 = \$97.16$ Insurance company's share

$\$280 - \$97.16 = \$182.84$ Amount of refund

12.8 *SOLVE THESE PROBLEMS:*

1. Determine the insurance company's earned premium and the amount of the return premium on a 1-year premium of $270 that was canceled by the company after 146 days.

2. A 2-year policy with a premium of $365 dated June 15 was canceled

on November 10 of the same year. Calculate the amount of the refund if the cancelation was at the insurance company's option.

3. A 3-year policy was canceled by the insurance company after 2 years and 141 days. If the premium was $730, calculate the amount of the refund.

4. A 1-year policy with a premium of $126 was cancelled after 45 days. Determine the refund if (a) the company cancelled, (b) the insured cancelled.

5. A building was rated at $6.53 per thousand for one year. The amount to be insured was $20,000, and the owner elected to reduce the cost by insuring for a term of 3 years. After 1 year and 70 days, the policy was cancelled by the insurance company. How much of the premium did the insurance company earn? How much was the refund?

3. Short-Term Rates. The cancelation or short-rate table (page 253) is also used to determine premiums for policies whose term is less than one year.

ILLUSTRATIVE PROBLEM. On November 1, the Blair Stationery Store decided to take out a 60-day fire insurance policy on its inventory. Because most of the goods on hand will be sold before Christmas, it is not necessary to carry the insurance beyond January 1. The amount of the inventory is $10,000 and the rate is $20.70 per thousand. Determine the cost of the policy.

SOLUTION:

1. To determine the annual premium

$10,000 = 10 thousands × $20.70 = $207.00

2. From the short-rate table it is determined that on a 1-year premium that runs for 60 days the insurance company earns 27 percent of the annual premium.

$207.00 × 27% = $55.89 Cost of 60-day policy

12.9 SOLVE THESE PROBLEMS:

1. Determine the premium on a 45-day policy if the amount to be insured is $8,000 and the rate is $7.75 per thousand.

2. If the term of the policy is from January 1 to but not including July 16, and the annual premium is $648, determine the short-rate premium.

3. Mr. Jameson insures the contents of his store for $70,000 for the period from August 1 to November 15. The annual rate is $10.26 per thousand. Determine the short-rate premium.

c. CO-INSURANCE

Most fire insurance policies contain a co-insurance clause. The effect of the clause is to limit the possible loss to the insurance company in cases where the insured carries less than a stipulated percentage (usually 80%) of the value of the property. For example, if the property is valued at $5,000 at the time of loss and there is an 80% co-insurance clause in the policy, the amount of the insurance to be carried should be $5,000 \times 80\% = \$4,000$. If the face of the policy is only $3,000, the insurance company will only bear $\frac{3}{4}(\$3,000/\$4,000)$ of the loss. Of course, in no case will the insurance company be liable for more than the face of the policy. In effect, the insured becomes a co-insurer in that, under certain conditions, he will share in the loss.

The formula for 80% co-insurance is:

$$\text{Insurance company's share of loss} = \text{Loss} \times \frac{\text{Amount of policy}}{80\% \text{ of value}}$$

ILLUSTRATIVE PROBLEM. A building worth $20,000 was insured for $16,000 under a policy containing an 80% co-insurance clause. A fire caused damages of $12,000. What was the insurance company's liability?

SOLUTION:

$$\text{Insurance company's liability} = \text{Loss} \times \frac{\text{Amount of policy}}{80\% \text{ of value}}$$

$$= \$12,000 \times \frac{\$16,000}{80\% \text{ of } \$20,000}$$

$$= \$12,000 \times \frac{\$16,000}{\$16,000}$$

$$= \$12,000 \times 1$$

$$= \$12,000$$

In this case, the amount of the insurance carried was equal to the co-insurance requirements, and the insurance company was responsible for the entire loss.

ILLUSTRATIVE PROBLEM. A building worth $20,000 was insured for $12,000 under a policy containing an 80% co-insurance clause. A fire caused damages of $12,000. What was the insurance company's liability?

SOLUTION:

$$\text{Insurance company's liability} = \text{Loss} \times \frac{\text{Amount of policy}}{80\% \text{ of value}}$$

$$= \$12,000 \times \frac{12,000}{16,000}$$

$$= \$12,000 \times \frac{3}{4}$$

$$= \$9,000$$

In this case, the amount of insurance carried was only $\frac{3}{4} \left(\frac{12,000}{16,000} \right)$ of the co-insurance requirements, and the insurance company was responsible for only $\frac{3}{4}$ of the loss, the insured becoming a co-insurer for the balance of the loss.

ILLUSTRATIVE PROBLEM. A building worth $20,000 was insured for $16,000 under a policy containing an 80% co-insurance clause. The building was completely destroyed by fire. What was the insurance company's liability?

SOLUTION:

$$\text{Insurance company's liability} = \text{Loss} \times \frac{\text{Amount of policy}}{80\% \text{ of value}}$$

$$= \$20,000 \times \frac{16,000}{16,000}$$

$$= \$20,000$$

However, the insurance company's loss can never exceed the face of the policy. Therefore, the answer is $16,000.

12.10 SOLVE THESE PROBLEMS:

1. An apartment house valued at $40,000 was insured for $32,000 under a policy containing an 80% co-insurance clause. Compute the insurance company's share of a fire loss of $12,500.

2. A fire completely destroyed a small office building worth $100,000 which had been insured for $80,000 under a policy that contained a 70% co-insurance clause. How much should the insurance company pay in settlement of the claim?

3. Peters bought a garage for $60,000 and insured it under a policy containing an 80% co-insurance clause for $42,000. Calculate the insurance company's share in a loss of $24,000.

4. A brick apartment house was valued at $90,000 and insured for $72,000, in accordance with the 80% co-insurance clause contained in the policy. Several years later, when the value of the building had increased to $110,000, there was a fire resulting in a loss of $40,000. What amount did the insurance company pay in settlement of the claim?

5. At the time of its complete destruction by fire, a building worth $75,000 was insured for $60,000 under a policy containing an 80%

co-insurance clause. What is the insurance company's responsibility in the loss?

6. A fire loss of $12,000 was sustained by a building that was valued at $16,000 and insured under a 70% co-insurance policy for $11,200. Determine the insurance company's liability.

CHAPTER REVIEW

1. Fred Kelly is single and has 2 additional dependents. His income and expenses for the year are as follows: salary, $32,000; taxable interest, $8,000; nontaxable interest, $200; deductible business expenses, $2,000; contributions, $400; health insurance, $400; medicines and drugs, $400; other medical expenses, $3,000; and allowable taxes $1,600. Using the tax table on page 243 of the text, calculate his income tax.

2. On March 1, Franklin received a $3,156, 110-day 5% note from a customer. The note was discounted at the bank on March 17 at a discount rate of 7%. Find the following:

> Maturity value =   Days in the discount period =
> Bank discount =   Net proceeds =

3. Find the premium on an insurance policy of $24,000 carrying an annual rate of $.15 per hundred.

4. Find the face of an insurance policy with an annual rate of $1.90 per thousand if the annual premium is $2,755.

5. Find the annual rate per thousand of an insurance policy whose face is $13,000 carrying an annual premium of $260.

6. An insurance policy of $8,000 carries a premium rate of $.158 per hundred. Calculate the 2-year premium; 3-year premium; 4-year premium; 5-year premium.

7. The Ace Novelty Company's insurance premium for 1 year cost $413.58. The policy was canceled after 95 days. Determine the refund, if the cancelation was made by the insurance company; by Ace Novelty.

8. A building that was completely destroyed by fire had a value of $80,000 at the time of the loss. The building was insured for $40,000 under a policy containing an 80% co-insurance clause. What is the insurance company's liability?

SEVEN
MATHEMATICS
IN
INVESTMENTS

Recent years have seen a considerable growth in investment in corporate securities. The amount of funds invested and the number of investors have grown to a point at which major fluctuations in security values affect a large segment of the American public. Many investors are directly involved by purchasing securities in their own account; others, through mutual funds, union surpluses, profit-sharing agreements and the like, find their financial position strongly related to stock market performance.

The investor reaches across all occupational lines from the housewife to the nuclear scientist. However, an understanding of mathematics in investments is necessary for all investors, regardless of their major occupational interest.

13

investment in stocks

1. NATURE OF CAPITAL STOCK

2. DIVIDENDS ON STOCK
   a. Preferred stock
   b. Common stock
   c. Cumulative preferred stock

3. BOOK VALUE OF STOCK

4. BUYING AND SELLING STOCK
   a. By the issuing corporation
   b. By the private investor

1. NATURE OF CAPITAL STOCK Corporate ownership is divided into units called shares of stock. These may be of various classes (types), but within each class each share has exactly the same rights as every other share. Thus the only difference between the owner of one share and the owner of 1,000 shares is in the number of shares held. The single share has the same rights as each of the 1,000 shares.

The actual owners of corporations are the stockholders. The owner of one share in a corporation that has 100 shares outstanding actually owns 1 percent of the corporation. Large corporations frequently have hundreds of thousands of shares outstanding, and a stockholder owning thousands of shares may have so small a percentage of ownership that the amount of his control of corporate affairs is negligible. Stocks are usually bought and sold for two reasons; to be resold later at a higher price, or to be kept by their owners for dividends (income).

2. DIVIDENDS ON STOCK

a. PREFERRED STOCK

In order to attract a wide variety of buyers to their stock offering, corporations frequently give some stocks preferences over others. Such stock is called preferred stock, and the preference is usually (not always) in dividends. Thus a corporation may state that its preferred stock must be paid a 6% dividend before common stock receives any dividend. The 6% is calculated on the par value (an arbitrary value set by the board of directors). The dividends for preferred stockholders usually do not exceed the stated percent.

The following formulas concern dividends on preferred stock:

$$\text{Total par value} = \text{Par value per share} \times \text{number of shares}$$

$$\text{Number of shares} = \frac{\text{Total par value}}{\text{Par value per share}}$$

$$\text{Amount of dividend} = \text{Par value} \times \text{Dividend rate}$$

264

$$\text{Dividends per share} = \frac{\text{Total dividends}}{\text{Number of shares}}$$

or Par value per share $\times$ Dividend rate

ILLUSTRATIVE PROBLEM. The Parker Corporation has $10,000 of $100 par value preferred stock outstanding. How many shares are outstanding? If the preferred stock pays 6% in dividends, what will the total dividend be?

SOLUTION:

To find the number of shares:

If the total value of the stock is $10,000, and each share is worth $100, then:

$$\frac{\text{Total par value } \$10,000}{\text{Par value per share } \$100} = 100 \text{ shares}$$

To find the total dividend:

Total par value 100 shares $\times$ $100 =	$10,000
Dividend rate	$\times$ .06
Total dividend	$ 600

13.1 *SOLVE THESE PROBLEMS:*

1. What is the total par value of the preferred stock of a corporation that has 1,000 shares of $20 par value preferred stock outstanding?

2. The total par value of the preferred stock of the Apex Corporation is $200,000. The number of shares outstanding is 4,000. Determine the par value per share.

3. If there is $400,000 of $50 par value preferred stock outstanding, how many shares are outstanding?

4. Ellen Jean Cosmetics, Inc., pays 6% on its preferred stock. Calculate the amount of cash needed for dividends if there is $500,000 of preferred stock outstanding.

5. The board of directors of the Shea Corporation voted to pay $60,000 in dividends to their common and preferred stockholders. The total par value of the 6% preferred is $600,000. Determine the total dividend available for common stockholders.

6. If 1,000 shares of preferred stock are to share in a dividend of $6,000, what is the amount of dividends per share?

7. A corporation that has 5,000 shares of $60, 6% preferred stock outstanding, has $75,000 available for dividends on common and preferred stock. How much will the common shareholders receive?

8. Complete the table.

	Shares Out-stand-ing	Par Value per Share	Total Par Value	Divi-dend Rate	Total Divi-dends Avail-able	Pre-ferred Total	Divi-dends Per Share Pre-ferred	Avail-able for Common
1.	—	$100	$ 100,000	6%	$ 12,000	—	—	—
2.	1,000	—	400,000	5%	60,000	—	—	—
3.	2,000	50	—	7%	10,000	—	—	—
4.	4,000	—	300,000	$4\frac{1}{2}\%$	30,000	—	—	—
5.	—	60	300,000	$6\frac{1}{2}\%$	95,000	—	—	—
6.	1,500	—	150,000	$5\frac{1}{2}\%$	115,000	—	—	—
7.	3,000	40	—	$7\frac{1}{2}\%$	10,000	—	—	—
8.	2,500	—	200,000	4%	6,000	—	—	—
9.	—	75	4,500,000	5%	200,000	—	—	—

b. COMMON STOCK

Voting rights are not usually granted to preferred stockholders. Therefore the common stockholders, who do have the right to vote, control the corporation. Common stockholders are given no dividend preferences, but unlike preferred stockholders whose dividends are generally limited to the stated rate, there is no limit to the amount of dividends common stockholders may receive. Because the amount of dividends received has a direct bearing on the market value of stock, common stock, whose dividends vary, is subject to wider fluctuations in value than preferred stock. Therefore common stock is considered to have greater risk as an investment, and preferred stock is the more conservative investment. Investors in preferred stock are generally interested in the dividends involved, while those that invest in common stock are usually seeking an increase in the market value of their shares. If a corporation has only one class of stock, it is common stock.

ILLUSTRATIVE PROBLEM. The board of directors of the Reeves Optical Corporation voted the payment of total dividends of $50,000 for the year. There are 1,000 shares of 6%, $50 par value, preferred stock outstanding, and 5,000 shares of $10 par value common stock. Find the total dividends and dividends per share for each class of stock.

SOLUTION:

To find the total dividends and dividends per share of preferred stock:

Total par value = Par value per share × Number of shares
= $50 × 1,000
= $50,000

$$\text{Total preferred dividend} = \text{Par value} \times \text{Dividend rate}$$
$$= \$50,000 \quad \times \quad 6\%$$
$$= \$3,000$$

$$\text{Dividends per share} = \frac{\text{Total dividends}}{\text{Number of shares}}$$

$$= \frac{\$3000}{1000}$$

$$= \$3 \text{ Dividends per share of preferred stock}$$

To find the total dividends and dividends per share of common stock:

Total dividends available to common stock
$$= \text{Total dividends available} - \text{Total preferred dividends}$$
$$= \$50,000 - 3,000$$
$$= \$47,000$$

$$\text{Dividend per share} = \frac{\text{Total dividends}}{\text{Number of shares}}$$

$$= \frac{\$47,000}{5,000}$$

$$= \$9.40$$

13.2 SOLVE THESE PROBLEMS:

1. A corporation has only one class of stock. This consists of $50,000 worth of stock at $10 par value per share. Calculate the amount of dividends per share if $10,000 is available for dividends.

2. The Concord Corporation is capitalized as follows:

   Preferred stock—4,000 shares, 7%, $60 par value
   Common stock—9,000 shares, $5 par value

   Determine the total dividends and the dividends per share for each class of stock, if there is $50,000 available for dividends.

3. K. Lawrence, Inc., is capitalized as follows:

   Preferred stock—$300,000, 5%, $50 par value
   Common stock—$750,000, $25 par value

   Determine the total dividends and the dividends per share for each class of stock on total dividends of $16,000.

4. The dividend policy of the Lifelong Workclothes Corporation is to distribute 80% of the profits in dividends and retain 20% for expansion purposes. The profits for the year were $140,000. There were outstanding 6,000 shares of $75 par, 6% preferred stock, and 20,000 shares of $15 par value common stock. Find the total

dividends and dividends per share to be distributed to each class of stock.

5. The board of directors of the Safe-Tread Tire Corporation voted to pay dividends for the year as follows:

  a. Pay the $5\frac{1}{2}\%$ preferred dividend in full on the 1,000 shares of preferred $60 par stock outstanding.

  b. Pay 70% of the balance of the profits to the 6,000 shares of $12 par common stock outstanding.

Calculate the total and per share dividends to be paid to each class of stock out of the year's profit of $200,000.

6. Calculate the total dividends and dividends per share to be paid to each class of stock.

  Available for dividends—$45,000
  Preferred stock—10,000 shares, 6%, $100 par value
  Common stock—50,000 shares, $2 par value

7. The dividend policy of the Nassau Gas and Oil Corporation is to apportion the amount available for dividends as follows:

  a. Pay the preferred dividend, or as much of it as there are funds available.

  b. Pay the balance to the common stockholder.

There are 10,000 shares of $2 par value common stock outstanding and 1,000 shares of $50 par value, 6%, preferred stock outstanding. The following chart indicates the amounts available for dividends for the last eight years. Complete the chart.

	Available for Dividends	Preferred Stock Total per Share		Common Stock Total per Share	
1.	$ 2,000	—	—	—	—
2.	3,500	—	—	—	—
3.	12,000	—	—	—	—
4.	22,000	—	—	—	—
5.	36,000	—	—	—	—
6.	50,000	—	—	—	—
7.	80,000	—	—	—	—
8.	150,000	—	—	—	—

c. CUMULATIVE PREFERRED STOCK

Because the investor in preferred stock is primarily interested in a safe dividend, the more confidence he has in the certainty of the dividend, the more apt he is to purchase the stock. Cumulative preferred stock increases the certainty of the dividend by providing that a dividend that is skipped (not paid), or not fully paid in any one year, will be paid in the following year in addition to the regular dividend for that year. Unpaid cumulative dividends are called dividends in arrears.

ILLUSTRATIVE PROBLEM. The Fluffy Soap Corporation has the following capital stock outstanding:

1. 1,000 shares outstanding, cumulative preferred 6%, par value $100
2. 20,000 shares outstanding, common stock, par $20.

During the first two years of its operation, the following amounts were available for dividends:

First year—None
Second year—$14,000

Determine the dividends per year for each class of stock for each of the two years.

SOLUTION: Find the regular annual dividend on preferred stock:

Total par value = Par value per share × Number of shares
= $100 × 1,000
= $100,000

Total annual dividend = Total par value × Dividend rate
= $100,000 × 6%
= $6,000

First year—Because there were no funds available for dividends, none were paid. However, there are $6,000 of preferred dividends in arrears.

Second year—The first $6,000 available for dividends must be used to offset the preferred dividends in arrears. This leaves $8,000 ($14,000 − $6,000) available for the current year's dividends of which preferred gets $6,000 and common, $2,000.

Preferred—For arrears $ 6,000
For current year   6,000
Total $12,000

$$\frac{\text{Total dividends}}{\text{Preferred shares}} = \frac{\$12,000}{1,000} = \$12 \text{ per share}$$

$$\text{Common—}\frac{\text{Total dividends}}{\text{Number of shares}} = \frac{\$2,000}{20,000} = \$.10 \text{ per share}$$

13.3 SOLVE THESE PROBLEMS:

1. The Kenneth Corporation has outstanding $100,000 of 5%, $25 par value, cumulative preferred stock and $500,000 of $5 par value

common. Determine the dividends per share for each class of stock for the two years in which the amounts available for dividends were $4,000 and $12,000.

2. During its first year in operation the Archer Corp. only paid 2% on its $200,000 7% cumulative, preferred stock. How much must the preferred dividend be if there is to be no arrears at the end of the second year?

Complete the chart.

	Available for Dividends	Arrears	Common Dividends Total	per Share	Preferred Dividends Total	per Share
1st year	$ 20,000	—	—	—	—	—
2nd year	10,000	—	—	—	—	—
3rd year	None	—	—	—	—	—
4th year	80,000	—	—	—	—	—
5th year	100,000	—	—	—	—	—
6th year	2,000	—	—	—	—	—
7th year	1,000	—	—	—	—	—
8th year	None	—	—	—	—	—
9th year	140,000	—	—	—	—	—

Common stock outstanding 10,000 shares; no par value preferred stock outstanding 1,000 shares, 6%, $100 par value, cumulative.

3. BOOK VALUE OF STOCK

The capital (worth) of a corporation has been described as the excess of its assets over its liabilities. Because the ownership of the corporation is divided up among the shares of capital stock outstanding, it is possible to determine the value of each share by dividing the total capital by the number of shares outstanding. The result is called the book value of each share of stock.

The formula for finding the book value of each share of stock when there is only one class of stock outstanding is:

$$\frac{\text{Total capital}}{\text{Number of shares outstanding}} = \text{Book value}$$

ILLUSTRATIVE PROBLEM. The balance sheet of the Kimmel Galleries, Inc., shows total assets of $75,000, and total liabilities of $52,000. The only stock outstanding is 500 shares of common stock. Determine the book value per share.

SOLUTION: To find the total capital:

Total assets — Total liabilities = Total capital
$75,000 — $52,000 = $23,000

To find the book value per share:

$$\frac{\text{Total capital}}{\text{Number of shares outstanding}} = \frac{\$23,000}{500}$$

$$= \$46 \text{ Book value per share}$$

13.4 *SOLVE THESE PROBLEMS:*

1. Find the book value per share of a corporation with a total capital of $37,500 and with one class of outstanding stock totaling 75 shares.

2. The Culver Corporation's outstanding stock is limited to 20 shares of common. What is the book value per share if the total assets are $714, and the total liabilities $327?

3. Complete the table.

	Assets	*Liabilities*	*Capital*	*Shares Out- standing*	*Book Value per Share*
1.	$125,000.00	$78,000.00	$47,000.00	1,500	$ —
2.	—	12,000.00	3,748.60	1,200	—
3.	62,827.00	—	18,473.80	4,000	—
4.	37.00	12.00	—	16	—
5.	4,386.00	—	—	2,000	.38
6.	—	6,000.00	—	1,000	14.00
7.	104,312.00	—	—	3,000	27.00
8.	—	27,000.00	72,000.00	—	36.00
9.	48,000.00	—	28,000.00	—	14.00

4. BUYING AND SELLING STOCK

There are two distinct purposes for trading in capital stock. The corporation issuing the stock trades for the purpose of raising money for business endeavors. The purchaser buys shares in a corporation for investment purposes. Once the corporation has issued the stock, it drops out of the picture. From then on trading (buying and selling shares of stock) is carried on between investors. Most of the trading that is done in corporate stock is between investors.

a. BY THE ISSUING CORPORATION

To raise money to finance its business endeavors, corporations sell stock. This is usually done through an underwriter, an individual or group of individuals who for a fee provide the customers and the marketing skill needed for such transactions. Frequently, an arbitrary value, known as par value, is placed on the stock. Because the amount for which shares are to be sold fluctuates rapidly, stocks are often sold above or below their par value.

The amount received in excess of par is called the premium, and the amount received below par is called the discount.

The formula for finding the premium or discount is:

Number of shares × Par value = Total par value
Number of shares × Selling price = Amount received
Total par value − Amount received = Premium or Discount

ILLUSTRATIVE PROBLEM. Spira Furs, Inc., sold 10,000 shares of $20 par value common stock through an underwriter and received $21 per share. Find the amount of premium or discount.

SOLUTION:

Number of shares × Par value = Total par value
10,000   × $20   = $200,000

Number of shares × Selling price = Amount received
10,000   × $21   = $210,000

Amount received − Par value = Premium or Discount
$210,000   − $200,000 = $10,000 Premium

13.5 *SOLVE THESE PROBLEMS:*

1. The Petroni Machinery Corporation issued 4,000 shares of 6% cumulative preferred stock, par value $100. The stock was sold at $96. Find the premium or discount.

2. Newman's Department Store, Inc., sold 10,000 shares of $2 par value common stock through an underwriter. After all of the stock was sold, the underwriter sent Newman's a check for $22,000. Find the premium or discount.

b. BY THE PRIVATE INVESTOR

An investor wishing to purchase or sell shares of stock does so through an agent or broker. Although it is not necessary to use a broker, it would be difficult to complete a transaction without one, because he has the facilities for matching buyers and sellers.

For his services, the broker charges a commission called brokerage. The amount of brokerage charged for stocks being traded varies with the number of shares and the amount of money involved. Stocks are traded in round lots or odd lots. A round lot is a unit of trading in which 100 shares are involved. (Some stocks that are not actively traded have round lot units of 10 shares.) An odd lot is a unit of trading of less than 100 shares (or less than 10 shares for those stocks whose round lot is 10). The board of governors of the New York Stock Exchange sets the rates which brokers may charge. The following is the portion of the commission schedule that deals with 100-share orders and odd-lot orders.

ROUND LOTS

Dollar Value of Stock	*Commission per Round Lot*
$100–$799	2% plus $6.40
$800–$2,499	1.3% plus $12.00
$2,500 and above	.9% plus $22.00

ODD LOTS

Same rates as above, less $2

When a purchase includes round and odd lots, the commission is determined by treating the round and the odd lots as separate transactions, and adding them.

ILLUSTRATIVE PROBLEM. Determine the commission on a purchase of 140 shares of stock selling at $20 per share.

SOLUTION: To find the round-lot commission:

Round lot value = 100 shares $\times$ $20 = $2,000
Commission per round lot = $2,000 $\times$ 1.3% + $12 = $38
Total round-lot commission = $38

To find the odd-lot commission:

Odd-lot value = 40 shares $\times$ $20 = $800
Odd-lot commission = Round commission less $2 = $20.40
= $800 $\times$ 1.3% + $12 − 2
= $20.40

Total commission = Round-lot commission + Odd-lot commission
= $38 + $20.40
= $58.40

13.6 SOLVE THESE PROBLEMS:

1. Determine the broker's round-lot commission on a purchase of 100 shares of stock selling at $46 per share.

2. Calculate the odd-lot commission on a purchase of 63 shares of a stock selling at $36 per share.

3. Determine the combined round- and odd-lot commission on the purchase of 165 shares of a stock selling at $16 per share.

The price at which stocks can be bought and sold depends upon the supply of stock being offered for sale, and the strength of the demand for that stock. If there are only 100 shares of a particular stock being offered for sale, and many investors are anxious to buy them, the prospective buyers will bid against one another and the price will rise. Because millions of shares are traded each day, there is a considerable amount of price fluctuation. The financial section of the nation's major newspapers publish a summary of each day's trading, and the prices quoted are generally regarded as the market value of the stocks listed.

The following is an excerpt of the summary of a day's trading:

High	Low	Stocks & Div. in Dollars	P/E	Sales 100s	High	Low	Last	Net Change
55	$45\frac{3}{8}$	AT&T	3.08	9	1403	$48\frac{1}{4}$	$47\frac{1}{4}$	$48\frac{1}{4}$	$+1\frac{1}{8}$
$26\frac{7}{8}$	$13\frac{1}{2}$	Boeing	.40	6	273	$14\frac{3}{4}$	$13\frac{5}{8}$	14	$+\frac{1}{8}$
52	25	CBS	1.46	8	147	$27\frac{1}{4}$	$26\frac{1}{2}$	27	$+1$
$76\frac{7}{8}$	$44\frac{1}{4}$	McDonald's		43	1681	$56\frac{5}{8}$	$52\frac{3}{4}$	$53\frac{1}{4}$	$-1\frac{3}{8}$
120	93	Proctor & Gamble	1.80	26	166	97	$95\frac{1}{8}$	$95\frac{1}{2}$	$-\frac{1}{4}$
$37\frac{1}{2}$	$26\frac{3}{4}$	U.S. Steel	1.60	6	683	$32\frac{7}{8}$	$31\frac{3}{4}$	$32\frac{3}{4}$	$+1\frac{1}{4}$
$20\frac{1}{2}$	$9\frac{5}{8}$	Warnaco	.80	3	373	$10\frac{1}{4}$	$9\frac{3}{8}$	$9\frac{3}{8}$	$-\frac{1}{2}$

The numbers indicate dollars, $\frac{1}{8} = \frac{1}{8}$ of \$1 or 12.5 cents, $17\frac{3}{8} = \$17.375$

The following is the information given from left to right:

1. The 1973 high–low indicates the highest and lowest price at which the stock sold during the year. American Telephone and Telegraph sold as high as 55 and as low as $45\frac{3}{8}$.
2. The name of the stock and the annual dividend; Boeing pays dividends of \$.40 per year.
3. P/E is the price–earnings ratio. It is found by dividing the annual earnings into the closing market price. CBS was last sold at 8 times earnings.
4. The day's sales in 100s: 1,681 hundreds or 168,100 shares of McDonald's were sold during the day.
5. The highest Proctor & Gamble sold during the day was \$97.
6. The lowest U.S. Steel sold for during the day was \$31.75.
7. The last sale of Warnaco was at \$9.375.
8. The difference between the last sale of the previous day and the last sale of this day for Warnaco was $-\frac{1}{2}$ (\$.50).

13.7 SOLVE THESE PROBLEMS:
1. Determine the day's change in total value for an investor holding 100 shares of AT&T.

2. An investor bought 200 shares of Boeing at the day's low and sold it at the day's high. What was his profit or loss (disregarding brokerage)?

3. Determine the increase or decrease to date in the holdings of an investor who bought 200 shares of McDonald's at the year's high.

4. Assuming that the last sale of CBS was 100 shares, determine the cost to the investor, including brokerage.

5. Complete the table.

	Cost per Share	Number of Shares	Cost of Stock	Commission	Total Cost of Purchase
1.	$55	100	—	—	—
2.	20	120	—	—	—
3.	15	60	—	—	—
4.	$1\frac{1}{2}$	100	—	—	—
5.	95	140	—	—	—
6.	$5\frac{1}{8}$	150	—	—	—
7.	$8\frac{3}{4}$	120	—	—	—
8.	$38\frac{1}{8}$	180	—	—	—

CHAPTER REVIEW

1. The capitalization of the Carr Corporation is as follows:

Preferred stock: $100 par value, $100,000
Common stock: 10,000 shares, par value $20

The preferred stock bears a 6% cumulative dividend which is in arrears for one year. At the close of the current year there are $50,000 available for dividends. Calculate the dividends per share for each class of stock.

2. The Dickinson Corporation's balance sheet indicates total assets of $120,000 and liabilities of $76,000. There are 2,000 shares of stock outstanding. Calculate the book value per share.

3. The Early Corporation sold 200 shares of its par value $100 preferred stock at $104 and 500 shares of its par value $10 common stock at $9. Calculate the premium or discount on each sale.

4. Calculate the broker's commission on a purchase of 110 shares of stock at $11 per share.

5. Calculate the profit or loss on a purchase of 100 shares of Warnaco at the year's high and sold at the day's low. Use the summary of stock trading on page 274 of the text. Disregard commissions.

14

investment in bonds

1. NATURE OF BONDS

2. BUYING AND SELLING BONDS
   a. Sale of bonds by the issuing corporation
   b. Sale of bonds by the private investor

3. INTEREST ON BONDS
   a. Current yield
   b. Yield to maturity

4. BUYING BONDS BETWEEN INTEREST PERIODS

1. NATURE OF BONDS

Financing a corporation by selling capital stock requires giving up part of the ownership and, consequently, a share in the future profits of the company. Many corporations raise necessary funds by means of long-term borrowing from the investing public. The vehicle for such borrowing is the corporate bond. A bond is evidence of long-term debt at a stated interest rate. A corporation that secures funds by use of bonds gives up none of its ownership, and when the bonds mature (become due) and are paid, the corporation has benefited by the financing and the original stockholders have maintained their percentage of ownership.

To the investor, bond interest offers more security than dividends. Dividends—even preferred dividends—are paid only by consent of the board of directors. A bondholder is a creditor of the corporation and, as such, he must be paid the principal plus interest on the maturity date, regardless of the wishes of the board of directors.

As in the case of stocks, bonds are issued, bought, and sold through brokers, who charge commissions for their efforts. Most bonds have the par value of $1,000 and are quoted at a percent of $1,000. In this section it will be assumed that all bonds have a par value of $1,000.

2. BUYING AND SELLING BONDS

The borrowing corporation issues bonds through an underwriter to the investing public. The underwriter deducts a commission from the total sales of the bonds and remits the remainder to the corporation. Further transactions in bonds are between investors who buy bonds for interest income, or in the hope that the bonds will increase in value. As in the case of stocks, there is a market where offerings to buy and sell cause price fluctuation. Unlike stocks, where dollar values are used, the selling price of bonds is quoted in percentages of par value. Thus a bond with a par value of $1,000 that is selling for 79 has a selling price of $790 ($1,000 × 79%).

277

14.1 SOLVE THESE PROBLEMS: Determine the selling price of the following $1,000 par value bonds:

1. Moray Corporation   106
2. Jameson, Inc.   37
3. Ray Company, Inc.   110
4. Applegates, Inc. $104\frac{1}{2}$
5. Carl's Company $98\frac{7}{8}$

a. SALE OF BONDS BY THE ISSUING CORPORATION

Because corporate bonds have a par value (usually $1,000) and are subject to price fluctuation, they are frequently bought at a premium (above par) or at a discount (below par).

The formula for determining the amount of money received from the sale of bonds is:

Amount received = Number of bonds $\times$ Par value $\times$ Price

The formula for determining the premium or discount is:

Total amount received $-$ Total par value = Premium or Discount

ILLUSTRATIVE PROBLEM. Zalka, Inc., sold 4,000 bonds to the general public at 102. Calculate (a) the amount the corporation received, and (b) the premium or discount.

SOLUTION: To find the amount of money received:

Amount received = Number of bonds $\times$ Par value $\times$ Price
= 4,000 $\times$ $1,000 $\times$ 102%
= $4,000,000 $\times$ 1.02
= $4,080,000

To find the premium:

Total amount received $-$ Total par value = Premium
$4,080,000 $-$ $4,000,000 = $80,000

14.2 SOLVE THESE PROBLEMS:
1. The Donavan Corporation sold 500 bonds at 98. How much did they receive? How much was the premium or discount?
2. Calculate the proceeds to the issuing corporation and the amount of premium or discount on 750 bonds which sold at 106.
3. Complete the table.

Numbers of Bonds	Par Value	Issue Price	Cash Received	Premium or Discount*
1000	$1000	102	—	—
800	1000	94	—	—
750	1000	96	—	—
2200	1000	107	—	—
2000	1000	100	—	—

* Use an asterisk to indicate a discount.

b. SALE OF BONDS BY THE PRIVATE INVESTOR

Although trading in corporate bonds is not nearly as extensive as is trading in stocks, it is considerable, and many large newspapers publish a daily summary of corporate bond transactions. The following is an example of this:

SUMMARY OF BOND TRADING

Bonds	Current Yield	Sales in $1,000	High	Low	Last	Net Change
ATT $6\frac{1}{2}$s 79	6.7	24	$96\frac{1}{2}$	$96\frac{1}{2}$	$96\frac{1}{2}$	$+\frac{1}{2}$
CON ED $7\frac{3}{4}$s 03	8.4	10	$93\frac{1}{2}$	92	92	$-1\frac{7}{8}$
RCA 9s 75	8.7	9	$103\frac{7}{8}$	$103\frac{1}{2}$	$103\frac{1}{2}$	$+\frac{1}{2}$
U.S. STL $4\frac{5}{8}$ 96	7.0	61	$65\frac{1}{4}$	65	$65\frac{1}{4}$	$+\frac{1}{8}$

The prices indicated are percentages of $1,000. Reading from left to right, the columns indicate:

1. American Telephone and Telegraph bonds pay interest of $6\frac{1}{2}\%$ (of par value, $1,000) and are due in 1979.
2. A purchaser of the Consolidated Edison bonds at the last price (92) would earn interest at the rate of 8.4% on his investment (the $7\frac{3}{4}\%$ on par value of $1,000. He would only pay $920 and receive $7\frac{3}{4}\%$ on $1,000).
3. During the day, $9,000 of RCA bonds were traded.
4. The highest price paid for the U.S. Steel bonds listed was $65\frac{1}{4}$ ($652.50).
5. The lowest price paid for the U.S. Steel bonds listed was 65 ($650.00).
6. The last price paid for the U.S. Steel bonds listed was $65\frac{1}{4}$.
7. U.S. Steel bonds closed $\frac{1}{8}$ higher than the previous day's close.

ILLUSTRATIVE PROBLEM. W. Fuori owns four Consolidated Edison bonds. Determine the amount of fluctuation in his investment during the day.

SOLUTION:

To find the par value of his investment:

Number of bonds × Par value = Par value of investment
   4   × $1,000 = $4,000

To find the value of the investment at the day's high:

Par value of investment × Day's high = High value of investment
   $4,000   × $93\frac{1}{2}\%$ = $3,740

To find the value of the investment at the day's low:

Par value of investment × Day's low = Low value of investment
   $4,000   ×   92%   = $3,680

To find the amount of fluctuation:

Day's high − Day's low = Amount of fluctuation
 $3,740   − $3,680   = $60

A simpler solution method is:

$$\begin{array}{ll} \text{Day's high} & 93\frac{1}{2}\% \\ \text{Day's low} & -92\% \\ \text{Percent of fluctuation} & -1\frac{1}{2}\% \end{array}$$

Value of investment × Day's fluctuation = Amount of fluctuation
   $4,000   × $1\frac{1}{2}\%$ = $60

14.3 SOLVE THESE PROBLEMS:

1. Determine the day's dollar change for an investor holding seven bonds of RCA.

2. An investor bought four U.S. Steel bonds at the day's high and sold them at the day's low. What was his loss?

3. N. Sterne bought eight RCA bonds at the day's low. By how much has her investment increased?

The commission that brokers charge for buying and selling bonds varies with each brokerage house. The following illustration is an example:

BROKER'S COMMISSION ON BONDS

Price per $1,000 *(of Principal) Bond*	*Rate per $1,000* *(of Principal) Bond*
Selling at less than $10 (1%)	$ .75
Selling at $10–$99 (10%)	1.25
Selling at $100 (10%) and over	2.50

To use the above table, convert the cost of the bond to dollars. Select the proper rate and multiply by the number of bonds.

ILLUSTRATIVE PROBLEM. Richard Small bought four American Telephone and Telegraph bonds at the day's low point. What was his total cost, including commission? (Use the summary of bond trading listed on page 279.)

SOLUTION: To find the cost of the bonds:

Par value × Day's low = Cost per bond
$1,000 × $96\frac{1}{2}\%$ = $965
4 Bonds at $965 each = $3,860 Total cost of bonds

To find the commission:

Cost per bond is $965. From the chart of broker's commission on bonds, it is found that the commission on bonds selling at $100 and over is $2.50 per bond.

Number of bonds × Commission per bond = Total commission
4 × $2.50 = $10

To find the total cost:

Total cost of bonds + Total commission = Total cost
$3,860 + $10 = $3,870

14.4 SOLVE THESE PROBLEMS:

1. Find the total cost, including commission, of seven Consolidated Edison bonds bought at the day's highest price. (Use the summary listed on page 279.)

2. Determine the total cost, including commission, of six RCA bonds that were bought at the day's high as indicated by the summary on page 279.

3. What is the total cost including commission of six bonds of Pacillo, Inc., purchased at $\frac{7}{8}$?

4. If a bond is sold at 6, what is the total cost, including commission, of eight bonds?

5. Complete the table.

	Par Value of Bonds	Selling Price	Number Bought	Cost of Bonds	Commission	Total Cost
1.	$1,000	102	6	—	—	—
2.	1,000	4	30	—	—	—
3.	1,000	37	2	—	—	—
4.	1,000	$1\frac{1}{2}$	80	—	—	—
5.	1,000	98	12	—	—	—
6.	1,000	101	9	—	—	—
7.	1,000	46	14	—	—	—
8.	1,000	6	105	—	—	—

Corporate bonds pay a stated interest *on par value*. The corporation that issues the bonds is not at all interested in the amount the investor paid for the bond. Its debt is the par value. That is the amount it will have to pay at maturity and that is the amount it pays interest on.

The interest is usually paid twice a year on specified dates. Because the interest is quoted at an annual rate, it is necessary to divide the annual interest in half to determine the amount of interest that will be received semi-annually.

The formula for determining semi-annual interest is:

Par value × Annual interest rate = Annual interest
Annual interest ÷ 2 = Semi-annual interest

ILLUSTRATIVE PROBLEM. Tom Black owns ten bonds of the Excellent T. V. Corp. for which he paid 87. The bonds have a par value of $1,000, and pay interest at $6\frac{1}{2}\%$ on February 1 and August 1. Determine the amount of interest Mr. Black will receive on each interest date.

SOLUTION: To find the annual interest per bond:

Par value × Annual interest rate = Annual interest
$1,000 × $6\frac{1}{2}\%$ = $65

To find the semi-annual interest per bond:

Annual interest ÷ 2 = Semi-annual interest
$65 ÷ 2 = $32.50

To find the total interest:

Semi-annual interest per bond × Number of bonds = Total semi-annual interest
$32.50 × 10 = $325.00

14.5 SOLVE THESE PROBLEMS:
1. John Fleming owns 100 Neighborhood Supermarkets, Inc., bonds. The bonds have a par value of $1,000, an interest rate of 7%, and pay interest on January 1 and July 1. If Mr. Fleming paid 104 for the bonds, calculate the interest he will receive on July 1.
2. The Elias Optical Corporation has $1,000,000 of $4\frac{1}{2}\%$ par value $1,000 bonds outstanding. The interest is payable on March 1 and September 1. Find the amount of interest the corporation must pay on each interest period.
3. Complete the table.

Number of Bonds	Par Value	Interest Dates	Interest Rates	Semi-annual Interest per Bond	Total Semi-annual Interest
10	$1,000	January–July	6%	—	—
6	1,000	February–August	$5\frac{1}{2}\%$	—	—
14	1,000	June–December	4%	—	—
30	1,000	March–September	$4\frac{1}{2}\%$	—	—
27	1,000	May–November	7%	—	—
72	1,000	April–October	$7\frac{3}{8}\%$	—	—
18	1,000	January–July	$4\frac{3}{4}\%$	—	—
44	1,000	May–November	$5\frac{1}{8}\%$	—	—
29	1,000	March–September	$6\frac{3}{8}\%$	—	—
36	1,000	June–December	$4\frac{5}{8}\%$	—	—
36	1,000	June–December	$4\frac{5}{8}\%$	—	—

a. CURRENT YIELD

The effective yield (return) on an investment is found by dividing the cost of the investment into the amount of the return. Because the interest rate stated on the bond is based on the par value of the bond rather than on the investor's cost, calculations, using the following formula, must be performed to find the effective current yield:

$$\frac{\text{Total annual interest}}{\text{Total cost}} = \text{Current yield}$$

ILLUSTRATIVE PROBLEM. Homer Flynn owns six Alexander Corp., 6% bonds which he purchased at 96. Commission on the purchase amounted to $15. What is the current yield on Flynn's investment?

SOLUTION:

$$\frac{\text{Total annual interest}}{\text{Total cost}} = \text{Current yield}$$

$$\frac{\$1,000 \text{ Par per bond} \times 6\% \text{ Annual rate} \times 6 \text{ Bonds}}{1,000 \text{ Par per bond} \times 96\% \text{ Cost per bond} \times 6 \text{ Bonds} + \$15 \text{ Commission}}$$

$$= \frac{360}{5775} = .0623 \text{ or } 6.2\%$$

14.6   SOLVE THESE PROBLEMS: Round off to the nearest decimal.
1. Determine the current yield on Wilson Corporation 5% bonds selling at 84, if there is no commission involved.
2. Western Finance $16\frac{1}{2}\%$ bonds are selling for 110. The brokerage (commission) is $2.50 per bond. How much will the holder of eight bonds receive annually? What will be the current yield?

3. Morgenstein holds eight Southern Railway 7% bonds for which he paid 8220 including brokerage. Calculate his current yield.

4. Determine the current yield on the following bonds. Round off to the nearest tenth of a percent.

Interest Rate	Selling Price	Current Yield
$6\frac{1}{4}\%$	96	—
$4\frac{3}{8}\%$	102	—
$5\frac{1}{2}\%$	82	—
$7\frac{3}{4}\%$	$83\frac{3}{4}$	—
$5\frac{5}{8}\%$	$106\frac{1}{2}$	—
$4\frac{1}{2}\%$	$110\frac{1}{4}$	—
$4\frac{3}{4}\%$	$94\frac{3}{8}$	—
$6\frac{3}{8}\%$	$91\frac{1}{8}$	—

b. YIELD TO MATURITY

Current annual yield is important to stockholders who do not plan to hold their bond investment until maturity. Those investors who expect to keep their bonds until they mature must take the amount of premium or discount they paid into account in determining their yield. Because the bond will be redeemed at par value at maturity, the cost of the bond in excess of par value (the premium) will be lost and must reduce the yield. Similarly, the discount, the amount paid below par, will be a profit and will increase the yield. There are tables available for determining the exact yield to maturity, but the following formulas will give a close approximation.

1. In the case of a premium:

$$\frac{\text{Annual interest} - (\text{Premium} \div \text{Number of years to maturity})}{\text{Average principal invested}}$$

$$= \text{Approximate yield to maturity}$$

2. In the case of a discount:

$$\frac{\text{Annual interest} + (\text{Discount} \div \text{Number of years to maturity})}{\text{Average principal invested}}$$

a. The annual interest may be found by multiplying the par value by the stated interest.

b. The premium is the amount by which cost exceeds par. The discount is the amount by which par exceeds cost.

c. Years to maturity is the time elapsed between the present date and the maturity date.

d. Average principal invested is the sum of the cost and the maturity value divided by 2.

ILLUSTRATIVE PROBLEM. Southeast Railroad 6% bonds, due in 1980, were purchased in 1968 at 90. Determine the approximate yield to maturity.

SOLUTION: Because the bonds were sold at a discount, the following formula is used:

$$\frac{\text{Annual interest} + (\text{Discount} \div \text{Number of years to maturity})}{\text{Average principal invested}}$$

$$= \text{Approximate yield to maturity}$$

$$\frac{(\$1,000 \times 6\%) + (\$1,000 - 900 \div 12)}{(\$900 + \$1,000) \div 2} = \frac{\$60 + \$8.33}{950} = \frac{68.33}{950} = 7.2\%$$

14.7 SOLVE THESE PROBLEMS: Round off to the nearest tenth of a percent.

1. Determine the annual rate of yield to maturity of a 6% bond with a maturity date of 1974 if the bond was purchased in 1968 at a cost of 106.
2. If a 6% bond that will mature in 8 years can be bought at 84, what is the rate of yield to maturity?
3. Find the approximate yield to maturity on the following bonds.

	Cost	Rate of Interest	Number of Years to Maturity	Yield to Maturity
1.	106	6%	15	—
2.	101	$5\frac{1}{2}$	5	—
3.	96	$4\frac{1}{2}$	20	—
4.	90	$7\frac{1}{2}$	5	—
5.	88	7	12	—
6.	60	5	10	—
7.	76	$4\frac{3}{4}$	8	—
8.	72	$5\frac{1}{4}$	14	—

**4. BUYING BONDS
BETWEEN
INTEREST PERIODS** Interest on bonds is calculated by multiplying the par value of the bonds by a stated interest rate. Interest is usually paid twice a year, with one half of the interest paid for each semi-annual interest period. In other words, a bond with a par value of $1,000, paying interest at 6% on January 1 and July 1, would pay the following on every interest date:

$$\text{Principal} \times \text{Rate} = \text{Annual interest}$$
$$\$1,000 \ \times \ .06 \ = \qquad \$60$$

and:

$$\frac{\text{Annual interest}}{2} = \text{Semi-annual interest}$$

$$\frac{\$60}{2} \qquad = \qquad \$30$$

Because the bonds will always pay $30 to the holder of the bond for the six months ended on every interest period, certain calculations are necessary for bonds that are bought and sold between interest periods. If the bond is held by the same person for the full six-month period, he is, of course, entitled to the full interest. But what about the person who bought the bond at the beginning of the sixth month of the interest period? As the holder of the bond, he will receive the full semi-annual interest payment. This obtains despite the fact that he held the bond for only one month, while the person he bought it from held it for five months and is entitled to $\frac{5}{6}$ of the interest for the period in question. This problem is solved by having the purchaser of the bond pay the seller, at the time of purchase, an amount equal to the interest that has accrued (accumulated) between the last interest period and the date of sale. In essence, the purchaser is buying the accrued interest. In calculating the number of days between the last interest date and the date of sale, consider all months to have 30 days.

The simple interest formula:

$$\text{Principal} \times \text{Rate} \times \text{Time} = \text{Interest}$$

is used to calculate accrued interest:

> Principal = Par
> Rate = Stated percent of interest
> Time = Time between last interest date and date of sale

ILLUSTRATIVE PROBLEM. A $1,000 par value 6% bond, paying interest on February 1 and August 1, was sold on April 13 for 102. Calculate the cost to the buyer including accrued interest.

SOLUTION: To find the cost of the bond:

$$\text{Par value} \times \text{Selling price} = \text{Cost}$$
$$\$1,000 \quad \times \quad 102\% \quad = \$1,020$$

To find the accrued interest:

$$\text{Principal} \times \text{Rate} \times \text{Time} = \text{Accrued interest}$$
$$\$1,000 \times 6\% \times \tfrac{72}{360} = \text{Accrued interest}$$
$$= \$12$$

The time was calculated as follows:

> February 1 to April 1 = 2 months = 60 days
> April 1 to April 13 $\qquad\qquad$ = 12 days
> $\qquad\qquad\qquad\qquad\qquad\qquad$ 72 days

$$\text{Cost of bond} + \text{Accrued interest} = \text{Total cost}$$
$$\$1,020 \quad + \quad \$12 \quad = \quad \$1,032$$

14.8 SOLVE THESE PROBLEMS:

1. S. Bettman purchased six American Telephone and Telegraph bonds on April 10 at 79. The bonds bear interest at 6%, payable on January 1 and July 1. What was the total cost of the bonds and the accrued interest?

2. An investor sold seven Consolidated Edison $4\frac{3}{4}$% bonds with interest dates of March 1 and September 1. If the sale took place on June 26, and the selling price was 109, how much money did the investor receive? (Disregard the commission.)

3. On July 6, G. Foster sold seven bonds at 116. The bonds bore interest at $6\frac{1}{2}$%, payble on April 1 and September 1. Calculate the total price of the bonds including accrued interest and commissions.

4. Determine the amount received including accrued interest and commission on the sale of five bonds bearing interest at $4\frac{1}{4}$%, payable on May 1 and October 1. The bonds were sold on December 9 at 87.

5. Complete the table.

Number of Bonds	Selling Price	Interest Rates	Interest Dates	Purchase Date	Accrued Interest	Com- mis- sion	Total Cost
1	102	$6\frac{1}{2}$%	January–July	April 10	—	—	—
3	68	4%	February–August	June 6	—	—	—
6	79	$4\frac{1}{4}$%	June–December	December 4	—	—	—
12	84	5%	March–September	May 11	—	—	—
14	$110\frac{1}{2}$	$6\frac{3}{4}$%	January–July	January 22	—	—	—
7	$96\frac{3}{4}$	6%	April–October	March 19	—	—	—
9	$114\frac{3}{4}$	7%	February–August	June 21	—	—	—
16	$107\frac{1}{8}$	$7\frac{1}{4}$%	May–November	January 7	—	—	—

CHAPTER REVIEW

1. Calculate the amount of money received and the premium or discount involved in the sale by a corporation of 10 of its $1,000 bonds at 105.

2. Allen bought 12 bonds at 104 and sold them at 101. Determine his profit or loss, taking commissions into account.

3. On January 1, Frank Thompson bought a $1,000, 6% bond at 106. The bond was sold one year later at 108. How much interest did he receive?

4. Calculate the current yield on twelve $1,000, 5% bonds purchased at 96.

5. Calculate the annual yield to maturity of a $1,000, 6% bond due in 10 years and purchased at 90.

6. On July 31 a $1,000, 6% bond was purchased at 105. The interest dates are January 1 and July 1. Commission on the purchase was $2.50. What is the total cost to the investor?

EIGHT
MATHEMATICS
IN
DATA PROCESSING

The effect of the new computer sciences on our way of life has been profound. Where at first only large businesses and complicated scientific research found uses for these devices, it is becoming more and more apparent that even smaller businesses are being forced to turn to electronic data processing to maintain their competitive position. Unquestionably, the near future will see all business students required to have a considerable understanding of data processing.

These amazing machines are nothing more than arithmetic morons. They are limited to the basic arithmetic operations: addition, subtraction, multiplication, and division. Their success lies in the speed with which they are capable of handling these functions. This is so great that their data-handling capabilities are truly phenomenal.

The understanding of the internal working of the computer must begin with an understanding of the arithmetic it performs. Because the base system used is different from the decimal (base 10) system we are familiar with, this section of the text will be devoted to the methods by which the computer performs the basic arithmetic operations.

binary arithmetic

1. BASE 10

2. BINARY SYSTEM
   a. Converting binary numerals to decimal numerals
   b. Converting decimal numerals to binary numerals
   c. Addition
   d. Subtraction
   e. Multiplication
   f. Division

1. BASE 10　　　In the same manner in which words in different languages can express the same meaning, different numbering systems can express the same values. Because there are similarities between computer arithmetic and decimal arithmetic, a thorough understanding of decimal arithmetic will be very helpful in the understanding of computer arithmetic.

The decimal system uses a base (radix) of 10 and a place value numeration system. The highest number that can appear in any one position is 9 (base minus 1).

The base 10 numeration system is positional. That is, the position (column) a digit is in affects its value. Thus 10 is not the same as 01, although the same digits are used. Not all numeration systems are positional. For example the Roman numeral V represents 5, no matter which position it falls in—e.g., XIV, LVI, VII.

The positional values of the base 10 (decimal) system are illustrated in the following chart:

Thousands	Hundreds	Tens	Ones
$10 \times 10 \times 10$	10×10	10×1	1

Because:　$10 \times 10 \times 10$ may be expressed as 10^3
10×10 may be expressed as 10^2
10 may be expressed as 10^1
1 may be expressed as 10^0 (by agreement)

The chart may then be shown as follows:

Thousands	Hundreds	Tens	Ones
$10 \times 10 \times 10$ or 10^3	10×10 or 10^2	10×1 or 10^1	1 or 10^0

To find the value of a base 10 numeral, it is necessary to multiply that number represented by the value of its position. For example, a 4 in the thousands position would have the value of 4×10^3 or $4 \times 10 \times 10 \times 10 = 4,000$.

To find the value of a numeral with several digits, each number must be multiplied by its positional value and individual positional values added.

ILLUSTRATIVE PROBLEM. Record the base 10 (decimal) numeral 5,362 according to its positional values:

$$\begin{aligned}
5 \times 10^3 &= 5 \times 10 \times 10 \times 10 = 5,000 \\
3 \times 10^2 &= 3 \times 10 \times 10 = 300 \\
6 \times 10^1 &= 6 \times 10 = 60 \\
2 \times 10^0 &= 2 \times 1 = 2 \\
\hline
& 5,362
\end{aligned}$$

15.1 SOLVE THESE PROBLEMS: Record the following base ten numerals according to their positional values:

1.	3,768	**6.**	126,804
2.	126	**7.**	54,260
3.	7	**8.**	3,088
4.	9,204	**9.**	406
5.	68	**10.**	78

2. BINARY SYSTEM

All electrical devices from light switches to computers have one characteristic in common; they can be in only two states, either off or on. The simplest numeration system for an electrical installation, then, is one that uses base 2. A subscript is used to define the base (radix). The numeral 127_{10} is a base 10 numeral and 10_2 is a numeral expressed in base 2. Arithmetic operations done with base 2 numerals are referred to as *binary arithmetic*.

The only difference between the binary system (base 2) and the decimal system (base 10) is in the base. Both are positional numeration systems. The numerals making up the decimal system are 0, 1, 2, 3, 4, 5, 6, 7, 8, 9. In the binary system there are only two numerals, 0 and 1. The value of a multidigit numeral can always be determined by adding the positional values of each of the digits.

Thus, starting with the rightmost column:

1 in the fourth column of a decimal numeral has the value of $1 \times 10 \times 10 \times 10 = 1 \times 10^3 = 1,000$

1 in the fourth column of a binary numeral has the value of $1 \times 2 \times 2 \times 2 = 1 \times 2^3 = 8$

As in the case of base 10 numerals, a chart of positional values may be constructed for base 2 numerals:

Sixteen	Eight	Four	Two	One
$2 \times 2 \times 2 \times 2$	$2 \times 2 \times 2$	2×2	2×1	1
or 2^4	or 2^3	or 2^2	or 2^1	or 2^0

Remember: $10^0 = 1$
 $2^0 = 1$

Remember: Because the digits making up a numeration system are equal to the base minus 1, the only digits available in the binary system are 1 and 0.

a. CONVERTING BINARY NUMERALS TO DECIMAL NUMERALS

To find the decimal equivalent of a binary numeral, you must multiply each digit by the value of its position. For example, a 1 in the fourth column = $1 \times 2 \times 2 \times 2 = 1 \times 2^3 = 8$. Again, a zero in the fifth column = $0 \times 2 \times 2 \times 2 \times 2 = 0 \times 2^4 = 0$.

To find the value of a binary numeral with several digits, multiply each digit by its positional value and add the individual positional values. To convert binary numeral to decimal numerals it is helpful to construct a table for each problem. As you familiarize yourself with the base 2 system, you may eliminate the table.

ILLUSTRATIVE PROBLEM. Determine the decimal equivalent of the binary numeral 1101.

SOLUTION: First construct a table and enter the binary number.

Eight	Four	Two	One
2^3	2^2	2^1	2^0
1	1	0	1

Find the positional value of each digit.

$$(1 \times 2^3) + (1 \times 2^2) + (0 \times 2^1) + (1 \times 2^0)$$

Add the individual positional values.

$$1 \times 2^3 = 8$$
$$1 \times 2^2 = 4$$
$$0 \times 2^1 = 0$$
$$1 \times 2^0 = \underline{1}$$
$$\overline{13} \text{ is the decimal equivalent of binary 1101}$$

This can be stated as $13_{10} = 1101_2$.

ILLUSTRATIVE PROBLEM. Determine the base 10 value of the binary numeral 10001.

SOLUTION: Construct a table and enter the digits of the binary numeral.

Sixteen 2^4	Eight 2^3	Four 2^2	Two 2^1	One 2^0
1	0	0	0	1

Find the positional value of each digit and add.

$$1 \times 2^4 = 16$$
$$0 \times 2^3 = 0$$
$$0 \times 2^2 = 0$$
$$0 \times 2^1 = 0$$
$$1 \times 2^0 = \underline{1}$$
$$\overline{17} \text{ Base 10 is the equivalent of binary 10001}$$
$$\text{or } 17_{10} = 10001_2$$

15.2 SOLVE THESE PROBLEMS: Determine the decimal equivalent of the following binary numerals.

1. 111_2
2. 101_2
3. 11_2
4. 1001_2
5. 1101_2
6. 1011_2
7. 1110_2
8. 1010_2
9. 1100_2
10. 11100_2

11. 10101_2
12. 10111_2
13. 11001_2
14. 11011_2
15. 11000_2
16. 11010_2
17. 101001_2
18. 1110001_2
19. 10010101_2
20. 10111001_2

Another method of converting from binary to decimal is to begin at the most significant digit (leftmost); this is doubled and the second most significant digit is added to it. This sum is doubled and the third digit is added. This procedure is continued, doubling each new sum and adding the 1 or 0 in each succeeding position. The final answer is found when the last digit is used.

ILLUSTRATIVE PROBLEM. Convert the binary numeral, 101100110 to its decimal equivalent.

	a	b	c	d	e	f	g	h	i
Binary number	1	0	1	1	0	0	1	1	0
Double and add
next digit	1	2	5	11	22	44	89	179	358

Answer: $101100110_2 = 358_{10}$

The problem was solved in the following manner:

The most significant (leftmost) binary digit (*a*) was doubled, $1 \times 2 = 2$ the binary digit in the second column (*b*) was added to it, $2 + 0 = 2$. The 2 was doubled and the binary third digit (*c*) added, $2 \times 2 + 1 = 5$. The 5 was doubled and the fourth binary digit (*d*) added, $5 \times 2 + 1 = 11$. This procedure was followed through column *i*.

15.3 SOLVE THESE PROBLEMS: Convert the following binary numerals to base 10 numbers by doubling and adding the next.

1. 01_2	**11.** 1101_2
2. 10_2	**12.** 11111_2
3. 001_2	**13.** 10111_2
4. 010_2	**14.** 11011_2
5. 101_2	**15.** 11101_2
6. 100_2	**16.** 11110_2
7. 1111_2	**17.** 101010_2
8. 1011_2	**18.** 110111_2
9. 1001_2	**19.** 110001_2
10. 1100_2	**20.** 100110_2

b. CONVERTING DECIMAL NUMBERS
TO BINARY DIGITS

The remainder method is commonly used to convert decimal numerals to binary numerals. The method involves dividing the decimal numeral by 2. The quotient, and all succeeding quotients, are similarly divided by 2. In each case, because we are dividing by 2, the remainder must be either 1 or 0, the digits that make up the binary numeration system. The remainders are kept in the order in which they occur with the final remainder the most significant (leftmost) digit in the resulting binary number.

ILLUSTRATIVE PROBLEM. What is the binary equivalent of 13_{10}?

SOLUTION:

$$
\begin{array}{r}
0 \quad \text{remainder } 1 \\
2\overline{|\ 1} \quad \text{remainder } 1 \\
2\overline{|\ \ \ 3} \quad \text{remainder } 0 \\
2\overline{|\ \ \ \ 6} \quad \text{remainder } 1 \\
2\overline{|\ \ \ \ \ 13}
\end{array}
$$

Answer: $13_{10} = 1101_2$

PROOF:

$$
\begin{array}{cccc}
8 & 4 & 2 & 1 \\
2^3 & 2^2 & 2^1 & 2^0 \\
\hline
1 & 1 & 0 & 1
\end{array}
$$

$$
\begin{array}{rcl}
1 \times 2^3 & = & 8 \\
1 \times 2^2 & = & 4 \\
0 \times 2^1 & = & 0 \\
1 \times 2^0 & = & 1 \\
\hline
& & 13
\end{array}
$$

ILLUSTRATIVE PROBLEM. What is the binary equivalent of 358_{10}?

SOLUTION:

$$
\begin{array}{r}
0 \quad \text{r } 1 \\
2\overline{|\ 1} \quad \text{r } 0 \\
2\overline{|\ \ \ 2} \quad \text{r } 1 \\
2\overline{|\ \ \ \ 5} \quad \text{r } 1 \\
2\overline{|\ \ \ \ \ 11} \quad \text{r } 0 \\
2\overline{|\ \ \ \ \ \ 22} \quad \text{r } 0 \\
2\overline{|\ \ \ \ \ \ \ 44} \quad \text{r } 1 \\
2\overline{|\ \ \ \ \ \ \ \ 89} \quad \text{r } 1 \\
2\overline{|\ \ \ \ \ \ \ \ \ 179} \quad \text{r } 0 \\
2\overline{|\ \ \ \ \ \ \ \ \ \ 358}
\end{array}
$$

Answer: $358_{10} = 101100110_2$

PROOF:

$$
\begin{array}{ccccccccc}
256 & 128 & 64 & 32 & 16 & 8 & 4 & 2 & 1 \\
2^8 & 2^7 & 2^6 & 2^5 & 2^4 & 2^3 & 2^2 & 2^1 & 2^0 \\
\hline
1 & 0 & 1 & 1 & 0 & 0 & 1 & 1 & 0
\end{array}
$$

$$1 \times 2^8 = 256$$
$$0 \times 2^7 = 0$$
$$1 \times 2^6 = 64$$
$$1 \times 2^5 = 32$$
$$0 \times 2^4 = 0$$
$$0 \times 2^3 = 0$$
$$1 \times 2^2 = 4$$
$$1 \times 2^1 = 2$$
$$0 \times 2^0 = 0$$
$$\overline{358}$$

15.4 SOLVE THESE PROBLEMS: Convert the following radix 10 numerals to their radix 2 equivalents and prove your work.

1. 12_{10}		**11.** 316_{10}
2. 27_{10}		**12.** 127_{10}
3. 92_{10}		**13.** 4_{10}
4. 41_{10}		**14.** 36_{10}
5. 126_{10}		**15.** 7_{10}
6. 147_{10}		**16.** 73_{10}
7. 136_{10}		**17.** 66_{10}
8. 118_{10}		**18.** 14_{10}
9. 275_{10}		**19.** 308_{10}
10. 292_{10}		**20.** 346_{10}

c. ADDITION

The addition of numbers in the binary system is similar to that of decimal numbers. There are only four basic facts involved:

$$0 + 0 = 0$$
$$0 + 1 = 1$$
$$1 + 0 = 1$$
$$1 + 1 = 10, \text{ written as 0 with a carry of 1}$$

As in the case of addition in the decimal system, the carried number is added to the next left column. Because binary digits are easily converted to their decimal equivalent, binary addition may be proven by converting the numbers to their decimal equivalents and adding.

ILLUSTRATIVE PROBLEMS. Add 1011_2 and 1010_2 and prove your work by converting to decimal numerals.

SOLUTION:

$$
\begin{array}{rcr}
\text{CC} & & \\
1\,011 & = & 11 \\
+\ \ 1\,0\,10 & = & +10 \\
\hline
10\,1\,01 & & 21 \\
\end{array}
$$

Note that C, the carried 1 resulting from $1 + 1$, is placed above the next column to the left and treated as a 1.

ILLUSTRATIVE PROBLEM.

$$
\begin{array}{r}
101101 \\
+\ \ 11011 \\
\end{array}
$$

SOLUTION:

$$
\begin{array}{rcr}
\text{CCCCCC} & & \\
1\,0\,1\,1\,0\,1 & = & 45 \\
+\ \ \ \ 1\,1\,0\,1\,1 & = & +27 \\
\hline
10\,0\,1\,0\,0\,0 & = & 72 \\
\end{array}
$$

15.5 SOLVE THESE PROBLEMS: Complete the following binary examples and prove your work by adding their base 10 equivalents.

1. 1101 +1001	**2.** 1111 + 101	**3.** 1010 +1110	**4.** 1100 +1111
5. 1111 +1001	**6.** 10010 +11101	**7.** 11011 +10001	**8.** 10101 +11111
9. 101 +11011	**10.** 1111 +11110	**11.** 10011 +11001	**12.** 11101 +11110
13. 11111 + 1	**14.** 10111 + 1101	**15.** 111 +111010	**16.** 100111 +111000
17. 110111 +110111	**18.** 111011 +101111	**19.** 1111011 +1111001	**20.** 1111101 +1111001

In the event that there are more than one carrier, $\overset{\text{C}}{\text{C}}$ is used and treated as $1 + 1$. Thus $1 + 1 + 1 + 1 = 0$ plus a carry of $\overset{\text{C}}{\text{C}}$ in the next column to the left.

ILLUSTRATIVE PROBLEM. Add the following binary digits and prove your work by adding their decimal equivalents.

$$
\begin{array}{r}
\text{C}\quad\text{C} \\
\text{CCCCCC} \\
10111 = 23 \\
11011 = 27 \\
+\ \underline{111011} = \underline{59} \\
1101101 \quad 109
\end{array}
$$

15.6 SOLVE THESE PROBLEMS: Add and prove the following examples.

	1.		2.		3.		4.
	1101		101		1110		11
	101		11011		10110		10011
	10101		10011		11		11001
	11		11111		1011		11111

	5.		6.		7.		8.
	11101		1011		101		1
	1010		1001		11		101
	111		1110		11		111
	111		10111		1011		1111

d. SUBTRACTION

All arithmetic operations that can be performed in the base 10 system can be done in a base 2 system. Like addition, binary subtraction consists of four basic facts:

$$
\begin{aligned}
1 - 1 &= 0 \\
1 - 0 &= 1 \\
0 - 1 &= 1 \quad \text{(1 must be borrowed from the next column)} \\
0 - 0 &= 0
\end{aligned}
$$

ILLUSTRATIVE PROBLEMS.

1.
$$
\begin{array}{r}
01 \\
1\cancel{1}0 = 6 \\
-\ \underline{1} = \underline{-1} \\
101 \quad 5
\end{array}
$$

SOLUTION: (1) Because the one in the rightmost column cannot be deducted from the 0 above it, the 1 in column 2 had to be borrowed, converting it to a zero.
(2) Then subtract as in the decimal system, moving from right to left.

2.   0100
$\quad\quad$ 1**0**1**1**0
$\quad$ − 1011
$\quad\quad$ 1011

SOLUTION: This problem is exactly the same as the one above with additional borrowing and lending. Note that the borrowing and lending is the same as you are accustomed to in the decimal system.

15.7 SOLVE THESE PROBLEMS: Complete the following problems. All are in base 2. Prove your answers.

1.	10111 − 10010	**2.**	10110 − 111	**3.**	10100 − 1101	**4.**	100 − 11
5.	11001 − 10111	**6.**	11011 − 100	**7.**	10001 − 1101	**8.**	1111 − 111
9.	100111 − 11011	**10.**	110111 − 1011	**11.**	11111 − 1001	**12.**	111011 − 10111
13.	11001 − 10110	**14.**	100011 − 11101	**15.**	11101 − 101	**16.**	111011 − 1111

e. MULTIPLICATION

Although the computer is not capable of performing multiplication and division (it uses repetitive addition and subtraction), it is felt that the student's understanding of the binary system will be improved by practice in multiplying and dividing binary numbers. The multiplication of numbers in the binary system is exactly the same as in the decimal system. That is:

$$0 \times 0 = 0$$
$$0 \times 1 = 0$$
$$1 \times 0 = 0$$
$$1 \times 1 = 1$$

ILLUSTRATIVE PROBLEMS. Multiply 1101_2 and 101_2.

SOLUTION:

$$
\begin{array}{r}
1101 \\
\times \quad 101 \\
\hline
\text{CCCC} \\
1101 \\
0 \\
1101 \\
\hline
1000001
\end{array}
$$

PROOF:

$$
\begin{array}{r}
1101 = 13 \\
\times \quad 101 = \times\ 5 \\
\hline
1000001 = \quad 65
\end{array}
$$

ILLUSTRATIVE PROBLEM. Multiply 111 × 1001.

SOLUTION:

$$
\begin{array}{r}
111 \\
\times 1001 \\
\hline
111 \\
0 \\
0 \\
111 \\
\hline
111111
\end{array}
$$

PROOF:

$$
\begin{array}{r}
111 = \quad 7 \\
\times \quad 1001 = \times\ 9 \\
\hline
111111 = \quad 63
\end{array}
$$

15.8 SOLVE THESE PROBLEMS: Find the products of the following numbers. All problems are base 2 numerals. Prove your answers using the decimal equivalents.

1. 11 11	**2.** 11 10	**3.** 111 11	**4.** 101 10
5. 101 11	**6.** 111 101	**7.** 1101 111	**8.** 1111 111
9. 1001 101	**10.** 1110 110	**11.** 1010 101	**12.** 1111 101
13. 1011 1111	**14.** 1101 1011	**15.** 1011 1101	**16.** 1110 1110

f. DIVISION

As in the case of the multiplication of binary numbers, binary division is included here to improve the student's ease in handling the binary system. Computers do not divide. The rules that apply to division of numbers in the decimal system are also applicable to division in the binary system.

ILLUSTRATIVE PROBLEM. Solve:

$$1001011_2 \div 1111_2$$

SOLUTION:

$$
\begin{array}{r}
101 \\
\hline
1111\overline{)1001011} \\
1111\text{xx} \\
\hline
1111 \\
1111 \\
\hline
\end{array}
$$

PROOF:

$$
\begin{array}{rcl}
1001011 &=& 75 \\
1111 &=& 15 \\
101 &=& 5 \\
1001011 \div 1111 &=& 101 \\
75 \div 15 &=& 5
\end{array}
$$

ILLUSTRATIVE PROBLEM.

$$111001 \div 110$$

SOLUTION:

$$
\begin{array}{r}
1001 \\
\hline
110\overline{)111001} \\
110\text{xxx} \\
\hline
1001 \\
110 \\
\hline
11 \quad \text{remainder}
\end{array}
$$

PROOF:

$$
\begin{array}{rcll}
110 &=& 6 \\
111001 &=& 57 \\
1001 &=& 9 \\
11 &=& 3 \\
111001 \div 110 &=& 1001 & \text{remainder } 11 \\
57 \div 6 &=& 9 & \text{remainder } 3
\end{array}
$$

15.9   SOLVE THESE PROBLEMS: Find the quotients of the following numbers. All problems are in base 2. Prove your answers using the decimal equivalents.

1. 1010 ÷ 101
2. 1110 ÷ 111
3. 1100 ÷ 11
4. 10100 ÷ 100
5. 11000 ÷ 110
6. 101100 ÷ 1011
7. 10110 ÷ 1011
8. 1101 ÷ 11

9. 11001 ÷ 101
10. 11011 ÷ 110
11. 10011 ÷ 1100
12. 10101 ÷ 1101
13. 110110 ÷ 1001
14. 101100 ÷ 1010
15. 1101110 ÷ 1011
16. 11101001 ÷ 11011

CHAPTER REVIEW

1. What are the decimal equivalents of the following binary numerals?

    11010 =   1001011 =   11010101 =

2. Find the binary equivalents of the following decimal numbers.

    80 =   101 =   214 =

3. Add the following binary numerals. Prove your work.

100	1111	10101
10	101	1010
101	1010	101
111	1001	1101

4. Subtract the following binary numbers. Prove your work.

100001	101101	11011
100	1001	1101

5. Multiply the following binary numerals. Prove your work.

1101	10111	1111
110	1011	111

6. Divide the following binary numbers. Prove your work.

    110⟌110110   111⟌100011   1011⟌1001101

16

arithmetic in base 8 and base 16

1. BASE 8
   a. Converting octal numerals to decimal numerals
   b. Converting decimal numerals to octal numerals
   c. Converting binary numerals to octal numerals

2. BASE 16
   a. Converting hexadecimal numerals to decimal numerals
   b. Converting decimal numerals to hexadecimal numerals

The binary numeration system allows basic arithmetic operations to be performed in a manner ideally suited to the computer. The major objection to the binary system is the number of bits (a contraction of the phrase *binary digits*) required to represent a large number. This has the effect of reducing computer speeds. The octal system may be used in many, but not all, computer operations, and results in a considerable savings in computer time and efficiency. In effect, the octal numeration system for computer purposes is a shorthand method of the binary system.

As in the case of decimal or binary systems, the octal system (base 8) is positional, and the digits involved in the system equal 1 less than the base, or the digits 0 through 7.

All basic arithmetic operations can be performed in the octal numeration system. However, we shall concern ourselves only with equivalent octal, decimal, and binary numerals.

a. CONVERTING OCTAL NUMERALS TO DECIMAL NUMERALS

Because octal numerals are positional, a chart of the positional values may be constructed for numbers in base 8.

4096	512	64	8	1
$8 \times 8 \times 8 \times 8$	$8 \times 8 \times 8$	8×8	8×1	1
8^4	8^3	8^2	8^1	8^0

The chart indicates the following:

1. The octal digit in the rightmost column must be multiplied by 8^0 or 1. (Any number with a 0 exponent $= 1$).

2. The octal digit in the second rightmost column must be multiplied by 8^1 or 8×1 or 8.

306

3. The octal digit in the third rightmost column must be multiplied by 8^2 or 8×8 or 64.

4. The octal digit in the fourth rightmost column must be multiplied by 8^3 or $8 \times 8 \times 8$ or 512.

5. The octal digit in the fifth rightmost column must be multiplied by 8^4 or $8 \times 8 \times 8 \times 8$ or 4096.

6. This chart could be extended indefinitely with the sixth column equal to 8^5, the seventh 8^6, and so on.

To find the decimal equivalent of a base 8 numeral it is necessary to multiply each digit by the value of the position of that digit as indicated by the chart. For example, the value of the four in the fourth position from the decimal (4000) is 4×8^3 or $4 \times 8 \times 8 \times 8$ or $4 \times 512 = 2048$. To find the decimal equivalent of an octal numeral containing many digits, the positional value of each digit must be found, and all of the positional values added to arrive at the decimal equivalent.

ILLUSTRATIVE PROBLEM. Convert 356_8 to its decimal equivalent.

SOLUTION: Construct a table of the positional values of the octal numeration system:

512	64	8	1
$8 \times 8 \times 8$	8×8	8×1	1
8^3	8^2	8^1	8^0

Multiply the digit in each position by the positional value of that position. Add the positional values.

$$6 \times 8^0 = 6 \times 1 \qquad = \quad 6$$
$$5 \times 8^1 = 5 \times 8 \qquad = \quad 40$$
$$3 \times 8^2 = 3 \times 8 \times 8 = \underline{192}$$

238 is the decimal equivalent of 356_8

This can be expressed as $356_8 = 238_{10}$

ILLUSTRATIVE PROBLEM. What is the decimal equivalent of 2322_8?

SOLUTION: Construct a table of the positional values of the octal numeration system.

4096	512	64	8	1
$8 \times 8 \times 8 \times 8$	$8 \times 8 \times 8$	8×8	8×1	1
8^4	8^3	8^2	8^1	8^0

Multiply the digit in each position by the positional value of that position. Add the positional values.

$$2 \times 8^0 = 2 \times 1 \qquad\qquad = \qquad 2$$
$$2 \times 8^1 = 2 \times 8 \qquad\qquad = \qquad 16$$
$$3 \times 8^2 = 3 \times 8 \times 8 \qquad = \qquad 192$$
$$2 \times 8^3 = 2 \times 8 \times 8 \times 8 = \overline{1024}$$
$$1234_{10} = 2322_8$$

16.1 SOLVE THESE PROBLEMS: Find the decimal equivalent of the following numbers.

1. 12_8	**11.** 1212_8
2. 126_8	**12.** 2216_8
3. 101_2	**13.** 3741_8
4. 237_8	**14.** 2416_8
5. 257_8	**15.** 2121_3
6. 635_8	**16.** 3467_8
7. 570_8	**17.** 3122_4
8. 706_8	**18.** 2780_9
9. 574_8	**19.** 3216_7
10. 370_8	**20.** 2174_8

**b. CONVERTING DECIMAL NUMERALS
TO OCTAL NUMERALS**

To convert decimal to octal numerals, the simplest approach is the remainder method used in the decimal to binary conversion. In this case, 8 is divided into the decimal number. The quotient and all succeeding quotients are similarly divided by 8. In each case, because we are using the base 8 system, the remainder must be equal to 0 through 7. The remainders are kept in the order in which they occur, and it is these remainders that result in the equivalent octal numeral with the last remainder the leftmost digit in the answer.

ILLUSTRATIVE PROBLEM. Find the octal equivalent of 127_{10}.

SOLUTION:

$$
\begin{array}{r}
0 \quad \text{r}\,1 \\
8\overline{|1} \quad \text{r}\,7 \\
8\overline{|15} \quad \text{r}\,7 \\
8\overline{|127}
\end{array}
$$

Answer: $127_{10} = 177_8$

PROOF:

$$7 \times 8^0 = 7 \times 1 \quad = \quad 7$$
$$7 \times 8^1 = 7 \times 8 \quad = \quad 56$$
$$1 \times 8^2 = 1 \times 8 \times 8 = \underline{\quad 64}$$
$$127$$

Proof: $127_{10} = 177_8$

ILLUSTRATIVE PROBLEM. Find the base 8 equivalent of the radix 10 numeral 345. Prove your work by converting the octal solution to its decimal equivalent.

SOLUTION:

$$\begin{array}{r} 0 \;\; r\,5 \\ 8\overline{|5} \;\; r\,3 \\ 8\overline{|\,43} \;\; r\,1 \\ 8\overline{|\,345} \end{array}$$

Answer: $345_{10} = 531_8$

PROOF:

$$1 \times 8^0 = 1 \times 1 \quad = \quad 1$$
$$3 \times 8^1 = 3 \times 8 \quad = \quad 24$$
$$5 \times 8^2 = 5 \times 8 \times 8 = \underline{320}$$
$$345$$

PROOF:

$$345_{10} = 531_8$$

16.2 SOLVE THESE PROBLEMS: Find the octal equivalents of the following decimal numerals. Prove your work by octal to decimal conversion.

1. 63	**11.** 729
2. 89	**12.** 876
3. 96	**13.** 935
4. 101	**14.** 1038
5. 126	**15.** 1168
6. 237	**16.** 1247
7. 268	**17.** 5063
8. 346	**18.** 7937
9. 378	**19.** 7364
10. 846	**20.** 9287

**c. CONVERTING BINARY NUMERALS
TO OCTAL NUMERALS**

As was mentioned earlier, the octal numbering system provides a shorthand method for handling binary digits. The method for converting binary to octal numerals is as follows:

    a. Separate the binary digits into groups of 3, beginning with the rightmost.

    b. Convert each group of 3 binary digits to its decimal equivalent ($101_2 = 5_{10}$, $111_2 = 7_{10}$).

    c. The decimal equivalent of each group of 3 binary digits is the octal equivalent of the binary numeral.

    Remember, do not add the equivalents.

The solution may be proven by converting the binary and octal equivalents to the same decimal numeral.

ILLUSTRATIVE PROBLEM. Convert 1101111_2 to its octal equivalent. Prove your work by converting the binary and octal numerals to their decimal equivalents.

SOLUTION: Separate the binary digits into groups of 3 beginning with the rightmost.

$$1/101/111$$

Convert each group to its decimal equivalent.

Binary		Decimal Equivalent
1	=	1
101	=	5
111	=	7

Answer: $1101111_2 = 157_8$

1 5 7
1/101/111   (Binary 1 = 1, Binary 101 = 5, Binary 111 = 7.)

PROOF:

Convert 1101111_2 and 157_8 to their decimal equivalents:

BASE 2 TABLE:

	64	32	16	8	4	2	1
Binary numeral	1	1	0	1	1	1	1

$$1 \times 64 = 64$$
$$1 \times 32 = 32$$
$$0 \times 16 = 0$$
$$1 \times 8 = 8$$
$$1 \times 4 = 4$$
$$1 \times 2 = 2$$
$$1 \times 1 = 1$$
$$= 111_{10}$$

BASE 8 TABLE:

	64	8	1
Octal numeral	1	5	7

$$1 \times 64 = 64$$
$$5 \times 8 = 40$$
$$7 \times 1 = 7$$
$$111_{10}$$

Then

$$1101111_2 = 111_{10}$$

and

$$157_8 = 111_{10}$$

therefore

$$1101111_2 = 157_8$$

ILLUSTRATIVE PROBLEM. What is the octal equivalent of 1101011111_2? Prove your solution.

SOLUTION: Separate the binary digits into groups of 3 beginning with the rightmost:

$$1/101/011/111$$

Convert each group to its decimal equivalent.

Binary		*Decimal Equivalent*
1	=	1
101	=	5
011	=	3
111	=	7

Answer: $1101011111_2 = 1537_8$

PROOF:

Convert 1101011111_2 and 1537_8 to their decimal equivalents.

BASE 2 TABLE:

Binary numeral	512	256	128	64	32	16	8	4	2	1
	1	1	0	1	0	1	1	1	1	1

$$1 \times 512 = 512$$
$$1 \times 256 = 256$$
$$0 \times 128 = 0$$
$$1 \times 64 = 64$$
$$0 \times 32 = 0$$
$$1 \times 16 = 16$$
$$1 \times 8 = 8$$
$$1 \times 4 = 4$$
$$1 \times 2 = 2$$
$$1 \times 1 = 1$$
$$\overline{863_{10}}$$

BASE 8 TABLE:

Octal numeral	512	64	8	1
	1	5	3	7

$$1 \times 512 = 512$$
$$5 \times 64 = 320$$
$$3 \times 8 = 24$$
$$7 \times 1 = 7$$
$$\overline{863_{10}}$$

$$\text{Binary } 1101011111 = 863_{10}$$
$$\text{Octal } 1537 \qquad = 863_{10}$$

16.3 **SOLVE THESE PROBLEMS:** Determine the equivalent numerals.

	Binary Numeral	Decimal Equivalent	Octal Numeral	Decimal Equivalent
1.	1011	—	—	—
2.	1101	—	—	—
3.	11101	—	—	—
4.	10111	—	—	—
5.	110110	—	—	—
6.	111011	—	—	—
7.	101101	—	—	—
8.	1011111	—	—	—
9.	1010101	—	—	—
10.	1101101	—	—	—
11.	1011011	—	—	—
12.	11100111	—	—	—
13.	11011011	—	—	—
14.	10111101	—	—	—
15.	10101101	—	—	—
16.	110001101	—	—	—
17.	101010111	—	—	—
18.	110110110	—	—	—
19.	101110111	—	—	—
20.	101111011	—	—	—

The final numeration system to be discussed is the hexadecimal system, base 16. It is used by an important family of computers, and must be understood by computer programmers. Like the binary, octal, and decimal systems, the hexadecimal system is positional, and the digits involved in the system are the base minus one, or the digits from 0 through 15. Because the digits larger than 9 require two places, it would be difficult to determine the positional value of the digit 12, because it covers two positions. To overcome this problem the digits involved in the hexadecimal system are as follows:

Decimal Equivalent	Hexadecimal Digits
0	0
1	1
2	2
3	3
4	4
5	5
6	6
7	7
8	8
9	9
10	A
11	B
12	C
13	D
14	E
15	F

Thus, the hexadecimal three digit numeral 3-12-4 would be written as 3C4.

a. CONVERTING HEXADECIMAL NUMERALS TO DECIMAL NUMERALS

Because the hexadecimal numeration system is positional, it is necessary to prepare a chart of base 16 positional values. This is done in the same manner as the charts that have been discussed previously. Then to find the decimal equivalent of a hexadecimal numeral, one must multiply that digit by the value of its position as indicated on a base 16 chart.

65,536	4,096	256	16	1
$16 \times 16 \times 16 \times 16$	$16 \times 16 \times 16$	16×16	16×1	1
16^4	16^3	16^2	16^1	16^0

Thus a 4 in the third column to the left of the decimal (400.) would have the decimal equivalent of $4 \times 256 = 1024$. As in the case with the other numeration systems discussed, the decimal equivalent of a hexadecimal numeral containing many digits is the sum of positional value of each hexadecimal digit.

ILLUSTRATIVE PROBLEM. Convert the hexadecimal number 423 to its decimal equivalent.

SOLUTION: Construct a table of the positional values of the hexadecimal numbering system.

65,536	4096	256	16	1
$16 \times 16 \times 16 \times 16$	$16 \times 16 \times 16$	16×16	16×1	1
16^4	16^3	16^2	16^1	16^0

Multiply the digit in each position by the positional value of that position.

Add the positional values.

$$3 \times 16^0 = 3 \times 1 \qquad = \quad 3$$
$$2 \times 16^1 = 2 \times 16 \qquad = \quad 32$$
$$4 \times 16^2 = 4 \times 16 \times 16 = \underline{1024}$$
$$1059 \text{ is the decimal equivalent of}$$
$$\text{hexadecimal 423 or } 423_{16} = 1059_{10}$$

ILLUSTRATIVE PROBLEM. What is the decimal equivalent of 3268_{16}?

SOLUTION:

$$8 \times 16^0 = 8 \times 1 \qquad\qquad = \quad 8$$
$$6 \times 16^1 = 6 \times 16 \qquad\qquad = \quad 96$$
$$2 \times 16^2 = 2 \times 16 \times 16 \qquad = \quad 512$$
$$3 \times 16^3 = 3 \times 16 \times 16 \times 16 = \underline{12{,}288}$$
$$12{,}904_{10} = 3{,}268_{16}$$

16.4 SOLVE THESE PROBLEMS: Find the decimal equivalents of the following numerals.

1. 12_{16}
2. 26_{16}
3. $A4_{16}$
4. $2B6_{16}$
5. $3F8_{16}$
6. $E24_{16}$
7. EFA_{16}
8. 127_{16}
9. $32A_{16}$
10. $1C3_{16}$

11. $9DD_{16}$
12. 1001_{10}
13. 101010111_2
14. 173_8
15. 264_8
16. 1110111_2
17. $3A51_{16}$
18. ABC_6
19. FBC_{16}
20. $FACB_{16}$

b. CONVERTING DECIMAL NUMERALS TO HEXADECIMAL NUMERALS

The most widely used system of decimal to hexadecimal conversion is the remainder method illustrated in decimal to binary and decimal to octal conversion. In this case, 16 is divided into the decimal number. The quotient and all succeeding quotients are similarly divided by 16. In each case, because we are dividing by 16, the remainder must be equal to 0 through 15. The remainders are kept in the order in which they occur, and it is these remainders that result in the hexadecimal answer. *Remember, the last remainder is the most significant (leftmost) digit.* Decimal to hexadecimal conversion may be proven by reconverting the hexadecimal solution to its decimal equivalent.

ILLUSTRATIVE PROBLEM. Find the hexadecimal equivalent of 158_{10}.

SOLUTION:

$$
\begin{array}{l}
0 \quad r\ 9 \\
16\overline{|9} \quad r\ 14 \qquad 158_{10} = 9 \quad 14_{16} \\
16\overline{|158} \\
\qquad \text{Answer:} \quad 158_{10} = 9E_{16}
\end{array}
$$

PROOF:

Construct a table of the positional values of the hexadecimal numeration system.

256	16	1
16×16	16×1	1
16^2	16^1	16^0

Multiply the digit in each position by the positional value of that position.
Add the positional values.

$$
\begin{array}{l}
E(14) \times 16^0 = 14 \times 1 = 14 \\
9 \times 16^1 = 9 \times 16 = \underline{144} \\
158_{10} = 9E_{16}
\end{array}
$$

ILLUSTRATIVE PROBLEM. What is the hexadecimal equivalent of 362_{10}?

SOLUTION:

$$
\begin{array}{l}
0 \quad r\ 1 \\
16\overline{|1} \quad r\ 6 \\
16\overline{\ 22} \quad r\ 10 \qquad 362_{10} = 16A_{16} \\
16\overline{\ 362}
\end{array}
$$

PROOF:

$$A(10) \times 16^0 = 10 \times 1 \qquad = \quad 10$$
$$6 \times 16^1 = 6 \times 16 \qquad = \quad 96$$
$$1 \times 16^2 = 1 \times 16 \times 16 = 256$$
$$\overline{362_{10}} = 16A_{16}$$

16.5 SOLVE THESE PROBLEMS: Find the hexadecimal equivalents of the following decimal numerals. Prove your answers by converting your hexadecimal solution to its decimal equivalent.

1. 26	**11.** 1527
2. 32	**12.** 1110
3. 74	**13.** 1016
4. 96	**14.** 2032
5. 123	**15.** 1446
6. 268	**16.** 2637
7. 459	**17.** 2868
8. 327	**18.** 3752
9. 716	**19.** 5268
10. 838	**20.** 7933

CHAPTER REVIEW

1. Convert the following octal numerals to their decimal equivalents:

$$1420 = \qquad 2747 = \qquad 4038 =$$

2. Convert the following binary numerals to octal numerals:

$$111101 = \qquad 101011 = \qquad 110110 =$$

3. Convert the following decimal numerals to their octal equivalents:

$$129 = \qquad 457 = \qquad 639 =$$

4. Convert the following hexadecimal numerals to their decimal equivalents:

$$FE3 = \qquad 62A = \qquad 4AA =$$

5. Convert the following decimal numerals to their hexadecimal equivalents:

$$284 = \qquad 327 = \qquad 198 =$$

NINE
MATHEMATICS
IN
MANAGEMENT

Management, to operate at maximum efficiency, requires a variety of statements of business conditions. The most common, and most important of these are the balance sheet and the income statement. The balance sheet has been described as "a still photograph" of the values of a business at a particular moment. On the balance sheet are listed the values of the things the business owns, the amounts it owes, and the difference between the two—the amount that it is worth. The income statement, rather than showing values at a particular moment, is a summary for a particular period of time. On the income statements the costs and expenses of doing business are deducted from the income to determine the net profit.

Because the understanding of statements is vital to effective managerial control, a considerable body of knowledge has been developed for the analysis of financial statements. In this chapter we shall discuss some of the more important methods of interpreting income statements and balance sheets.

17

analysis of financial statements

1. BALANCE SHEET
   a. Horizontal analysis
   b. Vertical analysis

2. INCOME STATEMENT
   a. Horizontal analysis
   b. Vertical analysis

3. OTHER ANALYTICAL PROCEDURES
   a. Working capital
   b. Current ratio
   c. Rate earned on average total assets
   d. Rate earned on average capital
   e. Earnings per share of common stock

1. BALANCE SHEET

A balance sheet is a statement showing the values of a business at a particular time. From the values *owned* by the business the values *owed* by the business are deducted. The result, the excess of the values owned over the values owed, is the net worth of the business. In other words, if a man has $50 and owes $30, he is worth $20. To convert this into accounting terminology:

$$\text{Assets} = \text{Values owned}$$
$$\text{Liabilities} = \text{Values owed}$$
$$\text{Capital} = \text{Worth or net worth}$$

The formula for a balance sheet is:

$$\text{Assets} - \text{Liabilities} = \text{Capital}$$
$$\$50 \quad - \quad \$30 \quad = \quad \$20$$

This can also be stated as:

$$\text{Assets} = \text{Liabilities} + \text{Capital}$$
$$\$50 \quad = \quad \$30 \quad + \quad \$20$$

Assets are generally divided into the categories of current assets and fixed assets. Current assets are those that will be used or converted into cash in a short period of time. Cash, accounts receivable, and inventories are current assets. Fixed assets are those which will not be used or converted to cash in the near future. Fixed assets include land, buildings, and equipment.

Liabilities are grouped under the headings "current liabilities" and "fixed" or "long-term liabilities." Current liabilities are those which will be paid shortly, such as accounts payable, taxes payable and salaries payable. Typical of fixed liabilities are mortgages payable and bonds payable which will not become due for a number of years.

Capital, the excess of all assets over all liabilities is also known as net worth, proprietorship, or stockholder's equity.

320

ILLUSTRATIVE PROBLEM. Bob Harrison, an attorney, had the following assets and liabilities on June 30, 19__: cash, $6,000; due from customers, $3,000; bank loan, $1,000; auto, $3,500 on which he owed a finance company $2,000. Prepare a balance sheet.

SOLUTION:

BOB HARRISON
BALANCE SHEET
JUNE 30, 19__

ASSETS

Cash	$6,000	
Accounts receivable	3,000	
Auto	3,500	
Total assets		$12,500

LIABILITIES

Bank loan	$1,000	
Auto loan	2,000	
Total liabilities		$ 3,000

CAPITAL

Bob Harrison, capital	9,500
Total liabilities and capital	$12,500

Note that Assets ($12,500) = Liabilities ($3,000) + Capital ($9,500)

17.1 SOLVE THIS PROBLEM: The following information was taken from the books and records of Allan Golden, Inc., an accountant, on June 30, 19__: Accounts Payable, $12,000; Cash, $16,000; Notes Payable, $4,000; Merchandise Inventory, $18,000; Accounts Receivable, $14,000. Determine the value of Mr. Golden's business by preparing a balance sheet at June 30, 19__.

Balance sheets generally are prepared according to a prescribed format. The following is a typical balance sheet.

J. TRUEMAN, INC.
BALANCE SHEET
JULY 31, 19__

CURRENT ASSETS

Cash	$10,000	
Merchandise inventory	8,000	
Accounts receivable	12,000	
Total current assets		$30,000

FIXED ASSETS

Land	$15,000	
Buildings	45,000	
Equipment	9,000	
Total fixed assets		69,000
Total assets		$99,000

Liabilities and Capital

CURRENT LIABILITIES

Accounts payable	$17,000	
Salaries payable	1,000	
Total current liabilities		$18,000

FIXED LIABILITIES

Mortgage payable	40,000
Total liabilities	$58,000
J. Trueman, capital	41,000
Total liabilities and capital	$99,000

17.2 SOLVE THE FOLLOWING PROBLEMS RELATED TO THE ABOVE BALANCE SHEET:

1. What is the amount of excess of assets over liabilities?
2. Numerically prove that assets equal liabilities plus capital.
3. What was J. Trueman worth on July 31, 19__?

a. HORIZONTAL ANALYSIS

Although the study of an individual balance sheet reveals much information concerning the financial condition of a business, it does not indicate the changes that have occurred between two successive periods. Thus a balance sheet showing capital of $1,000,000 might be quite impressive; it would be less so if the previous period's capital was $2,000,000. For this reason, when statements are being presented for analysis it is customary to present balance sheets for two consecutive periods. These are called comparative statements. By comparing the statements, side by side, for two periods, information concerning the changes in the individual items comprising the balance sheet may be determined. Management is vitally interested in such information as the amount and percent of change in various values making up the balance sheet.

Horizontal analysis requires calculating the amount of change in each item on the balance sheet, and the percent of the first year's change. Remember, the first year is always the base used in determining the percent.

ILLUSTRATIVE PROBLEM. The following is the current asset section of the balance sheets of Kauffman's and Company for the years ended December

31, 1968 and 1969. Calculate the amount and percent of difference for each of the current assets.

Current Assets	December 31, 1968	December 31, 1969	Increase or Decrease* Amount	Percent
Cash	$ 4,000	$ 7,000	3000	75%
Accounts receivable	12,000	9,000	(3000)	—
Notes receivable	8,000	12,000	4000	—
Merchandise inventory	6,000	8,000	2000	—
Total current assets	$30,000	$36,000	6000	—

* The asterisk indicates a decrease.

SOLUTION:

Current Assets	December 31, 1968	December 31, 1969	Increase or Decrease* Amount	Percent
Cash	$ 4,000	$ 7,000	$3,000	75%
Accounts receivable	12,000	9,000	3,000*	25%*
Notes receivable	8,000	12,000	4,000	50%
Merchandise inventory	6,000	8,000	2,000	$33\frac{1}{3}$%
Total current assets	$30,000	$36,000	$6,000	20%

* The asterisk indicates a decrease.

The problem was solved in the following manner:

1. First the differences between the December 31, 1968 and December 31, 1969 amounts were determined and entered in the increase or decrease amount column. Note that the accounts receivable decrease of $3,000 is indicated by an asterisk.

2. The second step required the calculation of the percent of change using the earliest year (December 31, 1968) as the base.

$$\text{Cash} \quad \frac{\$3,000}{\$4,000} = 75\%$$

$$\text{Accounts receivable} \quad \frac{\$3,000}{\$12,000} = 25\%$$

$$\text{Notes receivable} \quad \frac{\$4,000}{\$8,000} = 50\%$$

$$\text{Merchandise inventory} \quad \frac{\$2,000}{\$6,000} = 33\frac{1}{3}\%$$

3. The sum of the differences in the Increase or Decrease amount column (adding increases and deducting decreases) must equal the difference between the total current assets at December 31, 1968 and the total current assets at December 31, 1969. ($3,000 —

$3,000 + $4,000 + $2,000 = $6,000$ and $36,000 - $30,000 = $6,000.)

4. Note that the 20% increase in total current assets is *not* the total of the Increase or Decrease percent column. It was arrived at in the same manner as all of the percentages; that is, the increase of $6,000 over the base year of $30,000 = 20%.

$$\frac{\$6,000}{\$30,000} = 20\%$$

The percent column is never added in horizontal analysis.

17.3   SOLVE THIS PROBLEM: Prepare a horizontal analysis of the following balance sheet. Round out your answer to the nearest 1%.

J. JAMPOL AND SON
COMPARATIVE BALANCE SHEET
DECEMBER 31, 1968 AND 1969

Assets	*1968*	*1969*	Increase or Decrease Amount	Percent
CURRENT ASSETS				
Cash	$ 7,000	$ 10,500	3500	50
Accounts receivable	9,000	12,000	3000	33⅓
Notes receivable	15,000	12,500	(2500)	16
Merchandise inventory	30,000	36,000	6000	20
Supplies	520	390	(130)	25
Total current assets	$ 61,520	$ 71,390	9970	−7
FIXED ASSETS				
Land	$ 40,000	$ 40,000		
Building	75,000	70,000	5000	6
Total fixed assets	$115,000	$110,000	5000	—
Total assets	$176,520	$181,390	(4870)	—
Liabilities and Capital				
CURRENT LIABILITIES				
Accounts payable	$ 36,000	$ 42,000	6000	16
Salaries payable	3,000	3,500	500	—
Total current liabilities	$ 39,000	$ 45,000	6000	—
FIXED LIABILITIES				
Mortgage payable	$ 60,000	$ 54,000	(6000)	—
Total liabilities	$ 99,000	$ 99,500	500	—
Capital	$ 77,520	$ 81,890	4370	—
Total liabilities and capital	$176,520	$181,390	4870	

b. VERTICAL ANALYSIS

As we have seen, the major groupings in the balance sheet are total assets and total liabilities and capital. Vertical analysis is a method of statement analysis that indicates the importance of each item to the total of the major grouping. A vertically analyzed balance sheet is one that shows the percent that each asset bears to total assets, that each liability bears to total liabilities and capital, and that each element of capital bears to total liabilities and capital. By vertically analyzing comparative statements, trends may be discovered, the knowledge of which may be vital to management. For example, if the percent of cash to total assets has decreased while the percent of accounts receivable (money owed to the company from customers) to total assets has increased, it is possible that the methods of collecting from customers should be investigated.

Arithmetically, vertical analysis is very simple. It is merely a matter of finding the percent each asset is of total assets and each liability and element of capital is of total liabilities and capital. In each case, the total is the base, and the sum of all of the individual percents for any of the major groupings equals 100%.

ILLUSTRATIVE PROBLEM. From the comparative balance sheet of Roffis, Inc., for the years ended December 31, 1968 and 1969, compute a vertical analysis using total assets and total liabilities, and stockholders' equity as the bases.

ROFFIS, INC.
COMPARATIVE BALANCE SHEET
DECEMBER 31, 1968 AND 1969

	1968		1969	
Assets	*Amount*	*Percent*	*Amount*	*Percent*
CURRENT ASSETS				
Cash	$ 40,000	20%	$ 30,000	10%
Accounts receivable	70,000	35%	60,000	20%
Merchandise inventory	30,000	15%	45,000	15%
Total current assets	$140,000	70%	$135,000	45%
FIXED ASSETS				
Furniture	$ 40,000	20%	$ 75,000	25%
Equipment	20,000	10%	90,000	30%
Total fixed assets	$ 60,000	30%	$165,000	55%
Total assets	$200,000	100%	$300,000	100%

Liabilities

CURRENT LIABILITIES				
Accounts payable	$ 10,000	5%	30,000	10%
Taxes payable	30,000	15%	45,000	15%
Total current liabilities	$ 40,000	20%	$ 75,000	25%
FIXED LIABILITIES				
Bonds payable	$ 70,000	35%	$ 66,000	22%
Total liabilities	$110,000	55%	$141,000	47%
STOCKHOLDERS' EQUITY				
Capital stock	$ 80,000	40%	$150,000	50%
Retained earnings	10,000	5%	9,000	3%
Total stockholders' equity	$ 90,000	45%	$159,000	53%
Total liabilities and stockholders' equity	$200,000	100%	$300,000	100%

SOLUTION: Using the total assets of 1968 ($200,000) as a base, the percent of each of the assets to total assets was determined. For example:

$$\text{Cash} = \frac{\$40,000}{\$200,000} \text{ or } 20\% \text{ of the total assets}$$

$$\text{Accounts receivable} = \frac{\$70,000}{\$200,000} \text{ or } 35\% \text{ of the total assets}$$

This was continued taking each asset separately and finding its percent of the total assets of $200,000. The arithmetic accuracy of the solution was proven by adding all of the percents and finding the sum of 100%.

The total liabilities and stockholders' equity of $200,000 was used as a base against which each of the elements comprising that total was converted to a percent of $200,000. In other words,

$$\text{Accounts payable} = \frac{\$10,000}{\$200,000} \text{ or } 5\% \text{ of the total liabilities and}$$

$$\text{stockholders' equity}$$

Again, the individual percents must total 100 percent. The same procedure was followed for both years. Vertical analysis is frequently done using more bases than two. Current assets, fixed assets, current liabilities, fixed liabilities, and stockholders' equity might all have been bases.

In vertical analysis the percent column must total 100 percent.

17.4   SOLVE THIS PROBLEM:

M. GREENHOLZ AND COMPANY
COMPARATIVE BALANCE SHEET
DECEMBER 31, 1974 AND 1975

Assets	1974 Amount	1974 Percent	1975 Amount	1975 Percent
CURRENT ASSETS				
Cash	$ 15,000	11 %	$ 25,000	15 %
Accounts receivable	27,000	20	35,000	21
Notes receivable	9,000	7	15,000	9
Total current assets	$ 51,000	39 %	$ 75,000	45 %
FIXED ASSETS				
Land	$ 36,000	27 %	$ 45,000	27.5 %
Building	45,000	34	45,000	27.5
Total fixed assets	$ 81,000	61 %	$ 90,000	55 %
Total assets	$132,000	100 %	$165,000	100 %
Liabilities and Capital				
CURRENT LIABILITIES				
Accounts payable	$ 18,000	___ %	$ 20,000	___ %
Salaries payable	3,000	___	5,000	___
Total current liabilities	$ 21,000	___ %	$ 25,000	___ %
FIXED LIABILITIES				
Mortgage payable	$ 39,000	___ %	$ 35,000	___ %
Bonds payable	42,000	___	35,000	___
Total fixed liabilities	$ 81,000	___ %	$ 70,000	___ %
Total liabilities	$102,000	___ %	$ 95,000	___ %
M. Greenholz, capital	$ 30,000	___ %	$ 70,000	___ %
Total liabilities and capital	$132,000	100 %	$165,000	100 %

Complete the comparative balance sheet, using vertical analysis, and total assets and total liabilities and capital as the bases.

2. INCOME STATEMENTS

An income statement is a summary of all income (revenue) and expenses for a specified period of time. It is prepared by adding all of the revenues of a business and deducting all of the expenses. The excess of income over expense is called net profit. Unlike a balance sheet, it is not a "still photograph" at a particular moment but an accumulation of what took place for a particular period of time, such as a month or a year. Every item on a balance sheet can be converted into cash, while on an income statement, the items have no worth, they merely indicate results. For example, merchandise inventory, a balance sheet item, can be sold for cash and has value. Total sales, an income statement item, indicates the amount that has been sold, and has no value. The formula for an income statement is:

$$\text{Total income} - \text{Total costs and expenses} = \text{Net profit}$$

ILLUSTRATIVE PROBLEM. At the end of a year, G. Foster, a physician, summarized his records and arrived at the following totals: Income from regular practice, $20,000; rent, $2,400; salaries, $5,000; utilities, $1,200; supplies, $600; other expenses, $2,000; income from minor surgery, $5,000.

SOLUTION:

INCOME

From regular practice	$20,000
From surgery	5,000
Total income	$25,000

EXPENSES

Salaries	$5,000	
Rent	2,400	
Utilities	1,200	
Supplies	600	
Other expenses	2,000	
Total expenses		11,200
Net profit		$13,800

The preceding illustration described a typical income statement for a business dealing in services. Organizations that sell merchandise require additional information. Operators of merchandising concerns need to know the profit they make on the sale of merchandise before expenses are deducted. This is called the gross profit. Knowledge of the gross profit enables management to check the adequacy of its markup, and compare it with that of similar businesses or the gross profit of its own business in prior periods.

The formula for the income statement of a merchandising concern is:

$$\text{Sales} - \text{Cost of goods sold} = \text{Gross profit} - \text{Expenses} = \text{Net profit}$$

17.5 SOLVE THESE PROBLEMS:

1. At the end of the year the books of the law firm of William Rosen and Company revealed the following information: Fees from clients, $80,000; rent, $3,608; utilities, $2,612; salaries, $16,000; traveling expenses, $620; other expenses, $4,000. Determine the profit for the year.

2. Calculate the net income of the Value Clothing Store from the following information: expenses, $8,000; sales, $40,000; cost of goods sold, $25,000.

Of course, the more complicated the business, the more detailed the income statement. Revenues and expenses of similar nature are grouped together to arrive at important subtotals. However, all income statements are based on the formula Revenues − Costs and Expenses = Profits.

The following is a typical income statement for a merchandise type of business:

F. COGAN
INCOME STATEMENT
FOR THE YEAR ENDED DECEMBER 31, 19___

Sales		$85,812
Less sales returns		2,614
Net sales		$83,198
Cost of goods sold:		
Inventory January 1, 19___	$18,037	
Purchases	53,216	
Merchandise available for sale	71,253	
Inventory December 31, 19___	22,128	
Cost of goods sold	$49,125	
Gross profit		49,125
		$34,073
Operating expenses:		
Salaries	$ 8,212	
Rent	2,400	
Utilities	4,678	
Selling	3,295	
Miscellaneous	1,769	
Total operating expenses		20,354
Net profit for the year		$13,719

a. HORIZONTAL ANALYSIS

Vertical and horizontal analysis may be performed on comparative income statements as well as comparative balance sheets. The horizontal analysis of a comparative income statement affords management with information concerning the increase and the decrease of each of the items that make up the income statement. For example, such information as the fact that a 20% increase in advertising resulted in a 50% increase in sales is of great importance for future planning. As in the case of the balance sheet, the horizontal analysis of income statements requires finding the difference of each item for the two years, and then finding what percent that difference is of the earliest year. For example, if telephone expense was $3,600 for the earliest year and $2,400 for the second year, the difference is:

$$\$3,600 - \$2,400 = \$1,200$$

$$\text{The percent is} = \frac{\text{Difference } \$1,200}{\text{Earliest year } \$3,600} = 33\tfrac{1}{3}\%$$

ILLUSTRATIVE PROBLEM. Horizontally analyze the following income statement.

		1974	1975	INCREASE OR DECREASE* Amount	Percent
JAY-JAY GIFTS **COMPARATIVE INCOME STATEMENTS** **DECEMBER 31, 1974 AND 1975**					
Sales		$120,000	$150,000	$30,000	25%
Cost of goods sold		75,000	90,000	15,000	20%
Gross profit		$ 45,000	$ 60,000	$15,000	$33\frac{1}{3}$%
Expenses					
Selling	$ 3,000		$ 4,000	1,000	$33\frac{1}{3}$%
Administrative	10,000		7,000	3,000*	30%*
Miscellaneous	7,000		14,000	7,000	100%
Total		$ 20,000	$ 25,000	$ 5,000	25%
Net profit		$ 25,000	$ 35,000	$10,000	40%

* The asterisk indicates a decrease.

It is important to remember that in horizontal analysis the percents are not together.

The problem was solved in the following manner:

1. The difference between the two years was calculated for each item:

Sales = $150,000 − $120,000 = $30,000 increase
Cost of goods sold = $90,000 − $75,000 = $15,000 increase
Gross profit = $60,000 − $45,000 = $15,000 increase
and so forth.

These amounts are entered in the Increase or Decrease column. Note that the amount of decrease in administrative expense is indicated by the asterisk.

2. The percent of increase or decrease was determined by using the earliest year as a base.

$$\text{Sales} = \frac{\text{Increase } \$30,000}{\text{Earliest year } \$120,000} = 25\%$$

$$\text{Cost of goods sold} = \frac{\text{Increase } \$15,000}{\text{Earliest year } \$75,000} = 20\%$$

and so forth.

3. The increase or decrease amount column should total the increase in net profit. The increase or decrease percent column is not added.

17.6 *SOLVE THIS PROBLEM:*

FROMM'S
COMPARATIVE INCOME STATEMENT
FOR THE YEARS ENDED DECEMBER 31, 1974 AND 1975

		1974	1975	*INCREASE OR DECREASE** Amount	*Percent*
Sales		$450,000	$510,000	$ 60000	13 %
Less returns		25,000	35,000	10	40
Net sales		$425,000	$475,000	$ 50000	
Cost of goods sold		300,000	320,000	20600	7
Gross profit		$125,000	$155,000	$ 90000	60 %
Expenses					
Selling	$16,000		$28,000	$ 12000	75 %
Administrative	19,000		22,000	3000	16
Buying	24,000		25,000	1000	4
Advertising	16,000		14,000	1000 *	13 ✝
Miscellaneous	8,000		7,000	1000 *	13 ✝
Total expenses		$ 83,000	$ 96,000	$	%
Net profit		$ 42,000	$ 59,000	$	%

Complete this income statement, using the horizontal analysis method.

b. VERTICAL ANALYSIS

The vertical analysis of income statements is performed in the same manner as is done on balance sheets, with one difference. On balance sheets there may be a variety of bases, while on income statements, vertical analysis is generally performed with net sales as the only base. In other words, the percent of each item is determined using net sales as the base.

ILLUSTRATIVE PROBLEM. Vertically analyze the Bruckner's, Inc. comparative income statement at the top of page 332.

The problem was solved in the following manner:

1. With each year's net sales as the base, the percent of each item to that year's net sales was determined.

$$\text{Selling expense (1974)} = \frac{\$\ 5,000}{\$100,000} = 5\%$$

$$\text{Buying expense (1974)} = \frac{\$\ 8,000}{\$100,000} = 8\%$$

BRUCKNER'S, INC.
COMPARATIVE INCOME STATEMENT
FOR THE YEARS ENDED DECEMBER 31, 1974 AND 1975

	1974	%	1975	%
Sales	$110,000	110%	$206,000	103%
Less returns	10,000	10	6,000	3
Net sales	$100,000	100%	$200,000	100%
Cost of goods sold	60,000	60	140,000	70
Gross profit	$ 40,000	40%	$ 60,000	30%
Expenses				
Selling	$ 5,000	5%	$12,000	6%
Buying	8,000	8	10,000	5
Administrative	14,000	14	20,000	10
Total expenses	$ 27,000	27%	$ 42,000	21%
Net profit	$ 13,000	13%	$ 18,000	9%

And so on, with each year's net sales acting as the base for determining the percentage of each item in that year.

2. In vertical analysis, the percents must be added.

17.7 SOLVE THIS PROBLEM: Using net sales as 100 percent, prepare a vertical analysis of the following comparative income statement:

K. PASCAL
COMPARATIVE INCOME STATEMENTS
FOR THE MONTHS ENDED MAY 31, AND JUNE 30, 1974

Divide by net sales

	May 31	%	June 30	%
Sales	$51,000	102 %	$65,000	___%
Less returns	1,000	2	5,000	___
Net sales	$50,000	100%	$60,000	100%
Cost of goods sold	38,000	76	43,000	___
Gross profit	$12,000	24%	$17,000	___%
Expenses:				
Rent	$1,200	2.4 %	$1,200	___%
Telephone	300	.6	400	___
Electric	700	1.4	200	___
Stationery	100	.2	200	___
General	1,500	3	2,000	___
Total expenses	$ 3,800	16 %	$ 4,000	___%
Net profit	$ 8,200	___%	$13,000	___%

3. OTHER ANALYTICAL PROCEDURES

In addition to horizontal and vertical analysis, there are many other procedures for analyzing financial statements. These are often expressed as percentages or ratios.

a. WORKING CAPITAL

To measure the ability of a business to meet its current debts, the excess of current assets over current liabilities is determined. This is called working capital. The formula is:

$$\text{Current assets} - \text{Current liabilities} = \text{Working capital}$$

ILLUSTRATIVE PROBLEM. Determine the working capital of Nigel's Pet Shop, whose current assets are $10,000 and whose current liabilities are $4,300.

SOLUTION:

Current assets	$10,000
Current liabilities	4,300
Working capital	$ 5,700

17.8 SOLVE THIS PROBLEM: Samantha's Gift Shop had $8,300 of cash and assets that will shortly be converted to cash in the normal operation of the business. It is estimated that $6,812 will be required to pay all debts maturing in the next few months. Calculate the amount of working capital.

b. CURRENT RATIO

Another way of expressing the relationship between current assets and current liabilities is by means of a ratio. Working capital is the dollar amount by which current assets exceed current liabilities. The current ratio expresses this comparison by means of a ratio. The formula is:

$$\text{Current ratio} = \frac{\text{Current assets}}{\text{Current liabilities}}$$

ILLUSTRATIVE PROBLEM. The current assets of Fleming's, Inc., total $500,000, and the current liabilities are $200,000. Determine the current ratio.

SOLUTION:

$$\frac{\text{Current assets}}{\text{Current liabilities}} \frac{\$500,000}{\$200,000} = 2.5:1 \quad \text{Current ratio}$$

17.9 SOLVE THIS PROBLEM: The following current assets are listed on the balance sheet of the Kenny Garage: cash, $6,000; accounts receivable, $4,000; and notes receivable, $10,000. The current liabilities consist of: accounts payable, $5,000; salaries payable, $6,000; and taxes payable, $1,000. What is the current ratio?

c. RATE EARNED ON AVERAGE TOTAL ASSETS

A measure of the effectiveness of management's use of the assets entrusted to them may be found by dividing the average assets into the net profit. The resulting percentage when compared to the results of prior years, or that of competitors, might give indication of the quality of managerial control. The formula is:

$$\text{Rate earned on average total assets} = \frac{\text{Net income}}{\text{Average total assets}}$$

ILLUSTRATIVE PROBLEM. The total assets of a company at January 1 and December 31, 1974, were $140,000 and $220,000, respectively. If the profit for the year ended December 31, 1974 was $45,000, what was the rate earned on average total assets?

SOLUTION:

    1. To determine the average total assets:

Total assets January 1, 1974	$140,000
Total assets December 31, 1974	220,000
Total	$360,000

$$\frac{\$360,000}{2} = \$180,000 \text{ Average total assets}$$

    2. To determine the rate earned on average total assets:

$$\frac{\text{Net profit} \quad \$45,000}{\text{Average total assets} \quad \$180,000}$$

$$= 25\% \text{ Rate earned on average total assets}$$

17.10   *SOLVE THIS PROBLEM:* From the following information, determine the rate earned on average total assets:

	December 31, 1974	*December 31, 1975*
Current assets	$30,000	$35,000
Fixed assets	35,000	60,000
1974 Profit $5,000		

d. RATE EARNED ON AVERAGE CAPITAL

Another test of management's efficiency in handling the funds in their care can be made by determining the rate of profit based on the value of the business.

The formula is:

$$\frac{\text{Net profit}}{\text{Average capital}} = \text{Rate earned on average capital}$$

ILLUSTRATIVE PROBLEM. The Plainview Restaurant was worth $60,000 at the beginning of the year and $80,000 at the end of the year. The year's profit was $14,000. Determine the rate earned on average capital.

SOLUTION:

1. To determine the average capital:

Capital at beginning of year	$ 60,000
Capital at end of year	80,000
Total	$140,000

$$\text{Average capital} = \frac{\$140,000}{2} = \$70,000$$

2. To determine the rate earned on average capital:

$$\frac{\text{Net profit}}{\text{Average capital}} \frac{\$14,000}{\$70,000} = 20\% \text{ Rate earned on average capital}$$

17.11 SOLVE THIS PROBLEM: From the following information, determine the rate earned on average capital.

	January 1, 19___	*December 31, 19___*
Assets	$45,000	$65,000
Liabilities	15,000	25,000

The net profit for the year was $5,000.

e. EARNINGS PER SHARE OF COMMON STOCK

Of great interest to investors is the amount of annual earnings made by a corporation per share of common stock. The earnings per share is determined by dividing the net profit by the number of shares of common stock outstanding.

The formula is:

$$\text{Earnings per share of common stock} = \frac{\text{Net profit}}{\text{Shares of common stock outstanding}}$$

ILLUSTRATIVE PROBLEM. Bettman's, Inc., has 5,000 shares of common stock outstanding. Determine the earnings per share if the net profit was $27,500.

SOLUTION:

$$\text{Earnings per share} = \frac{\text{Net profit } \$27,500}{\text{Shares of common stock outstanding } 5,000}$$

$$= \$5.50$$

17.12 SOLVE THESE PROBLEMS:

1. If the White Machine Company earned $7,500 during the last year, and had 4,000 shares of common stock outstanding, what were the earnings per share?

2. The following information was taken from the books and records of M. Schrag, Inc.

	December 31, 1974	December 31, 1975
Current assets	$10,000	$12,000
Current liabilities	6,000	8,000
Fixed assets	38,000	40,000
Fixed liabilities	24,000	11,000
Shares of common stock outstanding	6,000 shares	

Net profit for the year ending December 31, 1975—$9,600.

Based on the above information, determine the following:
   a. Working capital
   b. Current ratio
   c. Rate earned on average total assets
   d. Rate earned on average capital
   e. Earnings per share of common stock

CHAPTER REVIEW

1. Prepare a balance sheet from the following information:

Amount owed on merchandise	$ 5,236
Amount due from customers	2,536
Merchandise on hand	9,520
Owing to employees	75
Cash	18,196

2. Prepare an income statement from the following information:

Sales	$21,576
Rent	7,200
Cost of goods sold	7,692

Telephone	126.36
Salaries	4,078
Other expenses	2,976
Electric	624

3. Complete the following comparative balance sheet.

R. BLAKE
BALANCE SHEET
DECEMBER 31, 1973 AND 1974

	1973	1974	INCREASE OR DECREASE		PERCENT OF TOTAL	
			Amount	Percent	1973	1974
ASSETS						
Current assets	$212,000	$242,000	$+30,000	%	%	%
Fixed assets	494,000	472,000	−22,000	%	%	%
Total assets	$706,000	$714,000	$ +8,000	%	100%	100%
LIABILITIES AND CAPITAL						
Current liabilities	$182,800	$181,000	$−10,000	%	%	%
Fixed liabilities	225,200	216,200	−9,000	%	%	%
Total liabilities	$408,000	$398,000	$−10,000	%	%	%
Capital	298,000	316,000	+18,000	%	%	%
Total liabilities and capital	$706,000	$714,000	$ +8,000	%	100%	100%

4. From the balance sheet presented in problem 3, determine the following for the year 1973:

Working capital
Current ratio

18

business statistics, graphs, annuities, and present value

1. BUSINESS STATISTICS
   a. The mean
   b. The median
   c. The mode

2. GRAPHS
   a. Bar graphs
   b. Circle graphs
   c. Line graphs

3. ANNUITIES
   a. Ordinary annuities
   b. Annuities due

4. PRESENT VALUE

5. SINKING FUNDS

Decision making is probably the most vital, as well as the most difficult role played by business executives today. Selecting the right market for a new product's distribution, selecting the best channel or channels of distribution, choosing the most pro ing package design, and determining inventory characteristics and a nt re just some of the perplexing decisions that must be made by ma In our sophisticated business world, *statistics* —collected numeri d ay an important part. The most common statistical terms are i *median*, and the *mode*. Each will be discussed separately.

a. THE MEAN

The mean is a statistical term signifying an arithmetical average. This average is arrived at by *adding* the available figures or items, and then dividing their sum by the number of figures or items. The formula is:

$$\frac{\text{Sum of the figures}}{\text{Number of items}} = \text{Mean}$$

ILLUSTRATIVE PROBLEM. Five stock clerks earn the following weekly salaries: $50, $50, $52, $55, and $63. Find the mean salary.

SOLUTION:

$$\frac{\text{Sum of the figures}}{\text{Number of items}} = \text{Mean}$$

$$\frac{\$50 + \$50 + \$52 + \$55 + \$63}{5} = \text{Mean}$$

$$\frac{\$270}{5} = \$54 \text{ Mean}$$

18.1   SOLVE THESE PROBLEMS:

1. Six secretaries typed the following number of letters for one week.

Secretary 1—73 letters
Secretary 2—84 letters
Secretary 3—79 letters
Secretary 4—86 letters
Secretary 5—88 letters
Secretary 6—92 letters

Determine the mean letter production for the secretarial group.

2. What is the mean production figure for these sewing machine operators?

Mary Jones—625
Sandra Paul—691
Myra Caffey—684
Susan Schmidt—714
Paula Beggs—723

3. Find the mean cost of newspaper advertising per paper for the Home-Rite Furniture Company, whose expenditures for the past week were:

Newspaper	Number of Printed Lines	Cost per Line
Chronicle	8,746	$.32
Gazette	6,452	.34
News-Record	9,423	.28
Evening Star	5,741	.35
Evening Press	7,415	.33

b. THE MEDIAN

The median is the central or the middle point of a series of numbers. It is found by arranging all the numbers, beginning with either the highest or the lowest, and counting until the *middle* number is reached. For example, if there are five items, the third item is the median. When the distribution contains an even number of items, it is impossible to pick the median value, so we must find the average of the two middle values. For example, if there are four items: 1, 2, 3, 4, the second and third, 2 and 3, are added and divided by two; the median is $2\frac{1}{2}$.

ILLUSTRATIVE PROBLEM. Find the median salary of these clerks.

> Clerk A—$45
> Clerk B—$48
> Clerk C—$50
> Clerk D—$52
> Clerk E—$55

SOLUTION: Count either up or down until you come to the middle figure. Because there are five items, Clerk C—$50 is the middle figure, the median.

ILLUSTRATIVE PROBLEM. Find the daily median output of these chair upholsterers.

> Sam Phillips— 5
> Art James— 5
> Phil Cantor— 7
> Pete O'Day— 8
> Ira Bord—10
> John McLish—11

SOLUTION:

1. Because there are six items, it is necessary to find the *two* middle positions. Counting from the top or bottom, items 7 and 8 are in the middle.
2. Divide the sum of these items by two:

$$\frac{7 + 8}{2} = 7\tfrac{1}{2} \text{ Median}$$

18.2 *SOLVE THESE PROBLEMS:*

1. The shoes sold in the Style Craft Shoe Shop from 10 A.M. until noon were sized as follows:

$$6, 6\tfrac{1}{2}, 7\tfrac{1}{2}, 8, \text{ and } 9$$

Find the median size that was sold.

2. Find the median salary for these salesmen who are paid on a straight commission of 3%.

Salesman	Amount Sold
Abe Morter	$6,845.18
Ed White	$7,263.25
Pat Cappa	$7,425.40
Carl Avery	$7,875.32
Sid Carter	$8,426.11

3. The number of daily stops made by house to house salesmen for the Major Housewares Company were:

26, 28, 32, 33, 35, and 37

Find the median number of stops for the group.

4. Phonograph assemblers are paid at the rate of $3.75 for every job they complete for the Atlas Company. This is a section from their payroll for the week ending January 25, 19___:

A. Forbes—41
S. Leman—46
P. Dogaer—47
R. Wright—51
S. Pauls—52
T. Frank—55

Find the week's salary for each worker and the median salary.

c. THE MODE

The mode is the item that appears most frequently in a distribution. In some distributions there might be two or more modes. The mode is arrived at purely by inspection.

ILLUSTRATIVE PROBLEM. Determine the mode from the following daily salary schedule of hosiery saleswomen:

$12, $12, $14, $14, $14, $13.75, $13, $15

SOLUTION: By inspecting the salary distribution we see that $14 appears three times, more frequently than any other number.

$14 is the Mode

ILLUSTRATIVE PROBLEM. From the following list of weekly salaries, determine the mode:

$75	$80
$75	$80
$75	$80
$78	$72
$78	$79

SOLUTION: **By** inspecting the distribution we find $75 and $80 each appearing the same number of times. Therefore, this distribution has two modes, $75 and $80.

18.3 SOLVE THESE PROBLEMS:

1. The following is a record of the bicycles sold by the Peddles Bicycle Shop for one day:

$32, $32.50, $32, $36, $38, $45, $37.50, $32, $45, $38
$39.50, $40 and $32

Find the mode.

2. Fifteen salesmen are paid the following hourly rates by the Look-Well Shirt Shops:

$2.75, $2.75, $2.75, $2.90, $2.90, $3.25, $3.25, $3.25,
$3.25, $3.25, $3.50, $3.50, $3.50, $3.50 and $3.50

Find the mode of these hourly rates.

3. Find the mean, median, and mode for the following weekly salaries of the Artform, Ltd., Sales Personnel. Round off to the nearest cent.

$85	$ 96
$85	$ 98
$88	$100
$90	$102
$92	

4. One of the criteria for hiring mechanics at the Mayfair Assembly Plant is the score on a finger dexterity test. The following is a list of scores achieved by 24 applicants.

38	40	42	43
38	40	42	43
38	40	42	44
39	40	42	45
39	41	43	48
40	42	43	49

Find the mean, median, and mode of these applicants. Round off to the nearest hundredth.

2. GRAPHS

Pertinent data can be more easily and quickly understood, and can make a more meaningful impression on businessmen if they are presented graphically. Although executives have the ability needed to understand and interpret data, the graphic presentation presents a longer-lasting impression. Equally vital, it also shows the visual relationships of figures.

The graphs most frequently used in business situations are the bar graph, the circle graph, and the line graph. The type of graph to use is often determined by the individual, but occasionally, particular data is best presented in one form rather than another. Three classifications of graphs will be presented separately.

a. BAR GRAPHS

A bar graph is generally used when comparisons and/or relationships are made on items of the same nature.

ILLUSTRATIVE PROBLEM. The Chic Hosiery Chain, operators of six retail units, reported the following sales for the week ending April 9, 19__:

	Sales
Store A	$ 900
Store B	1,200
Store C	850
Store D	1,400
Store E	1,600
Store F	1,850

Plot a bar graph to each store's sales volume.

SOLUTION:

1. Using graph paper, list each store, A through F, vertically. Leave a space between each store equal to the line that each store occupies. This separation will allow for quick and easy plotting and observation.

2. Horizontally, indicate dollar amounts from zero to 2,000. Make certain that these are equally spaced.

3. Plot the appropriate sales volume for each store in its assigned space. Each bar should end in line with its sales volume and should be darkened to make a more meaningful visual presentation. The completed bar graph should look like Figure 18-1.

Another type of bar graph frequently used in business is one which presents a comparison of data for two or more periods. This is important to the executive interested in advances or declines in sales volume, units sold, employee turnover, etc.

Figure 18-1

Bar Graph

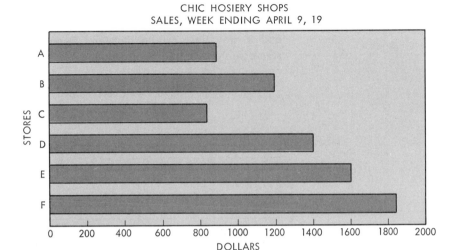

CHIC HOSIERY SHOPS
SALES, WEEK ENDING APRIL 9, 19

ILLUSTRATIVE PROBLEM. The Acme Tire Shop's records show the following figures for the two years it has been in business:

Months	First Year Units Sold	Second Year Units Sold
January	350	380
February	375	390
March	390	420
April	425	450
May	435	470
June	420	435
July	250	260
August	275	290
September	310	310
October	390	420
November	460	500
December	500	560

Plot the monthly unit sales for each year.

SOLUTION:

1. Vertically, on the lefthand side of graph paper, list each month of the year. Leave three lines, one for each year to be plotted, and one line for spacing between each month.

2. Next, after the last month, December, number each box, horizontally, beginning with zero, at intervals of 20, and ending with 600. This indicates the units sold.

3. Plot the appropriate number of units sold for every month, in each

year. The top lines should be for the first year's sales, the second lines for the next year's sales.

4. Select two different types of bars, one representing the first year's figures and the other the second year's figures. The key in Figure 18-2, at the upper righthand corner, indicates the use of a black line and a gray line for the plotting. The completed graph should resemble the graph in Figure 18-2.

Figure 18-2
Acme Tire Shop Units Sold

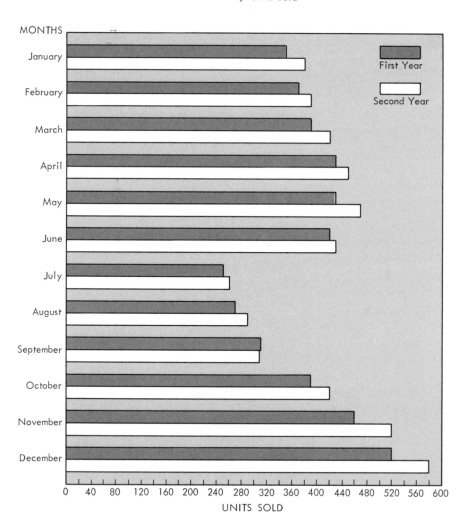

18.4 *SOLVE THESE PROBLEMS:*

1. Prepare a bar graph showing the number of employees in each department of the Noble Manufacturing Company.

Salesmen	—18
Cutters	—10
Machine operators	—35
Shippers	— 5
Clericals	— 3
Bookkeepers	— 6

2. The Pinto Novelty Company employs eight salesmen who travel throughout the United States. Prepare a bar graph showing each salesman's sales for June, 19__.

Salesman	Sales—June, 19__
Joe Williams	$26,000
Bill Harden	$22,000
Marv Shipp	$24,000
Al Cummins	$21,000
Pete Hobart	$28,000
Jack Mellons	$19,000
Bob Harris	$17,000
Andy Denton	$23,000

3. Handblock's Department Store records customer returns according to merchandise classifications. Prepare a bar graph showing last year's and this year's returns for each department during the month of January.

MERCHANDISE Classification	RETURNS Last Year	This Year
Men's suits	$ 825	$ 950
Men's accessories	$ 325	$ 600
Ladies' coats & suits	$1,250	$1,350
Ladies' dresses	$ 875	$ 925
Ladies' sportswear	$1,350	$1,450
Ladies' accessories	$ 625	$ 650
Children's wear	$1,225	$1,275
Shoes	$ 150	$ 75
Housewares	$ 275	$ 375
Furniture	$1,500	$1,625

b. CIRCLE GRAPHS

The circle graph is generally used when it is necessary to show separate components in relation to the whole in terms of percents. If the percents are not available, the data must be converted into percents. Because 100 percent equals 360 degrees in the circle, then each percent equals 3.6°. The circle graph is also referred to as a pie graph—its apportionment is similar to the dividend of a pie.

ILLUSTRATIVE PROBLEM. Construct a circle graph to show the breakdown of sales in a Ladies' Specialty Shop.

Coats and suits	50%
Shoes and accessories	25%
Sportswear	25%

SOLUTION:

1. Draw a circle (because there are only 3 divisions, the circle can be small; if there are many parts, the circle should be larger).

2. Multiply each percent by 3.6°, thus:

$$50 \times 3.6 = 180°$$
$$25 \times 3.6 = 90°$$
$$25 \times 3.6 = 90°$$
$$100\% = \overline{360°} \text{ or a circle}$$

3. Proceed to divide the circle according to the percents as in Figure 18-3.

Figure 18-3

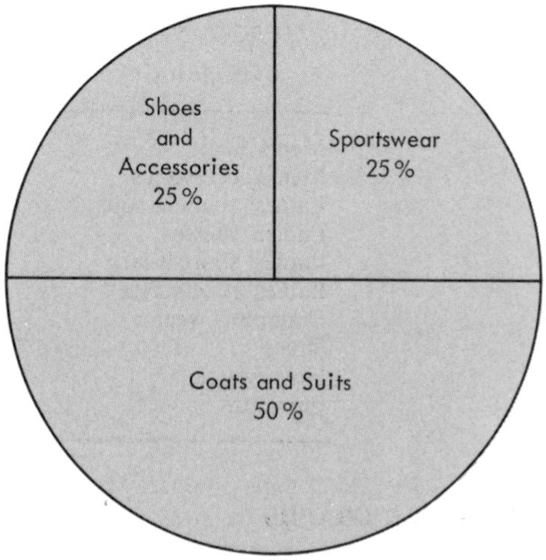

ILLUSTRATIVE PROBLEM. The Rite-Buy Supermarket spends the following for advertising in a typical week:

Newspapers $1,500
Direct mail $ 300
Circulars $ 200
Radio $1,000

Prepare a circle graph showing these advertising expenditures.

SOLUTION:

1. The figures must be converted into percents.

$1,500 + $300 + $200 + $1,000 = $3,000   Total expenditures

Newspapers: $\frac{\$1,500}{\$3,000} = 50\%$

Direct mail: $\frac{\$300}{\$3,000} = 10\%$

Circulars: $\frac{\$200}{\$3,000} = 6\frac{2}{3}\%$

Radio: $\frac{\$1,000}{\$3,000} = 33\frac{1}{3}\%$

Figure 18-4

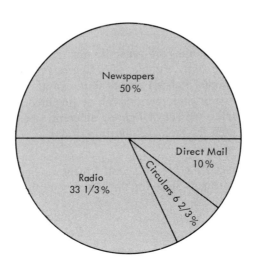

2. Each percent should be multiplied by 3.6°, thus:

$$50\% - 180°$$
$$10\% - 36°$$
$$6\frac{2}{3}\% - 24°$$
$$33\frac{1}{3}\% - 120°$$
$$\overline{100\% = 360° \text{ or a circle}}$$

3. Proceed to distribute percentages as in Figure 18-4.

18.5 *SOLVE THESE PROBLEMS:*

1. Prepare a circle graph to show the division of the publicity dollar for Lampart's Department Store.

Newspapers	38%
Display	32%
Magazines	5%
Special events	10%
Direct mail	15%

2. Using a circle graph, present the elements that comprise the pricing of a dress by its manufacturer.

Material	$3.00
Trimmings	.40
Construction (labor)	2.50
Salesman's commission	.60
Fixed expenses	.50
Profit	1.00

c. LINE GRAPHS

Line graphs are generally used when there is a time element pertinent to the data. For example, sales figures for a particular period are charted on line graphs. Related sets of data can also be plotted on a line graph. Sales for two or more periods can be prepared on one graph. When presenting more than one set of figures, different types of lines, clearly identified, must be used for each classification of data.

ILLUSTRATIVE PROBLEM. Prepare a line graph for sales at the Rancor Department Store for the first six months of the year.

January	$125,000
February	119,000
March	150,000
April	175,000
May	185,000
June	200,000

SOLUTION:

1. On graph paper (which is not necessary but easier to use) vertically, at the lefthand side of the paper, list sales figures beginning with $100,000 and ending at $200,000, with intervals of $5,000.

2. Horizontally, starting at $100,000, list the months, skipping 3 lines between each.

3. Plot each figure at the appropriate intersecting line.

4. Connect the dots with straight lines as in Figure 18-5.

Figure 18-5

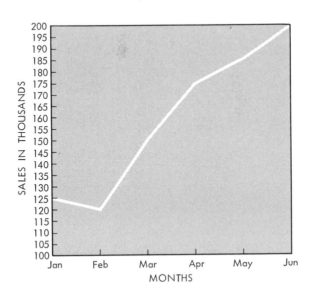

ILLUSTRATIVE PROBLEM. Plot a line graph for this year's sales, at the Harvey Specialty Shop, for the four weeks in June, and for the corresponding periods last year.

	SALES	
Weeks	*This Year*	*Last Year*
1	$2,500	$2,275
2	2,850	2,650
3	2,925	2,800
4	3,000	2,900

SOLUTION:

1. On graph paper, vertically list, at the lefthand side of the paper, sales beginning with $2,250 through $3,000, with intervals of $50.

2. Horizontally, at the $2,250 point, list weeks 1 through 4.

3. Plot each year's figures, making certain that each has a different type of line. The graph in Figure 18-6 uses a solid line for this year and a broken line for last year's figures. Connect the plot marks with appropriate lines.

Figure 18-6

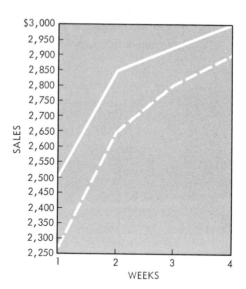

18.6 SOLVE THESE PROBLEMS: Prepare a line graph showing the telephone sales volume for the first six months at William's Department Store.

1.

Month	Telephone Sales
January	$14,625
February	12,750
March	16,000
April	18,900
May	22,500
June	23,000

2. The Reynold's Department Store lists sales in three categories; stores sales, telephone sales, and mail-order sales. On a line graph,

	SALES		
Months	At Store	Telephone	Mail Order
July	$40,000	$22,000	$26,000
August	36,000	14,000	18,000
September	52,000	27,000	29,000
October	58,000	30,000	32,000
November	65,000	34,000	36,000
December	80,000	38,000	42,000

plot sales in the three categories for the last six months of the preceding year.

3. ANNUITIES
Annuity, strictly defined, is a word that denotes yearly payment. In actual practice the term has come to mean periodic payments, generally of equal amounts, at regular interval periods. Commonly, the layman thinks of an annuity only as something purchased from an insurance agent for payment upon retirement. Although this is an annuity, there are many commercial applications which include installment payments, pensions, preferred stock dividend payments, bond interest payments, wages, and salaries. The two major classifications of annuities most often referred to are *contingent annuities* and *annuities certain*. The former term indicates an annuity that runs for an uncertain amount of time; the case where an individual is paid, periodically, by a life insurance company until the time of his death. The latter is an annuity that stipulates a definite number of determined payments; a mortgage on a home is an example of this type.

Annuities, categorized according to their time of payment, are:

1. *Ordinary annuity*—The regular payment is made at the end of a period.
2. *Annuity due*—The regular payment is made at the beginning of a period.

Each of these will be discussed separately, showing both the mathematical computations and the use of the tables necessary to determine the amount of the annuity.

a. ORDINARY ANNUITIES

The formula used to compute this type of annuity with payments made at the end of a period is based upon the compound interest principles. Each investment is multiplied by the interest rate, and the interest is added to determine the principal. For each subsequent year, the interest is determined on the preceding principal and continued until the final investment is made.

ILLUSTRATIVE PROBLEM. How much will John Phillips have at the end of five years if he invests $100 at the end of each year at 5% interest, compounded annually?

SOLUTION: Find the value at the end of the five annual investments by compounding the interest as follows:

$100	First investment
× .05	Interest rate
$5.00	
+100.	
105.00	First principal
+ 100.	Second investment
$205.00	
× .05	Interest rate
$10.25	
+ 205.	
$215.25	Second principal
+100.	Third investment
315.25	
× .05	Interest rate
15.7625	
+315.25	
331.0125	Third principal
+100.	Fourth investment
431.0125	
× .05	Interest rate
21.550625	
+431.0125	
452.563125	Fourth principal
+ 100.	Fifth investment
$552.563125	Final value

A table devised for faster, easier, and more accurate use is available on page 357. Working with the same figures as in the above problem, find the number of years under the period column, 5, then move along to the figure, on the same line, until you reach the designated interest rate, 5%. Because this chart is based upon a value of $1, it is necessary to multiply this figure, 5.5256313 (rounded off from 5.52563125), by $100, the value of each investment.

Thus the answer is the same as in the illustrative problem, $552.563125.

18.7 SOLVE THESE PROBLEMS:

1. At the end of each year, John Frazier deposits $500 in a bank account for his son. How much will be in the account at the end of four years if it accumulates interest, compounded annually, at a rate of 4%?

2. The employees at the Miller Packing Company invest their end-of-the-year bonuses in bonds which bring interest returns of 6%. How much will each employee have if they all invest their current bonuses for the number of years indicated?

Name	Annual Bonus	Number of Years
Al Jones	$100	8
Paul Sands	150	12
Harvey Smith	200	10
Joe Fredericks	250	14
Hank Arthur	300	15

Use the ordinary annuity table to solve the problem.

b. ANNUITIES DUE

In studying the ordinary annuity, we learned that payment was made at the end of a period; with annuities due, payment is made at the beginning. To find an annuity due, an ordinary annuity table (see page 356) is used. To determine an annuity due for a period in this table you find the value for one additional period less one investment. As an example, we will use the same figures as in the preceding illustrative problem.

ILLUSTRATIVE PROBLEM. How much will John Phillips have if he invests $100 at the beginning of each year for five years at 5% interest annually?

SOLUTION:
1. Using the ordinary annuity table on pages 356–357, proceed to 6 years (one year more than the number of years in the problem) and move across to 5%. This figure is 6.8019128.
2. Multiply the figure by $100 (the table is based on $1).

$$6.8019128 \times \$100 = \$680.19128$$

3. Subtract one investment:

$$\$680.19128 - \$100 = \$580.19128$$

18.8   *SOLVE THESE PROBLEMS:*
1. At the beginning of each year, Rafkin invests $800 at an interest rate of 6% to guarantee a sum sufficient to open an office for his son, who is entering medical school. If his son finishes all the necessary requirements within 6 years, how much will he have for the office?
2. How much will Sue Bennett have for her retirement years if for 20 years she invests, at the beginning of each year, $1,000 at an interest rate of 5%?

n	$2\frac{1}{2}\%$	3%	$3\frac{1}{2}\%$	4%	$4\frac{1}{2}\%$	n
1	1.000 0000	1.000 0000	1.000 0000	1.000 0000	1.000 0000	1
2	2.025 0000	2.030 0000	2.035 0000	2.040 0000	2.045 0000	2
3	3.075 6250	3.090 9000	3.106 2250	3.121 6000	3.137 0250	3
4	4.152 5156	4.183 6270	4.214 9429	4.246 4640	4.278 1911	4
5	5.256 3285	5.309 1358	5.362 4659	5.416 3226	5.470 7097	5
6	6.387 7367	6.468 4099	6.550 1522	6.632 9755	6.716 8917	6
7	7.547 4302	7.662 4622	7.779 4075	7.898 2945	8.019 1518	7
8	8.736 1159	8.892 3360	9.051 6868	9.214 2263	9.380 0136	8
9	9.954 5188	10.159 1061	10.368 4958	10.582 7953	10.802 1142	9
10	11.203 3818	11.463 8793	11.731 3932	12.006 1071	12.288 2094	10
11	12.483 4663	12.807 7957	13.141 9919	13.486 3514	13.841 1788	11
12	13.795 5530	14.192 0296	14.601 9616	15.025 8055	15.464 0318	12
13	15.140 4418	15.617 7904	16.113 0303	16.626 8377	17.159 9133	13
14	16.518 9528	17.086 3242	17.676 9864	18.291 9112	18.932 1094	14
15	17.931 9267	18.598 9139	19.295 6809	20.023 5876	20.784 0543	15
16	19.380 2248	20.156 8813	20.971 0297	21.824 5311	22.719 3367	16
17	20.864 7304	21.761 5877	22.705 0158	23.697 5124	24.741 7069	17
18	22.386 3487	23.414 4354	24.499 6913	25.645 4129	26.855 0837	18
19	23.946 0074	25.116 8684	26.357 1805	27.671 2294	29.063 5625	19
20	25.544 6576	26.870 3745	28.279 6818	29.778 0786	31.371 4228	20
21	27.183 2740	28.676 4857	30.269 4707	31.969 2017	33.783 1368	21
22	28.862 8559	30.536 7803	32.328 9022	34.247 9698	36.303 3780	22
23	30.584 4273	32.452 8837	34.460 4137	36.617 8886	38.937 0300	23
24	32.349 0380	34.426 4702	36.666 5282	39.082 6041	41.689 1963	24
25	34.157 7639	36.459 2643	38.949 8567	41.645 9083	44.565 2102	25
26	36.011 7080	38.553 0422	41.313 1017	44.311 7446	47.570 6446	26
27	37.912 0007	40.709 6335	43.759 0602	47.084 2144	50.711 3236	27
28	39.859 8008	42.930 9225	46.290 6273	49.967 5830	53.993 3332	28
29	41.856 2958	45.218 8502	48.910 7993	52.966 2863	57.423 0332	29
30	43.902 7032	47.575 4157	51.622 6773	56.084 9378	61.007 0697	30
31	46.000 2707	50.002 6782	54.429 4710	59.328 3353	64.752 3878	31
32	48.150 2775	52.502 7585	57.334 5025	62.701 4687	68.666 2452	32
33	50.354 0344	55.077 8413	60.341 2100	66.209 5274	72.756 2263	33
34	52.612 8853	57.730 1765	63.453 1524	69.857 9085	77.030 2565	34
35	54.928 2074	60.462 0818	66.674 0127	73.652 2249	81.496 6180	35
36	57.301 4126	63.275 9443	70.007 6032	77.598 3138	86.163 9658	36
37	59.733 9479	66.174 2226	73.457 8693	81.702 2464	91.041 3443	37
38	62.227 2966	69.159 4493	77.028 8947	85.970 3363	96.138 2048	38
39	64.782 9791	72.234 2328	80.724 9060	90.409 1497	101.464 4240	39
40	67.402 5535	75.401 2597	84.550 2778	95.025 5157	107.030 3231	40
41	70.087 6174	78.663 2975	88.509 5375	99.826 5363	112.846 6876	41
42	72.839 8078	82.023 1964	92.607 3713	104.819 5978	118.924 7885	42
43	75.660 8030	85.483 8923	96.848 6293	110.012 3817	125.276 4040	43
44	78.552 3231	89.048 4091	101.238 3313	115.412 8770	131.913 8422	44
45	81.516 1312	92.719 8614	105.781 6729	121.029 3920	138.849 9651	45
46	84.554 0344	96.501 4572	110.484 0314	126.870 5677	146.098 2135	46
47	87.667 8853	100.396 5010	115.350 9726	132.945 3904	153.672 6331	47
48	90.859 5824	104.408 3960	120.388 2566	139.263 2060	161.587 9016	48
49	94.131 0720	108.540 6478	125.601 8456	145.833 7343	169.859 3572	49
50	97.484 3488	112.796 8673	130.997 9102	152.667 0837	178.503 0283	50
60	135.991 5900	163.053 4368	196.516 8829	237.990 6852	289.497 9540	60
70	185.284 1142	230.594 0637	288.937 8646	364.290 4588	461.869 6796	70
80	248.382 7126	321.363 0186	419.306 7868	551.244 9768	729.557 6985	80
90	329.154 2533	443.348 9036	603.205 0270	827.983 3335	1145.269 0066	90
100	432.548 6540	607.287 7327	762.611 6567	1237.623 7046	1790.855 9563	100

n	5%	5½%	6%	7%	8%	n
1	1.000 0000	1.000 0000	1.000 0000	1.000 0000	1.000 0000	1
2	2.050 0000	2.055 0000	2.060 0000	2.070 0000	2.080 0000	2
3	3.152 5000	3.168 0250	3.183 6000	3.214 9000	3.246 4000	3
4	4.310 1250	4.342 2664	4.374 6160	4.439 9430	4.506 1120	4
5	5.525 6312	5.581 0910	5.637 0930	5.750 7390	5.866 6010	5
6	6.801 9128	6.888 0510	6.975 3185	7.153 2907	7.335 9290	6
7	8.142 0084	8.266 8938	8.393 8376	8.654 0211	8.922 8034	7
8	9.549 1089	9.721 5730	9.897 4679	10.259 8026	10.636 6276	8
9	11.026 5643	11.256 2595	11.491 3160	11.977 9888	12.487 5578	9
10	12.577 8925	12.875 3538	13.180 7949	13.816 4480	14.486 5625	10
11	14.206 7872	14.583 4983	14.971 6426	15.783 5993	16.645 4875	11
12	15.917 1265	16.385 5907	16.869 9412	17.888 4513	18.977 1265	12
13	17.712 9828	18.286 7981	18.882 1377	20.140 6429	21.495 2966	13
14	19.598 6320	20.292 5720	21.015 0659	22.550 4879	24.214 9203	14
15	21.578 5636	22.408 6635	23.275 9699	25.129 0220	27.152 1139	15
16	23.657 4918	24.641 1400	25.672 5281	27.888 0536	30.324 2830	16
17	25.840 3664	26.996 4027	28.212 8798	30.840 2173	33.750 2257	17
18	28.132 3847	29.481 2048	30.905 6526	33.999 0325	37.450 2437	18
19	30.539 0039	32.102 6711	33.759 9917	37.378 9648	41.446 2632	19
20	33.065 9541	34.868 3180	36.785 5912	40.995 4923	45.761 9643	20
21	35.719 2518	37.786 0755	39.992 7267	44.865 1768	50.422 9214	21
22	38.505 2144	40.864 3097	43.392 2903	49.005 7392	55.456 7552	22
23	41.430 4751	44.111 8467	46.995 8277	53.436 1409	60.893 2956	23
24	44.501 9989	47.537 9983	50.815 5774	58.176 6708	66.764 7592	24
25	47.727 0988	51.152 5882	54.864 5120	63.249 0377	73.105 9400	25
26	51.113 4538	54.965 9805	59.156 3827	68.676 4704	79.954 4152	26
27	54.669 1264	58.989 1094	63.705 7657	74.483 8233	87.350 7684	27
28	58.402 5828	63.233 5105	68.528 1116	80.697 6909	95.338 8298	28
29	62.322 7119	67.711 3535	73.639 7983	87.346 5293	103.965 9362	29
30	66.438 8475	72.435 4780	79.058 1862	94.460 7863	113.283 2111	30
31	70.760 7899	77.419 4293	84.801 6774	102.073 0414	123.345 8680	31
32	75.298 8294	82.677 4979	90.889 7780	110.218 1543	134.213 5374	32
33	80.063 7708	88.224 7603	97.343 1647	118.933 4251	145.950 6204	33
34	85.066 9594	94.077 1221	104.183 7546	128.258 7648	158.626 6701	34
35	90.320 3074	100.251 3638	111.434 7799	138.236 8784	172.316 8037	35
36	95.836 3227	106.765 1888	119.120 8667	148.913 4598	187.102 1480	36
37	101.628 1389	113.637 2742	127.268 1187	160.337 4020	203.070 3198	37
38	107.709 5458	120.887 3243	135.904 2058	172.561 0202	220.315 9454	38
39	114.095 0231	128.536 1271	145.058 4581	185.640 2916	238.941 2210	39
40	120.799 7742	136.605 6141	154.761 9656	199.635 1120	259.056 5187	40
41	127.839 7630	145.118 9229	165.047 6836	214.609 5698	280.781 0402	41
42	135.231 7511	154.100 4636	175.950 5446	230.632 2397	304.243 5234	42
43	142.993 3387	163.575 9891	187.507 5772	247.776 4965	329.583 0053	43
44	151.143 0056	173.572 6685	199.758 0319	266.120 8512	356.949 6457	44
45	159.700 1559	184.119 1653	212.743 5138	285.749 3108	386.505 6174	45
46	168.685 1637	195.245 5194	226.508 1246	306.751 7626	418.426 0668	46
47	178.119 4218	206.984 2339	241.098 6121	329.224 3860	452.900 1521	47
48	188.025 3929	219.368 3668	256.564 5288	353.270 0930	490.132 1643	48
49	198.426 6626	232.433 6270	272.958 4006	378.998 9995	530.342 7374	49
50	209.347 9957	246.217 4765	290.335 9046	406.528 9295	573.770 1564	50
60	353.583 7179	433.450 3717	533.128 1809	813.520 3834	1253.213 2958	60
70	588.528 5107	753.271 2042	967.932 1696	1614.134 1742	2720.080 0738	70
80	971.228 8213	1299.571 3869	1746.599 8914	3189.062 6797	5886.935 4283	80
90	1594.607 3010	2232.731 0160	3141.075 1872	6287.185 4268	12723.938 6160	90
100	2610.025 1569	3826.702 4668	5638.368 0586	12381.661 7938	27484.515 7043	100

357

3. The Belray Company plans to open three additional retail outlet in its chain of sporting goods stores. It expects to open these unit 4, 7, and 10 years from today. How much must they invest in thre separate funds at the beginning of each year to have enough for th estimated costs if the interest rates are 4%?

The estimated costs for each store are:

1. Store to be opened in 4 years

Fixtures	—$7,500
Lighting	—$1,500
Flooring	—$1,000
Windows	—$3,500
Decorating	—$1,200
Misc. expenses	—$2,000

2. Store to be opened in 7 years

Fixtures	—$9,000
Lighting	—$2,100
Flooring	—$1,200
Windows	—$4,000
Decorating	—$2,000
Misc. expenses	—$2,500

3. Store to be opened in 10 years

Fixtures	—$12,000
Lighting	—$ 3,200
Flooring	—$ 2,000
Windows	—$ 4,500
Decorating	—$ 3,000
Misc. expenses	—$ 3,500

4. PRESENT VALUE Present value is the worth now of a specified sum at a specific future date Individuals sometimes find it desirable to know from the beginning how much must be invested now to bring an amount needed at a future date To find value, the table on page 360 has been constructed for speed and accuracy of use. However, present value can also be calculated mathematically.

ILLUSTRATIVE PROBLEM. Tom Batton needs $10,000 ten years from now t pay for building improvements. How much would he have to pay now, if th interest rate is 5%, to have the required sum in ten years?

SOLUTION:

1. On the present value table, move down to period 10 and across t 5%. The figure you reach is .61391325.

2. Multiply by $10,000, because this table is based on $1.

.61391325 × $10,000 = $6,139.13 present value
($6,139.13 invested now at 5% will grow to $1,000 in 10 years)

18.9 SOLVE THESE PROBLEMS:
  1. Paul Harmon, upon retirement, wants in 20 years to receive a lump sum of $60,500. How much must his investment be if the interest rate is 6%?
  2. John Farley wants to set aside funds for his three children for their college years. The costs will vary because each child will attend a different college with different tuition and boarding expenses. Assuming each child begins college at age 18 and completes in four years, how much must each investment be if the interest is at 4%?

Children	Age	Estimated Cost for 4 Years
Mary	10	$18,000
Roger	12	$10,000
James	13	$16,000

5. SINKING FUNDS When a company expands its operation or requires large amounts of capital for its undertakings, it frequently borrows money, issuing bonds to cover the total amount. Money is set aside periodically and invested with interest to meet these obligations. The sum set aside is called a sinking fund. The table on page 362 is used in sinking fund calculations.

The sinking fund table illustrated on page 362 is a variation of the annuity table discussed earlier. This table takes into account the fact that sinking fund payments are made at the end of the period (annuity due) and the table is adjusted to this information. The other difference between this table and the annuity table is that the annuity table provides the total accumulation when the individual payments are known, and the sinking fund table is used to determine the individual payments when the necessary accumulation is known.

Illustrative Problem. The Archer Company issued bonds for $100,000 to be repaid in 10 years to finance a new factory. How much must be invested at the end of each year at 4% to pay off the bond issue at maturity due?

SOLUTION:
  1. On the compound interest table, the point where 10 periods and 4% meet is .0832909. This is the amount for $1.
  2. Multiply .0832909 by $100,000.

Answer: $8,329.09

PRESENT VALUE TABLE

Present Value of 1, $p = \dfrac{1}{(1+i)^n}$

Periods	1½%	2%	2½%	3%	3½%	4%
1	0.9852 2167	0.9803 9216	0.9756 0976	0.9708 7379	0.9661 8357	0.9615 3846
2	0.9706 6175	0.9611 6878	0.9518 1440	0.9425 9591	0.9335 1070	0.9245 5621
3	0.9563 1699	0.9423 2233	0.9285 9941	0.9151 4166	0.9019 4271	0.8889 9636
4	0.9421 8423	0.9238 4543	0.9059 5064	0.8884 8705	0.8714 4222	0.8548 0419
5	0.9282 6033	0.9057 3081	0.8838 5429	0.8626 0878	0.8419 7317	0.8219 2711
6	0.9145 4219	0.8879 7138	0.8622 9687	0.8374 8426	0.8135 0064	0.7903 1453
7	0.9010 2679	0.8705 6018	0.8412 6524	0.8130 9151	0.7859 9096	0.7599 1781
8	0.8877 1112	0.8534 9037	0.8207 4657	0.7894 0923	0.7594 1156	0.7306 9021
9	0.8745 9224	0.8367 5527	0.8007 2836	0.7664 1673	0.7337 3097	0.7025 8674
10	0.8616 6723	0.8203 4830	0.7819 8402	0.7440 9391	0.7089 1881	0.6755 6417
11	0.8489 3323	0,8042 6304	0.7621 4478	0.7224 2128	0.6849 4571	0.6495 8093
12	0.8363 8742	0.7884 9318	0.7435 5589	0.7013 7988	0.6617 8330	0.6245 9705
13	0.8240 2702	0.7730 3253	0.7254 2038	0.6809 5134	0.6394 0415	0.6005 7409
14	0.8118 4928	0.7578 7502	0.7077 2720	0.6611 1781	0.6177 8179	0.5774 7508
15	0.7998 5150	0.7430 1473	0.6904 6556	0.6418 6195	0.5968 9062	0.5552 6450
16	0.7880 3104	0.7284 4581	0.6736 2493	0.6231 6694	0.5767 0591	0.5339 0818
17	0.7763 8526	0.7141 6256	0.6571 9506	0.6050 1645	0.5572 0378	0.5133 7325
18	0.7649 1159	0.7001 5937	0.6411 6591	0.5873 9461	0.5383 6114	0.4936 2812
19	0.7536 0747	0.6864 3076	0.6255 2772	0.5702 8603	0.5201 5569	0.4746 4242
20	0.7424 7042	0.6729 7133	0.6102 0943	0.5536 7575	0.5025 6588	0.4563 8695
21	0.7314 9795	0.6597 7582	0.5953 8629	0.5375 4928	0.4855 7090	0.4388 3360
22	0.7206 8763	0.6468 3904	0.5808 6467	0.5218 9250	0.4691 5063	0.4219 5539
23	0.7100 3708	0.6341 5592	0.5666 9724	0.5066 9175	0.4532 8563	0.4057 2633
24	0.6995 4392	0.6217 2149	0.5528 7535	0.4919 3374	0.4379 5713	0.3901 2147
25	0.6892 0583	0.6095 3087	0.5393 9059	0.4776 0557	0.4231 4699	0.3751 1680

Periods	5%	6%	6½%	7%	7½%	8%	8½%
1	0.9523 8095	0.9433 9623	0.9389 6714	0.9345 7944	0.9302 3256	0.9259 2593	0.9216 5899
2	0.9070 2948	0.8899 9644	0.8816 5928	0.8734 3873	0.8653 3261	0.8573 3882	0.8494 5529
3	0.8638 3760	0.8396 1928	0.8278 4909	0.8162 9788	0.8049 6057	0.7938 3224	0.7829 0810
4	0.8227 0247	0.7920 9366	0.7773 2309	0.7628 9521	0.7488 0053	0.7350 2985	0.7215 7428
5	0.7835 2617	0.7472 5817	0.7298 8084	0.7129 8618	0.6965 5863	0.6805 8320	0.6650 4542
6	0.7462 1540	0.7049 6054	0.6853 3412	0.6663 4222	0.6479 6152	0.6301 6963	0.6129 4509
7	0.7106 8133	0.6650 5711	0.6435 0621	0.6227 4974	0.6027 5490	0.5834 9040	0.5649 2635
8	0.6768 3936	0.6274 1237	0.6042 3119	0.5820 0910	0.5607 0223	0.5402 6888	0.5206 6945
9	0.6446 0892	0.5918 9846	0.5673 5323	0.5439 3374	0.5215 8347	0.5002 4897	0.4798 7968
10	0.6139 1325	0.5583 9478	0.5327 2604	0.5083 4929	0.4851 9393	0.4631 9349	0.4422 8542
11	0.5846 7929	0.5267 8753	0.5002 1224	0.4750 9280	0.4513 4319	0.4288 8286	0.4076 3633
12	0.5568 3742	0.4969 6936	0.4696 8285	0.4440 1196	0.4198 5413	0.3971 1376	0.3757 0168
13	0.5303 2135	0.4688 3902	0.4410 1676	0.4149 6445	0.3905 6198	0.3670 9792	0.3462 6883
14	0.5050 6795	0.4423 0096	0.4141 0025	0.3878 1724	0.3633 1347	0.3404 6104	0.3191 4178
15	0.4810 1710	0.4172 6506	0.3888 2652	0.3624 4602	0.3379 6602	0.3152 4170	0.2941 3989
16	0.4581 1152	0.3936 4628	0.3650 9533	0.3387 3460	0.3143 8699	0.2918 9047	0.2710 9667
17	0.4362 9669	0.3713 6442	0.3428 1251	0.3165 7439	0.2924 5302	0.2702 6895	0.2498 5869
18	0.4155 2065	0.3503 4379	0.3218 8969	0.2958 6392	0.2720 4932	0.2502 4903	0.2302 8450
19	0.3957 3396	0.3305 1301	0.3022 4384	0.2765 0832	0.2530 6913	0.2317 1206	0.2122 4378
20	0.3768 8948	0.3118 0473	0.2837 9703	0.2584 1900	0.2354 1315	0.2145 4821	0.1956 1639
21	0.3589 4236	0.2941 5540	0.2664 7608	0.2415 1309	0.2189 8897	0.1986 5575	0.1802 9160
22	0.3418 4987	0.2775 0510	0.2502 1228	0.2257 1317	0.2037 1067	0.1839 4051	0.1661 6738
23	0.3255 7131	0.2617 9726	0.2349 4111	0.2109 4688	0.1894 9830	0.1703 1528	0.1531 4965
24	0.3100 6791	0.2469 7855	0.2206 0198	0.1971 4662	0.1762 7749	0.1576 9934	0.1411 5176
25	0.2953 0277	0.2329 9863	0.2071 3801	0.1842 4918	0.1639 7906	0.1460 1790	0.1300 9378

18.10 SOLVE THESE PROBLEMS:

1. John Forbes wishes to build a fund of $20,000 to purchase a business upon retiring from his present job. How much must he put aside, at the end of each year, for 10 years, if the interest he receives is compounded annually at 6%?

2. Peter Reynolds issued a bond amounting to $250,000, redeemable in 20 years. He wishes to set up a fund to provide the money necessary to redeem this bond. If he sets aside equal amounts of money at the end of every 3 months with interest compounded quarterly at 5% per quarter, how much must each payment be in the sinking fund?

3. In order to accumulate enough money to pay off a $100,000 mortgage due in 30 years on a farm, Collins plans to set aside equal amounts every 6 months which will earn interest at 4% compounded semi-annually. How much must Collins set aside for 1 year?

SINKING FUNDS TABLE

n	$\frac{1}{2}\%$	1%	2%	3%	4%	5%	6%
1	1.000 0000	1.000 0000	1.000 0000	1.000 0000	1.000 0000	1.000 0000	1.000 0000
2	0.498 7531	0.497 5124	0.495 0495	0.492 6108	0.490 1961	0.487 8049	0.485 4369
3	0.331 6722	0.330 0221	0.326 7547	0.323 5304	0.320 3485	0.317 2086	0.314 1098
4	0.248 1328	0.246 2811	0.242 6238	0.239 0271	0.235 4901	0.232 0118	0.228 5914
5	0.198 0100	0.196 0398	0.192 1584	0.188 3546	0.184 6271	0.180 9748	0.177 3964
6	0.164 5955	0.162 5484	0.158 5258	0.154 5975	0.150 7619	0.147 0175	0.143 3626
7	0.140 7285	0.138 6283	0.134 5120	0.130 5064	0.126 6096	0.122 8198	0.119 1350
8	0.122 8289	0.120 6903	0.116 5098	0.112 4564	0.108 5278	0.104 7218	0.101 0359
9	0.108 9074	0.106 7404	0.102 5154	0.098 4339	0.094 4930	0.090 6901	0.087 0222
10	0.097 7706	0.095 5821	0.091 3265	0.087 2305	0.083 2909	0.079 5046	0.075 8680
11	0.088 6590	0.086 4541	0.082 1779	0.078 0775	0.074 1490	0.070 3889	0.066 7929
12	0.081 0664	0.078 8488	0.074 5596	0.070 4621	0.066 5522	0.062 8254	0.059 2770
13	0.074 6422	0.072 4148	0.068 1184	0.064 0295	0.060 1437	0.056 4558	0.052 9601
14	0.069 1361	0.066 9012	0.062 6020	0.058 5263	0.054 6690	0.051 0240	0.047 5849
15	0.064 3644	0.062 1238	0.057 8255	0.053 7666	0.049 9411	0.046 3423	0.042 9628
16	0.060 1894	0.057 9446	0.053 6501	0.049 6109	0.045 8200	0.042 2699	0.038 9521
17	0.056 5058	0.054 2581	0.049 9698	0.045 9525	0.042 1985	0.038 6991	0.035 4448
18	0.053 2317	0.050 9821	0.046 7021	0.042 7087	0.038 9933	0.035 5462	0.032 3565
19	0.050 3025	0.048 0518	0.043 7818	0.039 8139	0.036 1386	0.032 7450	0.029 6209
20	0.047 6665	0.045 4153	0.041 1567	0.037 2157	0.033 5818	0.030 2426	0.027 1846
21	0.045 2816	0.043 0308	0.038 7848	0.034 8718	0.031 2801	0.027 9961	0.025 0046
22	0.043 1138	0.040 8637	0.036 6314	0.032 7474	0.029 1988	0.025 9705	0.023 0456
23	0.041 1347	0.038 8858	0.034 4681	0.030 8139	0.027 3091	0.024 1368	0.021 2785
24	0.039 3206	0.037 0734	0.032 8711	0.029 0474	0.025 5868	0.022 4709	0.019 6790
25	0.037 6519	0.035 4068	0.031 2204	0.027 4279	0.024 0120	0.020 9525	0.018 2267
26	0.036 1116	0.033 8689	0.029 6992	0.025 9383	0.022 5674	0.019 5643	0.016 9044
27	0.034 6857	0.032 4455	0.028 2931	0.024 5642	0.021 2385	0.018 2919	0.015 6972
28	0.033 3617	0.031 1244	0.026 9897	0.023 2932	0.020 0130	0.017 1225	0.014 5926
29	0.032 1291	0.029 8950	0.025 7784	0.022 1147	0.018 8799	0.016 0455	0.013 5796
30	0.030 9789	0.028 7481	0.024 6499	0.021 0193	0.017 8301	0.015 0514	0.012 6489
40	0.022 6455	0.020 4556	0.016 5558	0.013 2624	0.010 5235	0.008 2782	0.006 4615
50	0.017 6538	0.015 5127	0.011 8232	0.008 8655	0.006 5502	0.004 7767	0.003 4443
60	0.014 3328	0.012 2445	0.008 7680	0.006 1330	0.004 2019	0.002 8282	0.001 8757
70	0.011 9666	0.009 9328	0.006 6677	0.004 3366	0.002 7451	0.001 6992	0.001 0331
80	0.010 1970	0.008 2189	0.005 1607	0.003 1118	0.001 8141	0.001 0296	0.000 5725
90	0.008 8253	0.006 9031	0.004 0460	0.002 2556	0.001 2078	0.000 6271	0.000 3184
100	0.007 7319	0.005 8657	0.003 2027	0.001 6467	0.000 8080	0.000 3831	0.000 1774

1. The salesmen were paid on various commission rates and sold the following amounts last week. What was their mean pay?

Salesmen	Commission Rate	Sales
L. Blank	4%	$12,000
D. Grossman	6%	15,000
D. Samuels	5%	9,000
F. Terry	3%	18,000
T. Johnston	7%	8,000

2. What is the median pay of the following:

$$\$80, \$82, \$90, \$95, \$96, \$112, \$114$$

3. Find the mode from the following salary distribution:

$$\$84, \$89, \$92, \$85, \$86, \$92, \$97, \$114$$

4. Prepare a bar graph for the salaries of the following salespeople:

Helen	$150
Minna	165
Blanche	135
Elayne	170
Judy	155

5. Prepare a circle graph to show the year's promotional expenditures for the Steve and Judy Show if 50% goes to newspaper advertising and 10% each to direct mail, car cards, magazines, posters, and special events.

6. Using graph paper, chart the sales at Rona Carrie's Emporium for the past 10 weeks as follows:

1,200; 8,000; 2,600; 1,400; 1,250; 1,100; 2,900; 3,000; 3,100; 4,000

7. What amount will David receive at the end of 3 years if he invests $1,000 at the end of each year at 6% interest compounded annually?

8. How much must be deposited in a lump sum at 5% if $1,000 is required in 10 years?

9. Botwinick, Ltd. issued bonds for $200,000 to be repaid in 20 years. How much must Botwinick invest at the end of each year at 5% to pay off the bond at maturity?

GLOSSARY

Accounting. The process of recording, summarizing, and analyzing the financial transactions of a business.

Accrued Interest on Bonds. Money paid by the buyer of a bond for the accumulation of interest since the last interest payment.

Addends. Numbers to be added.

Adjusted Gross Income. Gross taxable income minus certain specified adjustments to income.

Aliquot Parts. Any number that can be divided into another number evenly is an aliquot part of that number.

Annuities. Periodic payments of equal amounts at regular periods.

Annuity Due. An annuity for which the payment is made at the beginning of a period.

Annuity, Ordinary. An annuity for which the payment is made at the end of a period.

Anticipation. A bonus discount to encourage customers to pay their bills before they are due.

Assessed Valuation. The value of property determined by examination and appraisal.

Assets. Those things of value that are owned.

Average Markup. The average addition in price (or mean) on all goods offered for sale.

Balance Sheet. A financial statement showing the assets, liabilities, and owner's equity in a business at a particular time.

Bank Discount. A bank's interest charge that is deducted in advance.

Bank Reconciliation. A computation used to prove that the bank's records agree with the depositor's records.

Bar Graph. A graph prepared by using solid blocks or bars to represent the various proportions.

364

Binary System. A positional numbering system based on the numeral 2.

Book Value of Stock. The value of each share of stock according to the value set forth in the corporate books.

Buyer's Wheel. A device used by buyers to automatically determine markup.

Cancellation Method. A method of multiplication of fractions by reducing numerators and denominators.

Capital. The net worth of a business.

Capital Stock. Shares in the ownership of a corporation.

Cash Discounts. A reduction of a debt to encourage prompt payment.

Cash Surrender Value. The amount of money paid to the insured if he decides to no longer retain the policy.

Change Memo. A method for determining the exact bills and coins for a payroll.

Change Tally. A form required by banks to enable them to break down a total payroll check into the proper denominations.

Circle Graph. A graph in which a circle is divided to show proportions.

Co-Insurance. A procedure in which the insured bears part of the risk if he carries less than the stipulated percentage of value on his property.

Commission, Quota Bonus. A method of remuneration in which the bonus is calculated on the excess over a specific quota.

Commission, Sliding Scale. A method of remuneration in which the commission rate changes according to the amount sold.

Commission, Straight. A method of remuneration by which earnings are computed as a percent of sales.

Commission, Straight Salary Plus. A method of remuneration in which a set salary is paid in addition to a percent paid on sales.

Common Stock. Voting or nonvoting stock that has no preferences and is evidence of ownership.

Comparative Statements. Accounting statements presented for two consecutive years to indicate changes in the various categories.

Compound Interest. Interest computed on the combined total of principal and prior interest.

Corporate Bond. A certificate indicating a corporation's debt.

Cumulative Markup. The markup on the goods about to be purchased and the markup on inventory.

Cumulative Preferred Stock. Preferred stock that gives owner the right to receive unpaid past dividends.

Current Assets. Assets used or converted into cash in a short time.

Current Liabilities. Debts that must be paid within the next business year.

Current Ratio. Current assets divided by current liabilities.

Current Yield. The return on an investment found by dividing the total annual interest by the total cost.

Decimal System. A positional number system based on the number 10.

Denominator. The lower portion of a fraction which indicates the number of parts into which the whole is divided.

Depreciation. A method of allocating the cost of a fixed asset over its useful life.

Depreciation, Declining-Balance. See Sum-of-the-Years Digits.

Depreciation, Straight-Line. A method of depreciation in which the cost of an item will be spread equally over its useful life.

Depreciation, Sum-of-the-Years Digits. A depreciation method that provides for the highest depreciation in the early years and the lowest in the final years.

Depreciation, Units of Production. A depreciation method that applies the cost of its asset to its actual use.

Differential Piecework. A piecework method in which the rate per piece varies with the number of pieces completed.

Discounting Notes. A procedure for cashing in a note before its due date.

Discount on Stock. The amount received below par value by a corporation for its capital stock.

Discount Terms. The amount of discount and the number of days allowed for payment.

Divisor. The amount by which a number is divided.

Endowment Insurance. Life insurance for a specific number of years at which time the insured, if alive, receives the face of the policy.

Equivalent Discount. A series of trade discounts calculated as a single rate.

Exemption. A deduction from adjusted gross income for dependents.

Federal Depositor Receipt. A form used to accompany the periodic payment of withholding and FICA taxes.

FICA. A payroll tax paid equally by the employer and employee that provides for old age pensions, survivors' benefits, disability insurance, and Medicare.

FIFO (First In, First Out). A method of pricing inventories that assumes that the first goods purchased were the first sold.

Fixed Assets. Assets that will not be used up in the next business year.

Fixed Liabilities. Debts that will not be due in the next business year.

Fraction. One or more equal parts of a whole number.

Graph. A pictorial representation of data.

Gross Margin. See Gross Profit.

Gross Profit. The difference between the cost and the actual selling price.

Gross Taxable Income. The total of all income subject to income taxes.

Hexadecimal System. A numbering system based on the numeral 16.

Horizontal Analysis. A means of comparing accounting statements for two consecutive years.

Improper Fractions. Fractions in which the numerator is greater than the denominator.

Income Statement. A financial statement which summarizes the revenue and expenses of a business for a specified period of time.

Installment Buying. A method of paying for a purchase by making equal payments over a period of time.

Interest. The rental charge for borrowing money.

Liabilities. The amounts owed.

LIFO (Last In, First Out). A method of pricing inventories that assumes that the last goods purchased were the first sold.

Limited Payment Life Insurance. Insurance that requires payment for a specified number of years but protection for life.

Line Graph. A graph in which a line is used to present pertinent information.

Long-Term Liabilities. See Fixed Liabilities.

Lowest Common Denominator. The smallest denominator that can be divided evenly by all of the denominators in the problem.

Maker. The person signing the note; the payer.

Markdown. The difference between the original retail price and the reduced price.

Markup. The difference between the cost of goods and the amount one hopes to sell it for.

Maturity Value. The value of an instrument when it is due (principal plus interest).

Mean. An arithmetic average.

Median. The middle number in a series of numbers arranged in ascending or descending order.

Merchandise Inventory Turnover. The number of times the average inventory is sold during a period.

Minuend. An amount from which a number is to be subtracted.

Mixed Numerals. A combination of units and fractions.

Mode. The number that appears most frequently in a distribution.

Multiplicand. An amount that is to be multiplied.

Multiplier. The amount by which the multiplicand is to be multiplied.

Negotiable Instrument. A business instrument that can be transferred from one party to another by endorsement.

Numerator. The upper portion of a fraction which indicates the number of parts of the whole.

Octal System. A numbering system based on the numeral 8.

Odd Lots. Units of trading of less than 100 (or 10) shares.

Open to Buy. The amount of merchandise that can be ordered during a period taking into account the difference between the total purchases planned and commitments already made.

Outstanding Checks. Those checks issued by the depositor not yet paid out by the bank.

Partnership. An association of two or more persons to carry on as co-owners of a business for profit.

Par Value. An arbitrary value placed on securities by the board of directors.

Payee. The person to be paid.

Percentage. The product of a number multiplied by a percent.

Percents. Fractions or decimals with the denominator of 100.

Personal Deductions. Allowable deductions from adjusted gross income of a personal nature.

Piecework. A method of remuneration in which the number of pieces completed is multiplied by a fixed rate per piece.

Positional Value. Numbering systems in which the value of a numeral is based on its position.

Preferred Stock. A class of capital stock that has a preference over other classes of stock with regard to dividends and assets in the event of liquidation.

Premium. Periodic payment to an insurance company.

Premium on Stock. The excess over par value that a corporation receives for its securities.

Present Value. The worth, now, of a specified sum at a specific future date.

Promissory Note. A written document indicating a debt.

Proper Fractions. Fractions in which the numerator is less than the denominator.

Quotient. The result of dividing two numbers.

Rate. A percent.

Ratio. A comparison of one number to another.

Retail Method of Estimating Inventory. A method of estimating inventory based upon the relationship between the cost and the selling price.

Round Lot. A unit of trading in stocks in which 100 shares are involved (some stocks have units of 10 shares).

Sinking Fund. An accumulation of funds generated by equal periodic payments.

Social Security Tax. See FICA.

Standard Deduction. A deduction from adjusted gross income that may be used as a substitute for personal deductions.

Stock Turnover. See Merchandise Inventory Turnover.

Straight Life Insurance. Insurance that allows for the payment of premiums each year until death of the insured or cancellation.

Subtrahend. An amount to be subtracted.

Sum-of-the-Years Digits. A method of depreciation which allows the highest amount of depreciation in the early years.

Term Insurance. Life insurance that allows for payment of premiums for a specific period of time.

Trade Discount. A reduction in cost used to differentiate among different classifications of customers.

Vertical Analysis. A method of analyzing financial statements by showing the percent of each item to the total.

Withholding Tax. Pay-as-you-go income tax deducted from gross salaries.

Working Capital. The excess of current assets over current liabilities.

Yield to Maturity. Return on investment based on the total income until maturity.

ANSWERS TO ODD-NUMBERED PROBLEMS

CHAPTER 1

1.1

1. 51,719
3. 1,954

1.2

1. 400.6484
3. 3844.427

1.3

1. 6,615
3. $7,986.85
5. $35,418.15

1.4

1. 16
3. 16
5. 18
7. 19
9. 292
11. 250
13. 160
15. 2,629
17. 3,086
19. 2,579
21. 2,851
23. 25,849
25. 21,585
27. 29,850
29. 315,212
31. 268,156
33. 247,697
35. 312,033

1.5

1. $645.42
3. $3,270.18
5. 28,931

1.6

1. 19,296
3. 259,877
5. 2,204,309

1.7

1. 15,868
3. 33,608
5. 47,521

1.8

1. 2590
3. 2221
5. 2475
7. 3953
9. 1552
11. 3009

1.9

1. 311
3. 776
5. 3,493
7. 3,682
9. 2,022
11. 13

1.10

1. 3.633 ✓
3. 27.47

5. 13.2
7. .393
9. .1121
11. 723.42166

1.11

1. 3,225
3. +1,414 diff.
5. $215.23

1.12

1. 376
3. 819
5. 1.163
7. 18.62

1.13

1. 51
3. 99
5. .328
7. .0033
9. .00091
11. .71998

1.14

1. 21
3. 852
5. .0307
7. 6.8

1.15

1. 39
3. 29

1.16

1. 1,401
3. 5,688
5. 14,904
7. 55,578
9. 251,865
11. 400,841

1.17

1. 12,062
3. 57,750
5. 61,614
7. 711,776
9. 5,552,085
11. 73,947,048

1.18

1. $677
3. $5,818

1.19

1. 4,680
3. 16,000
5. 9,260
7. 295,000

1.20

1. 2,370,000
3. 32,777,800
5. 172,972,720
7. 452,618,200
9. 239,652,000
11. 2,517,470,000

1.21

1. 32,864
3. 365,486
5. 18,604,872
7. 47,579,262

1.22

1. 4,762.8
3. .0034122
5. .063700
7. .01606807
9. .2840963
11. 14,409.730

1.23

1. $137.92
3. $1,308.97
5. $502.11

1.24

1. 220,725
3. 100,440
5. 187,563
7. .0127896
9. .3892418
11. 24,174

1.25

1. 94
3. $632\frac{1}{2}$
5. $214\frac{1}{9}$
7. $9,127\frac{1}{2}$
9. $6,098\frac{1}{9}$
11. $4,735\frac{3}{4}$

1.26

1. 31
3. 104.142
5. 56.010
7. 167.230
9. 134.782
11. 90,941

1.27

1. 382
3. .0375
5. .3781
7. .000638
9. .7638
11. .031

1.28

1. $3.8\frac{7}{12}$
3. $10.7\frac{3}{26}$
5. $11.4\frac{19}{21}$
7. $23.6\frac{3}{35}$
9. $2.29\frac{8}{9}$
11. 1.00333

1.29

1. $2.50
3. $4.25
5. $8\frac{1}{3}$ hours

1.30

1. 172.1052
3. .13583
5. .25259
7. .0024693

9. 24.982
11. 907.0552

1.31

1. 3182
3. 1728
5. 3268
7. 46,698
9. 249,018
11. 623,392

1.32

1. 12
3. 19
5. 7
7. 14
9. 17
11. 14

1.33

1. $37.28
3. $.59
5. $16.76
7. $.37

1.34

1. $1,053.12
3. .5029+ lb.
5. 15,792 minutes

1.35

1. 282—280
3. 1783—1800
5. 35,390—35,000

1.36

1. 25.2
3. 3.27
5. $30

1.37

1. 2.3
3. $.73

1.38

1. 7.6
3. 383.3

Chapter Review

1. $1,634.47
3. $3,229.44

5. $4.25
7. $12.37; $.10; $6.38; $.01

CHAPTER 2

2.1

1. $\frac{5}{7}$
3. $\frac{8}{11}$
5. $\frac{73}{161}$
7. $\frac{79}{185}$
9. $\frac{105}{107}$
11. $\frac{1}{3}$

2.2

1. $\frac{3}{7}$—42 GCD
3. $\frac{9}{62}$—12 GCD
5. $\frac{171}{284}$—2 GCD
7. $\frac{3}{5}$—63 GCD
9. $\frac{11}{31}$—12 GCD
11. $\frac{31}{41}$—18 GCD

2.3

1. $\dfrac{20}{24}$
3. $\dfrac{20}{36}$
5. $\dfrac{12}{96}$
7. $\dfrac{200}{250}$
9. $\dfrac{84}{132}$
11. $\dfrac{65}{85}$

2.4

1. $\frac{51}{8}$
3. $\frac{163}{16}$
5. $\frac{87}{7}$
7. $\frac{179}{16}$
9. $\frac{53}{37}$
11. $\frac{918}{19}$

2.5

1. $32\frac{1}{2}$
3. $9\frac{1}{5}$
5. $9\frac{1}{4}$
7. $40\frac{3}{4}$
9. $35\frac{5}{18}$
11. $7\frac{2}{23}$

2.6

1. $\frac{4}{12}, \frac{10}{12}, \frac{9}{12}$
3. $\frac{10}{20}, \frac{8}{20}, \frac{15}{20}$
5. $\frac{2}{12}, \frac{8}{12}, \frac{9}{12}$
7. $\frac{20}{30}, \frac{9}{30}, \frac{8}{30}, \frac{25}{30}$
9. $\frac{6}{28}, \frac{14}{28}, \frac{8}{28}, \frac{25}{28}$
11. $\frac{18}{45}, \frac{25}{45}, \frac{6}{45}, \frac{15}{45}$

2.7

1. $\frac{45}{120}; \frac{100}{120}; \frac{64}{120};$
120 L.C.D.
3. $\frac{45}{120}; \frac{50}{120}; \frac{42}{120};$
120 L.C.D.
5. $\frac{55}{210}; \frac{35}{210}; \frac{154}{210};$
210 L.C.D.
7. $\frac{42}{96}; \frac{84}{96}; \frac{28}{96}; \frac{21}{96}; 96$ L.C.D.
9. $\frac{25}{60}; \frac{28}{60}; \frac{9}{60}; \frac{54}{60}; 60$ L.C.D.
11. $\frac{50}{320}; \frac{45}{320}; \frac{60}{320}; \frac{176}{320};$
320 L.C.D.

2.8

1. $1\frac{7}{12}$
3. $\frac{13}{15}$
5. $2\frac{1}{24}$
7. $1\frac{7}{20}$
9. $1\frac{7}{32}$
11. $1\frac{17}{72}$

2.9

1. 8
3. $11\frac{7}{18}$
5. $14\frac{35}{72}$
7. $13\frac{7}{10}$
9. $18\frac{62}{99}$
11. $19\frac{43}{60}$

2.10

1. $414\frac{13}{24}$ feet
3. $21\frac{25}{28}$ feet
5. $7\frac{133}{240}$ inches

2.11

1. $\frac{1}{2}$
3. $\frac{1}{36}$
5. $\frac{7}{18}$
7. $\frac{11}{56}$
9. $\frac{11}{75}$
11. $\frac{13}{48}$

2.12

1. $3\frac{1}{12}$
3. $6\frac{5}{18}$

5. $112\frac{5}{18}$
7. 2
9. $16\frac{7}{16}$
11. $202\frac{15}{56}$

2.13

1. $5\frac{8}{15}$
3. $2\frac{7}{12}$
5. $11\frac{71}{80}$
7. $1\frac{9}{28}$
9. $30\frac{29}{35}$
11. $2\frac{37}{40}$

2.14

1. $\frac{37}{80}$ of one inch
3. $10\frac{7}{48}$
5. $63\frac{23}{48}$ feet

2.15

1. $\frac{5}{12}$
3. $\frac{3}{20}$
5. $\frac{24}{221}$
9. $\frac{1}{8}$
11. $\frac{1,820}{5,661}$

2.16

1. $11\frac{2}{3}$
3. $251\frac{43}{64}$
5. $62\frac{351}{512}$
7. $928\frac{152}{441}$
9. $16\frac{13}{25}$
11. $71\frac{7}{27}$

2.17

1. $\frac{1}{24}$
3. $\frac{1}{8}$
5. $4\frac{23}{52}$
7. $1\frac{19}{45}$
9. $11\frac{11}{35}$
11. $431\frac{1}{5}$

2.18

1. $\frac{1}{10}$
3. $49\frac{11}{14}$
5. $23.84

2.19

1. $\frac{1}{2}$
3. $\frac{9}{10}$
5. $1\frac{1}{3}$

7. $1\frac{13}{35}$
9. 1
11. $\frac{148}{205}$

2.20

1. 6
3. $\frac{3}{20}$
5. $\frac{1}{6}$
7. $1\frac{1}{3}$
9. $1\frac{11}{23}$
11. $\frac{325}{612}$

2.21

1. 192 pieces
3. 10 hours
5. $87\frac{1}{3}$

2.22

1. $\frac{3}{4}$
3. $\frac{13}{40}$
5. $1\frac{16}{25}$
7. $26\frac{7}{20}$
9. $19\frac{751}{2000}$
11. $4\frac{747}{2000}$

2.23

1. .125
3. .12
5. .583
7. .475
9. .375
11. .625

2.24

1. .5454
3. .6666
5. 3.4166
7. 7.1875
9. 2.4286
11. 11.4615

Chapter Review

1. $24\frac{13}{36}$
3. $\frac{10}{56}$; $\frac{100}{144}$; $\frac{70}{180}$
5. $\frac{1}{30}$; $\frac{1}{20}$
7. $10\frac{1}{4}$; $15\frac{3}{8}$; $1\frac{269}{2500}$; $1\frac{51}{80}$

CHAPTER 3

3.1

1. $\frac{21}{50}$
3. $\frac{43}{50}$

5. $1\frac{1}{4}$
7. $2\frac{3}{5}$
9. $7\frac{1}{2}$
11. $4\frac{1}{4}$

3.2

1. .76
3. 1.26
5. .63
7. .37
9. .10
11. .000004

3.3

1. $\frac{3}{4} = .75 = 75\%$
3. $\frac{3}{4} = .75 = 75\%$
5. $\frac{1}{3} = .33\frac{1}{3} = 33\frac{1}{3}\%$
7. $\frac{4}{5} = .8 = 80\%$
9. $1\frac{2}{5} = 1.4 = 140\%$

3.4

1. $60
3. $.84
5. $8.2476 = $8.25
7. $173.76

3.5

1. $37.50
3. $64.91
5. $1,113.50
7. $16.77
9. $287,337.60
11. $15.81

3.6

1. $1\frac{2}{3}\%$
3. $.78\%$
5. 1.94%
7. 1.5%

3.7

1. 8%
3. 5%
5. 96%
7. 25%
9. 12%
11. 2%

3.8

1. $350.00
3. $804.00

5. $220.00
7. $505.00

3.9

1. $520.00
3. $45,050
5. $86.00
7. $7,512
9. $1,802.00
11. $1,271.20

3.10

1. $27.00—$477.00
3. $11.52—$587.52
5. $.30—$1.05
7. $17.54—$430.22
9. $394.73—$5,657.85
11. $118.33+—$1,574.70

3.11

1. $180,056.00
3. $7,589.76
5. $8\frac{1}{4}$ lb.
7. $7.61
9. 32.96 in.
11. 2,225,047

3.12

1. $19.20—$300.80
3. $7.40—$177.60
5. $2.40—$4.80
7. $6.69—$5.47
9. $178.35—$1,248.45
11. $439.70—$2,198.42

3.13

1. 105.6 lbs
3. $8.03
5. 2,520.58 lbs
7. $7,160,010.67
9. $28,479.83
11. 7.56 miles

3.14

1. 197
3. 22
5. 21
7. 22
9. 243
11. 241
13. 550
15. 142

3.15

1. 129,000
3. 42,600
5. 21,600
7. $356\frac{1}{4}$
9. 2,100
11. 108,000
13. 2,640
15. 90

3.16

1. 43,416
3. 2,356
5. 9,100
7. 3,354
9. 13,332
11. 23,828
13. 33,390
15. 26,656

Chapter Review

1. $\frac{18}{25}$; $\frac{16}{25}$; $3\frac{13}{20}$; $2\frac{9}{25}$
3. $6,997.86
5. 6.2%
7. $472
9. $107.52

CHAPTER 4

4.1

1. $24
3. $19.35
5. $28.23
7. $587.90

4.2

1. $12
3. $12.80
5. $11.46
7. $65.06

4.3

1. $32.00
3. $4.00
5. $6.76
7. $45.60

4.4

1. 105
3. 97

5. 159
7. 113

4.5

1. $\frac{73}{360}$
3. $\frac{92}{360}$
5. $\frac{85}{360}$
7. $\frac{106}{360}$

4.6

1. 92
3. 44
5. 47
7. 146

4.7

1. $6.00
3. $1.20
5. $3.24
7. $5.00

4.8

1. $10
3. $5.40
5. $.02
7. $21.10
9. $101.68
11. $12.92

4.9

1. $3.75
3. $2.49
5. $2.65
7. $2.89+
9. $28.48
11. $84.07

4.10

1. $.92
3. $6.76+
5. $11.61
7. $.71

4.11

1. $720.00
3. $1,720.00
5. $1,810.00
7. $2,240.00

4.12

1. $4,800.00
3. $3,600.00
5. $7,812.50

4.13

1. 240 days
3. 30
5. 300
7. 36

4.14

1. 90 days
3. 40
5. 60

4.15

1. 3%
3. 2%
5. 10%
7. 7%

4.16

1. 6%
3. 8%
5. 3%

4.17

1. $36.72
3. $37.08
5. $84.93

4.18

1. $9.10
3. $4.04
5. $24.60

4.19

1. $129.99
3. $340.61
5. $1,062.78

4.20

1. $120.81
3. $132.11
5. $702.43

Chapter Review

1. $19.50; $29.33; $789.53
3. $7.40

5. 83 days; 144 days
7. $16.64; $2.40
9. 24 days
11. $97.92; $68.01

CHAPTER 5

5.1

1. a. $104.00; 19.2%
  b. $180.00; 53⅓%
  c. $430.00; 32%
  d. $276.00; 41.8%
  e. $481.20; 30.5%
  f. $715.68; 24.3%
  g. $996.00; 31.5%
  h. $1833.60; 17.2%
  i. $2090.20; 11.8%
  j. $2237.76; 9.9%

5.2

1. Sofa: $312
  Chair: $165
  Table: $140
  Bar: $292.50
  Stereo: $289.00
3. a. $885
  b. $135
  c. 25.3%
5. a. $1,226.75
  b. $1,354.01
  c. $127.26
  d. 22.5%

5.3

1. a. $210.40
  b. $183.45
  c. $183.75
  d. 162.58
  e. 102.39
3. $145.12

5.4

1. (1) Interest $ 80.00
   Principal $ 34.63
   Balance $15,965.37
  (2) Interest $ 79.83
   Principal $ 34.80
   Balance $15,930.57
  (3) Interest $ 79.65
   Principal $ 34.98
   Balance $15,895.59

Chapter Review

1. 126.28
3. $487; $37; 35.2%
5. Monthly Payment:
           $146.76
  1st month:
  Interest $ 133.33
  Payment $ 13.43
  Balance $19,986.57
  2nd month:
  Interest $ 133.24
  Payment $ 13.52
  Balance $19,973.05

CHAPTER 6

6.1

1. $1.13 per hundred
3. $11.12 per thousand

6.2

1. $2,000,269.54+
3. $429,820,980

6.3

1. $379.74
3. $853.20

6.4

1. $316.80
3. $.74 savings per thousand

6.5

1. a. $290
  b. $590
  c. $1,410
3. a. $3,150
  b. $5,180
  c. $2,310
  d. $1,060
  e. $580

6.6

1. $838.06
3. $1,165.45

Chapter Review

1. $.64
3. $1,958.07
5. $120; $1,040; $3,480

CHAPTER 7

7.1

1. 33⅓%
3. 36⅔%
5. 40%

7.2

1. $56
3. $40
5. $10.00

7.3

1. 50%
3. 84%
5. 50%

7.4

1. $66.67
3. $45
5. $4.05

7.5

1. Retail: $185.71
  Cost: $280
3. Retail: 46%
  Cost: 73%
5. Retail: $4.48
  Cost: 77%
7. Retail: $63.64
  Cost: $217
9. Retail: 48%
  Cost: $92.44

7.6

1. 66⅔%
3. $1,725.32

7.7

1. 53%
3. 45%

7.8

1. 33⅓%
3. 43%
5. a. 43%
  b. 50%
  c. 33⅓%
  d. 66⅔%
  e. 82%

Chapter Review

1. 40%
3. $25
5. $5.88
7. 51%
9. 43%

CHAPTER 8

8.1

1. $156,952.00
3. $35,082 G.P.
5. $4,400

8.2

1. 35%
3. 39%
5. $90
7. $210.00
9. $38\frac{1}{3}$%
11. 28.6%

8.3

1. $11,000
3. $158,000

8.4

1. $3\frac{3}{4}$
3. 4
5. Retail: 2.0
   Cost: 2.3+

8.5

1. 75%
3. $120,000
5. $60,000(R)
7. $30,680(C)
   $59,000(R)
9. $74,000(R)
   $44,178(C)

8.6

1. $34,000
3. $14,100
5. $4,600

Chapter Review

1. $47,381.47
3. $210

5. .95
7. $70,000

CHAPTER 9

9.1

1. $62.16

9.2

1. $156

9.3

1. a. 40; 1; $6.00; $166.00
   b. 40; 1; $4.20; $116.20
   c. 40; 6; $4.80; $156.80
   d. 40; 1; $3.60; $99.60
   e. 40; 1; $4.80; $132.80

9.4

1. $90.00

9.5

1. $104.00
3. a. 255; $127.50
   b. 338; $212.94
   c. 396; $190.08
   d. 392; $141.12

9.6

1. $12.28

9.7

1. $5.33
3. $7.24

9.8

1. $30.30
3. $8.70

Chapter Review

1. $131.25
3. $312
5. $166.50; $115.50; $323;
   $216; $266
7. $5.80; $6.46; $7.05;
   $7.37; $7.78

CHAPTER 10

10.1

1. $507.90
3. $64.41
5. $255.55
7. $618.56 due Carter

10.2

1. $2\frac{1}{2}$%
3. 9.375%

10.3

1. $13,566.67

10.4

1. $345.40
3. $568.87
5. $1,661.96
7. 5%
9. $3\frac{1}{2}$%
11. $13,733.33
13. $31,137.50
15. $22,656.15

10.5

1. $33.36
3. $128.38
5. $75.63

10.6

1. $150
3. $736.95
5. $432.50

10.7

1. $140.00
3. $150.11
5. $252.62

10.8

1. a. $615
   b. $1,296
   c. $392.75
   d. $1,680
   e. $955.60
   f. $467.13
   g. $1,000
   h. $1,141.80

i. $977.08
j. $1,549.00
3. $3,023.56 due

10.9

1. $71.00

10.10

1. $73.88

10.11

1. $10.70
3. $800
5. 6¼%

10.12

1. $401.90
3. $3.64

10.13

1. $183.67

10.14

1. $396

10.15

1. $165.11
3. a. $14.50—$85.50
    b. $123.47—$101.53
    c. $113.10—$261.90
    d. $126.82—$399.55
    e. $133.21—$205.93
    f. $397.68—$428.44
    g. $741.96—$505.04
    h. $314.03—$1,048.37
    i. $1,401.34—$1,394.34
    j. $4,921.02—$7,556.98

10.16

1. 37%; $148; $252
3. 52%; $650; $600
5. 43.30%; $55.06; $72.10

10.17

1. $249.90
3. $685.36
5. Peters: $969.54
    Jenkins: $750.69

10.18

1. $1,844.55
3. a. $121.83
    b. $3,700.72
    c. $2,755.92
    d. $3,661.87

Chapter Review

1. $1,500
3. $2,740
5. $20,000
7. $128
9. $6.50
11. 3⅓%
13. $252.00
15. $488.04

CHAPTER 11

11.1

1. $100, each year
3. $900

11.2

1. $780
3. a. $1,400
    b. $1,750
    c. $1,050

11.3

1. $2,666.67
    $2,133.33
    $1,600.00
    $1,066.67
    $ 533.33
    $8,000.00
3. a. $500
    b. $400
    c. $500
    d. $6.75
    e. $158.38
    f. $281.71
    g. $447.73
    h. $54.13

11.4

1. $1,600, 1st yr. dep.
    $960, 2nd yr. dep.
    $440, 3rd yr. limit
    $0, 4th and 5th yrs.

3. a. $187.50
    b. $518.40
    c. $358.40
    d. $693.33
    e. $532.97
    f. $428.09
    g. $288.62
    h. $533.67

11.6

1. a. $99.00
    b. $108.00
    c. $103.50

11.7

1. Collins: $6,000
    Dunn: $6,000

11.8

1. a. $10,000; $7,000;
      $3,000
    b. $12,000; $9,000;
      $5,000
    c. $8,500; $5,500;
      $1,500
3. a. $15,000; $9,000;
      $6,000
    b. $10,000; $4,000;
      $1,000

11.9

1. a. $3,820; $3,340;
      $6,220; $2,620
    b. −$3,180; −$3,660;
      −$780; −$4,380

11.10

1. a. $6,000; $2,400; $3,600
    b. $3,000; $1,200; $1,800

11.11

1. a. $18,440; $17,560
    b. $6,440; $5,560
3. a. $12,040; $10,968;
      $12,992
    b. $5,040; $2,568;
      $7,392

Chapter Review

1. 1: 2,500—4,000—6,000
      —1,200

2: 2,500—3,000—3,000
—2,650
3: 2,500—2,000—1,000
—3,250
4: 2,500—1,000—0—
2,900
3. a. $7,800—$14,400—
$8,000
b. $12,800—$19,400—
—$13,000

CHAPTER 12

12.1

1. $7,000
3. $1,300
5. $3,430.10

12.2

1. a. 67
b. 63
c. 47
d. 53
e. 47
f. 64

12.3

1. $1,515
3. $1,010.00
5. $1,530.90

12.4

1. a. $1,000—60—$10—
$990.00
b. $400—40—$1.78—
$398.22
c. $800—15—$1.67—
$798.33
d. $900—48—$7.80—
$892.20
3. $11.84 discount;
$2,018.16

12.5

1. $106.92
3. $20,000
5. $.1356

12.6

1. $65.42
3. $23.00
5. $420.78

12.7

1. a. $31.20
b. $88.80
3. a. $41.07
b. $36.43
5. $204.51

12.8

1. $108 earned
$162 refund
3. $149.33
5. $140.08 earned
$212.54 refund

12.9

1. $14.26
3. $287.28

12.10

1. $12,500
3. $21,000
5. limit to $60,000 face

Chapter Review

1. $10,051.50
3. $36
5. $20
7. $305.94; $260.56

CHAPTER 13

13.1

1. $20,000
3. 8,000
5. $24,000
7. $57,000

13.2

1. $2.00 per share
3. a. Preferred:
$15,000—$2.50
b. Common:
$1,000—$.03⅓
5. a. Preferred:
$3,300 = $3.30 per
share
b. Common:
$137,690 = $22.95
per share
7. a. $2,000—2.00—0—0

b. $3,000—3.00—500
—$.05
c. 3,000—3.00—9,000
—$.90
d. 3,000—3.00—19,000
—$1.90
e. 3,000—3.00—33,000
—$3.30
f. 3,000—3.00—47,000
—$4.70
g. 3,000—3.00—77,000
—$7.70
h. 3,000—3.00—147,000
—$14.70

13.4

1. $500
3. 1. $31.33⅓
2. $15,748.60—3.12
3. $44,353.20—4.62
4. 25—1.56
5. 760
6. $20,000—$14,000
7. 23,312—81,000
8. 99,000—2,000
9. 20,000—2,000

13.5

1. $16,000

13.6

1. $63.40
3. $56.32

13.7

1. +$112.50
3. −$4,725
5. 1. $ 5,500.00—$ 71.50
—$ 5,571.50
2. 2,400.00— 50.40
— 2,450.40
3. 900.00— 21.70
— 921.70
4. 150.00— 9.40
— 159.40
5. 13,300.00— 161.70
— 13,461.70
6. 768.75— 26.18
— 794.93
7. 1,050.00— 31.28
— 1,081.28
8. 6,862.50— 103.76
— 6,966.26

Chapter Review

1. Preferred: $12 per share
   Common: $3.80
3. $800 prem. on pref.
   $500 disc. on comm.
5. $1,112.50

CHAPTER 14

14.1

1. $1,060
3. $1,100
5. $988.75

14.2

1. $490,000;
   $10,000, discount
3. a. $1,020,000—$20,000
   b. $752,000—$48,000*
   c. $720,000—$30,000*
   d. $2,354,000—

   $154,000
   e. $2,000,000

14.3

1. $26.25
3. No change

14.4

1. $6,562.50
3. $57.00
5. 1. $ 6,120—$ 15.00—

   $ 6,135.00
   2. 1,200— 37.50—

   1,237.50
   3. 740— 5.00—

   745.00
   4. 1,200— 100.00—

   1,300.00
   5. 11,760— 30.00—

   11,790.00
   6. 9,090— 22.50—

   9,112.50
   7. 6,440— 35.00—

   6,475.00
   8. 6,300— 131.25—

   6,431.25

14.5

1. $3,500
3. 1. $30.00—$300.00

2. $27.50—$165.00
3. $20.00—$280.00
4. $22.50—$675.00
5. $35.00—$945.00
6. $36.87—$2,654.64
7. $23.75—$427.50
8. $25.62—$1,127.28
9. $31.87—$924.23
10. $23.12—$832.32

14.6

1. 6.0%
3. 7%

14.7

1. 4.9%
3. 1. 5.4%
   2. 5.3
   3. 4.8
   4. 10
   5. 8.5
   6. 11.3
   7. 8.8
   8. 8.4

14.8

1. $4,839
3. $8,257.57
5. a. $17.875; $2.50;
   $1040.38
   b. $13.888; $7.50;
   $2,089.17
   c. $2.125; $15.00;
   $4,757.13
   d. $116.667; $30.00;
   $10,226.67
   e. $55.125; $35.00;
   $15,560.13
   f. $196.00; $17.50;
   $6,959.75
   g. $245.00; $22.50;
   $10,595.00
   h. $212.667; $40.00;
   $17,392.67

Chapter Review

1. $10,500 received; $500
   premium
3. $60
5. 7.4%

CHAPTER 15

15.1

1. 3768
3. 7
5. 68
7. 54,260
9. 406

15.2

1. 7
3. 3
5. 13
7. 14
9. 12
11. 21
13. 25
15. 24
17. 41
19. 149

15.3

1. 1
3. 1
5. 5
7. 15
9. 9
11. 13
13. 23
15. 29
17. 42
19. 49

15.4

1. 1100_2
3. 1011100_2
5. 1111110_2
7. 10001000_2
9. 100010011_2
11. 100111100_2
13. 100_2
15. 111_2
17. 1000010_2
19. 100110100_2

15.5

1. $10110_2 = 22(13 + 9)$
3. $11000_2 = 24(10 + 14)$
5. $11000_2 = 24(15 + 9)$
7. $101100_2 = 44(27 + 17)$
9. $100000_2 = 32(5 + 27)$
11. $101100_2 = 44(19 + 25)$

13. $100000_2 = 32(31 + 1)$
15. $1000001_2 = 65(7 + 58)$
17. $1101110_2 = 110(55 + 55)$
19. $11110100_2 =$
  $244(123 + 121)$

15.6

1. $101010_2 =$
  $42(13 + 5 + 21 + 3)$
3. $110010_2 =$
  $50(14, 22, 3, 11)$
5. $110101_2 =$
  $53(29 + 10 + 7 + 7)$
7. $10110_2 = 22(5, 3, 3, 11)$

15.7

1. $101(23 - 18 = 5)$
3. $111(20 - 13 = 7)$
5. $10(25 - 23 = 2)$
7. $100(17 - 13 = 4)$
9. $1100(39 - 27 = 12)$
11. $10110(31 - 9 = 22)$
13. $11(25 - 22 = 3)$
15. $11000(29 - 5 = 24)$

15.8

1. $1001(3 \times 3 = 9)$
3. $10101(7 \times 3 = 21)$
5. $1111(5 \times 3 = 15)$
7. $1011011(13 \times 7 = 91)$
9. $101101(9 \times 5 = 45)$
11. $110010(10 \times 5 = 50)$
13. 10100101
  $(11 \times 15 = 165)$
15. 10001111
  $(11 \times 13 = 143)$

15.9

1. $10_2(10 \div 5 = 2)$
3. $100_2(12 \div 3 = 4)$
5. $100_2(24 \div 6 = 4)$
7. $10_2(22 \div 11 = 2)$
9. $101_2(25 \div 5 = 5)$
11. $1_{2R111}(19 \div 12 = 1_{R7})$
13. $110_2(54 \div 9 = 6)$
15. $1010_2(110 \div 11 = 10)$

Chapter Review

1. 26; 75; 213
3. 10010; 100111; 110001
5. 1001110; 11111101;
  1101001

CHAPTER 16

16.1

1. 10
3. 5
5. 175
7. 376
9. 380
11. 650
13. 2017
15. 70
17. 218
19. 1140

16.2

1. 77
3. 140
5. 176
7. 414
9. 572
11. 1331
13. 1647
15. 2220
17. 11,707
19. 16,304

16.3

1. $11_{10} = 13_8 = 11_{10}$
3. $29_{10} = 35_8 = 29_{10}$
5. $54_{10} = 66_8 = 54_{10}$
7. $45_{10} = 55_8 = 45_{10}$
9. $85_{10} = 125_8 = 85_{10}$
11. $91_{10} = 133_8 = 91_{10}$
13. $219_{10} = 333_8 = 219_{10}$
15. $173_{10} = 255_8 = 173_{10}$
17. $343_{10} = 527_8 = 343_{10}$
19. $375_{10} = 567_8 = 375_{10}$

16.4

1. 18_{10}
3. 164_{10}
5. 1016_{10}
7. 3834_{10}
9. 810_{10}
11. 2525_{10}
13. 343_{10}
15. 180_{10}
17. $14,929_{10}$
19. $4,028_{10}$

16.5

1. 1A
3. 4A

5. 7B
7. 1CB
9. 2CC
11. 5F7
13. 3F8
15. 5A6
17. B34
19. 1494

Chapter Review

1. 784; 1511; 2080
3. 201; 711; 1177
5. 11C; 147; C6

CHAPTER 17

17.1

1. Total Assets $48,000
  Capital $32,000

17.2

1. $41,000
3. $41,000

17.3

1. Increase in Total Assets
  $4,870
  Percent
  3%

17.4

1. Total Fixed Assets
  1974 61%
  1975 55%

17.5

1. Net Profit $53,160

17.6

1. Net Profit 40%

17.7

1. Net Profit
  1974 16.4%
  1975 $21\frac{2}{3}\%$

17.8

1. $1,488

17.9

1. $1\frac{2}{3}:1$

17.10

1. $6\frac{1}{4}\%$

17.11

1. $14\frac{2}{7}\%$

17.12

1. $1.875

Chapter Review

1. Total Assets $30,252
   Capital $24,941
3. Total Fixed Assets
   1973 70%
   1974 66.1%

CHAPTER 18

18.1

1. $83\frac{2}{3}$
3. $2,417.43

18.2

1. $7\frac{1}{2}$
3. $32\frac{1}{2}$

18.3

1. $32
3. $92.89
   $92
   $85

18.7

1. $2,123.23

18.8

1. $5,915.07
3. $3,781.43
   $2,532.19
   $2,258.47

18.9

1. $18,864.19

18.10

1. $1,517.36
3. $1,753.60

Chapter Review

1. $586
3. $92
5. —
7. $3,183.60
9. $6,048.52

INDEX

A

Addition, 4–11
  breaking columns, 10
  combinations of 10, 6, 7
  definitions, 4
  horizontal, 11
  positional numbering system, 4
  proving, 9
Aliquot Parts, 76–78
  aliquot parts of 100, 76
  in combinations, 78
  multiples of 10, 77
  multiplication by, 76–77
  table, 76
Annuities, 353–58
  due, 355
  ordinary, 353–54
    chart, 356–57
Assets
  current, 320–22
  fixed, 320–22

B

Balance Sheet, 320–21
Bank Reconciliation, 131–35
  checking account statement, 133
  common adjustments, 132–33
Base 8, 306–12
Base 10, 292, 293
Base 16, 313–16
Binary Arithmetic, 293–304
  addition, 298–99
  converting binary numerals to decimal
    numerals, 294–95
  converting decimal numerals to binary
    digits, 296–97
  division, 302–03
  multiplication, 301–02
  subtraction, 300–01
Bonds, 277–87
  buying and selling, 277–81
    sale of bonds by issuing corporation,
      278–79
    sale of bonds by the private investor,
      279–81
  buying between interest periods, 285–86
  interest on, 283
    current yield, 283–84
    yield to maturity, 284–85
Business Insurance, 250–58
  cancelation, 252
  cancelation or short-term rate table, 253
  finding the premium, 250–51
  short-term policies, 252
  short-term rates, 252
Business Statistics, 339–43

C

Capital Stock, 264
Change Memo, 185, 190
Change Tally, 190
Commissions, 198–206
  draw against, 199–200
  quota bonus, 205–06
  sliding scale, 203–04
  straight, 198–99
  straight salary plus, 204–05
Current Ratio, 333

D

Decimal Fractions, 55–59
  converting decimals to fractions, 56

Decimal Fractions (*Cont.*)
  converting fractions to decimals, 57
  remainders and repeating decimals, 58
Depreciation, 222–28
  declining balance, 226–28
  straight line, 222–28
  sum-of-the-years' digits, 225–26
  units of production, 224
Discounting Notes, 244–50
  days in discounting period, 245–56
  discounting notes receivable, 247–49
  interest on notes, 245
  maturity value, 246–47
  promissory notes, 245
    example of a promissory note, 245
Discounts, 207–16
  anticipation, 215–16
  cash, 207–08
  equivalent trade, 213–14
  other cash, 211
    EDM, 211
    ROG, 211
  series of trade, 211
  trade, 211
Division, 23–29
  decimals, 27
  definitions, 23
  long, 24, 25
  mental, 23, 24
  powers of 10, 25
  proving, 28, 29
  zero, 26
Division of Partnership Income, 231–35
  absence of agreement, 232
  investment of partners, 234
  services of the partners, 232–33

E

Earnings Per Share of Common Stock,
  335–36
Estimating, 30

F

Federal Depository Receipt, 193
Form 941, 192
Fractions, 37–54
  addition of, 45–46
  converting improper fractions to mixed
    numbers, 41–42
  converting mixed numbers to improper
    fractions, 40–41
  denominator, 38–39
  division of, 54–55
  divisor, 39

greatest common divisor, 39
improper, 37
lowest common denominator, 42–43
mixed numerals, 37
multiplication by cancelation, 52–53
multiplication of, 51–52
numerator, 38–39
proper, 37
raising, 39–40
reducing, 38–39
subtraction of, 47–48
types of, 37

G

Graphs, 343–53
  bar, 344–46
  circle, 347–50
  line, 350–53
Gross Margin, 155–59
Gross Profit, 155–59
  definition, 155
  method of estimating inventories, 158–5
    on sales, 155
  percent, 156–57

H

Hexadecimal System, 313–16
  converting decimals to hexadecimal
    315–16
  converting hexadecimals to decimal
    313–14
  positional value chart, 313
Home Mortgages, 110–13
  mortgage statement, 111
    escrow balance, 112
    interest, 112
    loan balance, 112
Horizontal Analysis, 322–24, 329–31

I

Income Statement, 327–29
Income Taxes, 239–44
  individual, 239–44
    adjusted gross income, 240
    adjustments to income. 240
    calculating the tax, 242
    deductions, 240–41
    gross taxable income, 293
    paying the tax, 243
    personal exemptions, 242
    standard deductions, 242
    tax-rate schedule, 243

Installment Buying, 108–10
  carrying charge, 108
  formula for cost, 108
  formula for interest, 108
  formula for service charge, 108
Interest, 81–100
  compound, 96–100
    arithmetic computation, 96–97
    using tables, 98–99
  simple, 81–96
    cancelation method, 87–88
    finding the principal, 92–93
    finding the rate, 94–95
    finding the time, 82–87, 93–94
      exact time—exact interest, 84–85
      in months, 82
      ordinary interest at exact time, 85
      thirty-day month ordinary interest,
        82–83
      using a table, 86
    6%–60 day method, 88–90
    using tables, 90–91

L

Life Insurance, 127–31
  cash surrender value, 129–31
  tables
    annual premium rates, 128
    cash value—endowment, 130
    cash value—straight life, 130
    cash value—twenty payment life, 130
  types of policies, 127–29
    endowment, 127–28
    limited payment life, 127
    straight life, 127
    term insurance, 127
Loan Repayment Schedules, 113–16

M

Markdown, 151–52
  definition, 151
  percentage, 152
Markup, 140–51
  average, 147–49
  basic equations, 140
  buyer's wheel, 145–47
    buyer's markup calculator, 147
    profit calculator, 146
  cumulative, 149–50
  definition, 140
  dollar, 140
  individual, 140
  percent based on cost, 143–44
  percent based on retail, 141–42

Mean, 339–40
Median, 340–41
Merchandise Inventory Turnover, 159–62
  average inventory, 160
  formulas, 159–60
Merchandise Inventory Valuation, 229–36
  FIFO, 229–30
  first in-first out, 229–30
  LIFO, 230
  last in-last out, 230
  weighted average, 230
Metric System, 31–34
  gram, 33
  linear measurement, 33
  liters, 34
  meters, 33
  metric equivalents and conversions, 32
  volume measure, 34
  weight, 33, 34
Mode, 342–43
Multiplication, 17–23
  decimals, 21–22
  definitions, 17
  long, 18
  mental, 17
  powers of 10, 19
  proving, 22, 23
  zeros, 21

O

Octal Numbers, 306–12
  converting binary to octal, 310–11
  converting decimals to octals, 308–09
  converting octals to decimals, 306–07
  positional value chart, 307
Open-to-Buy, 165–66
  definition, 165
  formula for OTB, 165

P

Payroll Deductions, 180–85
  FICA, 180–81, 191
  withholding tax, 184, 191
Payroll Time Card, 175
Percentages, 64–76
  converting percents to decimals, 65
  converting percents to fractions, 64–65
  finding the amount, 66, 72–73
  finding the base, 66, 70–71
  finding the difference, 66, 74
  finding the percentage, 66–67
  finding the rate, 66, 68–69
  formulas, 66–67

Personal Loans, 106–07
Present Value, 358–59
  table, 360–61

Rate Earned on Average Capital, 334–35
Rate Earned on Average Total Assets, 334
Real Estate Taxes, 124–27
  city, 124
  county, 124
  definitions, 124–25
    assessed valuation, 124–25
    tax, 124
    tax-rate, 125
  finding the assessed valuation, 126
  finding the rate, 125
  finding the tax, 126
  school districts, 124
  state, 124
  town, 124
Remuneration Methods, 172–80
  daily overtime, 176
  differential piece work, 179
  hourly wage, 174
  hourly wage formula, 174
  overtime pay formula, 176
  piece work, 178
  piece work formula, 178
Retail Method of Estimating Inventory,
  162–64
Rounding Off, 29

Sinking Funds, 359
  table, 362
Social Security, 172
  application blank, 173
  card, 173
  number, 172
Stocks, 262–74
  book value, 270–71
  buying and selling, 271–74
    by the issuing corporation, 271–72
    by the private investor, 272–73
  common, 266–67
  cumulative preferred, 268–69
  preferred, 264–65
Stock Turnover, 159–62
Subtraction, 12–16
  definitions, 12
  horizontal, 15
  mental, 16
  position, 12–13
  proving, 14

V

Vertical Analysis, 331–32, 325–26

W

Working Capital, 333